Critical Perspectives on Plurilingualism in Deaf Education

Full details of all our publications can be found on http://www.multilingual-matters.com, or by writing to Multilingual Matters, St Nicholas House, 31–34 High Street, Bristol BS1 2AW, UK.

Critical Perspectives on Plurilingualism in Deaf Education

Edited by
**Kristin Snoddon and
Joanne C. Weber**

MULTILINGUAL MATTERS
Bristol • Blue Ridge Summit

To Dr David Mason, who encouraged and trained many deaf teachers and strengthened the implementation of plurilingual education for deaf learners in Canada.

DOI https://doi.org/10.21832/SNODD00749
Library of Congress Cataloging in Publication Data
A catalog record for this book is available from the Library of Congress.
Names: Snoddon, Kristin, editor. | Weber, Joanne, editor.
Title: Critical Perspectives on Plurilingualism in Deaf Education/Edited by Kristin Snoddon and Joanne Weber.
Description: Bristol, UK; Blue Ridge Summit, PA: Multilingual Matters [2021] | Includes bibliographical references. | Summary: "This book is the first edited international volume focused on critical perspectives on plurilingualism in deaf education, which encompasses education in and out of schools and across the lifespan. It explores issues such as bimodal bilingualism, translanguaging, teacher education, sign language interpreting and parent sign language learning"— Provided by publisher.
Identifiers: LCCN 2021011541 (print) | LCCN 2021011542 (ebook) | ISBN 9781800410732 (paperback) | ISBN 9781800410749 (hardback) | ISBN 9781800410756 (pdf) | ISBN 9781800410763 (epub) | ISBN 9781800410770 (kindle edition) Subjects: LCSH: Deaf—Education. | Multilingualism. | Multilingual communication. | Multilingual education.
Classification: LCC HV2430 .C75 2021 (print) | LCC HV2430 (ebook) | DDC 371.91/2—dc23 LC record available at https://lccn.loc.gov/2021011541
LC ebook record available at https://lccn.loc.gov/2021011542

British Library Cataloguing in Publication Data
A catalogue entry for this book is available from the British Library.

ISBN-13: 978-1-80041-074-9 (hbk)
ISBN-13: 978-1-80041-073-2 (pbk)

Multilingual Matters
UK: St Nicholas House, 31–34 High Street, Bristol BS1 2AW, UK.
USA: NBN, Blue Ridge Summit, PA, USA.

Website: www.multilingual-matters.com
Twitter: Multi_Ling_Mat
Facebook: https://www.facebook.com/multilingualmatters
Blog: www.channelviewpublications.wordpress.com

The policy of Multilingual Matters/Channel View Publications is to use papers that are natural, renewable and recyclable products, made from wood grown in sustainable forests. In the manufacturing process of our books, and to further support our policy, preference is given to printers that have FSC and PEFC Chain of Custody certification. The FSC and/or PEFC logos will appear on those books where full certification has been granted to the printer concerned.

Typeset by Nova Techset Private Limited, Bengaluru and Chennai, India.
Printed and bound in the UK by the CPI Books Group Ltd.
Printed and bound in the US by NBN.

Contents

Contributors   vii

Foreword   xi
Jim Cummins

Introduction: Plurilingualism and (In)competence
    in Deaf Education   1
Kristin Snoddon and Joanne C. Weber

Part 1: Plurilingual Language Planning in Deaf Education

1   Four Decades of Sign Bilingual Schools in Sweden:
    From Acclaimed to Challenged   15
    Krister Schönström and Ingela Holmström

2   Sign Language Planning and Policy in Ontario
    Teacher Education   35
    Kristin Snoddon

3   Bourdieu, Plurilingualism and Sign Languages in the UK   60
    Dai O'Brien

4   Plurilingualism in Deaf Education in France: Language
    Policies, Ideologies and Practices for the Bimodal
    Bilingual Skills of Deaf Children   81
    Saskia Mugnier

5   Plurilingualism and Policy in Deaf Education   103
    Joanne C. Weber

Part 2: Plurilingual Education Practices and Models

6   Sign Bilingualism as Semiotic Resource in Science
    Education: What Does It Mean?   129
    Camilla Lindahl

7   Bimodal Bilingual Programming at a Canadian
    School for the Deaf   149
    Charlotte Enns, Karen Priestley and Shauna Arbuckle

8   Implementing a New Design in Parent Sign Language
    Teaching: The *Common European Framework of
    Reference for Languages*   173
    Joni Oyserman and Mathilde de Geus

9   Family Language Policy and Planning: Families with
    Deaf Children   195
    Julie Mitchiner and Christi Batamula

10 Critical Perspectives on Education Mediated by
    Sign Language Interpreters: Inclusion or the
    Illusion of Inclusion?   217
    Debra Russell

    Index   240

Contributors

Shauna Arbuckle is a speech-language pathologist with the Winnipeg School Division in Winnipeg, MB. She is also certified as a listening and spoken language specialist (AVEd) for educational settings. Shauna has worked with preschool and school-age children who are deaf or hard of hearing in the mainstream and at the Manitoba School for the Deaf. Prior to working in Winnipeg, she worked with Albuquerque Public Schools in Albuquerque, NM.

Christi Batamula is an Assistant Professor in the Department of Education at Gallaudet University. She has worked at Gallaudet University since 2005, when she began work as an early childhood educator at the Kendall Demonstration Elementary School. She earned a BA in elementary education from Geneva College, an MA in Deaf education from Gallaudet University and a PhD from George Mason University with specialization in international education and a secondary, interdisciplinary focus on early childhood education and teacher education. Christi's research interests involve working with culturally and linguistically diverse Deaf young children and the importance of bilingual and multilingual learning.

Jim Cummins is a Professor Emeritus in the Ontario Institute for Studies in Education at the University of Toronto. His research focuses on literacy development in educational contexts characterized by linguistic and socio-economic diversity. Since the late 1980s, members of the deaf community in Ontario have built on Jim's research and theoretical work on bilingual education and cross-linguistic relationships to argue for evidence-based policy changes in the education of deaf and hard-of-hearing students.

Mathilde de Geus is an independent researcher, advisor, certified teacher of the deaf and an educational designer who specializes in education for the deaf and hard of hearing in mainstream settings. She studied history, teacher training and educational design at Leiden University. From 1999–2013 Mathilde worked at schools for the deaf in the Netherlands. In 2009 she started her own consultancy firm concerning the upbringing and education of deaf and hard-of-hearing children. Since 2011 she has been developing sign language modules for parents of deaf and hard-of-hearing children. Together with parent foundations and other partners, she works on various research projects, both national and international.

Charlotte Enns is currently the Director of the Mauro Centre for Peace and Justice and a Professor in the Faculty of Education at the University of Manitoba. She teaches in the area of inclusive education, and her primary research interest is the bilingual education of deaf students. Together with her research team, she has created two standardized assessments of children's development of American Sign Language – the *ASL Receptive Skills Test* and the *ASL Expressive Skills Test*. Charlotte believes passionately in the need for all learners to realize their potential through the development of language and literacy practices.

Ingela Holmström is an Associate Professor in the Department of Linguistics at Stockholm University. Her research is directed towards communication issues in interaction between deaf, hard-of-hearing and hearing people. Ingela has a special interest in bilingualism and conducts research on teaching Swedish Sign Language as a second language.

Camilla Lindahl is Project Leader for the Teacher Education Program with a profile in Plurilingualism at Stockholm University. Her research interests center around sign bilingual education and include plurilingualism, translanguaging and multimodality. Camilla's research in sign bilingual science education and her experience as a mathematics and science teacher inform her development of the teacher education program with a focus on sign bilingual education. The project, in turn, contributes to research in what is required to develop sign bilingual education.

Julie Mitchiner is an Associate Professor in the Education Department at Gallaudet University, where she focuses primarily on early childhood education. She also directs the Deaf and Hard of Hearing Infants, Toddlers and their Families: Leadership and Collaboration Interdisciplinary Graduate Certificate Program at Gallaudet University. She received her BA in early childhood education and her MA in deaf education with a specialization in family centered early education at Gallaudet University. She received her PhD in education from George Mason University, with a specialization in early childhood education and a secondary concentration on multicultural/multilingual education. Julie has presented at many national and international conferences and has published several articles related to deaf families with children who have cochlear implants and on family language planning and policy with deaf and hard-of-hearing children.

Saskia Mugnier has been an Associate Professor at the Université Grenoble Alpes since 2007. Her work is mainly anchored in the field of sociolinguistics, and includes Langue des Signes Française (LSF) policies and discourse analysis of actors in the field of deafness: teachers, educators, speech therapists and parents. Part of her work also concerns educational matters in the context of deafness: educational policies; didactics of plurilingualism, place and relationship to languages (French and LSF); and analysis of language contact in the classroom. The third part of Saskia's work concerns the evaluation of the language skills of deaf children in order to better identify and understand deaf bilingualism in all its facets.

Dai O'Brien is a Senior Lecturer in BSL and Deaf Studies at York St John University in the UK. His research interests include Bourdieusian and Marxist theory, and he is interested in exploring creative and visual research methods. When not at work, Dai enjoys spending time with his family, yoga and running.

Joni Oyserman is a deaf scholar with an MA in sign linguistics. She is a qualified sign language teacher and has 20 years' experience of teaching and developing materials for the teaching of Sign Language of the Netherlands in higher education, at university and for parents, children and interpreters. Joni is currently studying for a PhD in sign linguistics and didactics at Leiden University, focusing on language teaching methods by sign language teachers. Her main research interests include sign language teaching and (second) language acquisition. Her publications and research interests focus on sign linguistics, prosody, assessment, curriculum, grammatical judgements, sociolinguistics, sign language teaching, second language acquisition, Sign Language of the Netherlands and Deaf Studies.

Karen Priestley has recently retired from her position as the Manitoba Provincial Coordinator of Deaf and Hard of Hearing (DHH) Services, which facilitated the provision of a wide range of programming and communication options for DHH students in order to meet their diverse learning needs. She continues to be involved in the field of inclusive special education and DHH education as an Adjunct Professor at the University of Manitoba. Karen's research interests are effective programming for DHH students and the development/implementation of universal design teaching practices – practices that meet the broad range of needs of our student populations.

Debra Russell is a Canadian certified interpreter, educator and researcher. As the previous David Peikoff Chair of Deaf Studies at the University of Alberta, her research interests include interpreter-mediated education, interpreting in legal settings and with legal discourse, and Deaf-hearing interpreter teams. Her interpreting focus is on medical, legal, mental health and employment settings. She is the former President of the World

Association of Sign Language Interpreters (WASLI) and serves as a Commissioner for the Commission on Collegiate Interpreter Education (CCIE). Debra is extensively published in the field of interpretation. She loves to travel and has presented in more than 62 countries.

Krister Schönström is an Associate Professor in the Department of Linguistics at Stockholm University. His primary research interests include several aspects within the topics of deaf bilingualism, including questions related to sign bilingualism, acquisition of written languages and sign languages in the deaf and second language acquisition of sign languages.

Kristin Snoddon is Associate Professor in the School of Early Childhood Studies at Ryerson University. Her research and professional experience includes collaborative work with deaf communities in developing sign language and early literacy programming for young deaf children and their parents. Additionally, she analyzes policy issues related to inclusive education, sign language rights and acquisition planning for ASL. Kristin has served as Coordinator for the World Federation of the Deaf's Expert Group on Deaf Education.

Joanne C. Weber is Canada Research Chair (Tier II) in Deaf Education and an Assistant Professor at the University of Alberta. Her research interests include language and literacy education, arts-based research, deaf education, posthumanism, applied linguistics and sign language studies. Joanne was awarded the Governor General's Academic Gold Medal in June 2019. She has taught in deaf education settings for 20 years and continues to work with deaf children and youth through her role as artistic director of Deaf Crows Collective, which aims to provide opportunities for theatre performance by deaf actors of all ages.

Foreword

When Kristin Snoddon and Joanne C. Weber initially invited me to write a Foreword to *Critical Perspectives on Plurilingualism in Deaf Education*, I was reluctant to take on this responsibility because I am not an 'insider' in Deaf education. My engagement with the Deaf community in Ontario came about in the late 1980s when members of the Deaf Ontario Now movement approached me about the empirical research on bilingual education involving spoken/written languages and its potential relevance for bilingual-bicultural education involving natural sign languages (American Sign Language [ASL] or Langue des signes québécoise [LSQ]). As Snoddon (this volume) lucidly documents, at the time the Deaf community in Ontario was pressuring a reluctant provincial government to rethink the predominant monolingual oralist approach to the education of deaf and hard-of-hearing (DHH) students. Thus, empirical research that strongly supported the legitimacy and effectiveness of bilingual education for minoritized students (e.g. Cummins, 2001) strengthened the case for implementing ASL/English bilingual education in provincial schools for the deaf.

In contributing to this volume, I see my role as engaging in dialogue similar to the dialogue about educational equity and effectiveness initiated by the Deaf community in Ontario more than 30 years ago that I was privileged to be part of. The authors of many of the chapters in this volume point out that the educational landscape for deaf students internationally has changed dramatically during the past 30 years. As Enns and colleagues (this volume) note, 'powerful hearing aids and cochlear implants are providing better access to speaking and listening as a viable option for DHH students'. One result of these changes is declining enrolments in schools for the deaf that have often employed deaf teachers and used natural sign languages for instructional purposes. Even in Sweden, long acclaimed for its enlightened policies regarding sign language instruction and provision of opportunities for parents to learn Swedish sign language (SSL), students' proficiency in SSL has declined as a result of more frequent placement in mainstream classes (Schönström & Holmström, this volume).

There is consensus among the authors of this volume that inclusion in mainstream classrooms is by no means a panacea for deaf students, with or without advanced technology supports. Russell (this volume) highlights the 'illusion of inclusion' and explicitly asks the central question that underlies the entire volume: 'In what ways can we re-imagine school environments that support deaf children?'

A general theme throughout the volume that responds to this question invokes the instructional possibilities that emerge when we shift from a monolingual (e.g. English-only) orientation to children's languages to an orientation defined by the Council of Europe's (2001) construct of *plurilingualism*. In their Introduction, Snoddon and Weber draw on this construct to highlight the pedagogical benefits of enabling students to utilize their entire set of linguistic resources, including their partial competencies in different languages, varieties and modalities. The construct of plurilingualism also highlights the fact that boundaries between languages are fluid and permeable rather than rigid and fixed. The history of Deaf education illustrates all too well the academic and linguistic deficits that are created when evidence-free educational policies and monolingual instructional practices deny students access to their plurilingual resources. These ideologies, unhinged from empirical evidence, constitute a brutal denial of human rights and unfortunately, as the contributors to this volume document, the residues of these ideologies continue to impact the lives and academic potential of DHH students. In Ontario, for example, government policies force parents to choose between spoken language or sign language services (but not both), with the result that children who receive cochlear implants are effectively prevented from learning ASL or LSQ (Snoddon, this volume).

Linked to plurilingualism is the construct of *translanguaging pedagogy*, broadly understood as the instructional mobilization of students' full linguistic repertoire and the promotion of productive contact across languages. During the past 20 years, educators of emergent bilingual students have demonstrated the potency of these instructional strategies to increase students' access to the curriculum and to enable them to showcase their creative, intellectual, artistic and linguistic abilities (e.g. Cummins & Early, 2011; DeFazio, 1997; Lau & Van Viegen, 2020).

The theoretical and educational significance of the present volume lies in its exploration of how these emerging insights about plurilingual/translanguaging pedagogies might be applied to the education of DHH students. This exploration entails a direct challenge to the persistence of monolingual oralist pedagogical assumptions within mainstream education. The instructional power of translanguaging pedagogy in the education of DHH students is vividly illustrated in Camilla Lindahl's analysis (this volume) of how Swedish sign language and Swedish in written form contribute to joint meaning-making in science education. She illustrates how teachers and 13–15 year-old students draw on their entire linguistic repertoire to explore scientific concepts and, in the process of translanguaging across semiotic modes, deepen and refine their understanding of scientific content. Not only is knowledge of academic content enriched, but because the languages interact in the process of communication, 'language proficiency in sign language strengthens language proficiency in spoken/written language and ... one language helps to enrich the second language with more possible meanings for different terms'.

A first step in re-imagining school environments that support DHH children is to examine the extent to which theoretical understandings that have emerged in the broader empirical research on minoritized bilingual students apply equally to the education of DHH children. In other words, what evidence exists upon which to base policy and instructional decisions? This question can be addressed in relation to four central issues, expressed here as questions:

- What are the causes of underachievement among DHH students?
- To what extent does the development of sign language proficiency in the preschool years contribute to subsequent academic development?
- To what extent is there evidence of a positive relationship between sign language proficiency and the development of literacy in the dominant language?
- To what extent will DHH students benefit from a bilingual and/or plurilingual instructional approach focused on developing students' abilities in both a natural sign language and the dominant spoken/written language?

This dialogue between the mainstream research on minoritized bilingual students and the emerging research on DHH students shows clearly that the same developmental and instructional principles operate in both contexts.

Causes of Underachievement

Based on extensive empirical evidence, I have argued that the historical underachievement of minoritized students is rooted in the operation of societal power relations and their reflection in patterns of teacher-student identity negotiation (Cummins, 1986, 2001, 2017a). A major reason why mainstream initiatives aimed at closing the achievement gap between social groups have produced such meager results is that issues related to societal power relations and identity negotiation in schools have been largely ignored. An implication of this analysis is that the effective instruction of minoritized students *requires* educators to challenge coercive relations of power.

The operation of coercive power relations in the historical and current education of DHH students is amply demonstrated in this volume. O'Brien (this volume), for example, points out that 'when a student or family attempts to campaign for language access or for recognition of their linguistic capital in sign language, they are not just fighting against a single teacher or school, but the whole educational establishment and the weight of history' (p. 72). Weber (this volume) likewise documents the ways in which cognitive-imperialist discourse positions DHH students as deficient and in need of a 'cure' in order to succeed in school. In short, medical, social and educational structures still systematically deny DHH children early and appropriate access to a strong primary language in their early developmental years. As a result, cognitive stimulation and linguistic interaction within the classroom have been severely limited for many students, both historically and currently.

The Need for a Strong Conceptual Base in the Early Years

Research in contexts around the world has demonstrated that the level of development of children's primary language is a strong predictor of their second language development (National Academies of Sciences, Engineering, and Medicine, 2017). To what extent does this relationship hold when the primary language is a visual language and the second language an auditory/oral language? The research synthesis carried out by the National Academies of Sciences, Engineering, and Medicine answered this question unambiguously:

> Studies of deaf children learning American Sign Language (ASL) and English offer strongly compelling evidence that L1 development facilitates L2 development, illustrating the effect even across different modalities. ... Thus, it appears that learning a language early establishes a general foundation that can be engaged for later language learning and literacy. (National Academies of Sciences, Engineering, and Medicine, 2017: 4–16)

In short, there is consensus in the research literature that acquisition of a strong language and conceptual foundation during the child's early development is a prerequisite for subsequent language and literacy development in the dominant language of the school. The natural language of the Deaf community in any country clearly constitutes an appropriate language for early conceptual development for those children who have, or are provided with, access to a signing community. Deaf children, with or without cochlear implants, who are not provided with access to a signing community, are likely to spend considerable time trying to acquire the oral language code and this instructional focus on 'code-breaking' may limit the extent to which they are enabled to use language for communication, conceptual development and engagement with their experience.

Linguistic Interdependence

The principle of cross-lingual interdependence posits that there is a common underlying proficiency that enables transfer of conceptual and linguistic skills and knowledge across languages (Cummins, 1981). The evidence supporting cross-lingual interdependence is clearly summarized by Dressler and Kamil as part of the Report of the National Literacy Panel on Language-Minority Children and Youth (August & Shanahan, 2006). They conclude:

> In summary, all these studies provide evidence for the cross-language transfer of reading comprehension ability in bilinguals. This relationship holds (a) across typologically different languages …; (b) for children in elementary, middle, and high school; (c) for learners of English as a foreign language and English as a second language; (d) over time; (e) from both first to second language and second to first language. (August & Shanahan, 2006: 222)

Numerous research studies conducted in North America during the past 20+ years have demonstrated that deaf children and adults who develop strong ASL signing skills also perform better on measures of English literacy than those who fail to develop strong ASL skills (e.g. Strong & Prinz, 1997). Research studies conducted in contexts outside North America have also demonstrated positive relationships between the development of expertise in natural sign languages and overall academic performance. Transfer between sign language and written/spoken language has been reported at lexical, morphological, syntactic and pragmatic levels (e.g. Andrew et al., 2014; Hermans et al., 2010; Kontra, 2020; Malaia & Wilbur, 2020; Menéndez, 2010; Padden & Ramsey, 1998). The positive relationships can be attributed to transfer of conceptual elements (knowledge of the world) across languages, transfer of metacognitive and metalinguistic elements, and some specific linguistic elements (e.g. fingerspelling, initialized signs). In addition, cross-language activation studies demonstrate that proficient signers activate signs while working in a spoken/written language (Morford et al., 2014). This provides behavioral evidence of two phonological systems in bilingual signers that interact with each other despite the different modalities of the two systems.

The interdependence principle has relevance for several controversial issues in the education of DHH students. First, although rigorous evaluation findings are sparse, the reality of cross-lingual transfer explains why students in bimodal bilingual programs appear to perform at least as well in written literacy as those in non-bilingual programs (Svartholm, 2010). Concepts, thinking skills and learning strategies developed through sign language instruction support the development of literacy in the dominant school language.

Second, the strong evidence for ASL/English interdependence refutes the claim put forward by Mayer and Wells (1996) that direct transfer between ASL and English cannot take place because the structure and modalities of the languages are so different. They argue that manually coded versions of the spoken language are an essential mediator in enabling DHH students to acquire reading (and writing) skills. Their argument that transfer cannot take place is refuted by the overwhelming evidence that transfer *does* take place.

Third, the refusal by auditory-verbal therapy professionals in some contexts to provide services to children who start learning a natural sign language is inconsistent with the extensive evidence showing positive relationships between sign language expertise and development of spoken and written language proficiency (Edelist, 2015; Snoddon & Paul, 2020).

Plurilingual Instruction

Partly because of the paucity of genuine bilingual programs for DHH children, there is a lack of coherent research evidence regarding the outcomes of such programs (see Howerton-Fox & Falk, 2019). Even in Sweden, where a sustained effort was made to implement bilingual education involving SSL and spoken/written Swedish as mediums of instruction, interpretation of results is complex (Schönström & Holmström, this volume). Early findings indicated the development of stronger literacy skills in Swedish compared to previous outcomes in monolingual/oralist programs, but the gap between DHH and 'mainstream' students in graduation rates remained significant (Svartholm, 2010). National data reported in 2008 showed that DHH students in special schools had significantly lower passing rates in Swedish, mathematics and English than was the case for hearing students whose first language was Swedish (Swedish: 69% versus 97%; mathematics: 55% versus 93%; English: 59% versus 94%). Svartholm points out that these data must be interpreted cautiously because many of the students in the special schools had additional learning difficulties that compounded the learning challenges resulting from their lack of access to a solid linguistic base in their early years. In addition, the special schools had a large number of children (25%) from immigrant backgrounds and almost one-third (32%) had enrolled as late as Grades 7–10.

An additional consideration relates to the problematic pedagogical assumptions underlying the model of bilingual education implemented in Swedish schools. Bagga-Gupta (2004) critiqued the assumptions that (a) instruction in Swedish reading and writing should be delayed until the age of 6–7 years to allow SSL to become well established, (b) the two languages should be kept separate for instructional purposes and (c) the teaching of Swedish should be carried out through an explicit comparative grammar instructional method. None of these pedagogical assumptions is consistent with current understandings of effective pedagogy in general or within bilingual education for minoritized students (Cummins, 2017b). For example, there is overwhelming evidence that (a) literacy engagement is a primary determinant of literacy attainment, (b) teaching for cross-linguistic transfer is a crucial component of effective instruction in bilingual programs and (c) connecting instruction to students' lives, experiences and imaginations is a prerequisite for academic engagement. The implications of this evidence are that we should: expose children to books and draw their attention to print from a very early age; encourage students to draw on their entire plurilingual repertoire rather than insisting on language separation; and develop language awareness (focus on form) not in isolation but rather in the context of experiential learning that engages students in intellectually challenging projects and tasks.

Re-imagining School Environments for DHH Children

These considerations bring us back to the question posed by Debra Russell (this volume): *In what ways can we re-imagine school environments that support deaf children?*

It is clear that a large majority of DHH students, with or without cochlear implants and/or other auditory technological supports, are being educated in purportedly 'inclusive' settings in mainstream schools. In many cases, comprehension of classroom instruction is mediated by an educational assistant or interpreter who attempts to help students understand instruction by using some form of sign language. However, as illustrated in Russell's chapter (this volume), interpreters are frequently not fluent in a natural sign language or use a manually coded system of the dominant spoken language. Consequently, the input that students receive is often both conceptually and linguistically fragmented. Furthermore, as Enns and colleagues (this volume) point out, 'even with access to spoken language through their implants or hearing aids, these students can and do feel isolated and segregated in a mainstream environment'. They highlight the fact that when parents are given a choice, many will opt for instructional environments that create opportunities for their children to develop proficiency in both spoken and sign language.

Several of the chapters in this volume point to an emerging consensus among many researchers and Deaf education experts regarding the benefits of providing opportunities for DHH children to develop proficiency in both spoken and sign languages through bimodal bilingual education. A bimodal bilingual instructional approach is inspired by the concepts of plurilingualism and translanguaging which highlight the interpersonal and cognitive affordances generated by access to multiple languages and varieties that can be used in flexible and creative ways according to the context. This approach views sign language and assistive hearing devices as mutually reinforcing – complementing each other rather than competing with or being in opposition to one another.

Enns and colleagues (this volume) similarly point to the recently emerging views of various researchers who advocate for more equitable use of both ASL and spoken English for DHH students with cochlear implants at schools for the deaf and in mainstream schools. These researchers have highlighted the benefits of positive identity development in both languages as well as improved access to language and communication, better learning potential and the ability to move between the Deaf and the hearing worlds.

Enns and colleagues also review recent research into co-enrolment programs in which DHH and hearing students are educated in the same classrooms, co-taught by a specialist in DHH education and a regular teacher, with the goal of enabling students to develop skills in both spoken and sign language. Multiple benefits appear to be associated with this approach. DHH students appeared to benefit academically; they experienced increased social interaction and were fully part of the classroom community. This pattern of findings, albeit preliminary, parallels the positive outcomes of two-way dual-language programs in which, for example, Spanish-dominant and English-dominant students are educated together, with Spanish and English as languages of instruction (e.g. Valentino & Reardon, 2015).

An additional advantage of the pedagogical philosophy underlying co-enrolment programs is that they focus on students' personal, cognitive, linguistic and creative assets rather than on presumed deficits, thereby challenging the oppressive hierarchy of languages that is characteristic of more conventional mainstream programs. All students are adding an additional language to their repertoire of skills and both hearing and DHH students are contributing to the linguistic enrichment of the entire classroom community.

Conclusion

Unfortunately, however, provision of a similar instructional environment through bimodal bilingual education, with or without co-enrolment of DHH and hearing children, is increasingly challenging to implement in many countries because of the declining numbers of teachers and/or instructional assistants fluent in natural sign languages. This decrease is directly linked to the reduced numbers of students enrolled in schools for the deaf, which historically have provided socialization opportunities for the acquisition of sign languages. Thus, ironically, the provision of effective supports for DHH students in mainstream schools is being undermined by the erosion of opportunities for children to acquire a strong linguistic and conceptual foundation in a natural sign language.

The unfolding of this situation is not innocent – it didn't just happen by accident. It is a direct result of the continuing operation of coercive power relations to which the Deaf community and DHH children have been subjected since evidence-free monolingual oralist ideologies were ushered in by the 1880 International Congress for the Improvement of the Conditions of Deaf-Mutes in Milan. These societal power relations are manifested both in discriminatory structures and in the vehement opposition by medical professionals, policymakers and some educators in many countries to the provision of opportunities for DHH children and their parents to acquire sign language. Discriminatory structures are exemplified most egregiously in exclusionary teacher education programs such as the teacher-of-the-deaf program in York University in Toronto, which includes no full-time deaf faculty member, offers no ASL courses for future teachers of DHH students and has significantly restricted access by deaf university graduates to the program (Snoddon, this volume).

Obviously, we still have a long way to go before evidence-based educational policies for DHH students are implemented and the misinformation disseminated to parents by policymakers and medical professionals is acknowledged and repudiated. But the evidence and insights assembled by the contributors to this inspirational book represent a very significant beginning that hopefully will gather momentum as more schools explore the educational potential of plurilingual pedagogies and bimodal bilingual instructional approaches.

Jim Cummins

References

Andrew, K.N., Hoshooley, J. and Joanisse, M.F. (2014) Sign language ability in young deaf signers predicts comprehension of written sentences in English. *PLoS One* 9 (2). See https://journals.plos.org/plosone/article?id=10.1371/journal.pone.0089994.

August, D. and Shanahan, T. (eds) (2006) *Developing Literacy in Second-Language Learners: Report of the National Literacy Panel on Language-Minority Children and Youth.* Mahwah, NJ: Lawrence Erlbaum.

Bagga-Gupta, S. (2004) *Literacies and Deaf Education: A Theoretical Analysis of the International and Swedish Literature.* Forskning i Fokus no. 23. Stockholm: Swedish National Agency for School Improvement.

Council of Europe (2001) *Common European Framework of Reference for Languages: Learning, Teaching, Assessment.* Strasbourg: Cambridge University Press. See https://rm.coe.int/1680459f97.

Cummins, J. (1981) The role of primary language development in promoting educational success for language minority students. In California State Department of Education (eds) *Schooling and Language Minority Students: A Theoretical Framework* (pp. 3–49). Los Angeles, CA: Evaluation, Dissemination and Assessment Center, California State University.

Cummins, J. (1986) Empowering minority students: A framework for intervention. *Harvard Educational Review* 56, 18–36.

Cummins, J. (2001) *Negotiating Identities: Education for Empowerment in a Diverse Society* (2nd edn). Los Angeles, CA: California Association for Bilingual Education.

Cummins, J. (2017a) Teaching minoritized students: Are additive approaches legitimate? *Harvard Education Review* 87 (3), 404–425.

Cummins, J. (2017b) Teaching for transfer in multilingual educational contexts. In O. García and A. Lin (eds) *Bilingual Education: Encyclopedia of Language and Education* (3rd edn) (pp. 103–115). New York: Springer Science+Business Media.

Cummins, J. and Early, M. (2011) *Identity Texts: The Collaborative Creation of Power in Multilingual Schools.* Stoke-on-Trent: Trentham Books.

DeFazio, A.J. (1997) Language awareness at The International High School. In L. Van Lier and D. Corson (eds) *Knowledge About Language: Encyclopedia of Language and Education* (pp. 99–107). Dordrecht: Kluwer Academic.

Dressler, C. and Kamil, M. (2006) First- and second-language literacy. In D. August and T. Shanahan (eds) *Developing Literacy in Second-Language Learners: Report of the National Literacy Panel on Language-Minority Children and Youth* (pp. 197–238). Mahwah, NJ: Lawrence Erlbaum.

Edelist, T. (2015) Listen and speak: Power-knowledge-truth and cochlear implants in Toronto. *Disability Studies Quarterly* 35 (1). doi:10.18061/dsq.v35i1.4312

García, O. (2009) *Bilingual Education in the 21st Century: A Global Perspective*. Malden: Wiley.

Hermans, D., Ormel, E. and Knoors, H. (2010) On the relation between the signing and reading skills of deaf bilinguals. *International Journal of Bilingual Education and Bilingualism* 13, 187–199.

Howerton-Fox, A. and Falk, J.L. (2019) Deaf children as 'English learners': The psycholinguistic turn in deaf education. *Education Sciences* 9 (2), 133. doi:10.3390/educsci9020133

Kontra, E.H. (2020) Sign bilingual education of foreign languages. In S. Laviosa and M. González-Davies (eds) *The Routledge Handbook of Translation and Education* (pp. 353–367). New York: Routledge.

Lau, S.M.C. and Van Viegen, S. (2020) *Plurilingual Pedagogies: Critical and Creative Endeavors for Equitable Language in Education*. Cham: Springer.

Malaia, E.A. and Wilbur, R.B. (2020) Syllable as a unit of information transfer in linguistic communication: The entropy syllable parsing model. *WIREs: Cognitive Science* 11 (1), e1518. doi:10.1002/wcs.1518

Mayer, C. and Wells, G. (1996) Can the linguistic interdependence theory support a bilingual bicultural model of literacy education for deaf students? *Journal of Deaf Studies and Deaf Education* 1, 93–107.

Menéndez, B. (2010) Cross-modal bilingualism: Language contact as evidence of linguistic transfer in sign bilingual education. *International Journal of Bilingual Education and Bilingualism* 13, 201–223.

Morford, J.P., Kroll, J., Piñar, P. and Wilkinson, E. (2014) Bilingual word recognition in deaf and hearing signers: Effects of proficiency and language dominance on cross-language activation. *Second Language Research* 30 (2), 251–271. doi:10.1177/0267658313503467

National Academies of Sciences, Engineering, and Medicine (2017) *Promoting the Educational Success of Children and Youth Learning English: Promising Futures*. Washington, DC: National Academies Press. doi:10.17226/24677

Padden, C. and Ramsey, C. (1998) Reading ability in signing deaf children. *Topics in Language Disorders* 18, 30–46.

Snoddon, K. and Paul, J.J. (2020) Framing sign language as a health need in Canadian and international policy. *Maternal and Child Health Journal* 24 (11), 1360–1364. doi:10.1007/s10995-020-02974-8

Strong, M. and Prinz, P. (1997) A study of the relationship between American Sign Language and English literacy. *Journal of Deaf Studies and Deaf Education* 2, 37–46.

Svartholm, K. (2010) Bilingual education for deaf children in Sweden. *International Journal of Bilingual Education and Bilingualism* 13, 159–174.

Valentino, R.A. and Reardon, S.F. (2015) Effectiveness of four instructional programs designed to serve English Learners: Variation by ethnicity and initial English proficiency. *Educational Evaluation and Policy Analysis* 20, 1–26. doi:10.3102/0162373715573310

Introduction: Plurilingualism and (In)competence in Deaf Education

Kristin Snoddon and Joanne C. Weber

The idea for this book came in part from a colloquium about American Sign Language (ASL) revitalization in bilingual deaf education which the editors hosted at the 2017 American Association of Applied Linguistics conference. This colloquium included Joanne's research and practice involving arts-based approaches to supporting language and literacy learning for deaf youth with language delays, and Kristin's work in developing an ASL curriculum for parents of deaf children which is based on the *Common European Framework of Reference for Languages* (CEFR) (see also Oyserman & de Geus, this volume). However, the impetus behind the colloquium was what we saw as an unbalanced revitalization (De Meulder, 2019a) of ASL and other national sign languages, particularly in the global North. However, sign language vitality is also threatened in the global South when countries seek to implement a so-called inclusive education agenda (Goico, 2019).

While ASL has become an increasingly popular modern language offering in schools and postsecondary contexts in Canada and the United States, its learning and use by deaf children has been in decline since the last two decades of the 20th century (Snoddon, 2016). For example, Snoddon (2016) reported that in 2014–2015 fewer than 300 students were enrolled in the four provincial schools for the deaf in Ontario, Canada. During the same year, over 1000 mostly nondeaf learners were enrolled in ASL classes at what was then the author's university. This situation is similar in contexts around the world, including Australia, Denmark, Ireland, New Zealand, Sweden and the United Kingdom (De Meulder, 2019a; Johnston, 2004; McKee, 2017; Schönström & Holmström, this volume). This unbalanced revitalization is tied to the increasing medicalization of deaf children within the framework of universal neonatal hearing screening and early intervention systems. The near-universal provision of cochlear implants is often accompanied by policies that restrict children's and parents' learning of sign language (Mauldin, 2016; Snoddon &

Paul, 2020). In several contexts, the perceived decline of sign language vitality is also linked to the shrinkage and closure of deaf schools (Murray et al., 2020).

This book seeks both to tell the story of bilingual deaf education, which was paradoxically introduced at schools for the deaf in several countries during the same late 1980s–early 1990s period when deaf children's access to sign language began its decline, and to showcase a range of critical insights and new approaches that are driving the bilingual education project forward. We note that in the present day, when for many deaf learners the contexts for sign language acquisition and maintenance have changed considerably, this project cannot only be driven by instrumental or deficiency-based arguments (De Meulder, 2019b; Snoddon & De Meulder, 2020). Such arguments are rooted in notions of deaf people's dependency on sign languages and sign languages as communication accommodations (De Meulder, 2019b). In line with the concept of plurilingualism and as the chapters in this book express, we urge that the bilingual education project be driven with regard to deaf learners' broad linguistic repertoires, which may include spoken languages. We also advocate for the right to opportunities and incentives for lifelong learning of sign languages by deaf children and their parents (De Meulder, 2019b). This requires more commitment from governments, policymakers and educational leaders to provide the resources for researching, developing and maintaining bilingual programs.

Historical Perspective

Bilingual education for deaf learners became a phenomenon for researchers to explore during a relatively short time period (see Johnson et al., 1989). This period followed the flowering of sign language research and the recognition of deaf cultures in the latter half of the 20th century. Sweden and Denmark emerged as internationally renowned leaders in the field of bilingual education (Mahshie, 1995). These developments also followed and were accompanied by a flurry of research on spoken-language bilingual education in the United States and elsewhere (e.g. Cummins, 1981; Lambert & Tucker, 1972; Swain & Lapkin, 1991; Thomas & Collier, 1997). In many global North contexts, however, the development of bilingual education programs for deaf learners has been overshadowed by medical advances in the form of cochlear implants and by the inclusive education movement (Blume, 2010; Mauldin, 2016), both of which have led to fewer deaf children learning sign language and attending schools where sign language is a language of instruction (Holmström & Schönström, 2017). This is symbolized by the closure of the Centre for ASL and English Bilingual Education Research in the United States, which formerly provided bilingual education teacher training (Nover et al., 2001). In our observation, attempts to meet the needs of language-deprived children often remain contingent upon the efforts of committed individual teachers of the deaf and deaf communities rather than being supported by governments, policymakers or educational leaders. Thus, in many ways deaf education suffers from the collective incompetence of and neglect by the latter groups. Meanwhile, the symptoms and prevalence of language deprivation in deaf children and youth continue to be documented and the needs of this group of learners are left largely unaddressed (Gulati, 2014; Hall *et al.*, 2017; Humphries *et al.*, 2012, 2016). Language deprivation is the persistent lack of access to a natural language in early childhood which leads to poor education and health outcomes for deaf individuals (Murray *et al.*, 2019). Schools for the deaf which previously initiated exemplary bilingual education programs have dwindled in many parts of the world, including Canada and Sweden (see Schönström & Holmström, this volume; Snoddon, this volume; Weber, this volume). In addition to causing the vitality of sign languages to be threatened in several contexts (De Meulder *et al.*, 2019b), the loss of deaf schools means that deaf children rarely receive an education in sign language.

Theoretical Framing

Plurilingualism, a guiding theme for this book and a foundation of the CEFR, is a term that signifies multilingualism at the level of the individual (Council of Europe, 2001). We chose plurilingualism for our theme because this concept was seen as more expansive and promising of a multiplicity of languages, modalities and channels than a more traditional, binary view of bilingualism. These traditional views can hierarchize languages as well as marginalize other semiotic resources that are used in human communication. As cited in Mugnier (this volume), the prefix 'bi' summons up opposing 'images of balance or imbalance, community or difference, dialogue or opposition' (Coste *et al.*, 2009: 10). However, we recognize that views of bilingualism have evolved, and our use of plurilingualism is intended to complement rather than replace bilingualism (Marshall & Moore, 2016). The term was also chosen for what we saw as plurilingualism's embrace of partial competences in languages as integral to the individual's whole linguistic repertoire. While recently we have witnessed suggestions that the CEFR should place less emphasis on partial competences, we see plurilingualism's embrace of partiality as radical and emancipatory precisely because it challenges us to value the incompetence, disability and life experiences that have granted us less than optimal acquisition of languages (Canagarajah, 2018). For example, in Kristin's research with developing an ASL curriculum for nondeaf parents of deaf children, plurilingualism provides a framework for adult second language learning of sign language. This framework supports a functional competence for parenting a deaf child even though parents may not possess native-like proficiency (Snoddon, 2015).

The framing device of plurilingualism is intended to honor the repertoires of linguistically diverse deaf learners and their families who, in addition to using one or more national languages (signed, written and possibly spoken), may possess knowledge of other minority languages (Swanwick, 2017). As this volume shows, there remains a need to explore what plurilingualism looks like in terms of classroom pedagogy, policy, and social and cultural discourses. The result is a patchwork of attempts to revitalize sign languages as a medium of instruction and the deaf communities that support the use of sign languages. This volume is meant to reflect the efforts of those who are working under duress, with limited resources, time and support from larger funding bodies.

Frequently, for deaf students in the advent of increased opportunities for so-called inclusive education and advanced technological interventions such as cochlear implants, plurilingualism has been delegated to the margins of education. In over 20 years of experience as a deaf resource room teacher in Saskatchewan, Canada, Joanne has provided tutorials and direct instruction in ASL to deaf youth. In this context, ASL is often regarded as a belated intervention to alleviate language deprivation that has already occurred. Despite the widespread availability of technological and auditory habilitation for deaf children, as a frontline educator Joanne continues to face a significant number of children and youth who need sign language in order to communicate, learn and access the curriculum. She experiences daily confrontations with the paucity of resources, knowledge and commitment for this pool of students (Weber, 2012), and experiments with fostering plurilingualism in the classroom where Joanne teaches and supports all students, regardless of whether they prefer to speak or to sign. In so doing, she has been prompted to ask the following questions of her students: (1) What can they know? (2) What can be expected from them? (3) What can they do with limited access to signed language and spoken language? and (4) What and how much of the curriculum can they learn despite the limited linguistic resources available to them? Joanne's observations of what students were doing with partial competences while coping with limited access to language and formulating new ways of expressing what they saw, did and felt provided a new perspective on plurilingualism. The plurilingual practices in her classroom attest to the resourcefulness of all deaf students as they engage with multiple semiotic resources, including spatial and material repertoires, to increase their facility with languages in the context of a community of learning. In so doing, the students emerge as competent, confident and engaged learners, more ready to accept further challenges and opportunities. For instance, one of Joanne's deaf students, who is also a Syrian refugee, landed a role in a Netflix series and garnered media attention (Martin, 2018).

Plurilingual teaching promotes linguistic tolerance, partial competences and translanguaging. Translanguaging is defined as the individual's deployment of their full linguistic repertoire without regard for boundaries between languages (García *et al.*, 2015). However, there is a concern that endorsing plurilingualism and translanguaging may dismiss the need for standard sign language models (see De Meulder *et al.*, 2019a). For instance, current thinking in applied linguistics disputes the notion of languages as bounded, discrete and defined systems (Canagarajah, 2013; Pennycook, 2018). From this viewpoint, everyone possesses partial linguistic repertoires and engages in the negotiation of meanings. As a result of translanguaging practices, standard phrases and code-meshed terms become settled over time, while new words, phrases and meanings crop up. As languages continue to evolve and borrow from other languages, and as global migration patterns continue, languages are no longer defined by geographical or political boundaries. This position also applies to the evolving nature of sign languages, and in particular to International Sign, which is a dynamic and constantly evolving system used by signers of different national sign languages when communicating with each other (Crasborn & Hiddinga, 2015).

For most nondeaf people, plurilingualism rests on the assumption that the individual's repertoire expands through guaranteed access to spoken languages, even if some languages are not immediately understood by the listener. Over time and multiple negotiations, meanings eventually become clear. Therefore, where spoken languages used by typically hearing speakers are concerned, plurilingualism involves the deployment of partial repertoires facilitated by full access to all participants' input. On the other hand, deaf children's access to languages is always precarious. For a variety of reasons, including the limitations of technology and a lack of access to proficient signers, deaf children may not fully access spoken or signed languages in every – or any – context. While translanguaging between multilingual nondeaf people is a complex endeavor, communication between deaf and nondeaf persons and between deaf people of different backgrounds is further complicated by uneven access to varying degrees of linguistic complexity. In the classroom, plurilingualism is a useful concept for viewing deaf learners holistically, albeit in ways that are sometimes different from approaches to educating nondeaf plurilingual learners.

There have been a number of critiques of plurilingualism among nondeaf populations that bear significance for deaf plurilinguals. For example, Marshall and Moore (2016) argue that current theorizing about plurilingualism may overlook social and cultural restrictions and affordances that shape learners' agency and repertoires. An over-agentive view of individuals' language practices is of concern for deaf learners who are often restricted in their access to signed and spoken languages. As a result, deaf individuals may produce what are perceived as truncated and nonstandard varieties of signed, written and spoken languages. In presenting the individual as overly agentic, plurilingualism is seen as the result of the individual's innate abilities, interests and motivations (Marshall & Moore, 2016). Such emphasis on individual agency can exacerbate the continued struggle of deaf people to obtain their rights to learn, communicate and contribute to society using sign language. In this way, social inequality is reified. Therefore, it is important to remember that plurilingualism considers language learners as social actors with particular social positions (Marshall & Moore, 2016). In previous work, we linked plurilingualism to the social relational model of deaf childhood, which recognizes the 'emergent, hybrid, yet often functional linguistic and cultural competences' of deaf children and their parents (Snoddon & Underwood, 2014: 533). These competences come into play when children and parents negotiate the social relationships needed to support a positive deaf identity.

For these reasons, we caution those who may infer that a plurilingual approach to deaf education does not require teachers who are proficient in a standard sign language variety. Deaf students' access to standard varieties of sign language is needed in order to support learners' access to linguistic complexity and development of plurilingual repertoires. Critical perspectives on plurilingualism in deaf education must address learners' precarious access to speech and sound, the need for access to linguistic complexity and the sustainable revitalization of sign languages within educational environments. Together, the chapters in this book address all of these themes.

In Joanne's classroom, structured English and ASL lessons continue to be taught during the day. In the first half of the book, this point regarding the continued need for rigorous and exemplary models of sign language teaching in classrooms with deaf students is addressed from a historical and policy level in chapters by Krister Schönström and Ingela Holmström; Kristin Snoddon; Dai O'Brien; Saskia Mugnier; and Joanne C. Weber. This point is also reinforced in the chapters in the second half of the book regarding on-the-ground bilingual education practices that feature contributions from Camilla Lindahl; Charlotte Enns, Karen Priestley and Shauna Arbuckle; and Joni Oyserman and Mathilde de Geus. These chapters highlight the central role in plurilingual education of deaf teachers proficient in sign language. Other chapters in this section, namely those by Julie Mitchiner and Christi Batamula; and Debra Russell, demonstrate the need for added resources from early childhood onwards to support deaf students' access to language and curricular content.

Critical Reflections on the Diversity of Nomenclature

While not all of the chapters in this book name plurilingualism directly, each presents theory, policy and/or practice-informed insights which set the stage for a new conversation about plurilingualism for deaf children and youth. This conversation stretches beyond the confines of binarizing discourses, essentializing perspectives and language hierarchies. Rather than attempting to unify the field through one common definition and approach to be used by everyone, such as translanguaging, bilingualism or plurilingualism, we employ a heterogeneous approach and seek to use terms embraced by researchers in their own contexts. Our theoretical framework embraces the notion of partiality and of shifting, multiple truths which contribute to scientific objectivity (Haraway, 1991). The multiplicity of the nomenclature is an attempt by researchers to describe their community's perspective on the mapping of or relationships between multiple languages and modalities. Some researchers frame this mapping as a dual-language relationship (bilingualism), whereas other researchers may refer to the unboundedness of languages and to the partial repertoires of users (plurilingualism). Others may emphasize the difference in modalities occurring between signing and speaking (bimodal bilingualism), and still other researchers emphasize the actions associated with plurilingualism (translanguaging). The inclusion of this variety of terms in this book promotes a multifaceted and complex appreciation of the relationships between signed and spoken languages. The range of nomenclature also shows how multiple languages in multiple forms are held in tension in order to address the learning needs of deaf children and youth. When these terms are considered against the backdrop of deaf ontologies, the differences become unified through the 'preferential focus given to visual and tactile experiences, languages, and ways of understanding the world' (O'Brien, 2017: 59).

The conversation is ongoing between educators and researchers who promote a monolingual framework in deaf education that privileges spoken languages, and educators who promote a plurilingual framework. However, the parameters of this ongoing conversation have often been confined to a deficit view of deaf people who are compelled to reach able-bodied norms. For this reason, deaf education researchers who use deaf ontologies as their frame may often find themselves on the defensive and struggling to gain a footing within the uneven terrain created by power imbalances. Deaf ontologies involve the examination of what deaf people do in the contexts of language use (signed, written and/or spoken), and privilege the principles of self-determination, identity preservation and community development (O'Brien, 2017). The defensive positioning in which deaf education researchers are often placed distracts from the crux of our project of meeting the sign language learning needs of deaf people. We argue for the necessity of a new conversation, which requires a focus on deaf ontologies. Such inquiry helps to shape the conversation in new trajectories and develop further lines of questioning.

Thus, this book is framed according to our own experiences and practices as deaf individuals and nondeaf allies, embedded in our communities, working in educational environments and examining our own language ideologies and practices. The deaf and nondeaf contributors in this volume have years of experience in classroom teaching and/or research and interaction with deaf learners, and are fluent in one or more sign languages in addition to spoken and/or written languages. The ability to converse in sign language with deaf people, and emotional and personal investment in the communities where one does research, yields critical insights that are deaf-authored or influenced by deaf perspectives (Kusters *et al.*, 2017). As such, this book covers theoretical trends in Deaf Studies from a deaf education perspective (Kusters *et al.*, 2017).

Overview of the Book

This book begins with a policy lens on plurilingual education for deaf students. Krister Schönström and Ingela Holmström's chapter provides a snapshot of the current state of sign bilingual education in Sweden, one of the first countries in the world to introduce bilingual education for deaf students. Bilingual approaches frequently face claims that empirical evidence for their efficacy is lacking in terms of providing educational outcomes equal to those of nondeaf students (e.g. Knoors & Marschark, 2012). Nonetheless, there is evidence of higher academic outcomes using these approaches, and '[a] discussion of what is a superior bilingual education for the deaf should, however, continue' (Schönström & Holmström, this volume, p. 29). Kristin Snoddon's chapter discusses the history of sign language planning and policy in teacher education in Ontario, Canada, following the Deaf Ontario Now movement of 1988. This chapter cautions that continued restrictions to teacher education faced by deaf people threaten the advances made by the Deaf Ontario Now movement.

Dai O'Brien's chapter surveys the history of deaf education in the United Kingdom through the lens of Bourdieusian theory. This chapter presents a clear-eyed picture of the damage to deaf students and communities that has historically been wrought by oralism and monolingualism. However, the chapter also suggests a way forward using innovative approaches, such as adding British Sign Language to the national curriculum. Saskia Mugnier's chapter studies the historical construction of social representations of deafness in France, the evolution of official policy on language learning and use, and special education for deaf children. The chapter then presents data from an exploratory classroom study of language use by deaf children to show the need to move towards a 'multimodal plurilingual' model of deaf education. Using an epistemological frame of posthumanism, Joanne C. Weber's chapter rounds off this section with a study of monolingual and plurilingual language planning discourses embedded in policy and artistic texts produced in Saskatchewan, Canada.

The second half of the book moves to a practice-oriented perspective on plurilingualism in deaf education. Camilla Lindahl's chapter analyzes sign bilingualism as a semiotic resource in science education. This chapter shows how translanguaging between Swedish Sign Language and Swedish takes place during learning, teaching and discussion. As an exemplar of high-quality plurilingual education, this chapter is joined by Charlotte

Enns, Karen Priestley and Shauna Arbuckle's study of the introduction of bimodal bilingual programming and a co-enrolment model with deaf and nondeaf young children. These children attend a Canadian school for the deaf that faced a declining student population.

Joni Oyserman and Mathilde de Geus's chapter studies the implementation of advanced parent Sign Language of the Netherlands courses. These courses are aligned with the CEFR. Julie Mitchiner and Christi Batamula's chapter presents a clear overview of and model for developing a family language plan to support plurilingualism in families with young deaf children. Debra Russell's chapter provides a critical overview of a mediated education for deaf students via a sign language interpreter. This chapter reports study findings regarding the inadequacy of sign language interpretation for effective teaching. Russell's chapter recommends that policymakers take a harder look at inclusive education for deaf learners and consider interventions to improve interpreter training and quality.

Together, the chapters present a snapshot of the state of plurilingual deaf education in countries and languages around the world. However, this book does not cover successful initiatives in contexts such as Tokyo, Japan, home to the bilingual bicultural Meisei Gakuen school. This school was founded by deaf people educated under an oralist system (Morita et al., 2017). The book also does not cover the Happy Hands School for the Deaf (n.d.) in Sindurpur, India, which implements a bilingual education in Indian Sign Language and English. The book excludes other countries in a global South context where most deaf people reside but deaf learners often have much less access to education (Friedner, 2017). In these contexts, issues of sign language vitality may differ in several ways from those in the global North. In future work, we will seek to rectify these omissions. We begin and end this book with an embrace of the partial in our knowledge, our competences and our hope.

References

Blume, S. (2010) *The Artificial Ear: Cochlear Implants and the Culture of Deafness.* Piscataway, NJ: Rutgers University Press.

Canagarajah, S. (2013) *Translingual Practice: Global Englishes and Cosmopolitan Relations.* New York: Routledge.

Canagarajah, S. (2018) Yet 'another fucking cancer diary': Embracing language incompetence and disability. American Association of Applied Linguistics Distinguished Scholarship and Service Award Address, Chicago, IL, 26 March. See https://www.youtube.com/watch?v=jgohn7mhVT0&t=41s.

Coste, D., Moore, D. and Zarate, G. (2009) *Plurilingual and Pluricultural Competence: Studies Toward a Common European Framework of Reference for Language Learning and Teaching.* Strasbourg: Language Policy Division, Council of Europe.

Council of Europe (2001) *Common European Framework of Reference for Languages: Learning, Teaching, Assessment.* Strasbourg: Language Policy Unit. See http://www.coe.int/t/dg4/linguistic/source/framework_en.pdf.

Crasborn, O. and Hiddinga, A. (2015) The paradox of International Sign: The importance of deaf-hearing encounters for deaf-deaf communication across sign language borders. In M. Friedner and A. Kusters (eds) *It's a Small World: International Deaf Spaces and Encounters* (pp. 59–69). Washington, DC: Gallaudet University Press.

Cummins, J. (1981) The role of primary language development in promoting educational success for language minority students. In California State Department of Education (eds) *Schooling and Language Minority Students: A Theoretical Framework* (pp. 3–49). Los Angeles, CA: Evaluation, Dissemination and Assessment Center, California State University.

De Meulder, M. (2019a) 'So, why do you sign?' Deaf and hearing new signers, their motivation, and revitalization policies for sign languages. *Applied Linguistics Review* 10 (4), 705–724. doi:10.1515/applirev-2017-0100

De Meulder, M. (2019b) Sign language rights for all, and forever? Plenary presentation at the XVIII World Congress of the World Federation of the Deaf, Paris, France, 25 July.

De Meulder, M., Kusters, A., Moriarty, E. and Murray, J.J. (2019a) Describe, don't prescribe: The practice and politics of translanguaging in the context of deaf signers. *Journal of Multilingual and Multicultural Development* 40 (10), 892–906. doi:10.10 80/01434632.2019.1592181

De Meulder, M., Murray, J.J. and McKee, R.L. (eds) (2019b) *The Legal Recognition of Sign Languages: Advocacy and Outcomes Around the World*. Bristol: Multilingual Matters.

Friedner, M. (2017) Doing deaf studies in the global South. In A. Kusters, M. de Meulder and D. O'Brien (eds) *Innovations in Deaf Studies: The Role of Deaf Scholars* (pp. 129–149). Oxford: Oxford University Press.

García, O., Otheguy, R. and Reid, W. (2015) Clarifying translanguaging and deconstructing named languages: A perspective from linguistics. *Applied Linguistics Review* 6 (3), 281–307. doi:10.1515/applirev-2015-0014

Goico, S.A. (2019) The impact of 'inclusive' education on the language of deaf youth in Iquitos, Peru. *Sign Language Studies* 19 (3), 348–374. doi:10.1353/sls.2019.0001

Gulati, S. (2014) Language deprivation syndrome lecture, *Brown University*, 2 April. See https://www.youtube.com/watch?v=8yy_K6VtHJw.

Hall, W.C., Levin, L.L. and Anderson, M.L. (2017) Language deprivation syndrome: A possible neurodevelopmental disorder with sociocultural origins. *Social Psychiatry and Psychiatric Epidemiology* 52 (6), 761–776. doi:10.1007/s00127-017-1351-7

Happy Hands School for the Deaf (n.d.) *Happy Hands School for the Deaf: A School for Unique Education*. See http://hhsd.rurallifeline.in/.

Haraway, D. (1991) *Simians, Cyborgs and Women: The Reinvention of Nature*. London: Free Association Books.

Holmström, I. and Schönström, K. (2017) Resources for deaf and hard-of-hearing students in mainstream schools in Sweden: A survey. *Deafness & Education International* 19 (1), 29–39. doi:10.1080/14643154.2017.1292670

Humphries, T., Kushalnagar, P., Mathur, G., Napoli, D., Padden, C., Rathmann, C. and Smith, S. (2012) Language acquisition for deaf children: Reducing the harms of zero tolerance to the use of alternative approaches. *Harm Reduction Journal* 9 (1), 16. doi:10.1186/1477-7517-9-16

Humphries, T., Kushalnagar, P., Mathur, G., Napoli, D., Padden, C., Rathmann, C. and Smith, S. (2016) Avoiding linguistic neglect of deaf children. *Social Service Review* 90 (4), 589–619. doi:10.1086/689543

Johnson, R.E., Liddell, S.K. and Erting, C.J. (1989) *Unlocking the Curriculum: Principles for Achieving Access in Deaf Education*. Gallaudet Research Institute Working Paper No. 89-3. Washington, DC: Gallaudet University.

Johnston, T. (2004) W(h)ither the deaf community? Population, genetics, and the future of Australian Sign Language. *American Annals of the Deaf* 148 (5), 358–375. doi:10.1353/aad.2004.0004

Knoors, H. and Marschark, M. (2012) Language planning for the 21st century: Revisiting bilingual language policy for deaf children. *Journal of Deaf Studies and Deaf Education* 17 (3), 291–304.

Kusters, A., De Meulder, M. and O'Brien, D. (2017) Innovations in deaf studies: Critically mapping the field. In A. Kusters, M. De Meulder and D. O'Brien (eds) *Innovations in Deaf Studies: The Role of Deaf Scholars* (pp. 1–53). Oxford: Oxford University Press.

Lambert, W.E. and Tucker, G.R. (1972) *Bilingual Education of Children: The St. Lambert Experiment*. Rowley, MA: Newbury House.

Mahshie, S.N. (1995) *Educating Deaf Children Bilingually: With Insights and Applications from Sweden and Denmark*. Washington, DC: Gallaudet University Press.

Marshall, S. and Moore, D. (2016) Plurilingualism amid the panoply of lingualisms: Addressing critiques and misconceptions in education. *International Journal of Multilingualism* 15 (1), 19–34. doi:10.1080/14790718.2016.1253699

Martin, A. (2018) Mustafa Alabssi's incredible journey: Netflix debut the latest feat for deaf Syrian refugee. *Regina Leader-Post*, 13 October. See https://leaderpost.com/ entertainment/local-arts/mustafa-alabssis-incredible-journey-deaf-syrian-refugee-to-make-his-netflix-debut-in-2019/.

Mauldin, L. (2016) *Made to Hear*. Minneapolis, MN: University of Minnesota Press.

McKee, R. (2017) Assessing the vitality of New Zealand Sign Language. *Sign Language Studies* 17 (3), 322–362. doi:10.1353/sls.2017.0008

Morita, A., Kaya, Y. and Oka, N. (2017) Bilingual education can make a difference: Key to empowering the diminishing deaf society. Presentation at World Federation of the Deaf Conference, Budapest, Hungary, 15 November.

Murray, J.J., Hall, W.C. and Snoddon, K. (2019) Education and health of children with hearing loss: The necessity of signed languages. *Bulletin of the World Health Organization* 97. See https://www.who.int/bulletin/volumes/97/10/19-229427.pdf.

Murray, J.J., Snoddon, K., De Meulder, M. and Underwood, K. (2020) Intersectional inclusion for deaf learners: Moving beyond General Comment No. 4 on Article 24 of the UNCRPD. *International Journal of Inclusive Education* 24 (7), 691–705. doi:10. 1080/13603116.2018.1482013

Nover, S.M., Andrews, J.F. and Everhart, V.S. (2001) *Critical Pedagogy in Deaf Education: Teachers' Reflections on Implementing ASL/English Bilingual Methodology and Language Assessment for Deaf Learners. Year 4 Report (2000–2001). USDLC Star Schools Project Report*. Washington, DC: Office of Educational Research and Improvement.

O'Brien, D. (2017) Deaf-led deaf studies: Using Kaupapa Māori principles to guide the development of deaf research practices. In A. Kusters, M. De Meulder and D. O'Brien (eds) *Innovations in Deaf Studies: The Role of Deaf Scholars* (pp. 57–76). New York: Oxford University Press.

Pennycook A. (2018) *Posthuman Applied Linguistics*. New York: Routledge.

Snoddon, K. (2015) Using the *Common European Framework of Reference for Languages* to teach sign language to parents of deaf children. *The Canadian Modern Language Review* 71 (3), 270–287. doi:10.3138/cmlr.2602

Snoddon, K. (2016) Whose ASL counts? Linguistic prescriptivism and challenges in the context of parent sign language curriculum development. *International Journal of Bilingual Education and Bilingualism* 21 (8), 1004–1015. doi:10.1080/13670050.201 6.1228599

Snoddon, K. and De Meulder, M. (2020) Introduction: Ideologies in sign language vitality and revitalization. *Language & Communication* 74, 154–163. doi:10.1016/j. langcom.2020.06.008

Snoddon, K. and Paul, J.J. (2020) Framing sign language as a health need in Canadian and international policy. *Maternal and Child Health Journal* 24 (11), 1360–1364. doi:10.1007/s10995-020-02974-8

Snoddon, K. and Underwood, K. (2014) Toward a social relational model of Deaf child-hood. *Disability & Society* 29 (4), 530–542. doi:10.1080/09687599.2013.823081

Swain, M. and Lapkin, S. (1991) Additive bilingualism and French immersion education: The roles of language proficiency and literacy. In A.G. Reynolds (ed.) *Bilingualism, Multiculturalism, and Second Language Learning* (pp. 203–216). Hillsdale, NJ: Lawrence Erlbaum.

Swanwick, R. (2017) *Languages and Languaging in Deaf Education: A Framework for Pedagogy.* New York: Oxford University Press.

Thomas, W.P. and Collier, V.P. (1997) School effectiveness for language minority stu-dents. *National Clearinghouse on Bilingual Education Resource Collection Series* 9, 1–96.

Weber, J. (2012) *Community Literacy Plan for the Deaf and Hard of Hearing Learners of Saskatchewan.* Regina, SK: Literacy Office, Ministry of Education.

Part 1

Plurilingual Language Planning in Deaf Education

1 Four Decades of Sign Bilingual Schools in Sweden: From Acclaimed to Challenged

Krister Schönström and Ingela Holmström

This chapter provides insight into the progress and current status of a national sign bilingual program, with a special focus on the linguistic situation. The chapter begins with a historical overview and a description of sign bilingual education in Sweden and how it has changed during the last four decades, due in great part to advancements in hearing technology, i.e. cochlear implantation. Based on semi-structured interviews with teachers of deaf and hard-of-hearing students, the chapter then provides an empirical account of the current linguistic situation of sign bilingual education in Sweden. Approaching this situation from a bilingual perspective sheds some light on the schooling of the new generation of deaf and hard-of-hearing students and shows that the linguistic situation for deaf students has changed. The chapter ends with a discussion of how sign bilingual education in Sweden has shifted from a position of being acclaimed to one of being challenged, driven by various factors that are basically derived from monolingual norms.

Introduction

Since 1983, Sweden has provided sign bilingual education at the national level for all deaf students. As one of the first countries to provide such an education, Sweden initially gained considerable attention and acclaim internationally. However, in recent years, sign bilingual deaf education in Sweden has been affected by a changing pattern in the demographics within the deaf community, namely, increased rates of cochlear implantation (CI) in deaf and hard-of-hearing children (SOU 2016:46). This has had consequences for sign bilingual schools, including a decline in enrolment. While in the past deaf students were placed primarily in sign bilingual schools, they are now also being placed in mainstream public schools, as well as in schools with special programs for hard-of-hearing students. In both kinds of schools, the language of instruction is primarily spoken Swedish. In sign bilingual schools, there has been a growing desire among parents that their deaf children should receive instruction not only through Swedish Sign Language (*Svenskt teckenspråk* [STS]) and written Swedish, but also through spoken Swedish (Holmström, 2013; see also Leigh, 2008; Simonsen *et al.*, 2009). As a result, the foundation of a strong visual and sign language base for learning that has characterized sign bilingual education in Sweden for more than 30 years has, to some degree, been diminished in recent years (cf. Nilsson & Schönström, 2014; Swanwick *et al.*, 2014; for an overview of Swedish sign bilingual education, see Svartholm, 2010, as well as Bergman & Engberg-Pedersen, 2010). In addition, the number of settings where STS naturally occurs has decreased, and therefore fewer children with hearing loss are finding opportunities to develop this language in interaction with others in contexts outside of school settings (cf. Holmström & Schönström, 2017). Even in children's homes, STS seems no longer prevalent, despite the fact that hearing parents in Sweden have the opportunity to receive up to 240 hours of STS courses (TUFF or *Teckenspråksutbildning för föräldrar* [Sign language courses for parents]) free of charge through the government (Lyxell, 2013). The diminishing use of STS in children's homes may be the reason for the declining interest in TUFF courses in recent years, not in number but in regard to persons who have completed all 240 hours that are offered (Lyxell, 2013). Taken together, this description indicates a change both in deaf education and in the linguistic situation of deaf children. Therefore, the aim of this chapter is to supplement accounts of change within sign bilingual education for the deaf in Sweden and its effects on the linguistic situation of the deaf students. The first part of this chapter provides a historical account. The second part provides a description of the current situation. The third part describes the change through the perspectives of teachers. Through teachers' perspectives, the linguistic situation of deaf and hard-of-hearing students will be specifically highlighted. The final part of the chapter will discuss how sign bilingual education in Sweden has changed from being acclaimed to being challenged and how, as a result, its efficacy has recently been brought into question.

The Emergence and Establishment of Sign Bilingual Education in Sweden

The emergence of the sign bilingual approach has its origins in the Swedish parliament's recognition of STS in Proposition 1980/81:100, where it was stated that Swedish deaf people should be bilingual in the sense that they should master both STS and Swedish in order to become fully involved citizens in Swedish society. This was a core component that led to a number of changes within Swedish deaf education, and a few years later, in 1983, the national school agency published a supplementary to the existing national curriculum (Lgr 80/83) to meet the new bilingual demand as expressed by the Swedish parliament. This supplementary curriculum stated that the development of deaf students with respect to STS and Swedish would be ensured, and that the goal for instruction in deaf schools was that these students should become bilingual (see also Bagga-Gupta & Domfors, 2003; Svartholm, 2010). In this chapter we use the internationally common term 'deaf schools' instead of the official Swedish term 'special schools for the deaf and hard-of-hearing'. Regarding the students' hearing abilities, Swedish should be handled differently in school: 'For deaf students, Swedish as language for instruction means the written form, while hard-of-hearing students with the help of hearing aids and a good listening environment can also utilize spoken Swedish. They also shall get training in and should be encouraged to use speech' (Lgr 80/83: 13, our translation). In the following years, instruction of deaf students in all school subjects was increasingly conducted via STS, and the language gradually attained a stronger position in deaf schools. As a consequence, in the 1990s, teachers of the deaf began attending STS courses, which were provided by Stockholm University with governmental support in order to develop their proficiency in STS (Nilsson & Schönström, 2014).

One decade later, in 1994, the Lgr 80/83 curriculum was replaced with a new one, Lpo 94. This new curriculum still emphasized a sign bilingual view of education, which was more strictly based on a visual mode of learning, as depicted in the following passage:

> The deaf school is responsible for ensuring that each deaf or hard-of-hearing student upon graduation from a special school
> – is bilingual, i.e. can understand sign language and read Swedish as well as exchange thoughts and ideas in sign language and in writing, and
> – is able to communicate in English writing. (Lpo 94: 11, our translation)

As a result, the teaching of Swedish or English was decreed to be conducted solely through sign language and reading and writing, and as second languages (Mahshie, 1995; Schönström, 2014). The role of spoken Swedish that was emphasized in Lgr 80/83 was not mentioned at all in Lpo 94. This can be seen in relation to the curricula of public schools (including those with special programs for hard-of-hearing students) which did not have such an emphasis. Within these schools, reading/writing activities are equally as central as in deaf schools, with the difference that Swedish does not only come in the written mode, as in the sign bilingual deaf schools.

In the 1990s, CI surgeries on children began to be performed in Sweden, and as the number of children with CIs steadily grew, parents began to question the strictly visual sign bilingual model used in most deaf schools, as outlined by the Lpo 94 curriculum. These parents began requesting speech-based education to be offered in deaf schools, in parallel with instruction in and through STS. When their requests were first denied by most deaf schools, the parents began to choose other schools (Bagga-Gupta & Holmström, 2015). That is, parents elected to send their deaf children to regular public schools or mainstream schools with some classes for hard-of-hearing students and specifically designed municipal schools for hard-of-hearing students. Thus, in order to avoid decreases in the enrolment of deaf students, deaf schools gradually changed their approach to also include a speech-based option as part of their sign bilingual programs. This meant that the deaf schools once again offered teaching in STS and both written and spoken Swedish, dependent on the student's abilities and desires (Bagga-Gupta & Holmström, 2015; Holmström, 2013; SOU 1998:66).

When the current curriculum, Lgr 11, was implemented, a more flexible version of sign bilingualism was adopted. This meant a curriculum that once again included both sign-print bilinguals and sign-spoken bilinguals:

> The school is responsible for seeing that each student upon graduation from the deaf school
> – can use the Swedish language in speech and writing in a rich and balanced way
> – can communicate in English in speech and writing, and has the possibility of communicating in one other foreign language at a functional level.
> In addition, the goal of the deaf school is that each deaf or hard-of-hearing student is developing their ability to use sign language in a rich and balanced way. (Lgr 11: 15f., our translation)

To summarize the three school reforms during the last four decades, there has been a change from a strictly oral approach before the 1980s to the development of a sign bilingual model with STS and Swedish (in both written and spoken form) as the languages of instruction during the 1980s and early 1990s. In the mid-1990s, education policy was directed towards a more strictly visual bilingual education in which the languages that were used were primarily STS and *written* Swedish. In the early 2010s, the curriculum again mentions a more flexible bilingual model in which the instruction is to be STS and Swedish in both spoken and written forms. This flexibility was further addressed in the language plan for sign bilingual schools, in which STS and *written* Swedish are stated to be *common* languages for all children enrolled in the schools, and spoken Swedish is used where applicable, i.e. depending on the students' individual oral abilities (SPSM, 2017).

Evaluation of the Effectiveness of the Swedish Sign Bilingual Model

Early efforts to evaluate the bilingual model used in Sweden were presented in Svartholm (1993) and Mahshie (1995), and indicated changes in attitude and positive social and emotional developmental effects, as well as improved literacy skills of deaf students. Heiling (1993, 1996), in turn, also demonstrated progress in deaf students' knowledge of school subjects after the implementation of the sign bilingual model. Thus, the 1990s were marked by a general air of enthusiasm and a strong belief in a sign bilingual approach as a model for deaf education, and Swedish bilingual education was internationally acclaimed. In that way, Sweden focused on maintaining and developing bilingual education as the only model for deaf students, and as a consequence there was never really a need for evaluation of the model itself from the Swedish perspective, but only the expected educational development work.

In the past years, in the international literature on deaf education, discussions have emerged regarding the success rate of sign bilingual education as a model and its effects on deaf students' academic achievement, specifically with respect to literacy skills (Dammeyer, 2014; Hermans *et al.*, 2014; Knoors & Marschark, 2012; Swanwick *et al.*, 2014). For example, because deaf students in bilingual programs are instructed through a sign language, it was expected that they should perform on a par with their hearing peers, but several studies have shown that this has not been the case. Results from bilingual schools have shown that deaf students still lag behind hearing students in mathematics, spelling and reading comprehension (e.g. Hermans *et al.*, 2014). Furthermore, a recurring theme in these discussions is the absence of robust evidence regarding the benefits of sign bilingual programs as successful programs for deaf students with regard to academic and literacy achievement (Knoors & Marschark, 2012; Marschark & Spencer, 2010). For the Swedish context, Hendar and O'Neill (2016) reported lower outcomes for deaf and hard-of-hearing students in Sweden and Scotland, including students from sign bilingual schools, compared to the general hearing population. However, it should be noted that sign bilingual programs for the deaf are relatively rare worldwide, and hence there are very few studies evaluating the outcomes of an (adequate) sign bilingual education. Obtaining comparable and generalizable results has proven to be difficult, especially in the Swedish context. The challenge is that the deaf population in Sweden is very small, as are the numbers of deaf students in deaf schools. In addition, some of these students may have additional disabilities or may have enrolled in the schools at a later stage. During the school year 2014/2015, for example, there were a total of 361 students in the five deaf schools in Sweden (SOU 2016:46). According to the Swedish National Agency for Education (SPSM) annual reports for 2014–2016, the number of deaf students who obtained grades required for entry into higher education studies ranged between 50% and 62% of the total number of students (there were between 34 and 47 students per year during these years) (SPSM, 2016). As a comparison, earlier statistics provided in Hendar and O'Neill (2016) reported 38% of deaf children from sign bilingual schools qualifying for higher education studies. Apparently, it is difficult to provide an interpretation of these results that has any statistical validity; rather, at best they only provide an indication. Another possible way to evaluate student outcomes is to look at achievement in Swedish literacy. Svartholm (2010), for example, refers to deaf school achievement statistics in which 50% of the students on average succeeded in passing Swedish curriculum requirements. More recent statistics for the years 2014, 2015 and 2016 show a range of between 56% and 71% of the students passing Swedish (SPSM, 2016). For the years 2017, 2018 and 2019, SPSM does not report on Swedish statistics, but the overall grades required for entry into higher education have ranged between 35% and 48%, i.e. there has been lower achievement compared to the years 2014–2016. According to SPSM (2019), this correlates with an increased number of newly arrived deaf students, who become enrolled in the sign bilingual schools at a later age.

Another issue linked to quality in bilingual instruction is access to qualified teachers. With the birth of bilingual schools in Sweden, there was a need for qualified teachers who could sign fluently and follow a bilingual curriculum. Svartholm (1993) described this new and challenging teaching situation that many teachers of the deaf experienced. As a consequence, different training programs were established in an effort to increase teachers' skills and competency, particularly in STS, in order to educate deaf students in the new curriculum. In the mid-1990s, teacher-training programs with sign bilingual profiles were established for the first time at the university level. Other Swedish researchers are concerned with evaluating the quality of teaching from a linguistic point of view. Bagga-Gupta and Domfors (2003) point out the problem of applying bilingual teaching methods in a monolingual system in which deaf students are 'required to follow almost the same curriculum and guidelines that have been established for monolingual hearing children' (Bagga-Gupta & Domfors, 2003: 76). They mention that teachers lack not only linguistic competency in STS but also communicative competency in STS.

Demographic Changes and their Impact on Sign Bilingual Education for the Deaf

In the early 2000s, due to an increasing number of deaf children with CIs, deaf education in Sweden started to face a new reality. Although today there still are Swedish deaf children without hearing aids and with fluency in STS, the rising number of CI infant surgeries since the early 2000s has had an impact on the group, contributing to a demographic change (SOU 2016:46). This has had some consequences for the linguistic and educational situation among the deaf. Despite the fact that many parents still attend TUFF courses, many of them cancel their studies when their children's spoken language develops, and thus the use of STS in the home decreases (Lyxell, 2013). In addition, during the early school years many parents choose to place their children in mainstream schools close to their homes. Most of these children do not learn STS fluently; they only learn some signs or no signs at all (Holmström & Schönström, 2017). The number of deaf children who are STS signers has therefore decreased, which in turn has had an impact on sign bilingual education. Nevertheless, in the last decade, many mainstreamed students have changed schools in later grades, opting to attend deaf schools, often without prior STS knowledge (SOU 2016:46; Wikström, 2018). This poses a challenge to sign bilingual education in several ways, in that the languages of instruction are not shared by all students in the class. Another important factor that influences the schools is the comparatively large number of refugees and immigrants who have come to Sweden during the last decade (SOU 2016:46; Wikström, 2018). Deaf children from these groups have been placed in deaf schools, where they have to learn both STS and Swedish from the beginning. Often, they do not have a CI or a fluent sign language from their home country. In addition, they are often placed in upper-level grades, contributing to difficulties in achieving academic goals in time for qualification from deaf schools. This is a challenging situation, especially as their families also struggle with their own learning and integration within Swedish society (SOU 2016:46). This situation seems also to have contributed to the lower achievements in the sign bilingual schools during 2017–2019 according to SPSM (2019) (see above).

The demographic changes described above have led to a wide variation in STS proficiency among students. To deal with this variation, the National Agency for Education decided to make changes to the Lgr 11 syllabus for the school subject STS, which took the name *Swedish Sign Language for the deaf and hard-of-hearing*. In practice, the students follow the same syllabus (i.e. learning content), but there are two different regulations concerning the evaluation of proficiency in STS. The first regulation recognizes that STS is the students' primary language, and the other regulation recognizes that the students' STS proficiency is at a beginner level. The latter regulation is followed when a student has enrolled in a deaf school after the lower grades or is a refugee or immigrant, or when there are other special reasons to consider. The school principal decides which regulation is to be followed for an individual student.

As a result of these changes, deaf schools today struggle with an array of language and communication issues (instruction through STS, spoken Swedish or a combination of both languages). This situation received attention in SOU 2016:46, with the investigation showing that in 2015, 55% of the students were instructed through STS, while 12% received instruction mainly through spoken Swedish and 32% through a combination of both languages. The remaining 1% of the students received instruction through an alternative communication method. However, regardless of this more varied approach to educating deaf children through sign, oral and mixed instruction, it should be noted that the main language of instruction is still STS, and that students who do not have enough proficiency to understand STS get support in the classroom through spoken Swedish interpreters. All students attending Swedish deaf schools are today required to learn STS because it is a language that all students can access and have in common. Spoken Swedish is only the language of instruction in particular language subjects, such as Swedish and English, for those students who are judged to be able to receive instruction in oral mode (SPSM, 2017).

Schools for the hard of hearing have also garnered attention as an alternative to deaf schools and mainstream schools. The difference between deaf schools and those for the hard of hearing is that the former offer sign bilingual education, while the latter are public schools with classes made up of hard-of-hearing students who are instructed primarily through spoken Swedish with a range of supports (e.g. hearing technology and adjusted classroom sizes) (Heiling, 1999; SOU 2016:46). Most of these schools are programs within mainstream hearing schools, some with their own buildings or classrooms. Today, a larger number of students are shifting between the different school forms. Many students begin in mainstream schools and move to hard-of-hearing programs or deaf schools in later grades. For example, in 2016, 50% of the deaf schools' student population were enrolled in the higher grades (7–10) because students had transferred from hard-of-hearing schools or mainstream education environments in their later years (SPSM, 2016). However, due to demographic changes, all forms of schooling today are facing new challenges regarding languages of instruction and communication modes when teaching deaf and hard-of-hearing students. For example, as we will show in the next section, deaf schools today have a larger number of students who do not master STS well enough to follow instruction in this language, nor hear well enough to be instructed in spoken Swedish. This leads to teachers facing challenges as to how to conduct teaching in a language or communication system that includes all students in a class.

Teachers' Perceptions of Sign Bilingual Education and the Language Situation of the Deaf

With the aim of increasing knowledge about the challenges facing sign bilingual education, a project was initiated in 2012 with support from Stockholm University's fund for the development of teacher education for the deaf and hard of hearing (Schönström, 2013). The project surveyed the current state of sign bilingual education for the deaf in Sweden in general. Although the main focus was on sign bilingual education, it was necessary to include schools for the hard of hearing due to the growing number of deaf students with CIs who might have been enrolled there instead of in bilingual deaf schools.

From a sociocultural perspective (Säljö, 2000, 2005; Vygotsky, 1978; Wertsch, 1998), teachers' perceptions of students' language profiles and changes in teaching from the implementation of bilingual education in the 1980s–1990s to the current situation may give unique insights into their practice, with uneven pedagogical disparities in using a bilingual approach with STS or a monolingual approach with oral Swedish and sign-supported speech. Therefore, teachers' perceptions, experiences, attitudes and feelings were investigated concerning the language situation in deaf bilingual and hard-of-hearing monolingual schools. The rationale for interviewing teachers was that they meet with students on a daily basis. They work and communicate with students and have a range of experiences with students during their everyday school life. Accessing teachers' views and experiences will thus give us valuable knowledge of and insights into the current language situation in the schools and a comparable view of the past and present.

Semi-structured interviews were conducted with teachers of deaf and hard-of-hearing students in both deaf schools and schools for the hard of hearing. The purpose was to 'generate interviewees' accounts of their own perspectives, perceptions, experiences, understandings, interpretations, and interactions' (Mason, 2004: 1021). The study included two deaf schools and one school for the hard of hearing (see Table 1.1). In order to compare the past with the present, the project focused on teachers who had taught during the earlier phases of sign bilingual education as well as in hard-of-hearing schools. Also, it was important for teachers to be proficient in STS in order for them to be able to make general judgements about students' bilingual abilities and development. The participant criteria for teachers was thus that they must have (1) long and extensive experience in teaching, and (2) full proficiency in STS. In collaboration with the schools, nine teachers were invited to participate in the study, and all agreed to do so. Three of these participants were deaf and one was hard of hearing, while five were hearing; one of the hearing participants had deaf parents. It was important to the project to include perspectives from deaf and hard-of-hearing as well as hearing teachers, in order to amass diverse perspectives.

Table 1.1 Data overview

School	Kind of school	Education approach	Teachers interviewed	Total minutes	Subject ID
School 1	Deaf school	Sign bilingual	3	156	S1, S4, S7
School 2	Deaf school	Sign bilingual	3	132	S2, S6, S9
School 3	School for hard of hearing	Speech monolingual	3	138	S3, S5, S8
Total			9	426	

The interviews were conducted in STS at the teachers' schools while being video-recorded by the first author. Thereafter, teachers' perceptions were examined in an analysis of the interviews. Here, three recurring themes strongly linked to language and bilingualism appeared that will be presented below: (i) issues of variability; (ii) sign language issues; and (iii) students' spoken language skills. The section concludes with a general description of the teachers' views on the future of bilingualism and sign bilingual schools, partly grounded in the views of the teachers, and partly in investigations of current trends in Sweden.

Issues of variability

According to the teachers in deaf schools, a common view is that in the past it was less complicated to instruct students. By this they mean that there are many more factors that need to be taken into consideration in the classroom today. Although there was also variability among deaf students in the 1980s and 1990s in terms of prerequisites and abilities to learn and acquire school subjects, the teachers pointed out that there was less variability regarding the preferred language of instruction. While sub-grouping in classes was a common practice that was previously dependent on students' perceived cognitive capacities and abilities to learn a particular subject, sub-grouping today is made more complicated by students' choice of language and their linguistic skills. At the same time, there has been a decline in the number of students in deaf schools, resulting in smaller class sizes. Taken together, this makes teaching a real challenge. As one teacher (S4) put it: 'one class could consist of six students, and each of them with their own individual prerequisites [...] To further divide them would be impossible.' Furthermore, teachers felt anxious that the smaller class sizes mean limited possibilities for peer socialization: 'They get so isolated. I wish we could have more students in our classes' (S2).

Similar views were revealed by teachers who worked in the hard-of-hearing school and experienced an increased variability among the students due to an increased number of deaf and hard-of-hearing students with additional needs. Previously, there were only hard-of-hearing students using hearing aids, but today there are also deaf students with CIs who do not always function as either deaf or hard of hearing and, in turn, make the classes more varied. Some of these students may function as a more traditional deaf learner, i.e. with confidence in STS, whereas others may have more confidence in communicating in oral Swedish in addition to STS but have limited functional hearing. Some students have no problem with functional hearing or oral Swedish but may be in need of STS in particular environments (and are lacking in STS abilities).

Sign language issues

As the number of students using speech with each other increases, it has become a challenge for bilingual deaf schools to maintain signing environments. Therefore, a language plan was developed and implemented in 2017, with the aim of reinforcing the STS environment (SPSM, 2017). This was made after the interviews were conducted. According to the interviews, there has been a concern among personnel in deaf schools and in the SPSM regarding strategies for maintaining a bilingual environment without excluding anyone. Teachers in the deaf schools described the mingling of deaf students who can hear and speak with others who do not have these abilities. There have thus been situations where groups of students speak in the schoolyard or during breaks, which creates an inaccessible linguistic environment for those who cannot hear and speak.

As indicated in the introduction to this chapter, there also has been a shift in language use in students' homes. The teachers explicitly mentioned this shift as having implications for the sign language environment at deaf schools. According to the teachers, the 'older generation' of deaf students used STS both at home and at school, but the 'younger generation', with its increased ability to hear and speak, instead uses spoken Swedish to a greater extent at home. The younger generation therefore does not have the same proficiency in STS as the older students, which hampers their ability to participate in STS instruction and to demonstrate the language proficiency required to learn academic content (cf. Cummins, 1996).

A notable observation links to past discussions in the literature regarding deaf family background as a success factor in language and cognitive skill development (Mitchell & Karchmer, 2004). Some teachers pointed out that deaf students from deaf families are the only ones who really master STS nowadays. As one teacher (S4) put it:

> When I began to educate deaf students in a deaf school in the 1990s, I remember there were international visitors surprised at the high STS skills shown by our deaf students, asking me if all of them had deaf parents, specifically asking who among them were from deaf families. At this time, I had no clue; I couldn't see the difference, and we really used not to think that way. But nowadays, I see clearly which of the students are from deaf families. (S4)

In addition, there are students who do not have a high STS communicative proficiency level, which means that teaching has to be at an appropriate level to meet the students' individual prerequisites. Some of the students may have difficulties with understanding different STS variants and contexts in which STS is used; for example, a STS interpreter at a visit to a museum as part of a school excursion. Regarding this scenario, S4 said: 'More than previously, the teacher often explains to the students what the sign language interpreter has just said. There are students who are not able to understand the interpreters' sign language today.'

Mastering linguistic rules for turn-taking in sign languages is important in order to maintain a functional dialogue, especially in the classroom context. As sign languages are visual languages, the teachers and students need to establish sightlines and know when to take turns and when they may interrupt each other. However, the interviews indicate that some teachers experienced problems in helping students with mastering and maintaining turn-taking rules. In addition, teachers claimed that STS linguistic properties are lacking in some students, such as the use of spatiality and non-manual markers, indicating an early level of STS competency that relies on lexical ('frozen') signs. (Sign language linguistics usually divided signs into three categories: lexical signs, productive signs and fingerspelling. Lexical signs typically consist of 'frozen' signs that are highly conventionalized in form; e.g. signs for CAR, APPLE and HOUSE. These signs are usually included in sign language dictionaries (e.g. Hodge & Johnston, 2014).)

In contrast to the deaf schools, teachers in the hard-of-hearing program referred to a tradition of little to no use of STS, but also that during the last decade a growing number of deaf students with CIs have arrived at the school. Some of these students are bilingual and vary in their spoken language skills. This has led to an increase in consciousness among the teachers in this type of school about the importance of STS skills, and discussions have taken place regarding how to meet this new demand.

With regard to educating hard-of-hearing students and students with CIs at the school for the hard of hearing, there are issues related to language choice based on students' language proficiencies and access. One common phenomenon identified in interviews with teachers from the hard-of-hearing school was the use of 'mixed' languages, i.e. sign-supported speech. The reason behind this approach was that the students' STS skills were not developed enough to rely only on STS, and their hearing capability was not functional enough to absorb all the instruction solely through spoken Swedish. Thus, teachers are using sign-supported speech, or spoken Swedish with partial and simultaneous production of STS signs. As S3 put it, 'Neither STS nor Swedish can be used, but a mix of languages'. Or, as S5, a teacher who is hard of hearing, said in regard to the language choice of the students: 'It depends on the situation: if I am in the classroom teaching my students, most of them will sign to me.' However, S5 emphasized that it was not standard sign language that was used, but a sign-supported variety of Swedish. There were also situations in which any kind of sign language use between the students, for example in the dining hall, was more extensive due to a noisy environment.

The interviews also reveal that some of the teachers felt that there were unanswered questions regarding a mixed sign-supported speech approach and its consequences, as this is a relatively unknown topic in Sweden. It also stands in opposition to the STS-based approach, which employs a standard language with deaf cultural aspects. Furthermore, determining the situations in which a specific language (Swedish or STS) should be used was an issue deemed to be problematic, in terms of how to provide both languages without diminishing the quality of education for students. First, not all students master STS, but all students are using sign-supported speech to various degrees in the classroom. So, if the teacher uses standard STS, the content will be inaccessible to some students. Second, it is unclear how much the students understand spoken Swedish without visual enhancements, i.e. sign-supported speech. Another issue discussed by the teachers was the responsibility of the schools to provide students with opportunities to develop their proficiency in STS.

Students' spoken language skills

To a greater extent than the previous generation of students (i.e. pre-CI generations), students in deaf schools today have spoken Swedish as their primary language (SOU 2016:46). In earlier years, they were expected to have little or no knowledge of Swedish upon school enrolment and, accordingly, learned it as a second language (cf. Svartholm, 2008). The greater knowledge of spoken Swedish among the new generation of students has educational implications, as it now is possible to teach Swedish using spoken Swedish as the language of instruction for some groups of deaf and hard-of-hearing students.

Teachers, especially those from the hard-of-hearing schools, generally experienced no problem in communicating in spoken Swedish with the students. However, they reported very few students speaking fluently without errors, although they did not describe in detail what these errors are or the implications of these errors. Also, as mentioned in the previous section, the teachers agreed that spoken Swedish as the sole language of instruction was not always sufficient, even with hearing technology (e.g. frequency modulation [FM] systems). Rather, many of the teachers in the interviews used a variation of sign-supported speech. The teachers pointed out the importance of visual enhancement, such as making information visually accessible through writing on the whiteboard and using spoken communication based upon sign-supported speech and visualizing lip movements, together with pedagogic strategies such as making the class-room more visually friendly through pictures, print, etc. Such strategies have been mentioned by researchers as chaining (e.g. Bagga-Gupta, 2004; Humphries & MacDougall, 1999) and, more recently, as multimodal or visually oriented translanguaging (Allard & Chen Pichler, 2018; Holmström & Schönström, 2018).

Looking into the future of sign bilingualism

The teachers working at the deaf and hard-of-hearing schools have different educational backgrounds, as some have gained a sign bilingual based teacher education while others have not, but have taken additional courses in STS. Concerning the future and what the education of a future teacher of deaf and hard-of-hearing students should include, on the topic of bilingualism the answers were united among the teachers, even among the teachers from the hard-of-hearing school. The interviewees think it is important to learn how to teach bilingually. Future teachers also need to learn how to use Swedish and STS in different educational contexts. As S8 put it: 'as it seems nowadays, a habit [of being bilingual] is missing. There is always a language that comes in first place. And the other language is merely like a card up the sleeve.' The teachers accordingly expressed a need for knowledge about how to work bilingually with both languages.

Another problem for sign bilingualism highlighted by the teachers was that there is a monolingual norm in Swedish society, as there is an expectation that most deaf and hard-of-hearing children should primarily learn to hear and speak, and only secondarily learn STS. Therefore, placement in deaf schools is often regarded as the last option. The teachers' perception seems to be confirmed by SOU 2016:46, in which the investigation argued that the primary school form for deaf and hard-of-hearing students was to be in mainstream settings, close to the students' homes. Only children in need of bilingual education in a sign language-based setting were to attend deaf schools. This is decided by a committee within SPSM that is responsible for admitting students to special schools and other education customized for children with a disability. Their work follows the regulations of the Swedish school act. Decisions about placing students in deaf schools depend upon the medical, audiological and pedagogical needs of the student. The key issue regarding students with CIs lies in the pedagogical needs that ensure students' success in a mainstream school setting. If students with CIs succeed relatively well in mainstream settings, there will be no pedagogical reason for applying to deaf schools. This means that, in the future, the total number of students considered for this form of schooling may be smaller. Therefore, the investigation suggests that the number of deaf schools should decrease in order to gather more students in each of the remaining schools. At the same time, the investigation concluded that the STS environment at these deaf schools should be strengthened to provide good opportunities for the students to develop proficiency in STS. However, the students who are not deemed as being in need of STS are inadmissible. It is therefore worth considering that prior to the investigation's suggestions, teachers in the hard-of-hearing program have described an increased demand to become *more* bilingually oriented in their educational approach due to the growing number of students who are helped by a more sign-based approach. In fact, all the teachers interviewed in the study emphasized the need for a bilingual orientation in teaching hard-of-hearing students, which stands in strong contrast to the SOU 2016:46 suggestion of limiting access to sign bilingual education.

S8 stated that:

it is hard to understand why. What about the children's identity as a CI user or as a hard-of-hearing individual? Sometimes hearing, sometimes deaf. The risk of being alone [in mainstream schools]. What if the CI gets damaged, the battery runs out? (S8)

The bilingual option could also stand for flexibility and assurance, as pointed out by S5: 'with bilingualism one doesn't need to choose, you can participate in everything.'

Discussion

Sweden was one of the first countries to adopt sign bilingual programs in the 1980s. However, according to Marschark *et al.* (2014), empirical evidence for the effectiveness of sign bilingual education is limited. Nevertheless, the existing evaluative studies have shown positive tendencies. In Sweden, for example, better academic outcomes have been found among deaf students who attended sign bilingual education, in comparison to students from earlier generations who were educated orally (Heiling, 1993, 1996). Also, in comparison with deaf education internationally, Sweden reports higher academic outcomes, although in-group comparisons with monolingual Swedish hearing peers indicate that they still lagging behind (Svartholm, 2010). Although there is a lack of research showing the benefits of sign bilingual programs, the grades and achievements of Swedish students as reported in Svartholm (2010) grant them access to higher education, and this is evidence that the model actually provides a good foundation for further studies. A discussion of what is a superior bilingual education for the deaf should, however, continue. For instance, after decades of longitudinal studies and the creation of an extensive database, Collier and Thomas (2004) arrived at conclusions that some types of bilingual education programs for English language learners were more successful than others.

Thus, the question of language choice remains an issue even after four decades of bilingual education. Although Sweden has extensive experience in sign bilingualism and a relatively robust language policy, it continues to experience challenges on a practical level pertaining to the linguistic foundation of deaf education. With its monolingual norm, Swedish society exerts a strong influence on the process of educating deaf and hard-of-hearing students that sometimes clashes with solutions proposed by linguistic and educational research. Bilingual deaf education needs to establish its own 'bilingual norm' using both the majority language (e.g. Swedish) and the minority language (e.g. STS) as parts of the students' whole language repertoire. The concept of *translanguaging* could be a point of departure in further investigations. Translanguaging can be described as a theory of bilingualism and a pedagogical stance, but also as a language ideology (Mazak, 2017). When translanguaging, the individual's entire linguistic repertoire is used, and the languages work together as part of the complexity of language interrelations from the perspective of language practice (García, 2009; García & Li Wei, 2014). A Swedish study by Lindahl (2015; this volume) constituted the first attempt to take such a perspective on instruction in deaf schools, showing examples of complex constructions and interaction between teacher and students in STS as well as written Swedish in a science class. In forthcoming investigations, we also need to look more closely at the language mixing that is apparently being used to a high degree in both the deaf schools and the hard-of-hearing program. For example, Swanwick (2016) argues that we need to know more about how bimodal bilingual communication, i.e. the simultaneous mixing of sign and speech, can improve classroom talk with the aim of exploiting teachers' and students' language repertoires in different ways. She argues that such mixing can be included within the concept of translanguaging since the students' full language repertoires are used, and that how the learners use languages in this context is of interest. Within the signing deaf community, however, such bimodal communication is considered to be negative and oppressive because students who rely solely on STS may be excluded. This is because it is spoken Swedish that is the matrix language, and many of the STS features disappear (cf. Snoddon, 2017). In order to understand bimodal communication or, in other words, sign-supported Swedish, one must know and master *spoken Swedish*. Therefore, the student needs to learn both languages – i.e., spoken Swedish and STS – in order to be able to communicate bimodally (see also De Meulder *et al.*, 2019).

Regarding students with CIs in Sweden, there are no studies evaluating their academic achievements. Part of the issue lies in the fact that once students with CIs are enrolled in mainstream programs, due to confidentiality protocols it is almost impossible to get information from the schools about these students. However, late-enrollers in deaf schools bear witness that mainstream programs are not suitable for all, and even if the program works well, it can be hard for deaf children to keep pace with their peers (cf. Holmström, 2013). Some international investigations, moreover, report that students with CIs are still lagging behind their hearing peers. Nevertheless, none of the investigations employ a bilingual framework; that is, they do not have variability as the norm and rather have monolingual norms regarding academic achievement. This bilingual framework is a missing component in the whole picture of deaf education.

Summary

In this chapter, we have described changes in Swedish bilingual education during the past four decades and teachers' views on the current bilingual situation. The interviews may be associated with changes in student demographics and language situations. The first change relates to a high language variability among students today, which indeed makes a bilingual approach to educating the deaf even more relevant than before. The second change relates to sign language issues. We have shown that communication in deaf schools has shifted from being solely sign-based to more bimodal-bilingual based, even if a signing environment is the goal and profile of deaf schools. Also, STS fluency among deaf students seems to have changed, leading to a greater variability of signing skills compared to earlier generations. Only a few students remain fluent in STS because they are primarily from deaf families. The third change is that, in practice, spoken language skills present a complicated picture. The teachers in our study stressed that students' abilities to participate in spoken communication are highly idiosyncratic: some students are totally dependent upon signing, whereas others can rely on listening strategies. In the last section, we have also taken a look into the future, and we anticipate that there may be many changes to come in bilingual education. Among other things, the teachers in our study indicated that they desire access to deeper knowledge of bilingual education practices and strategies.

In interviews, the teachers described a range of individual experiences associated with diversity. These experiences contribute to the conclusion that educating deaf and hard-of-hearing students is very complex, not least because of demographic changes and the students' skills in STS and spoken Swedish. Teachers also expressed the perception that society needs a better understanding of the benefits of the sign bilingual approach.

The ultimate purpose of a CI is to 'cure' deafness and therefore give children opportunities to hear and speak. The assumption is that if the children gain such abilities, society may decide that there is no longer any need for sign bilingual education, as there is no pedagogical basis for the students to receive such an education. For some, successful inclusion in mainstream schools has thus been a mark of success in terms of meeting societal norms and achieving one of the ultimate CI outcomes. Deaf schools are seen as a last resort for deaf students *in case* children's speech communication abilities are limited. In comparison, four decades ago, deaf schools were practically the only option for deaf children, with the exception of hard-of-hearing schools, and when a sign bilingual profile was implemented, it was an attractive model with no other practical alternatives. It also stood for an empowering education based on the movements during this period related to deaf culture and sign language rights.

References

Allard, K. and Chen Pichler, D. (2018) Multi-modal visually-oriented translanguaging among Deaf signers. *Translation and Translanguaging in Multilingual Contexts* 4 (3), 384–404.

Bagga-Gupta, S. (2004) Visually oriented language use: Discursive and technological resources in Swedish Deaf pedagogical arenas. In M. Van Herreweghe and M.

Vermeerbergen (eds) *To the Lexicon and Beyond: Sociolinguistics in European Deaf Communities* (pp. 171–207). Washington, DC: Gallaudet University Press.

Bagga-Gupta, S. and Domfors, L. (2003) Pedagogical issues in Swedish deaf education. In L. Monaghan (ed.) *Many Ways to be Deaf: International Variation in Deaf Communities* (pp. 67–88). Washington, DC: Gallaudet University Press.

Bagga-Gupta, S. and Holmström, I. (2015) Language, identity and technologies in classrooms for the differently-abled. *Journal of Communication Disorders, Deaf Studies & Hearing Aids* 3 (4). doi:10.4172/2375-4427.1000145

Bergman, B. and Engberg-Pedersen, E. (2010) Transmission of sign languages in the Nordic countries. In D. Brentari (ed.) *Sign Languages* (pp. 74–94). Cambridge: Cambridge University Press.

Collier, V.P. and Thomas, W.P. (2004) The astounding effectiveness of dual language education for all. *NABE Journal of Research and Practice* 2 (1), 1–20.

Cummins, J. (1996) *Negotiating Identities: Education for Empowerment in a Diverse Society*. Ontario, CA: California Association for Bilingual Education.

Dammeyer, J. (2014) Literacy skills among deaf and hard of hearing students and students with cochlear implants in bilingual/bicultural education. *Deafness & Education International* 16 (2), 108–119.

De Meulder, M., Kusters, A., Moriarty, E. and Murray, J. (2019) Describe, don't prescribe: The practice and politics of translanguaging in the context of deaf signers. *Journal of Multilingual and Multicultural Development* 40 (11), 892–906.

García, O. (2009) *Bilingual Education in the 21st Century: A Global Perspective*. Oxford: Wiley/Blackwell.

García, O. and Li Wei (2014) *Translanguaging: Language, Bilingualism and Education*. Basingstoke: Palgrave Macmillan.

Heiling, K. (1993) *Döva barns utveckling i ett tidsperspektiv: kunskapsnivå och sociala processer* [Deaf Childrens' Development in a Temporal Perspective: Academic Achievement Levels and Social Processes]. Studia psychologica et paedagogica. Series altera 108. Stockholm: Almqvist & Wiksell International.

Heiling, K. (1996) Deaf children's reading and writing: A comparison between pupils in different ages from oral and bilingual schools. In A. Muruvik Vonen, K. Arnesen, T.R. Enerstvedt and A. Varran Nafstad (eds) *Bilingualism and Literacy Concerning Deafness and Deaf-blindness. Proceedings of an International Workshop, 10th–13th November 1994* (pp. 101–114). Skådalen Publication Series No. 1. Oslo: Research and Development Unit, Skådalen Resource Centre.

Heiling, K. (1999) *Teknik är nödvändigt – men inte tillräckligt: en beskrivning av lärarsituationen i undervisningen av hörselskadade elever*. Pedagogisk-psykologiska problem. Malmö: Malmö högskola.

Hendar, O. and O'Neill, R. (2016) Monitoring the achievement of deaf pupils in Sweden and Scotland: Approaches and outcomes. *Deafness & Education International* 18 (1), 47–56.

Hermans, D., Wauters, L., de Klerk, A. and Knoors, H. (2014) Quality of instruction in bilingual schools for deaf children. In M. Marschark, G. Tang and H. Knoors (eds) *Bilingualism and Bilingual Deaf Education* (pp. 273–292). Oxford: Oxford University Press.

Hodge, G. and Johnston, T. (2014) Points, depictions, gestures and enactment: Partly lexical and non-lexical sign as core elements of single clause-like units in Auslan (Australian Sign Language). *Australian Journal of Linguistics* 34 (2), 262–291.

Holmström, I. (2013) Learning by hearing? Technological framings for participation. Doctoral dissertation, Örebro University.

Holmström, I. and Schönström, K. (2017) Resources for deaf and hard-of-hearing students in mainstream schools in Sweden: A survey. *Deafness & Education International* 19 (1), 29–39.

Holmström, I. and Schönström, K. (2018) Deaf lecturers' translanguaging in a higher education setting: A multimodal multilingual perspective. *Applied Linguistics Review* 9 (1), 90–111.

Humphries, T. and MacDougall, F. (1999) 'Chaining' and other links: Making connections between American sign language and English in two types of school settings. *Visual Anthropology Review* 15 (2), 84–94.

Knoors, H. and Marschark, M. (2012) Language planning for the 21st century: Revisiting bilingual language policy for deaf children. *Journal of Deaf Studies and Deaf Education* 17 (3), 291–305.

Leigh, G. (2008) Changing parameters in deafness and deaf education: Greater opportunity but continuing diversity. In M. Marschark and P.C. Hauser (eds) *Deaf Cognition: Foundations and Outcomes* (pp. 24–51). New York: Oxford University Press.

Lgr 80/83. *Läroplan för specialskolan. Kompletterande föreskrifter till Lgr 80* [*Curriculum for the Special School. Supplementary Directives to Lgr 80*]. Stockholm: Skolöverstyrelsen, Liber utbildningsförlaget.

Lgr 11. *Läroplan för specialskolan, förskoleklassen och fritidshemmet 2011* [*Curriculum for the Special School, Preschool Class and the After-School Centre 2011*]. Stockholm: Skolverket, Fritzes.

Lindahl, C. (2015) Tecken av betydelse: En studie om dialog i ett multimodalt, teckenspråkigt tvåspråkigt NO-klassrum [The sign of meaning: A study on the dialogue in a multimodal, sign bilingual STEM-classroom]. Doctoral dissertation, Stockholm University.

Lpo 94. *Läroplan för det obligatoriska skolväsendet* [*Curriculum for the Compulsory School*]. Stockholm: Utbildnings-departmentet.

Lyxell, T. (2013) *Se språket: Barnets tillgång till språket* [*See the Language: Children's Access to the Language*]. Stockholm: Språkrådet [Language Council of Sweden].

Mahshie, S.N. (1995) *Educating Deaf Children Bilingually: With Insights and Applications from Sweden and Denmark*. Washington, DC: Pre-College Programs, Gallaudet University.

Marschark, M. and Spencer, P.E. (2010) The promises (?) of deaf education: From research to practice and back again. In M. Marschark and P.E. Spencer (eds) *The Oxford Handbook of Deaf Studies, Language, and Education, Vol. 2*. Oxford: Oxford University Press. doi:10.1093/oxfordhb/9780195390032.013.0001

Marschark, M., Tangs, G. and Knoors, H. (2014) Bilingualism and bilingual deaf education: Time to take stock. In M. Marschark, G. Tang and H. Knoors (eds) *Bilingualism and Bilingual Deaf Education* (pp. 1–22). Oxford: Oxford University Press.

Mason, J. (2004) Semi-structured interview. In M.S. Lewis-Beck, A. Bryman and T. Futing Liao (eds) *The SAGE Encyclopedia of Social Science Research Methods* (pp. 1021–1022). Thousand Oaks, CA: Sage.

Mazak, C.M. (2017) Introduction: Theorizing translanguaging practices in higher education. In C.M. Mazak and K.S. Carroll (eds) *Translanguaging in Higher Education: Beyond Monolingual Ideologies* (pp. 1–10). Bristol: Multilingual Matters.

Mitchell, R.E. and Karchmer, M.A. (2004) Chasing the mythical ten percent: Parental hearing status of deaf and hard of hearing students in the United States. *Sign Language Studies* 4 (2), 138–163.

Nilsson, A.-L. and Schönström, K. (2014) Swedish Sign Language as a second language: Historical and contemporary perspectives. In D. McKee, R.S. Rosen and R. McKee (eds) *Teaching and Learning Signed Languages: International Perspectives and Practices* (pp. 11–34). Basingstoke: Palgrave.

Proposition 1980/81:100. Bilaga 12. Stockholm: Utbildningsdepartementet.

Säljö, R. (2000) *Lärande i praktiken: Ett sociokulturellt perspektiv* [*Learning in Practice: A Sociocultural Perspective*]. Stockholm: Prisma.

Säljö, R. (2005) *Lärande och kulturella redskap: Om lärprocesser och det kollektiva minnet* [*Learning and Cultural Tools. Learning Processes and the Collective Memory*]. Falun: Norstedts Akademiska Förlag.

Schönström, K. (2013) *Kartläggning av dövas och hörselskadades tvåspråkighet med särskilt avseende på svenskt teckenspråk* [*Survey of Bilingualism of the Deaf and Hard-of-Hearing with a Special Focus on Swedish Sign Language*]. Projektrapport [Project report].

Schönström, K. (2014) Visual acquisition of Swedish in deaf children: An L2 processability approach. *Linguistic Approaches to Bilingualism* 4 (1), 61–88.

Simonsen, E., Kristoffersen, A.-E., Hyde, M.B. and Hjulstad, O. (2009) Great expectations: Perspectives on cochlear implantation of deaf children in Norway. *American Annals of the Deaf* 154 (3), 263–273.

Snoddon, K. (2017) Uncovering translingual practices in teaching parents classical ASL varieties. *International Journal of Multilingualism* 14 (3), 303–316.

SOU 1998:66. *Utredningen om Funktionshindrade elever i skolan* [*The Investigation of Disabled Students in School*]. Stockholm: Utbildningsdepartementet.

SOU 2016:46. *Samordning, ansvar och kommunikation – vägen till ökad kvalitet i utbildningen för elever med vissa funktionsnedsättningar* [*Coordination, Responsibility and Communication – the Way to Increased Quality in Education for Students with Certain Disabilities*]. Stockholm: Utbildningsdepartementet.

SPSM (2016) *Årsredovisning 2016* [*Annual Report 2016*]. Härnösand: Specialpedagogiska skolmyndigheten.

SPSM (2017) *Språkplan för specialpedagogiska skolmyndigheten* [*Language Plan for the Swedish National Agency for Education*]. Härnösand: Specialpedagogiska skolmyndigheten.

SPSM (2019) *Årsredovisning 2019* [*Annual Report 2019*]. Härnösand: Specialpedagogiska skolmyndigheten.

Svartholm, K. (1993) Bilingual education for the deaf in Sweden. *Sign Language Studies* 81 (1), 291–332.

Svartholm, K. (2008) The written Swedish of Deaf children: A foundation for EFL. In C.J. Kellett Bidoli and E. Ochse (eds) *English in International Deaf Communication* (pp. 211–249). Bern: Peter Lang.

Svartholm, K. (2010) Bilingual education for deaf children in Sweden. *International Journal of Bilingual Education and Bilingualism* 13 (2), 159–174.

Swanwick, R. (2016) Scaffolding learning through classroom talk: The role of translanguaging. In P.E. Spencer and M. Marschark (eds) *The Oxford Handbook of Deaf Studies in Language* (pp. 420–430). Oxford: Oxford University Press.

Swanwick, R., Hendar, O., Dammeyer, J., Kristoffersen, A.-E., Salter, J. and Simonsen, E. (2014) Shifting contexts and practices in sign bilingual education in Northern Europe. In M. Marschark, G. Tang and H. Knoors (eds) *Bilingualism and Bilingual Deaf Education* (pp. 293–311). Oxford: Oxford University Press.

Vygotsky, L. (1978) *Mind in Society: The Development of Higher Psychological Processes*. London: Harvard University Press.

Wertsch, J.C. (1998) *Mind as Action*. Oxford: Oxford University Press.

Wikström, L. (2018) *Den tvåspråkiga verkligheten i specialskolan. Språk-, läs- och skrivutveckling*. Modul: Tvåspråkig undervisning – teckenspråk och svenska, del 2: Teckenspråkig tvåspråkig undervisning [*The Bilingual Reality in the Special School. Language, Reading and Writing Development*. Module: Bilingual teaching – sign language and Swedish, Part 2: Sign bilingual teaching]. Stockholm: Skolverket.

2 Sign Language Planning and Policy in Ontario Teacher Education

Kristin Snoddon

The Deaf Ontario Now movement of 1988 called for more hiring of deaf teachers and the full implementation of American Sign Language (ASL) across the curriculum in schools with deaf students. In 1989, the Review of Ontario Education Programs for Deaf and Hard of Hearing Students recommended that ASL become a language of instruction at the Ernest C. Drury School for the Deaf in Milton, Ontario. Subsequently, the school became the site of a pilot bilingual bicultural project that led to the ratification of a policy statement on bilingual bicultural education for deaf children at all three Anglophone provincial schools for deaf students in Ontario. In 1993, Bill 4 was incorporated into the Ontario Education Act, sanctioning the use of ASL and Langue des signes québécoise (LSQ) as languages of instruction in all schools for deaf students in Ontario. Despite this seeming progress at the policy level in sign language planning in Ontario deaf education, there has been a marked pattern of resistance to systemic change at levels of government and teacher accreditation, the university teacher of the deaf preparation program established in 1991 and provincial school administration. This chapter outlines the trajectory of deaf community activism, policy change and subsequent resistance.

Introduction

This chapter surveys the history of sign language planning and policy in teacher-of-the-deaf education in Ontario, Canada, with regard to the issue of teachers' sign language proficiency. From the perspective of deaf communities and bilingual education researchers, teachers' lack of sign language ability is frequently considered to be a root cause of deaf students' low achievement levels (Hoffmeister, 2007; Johnston *et al.*, 2002; Komesaroff, 2008; O'Neill, 2017). Despite the history of Ontario deaf community advocacy, gaps in sign language status and acquisition planning as pillars of language-in-education planning continue to impact the availability of bilingual education for deaf students by delaying or waiving the requirement that teachers of the deaf be proficient in sign language (Hult & Compton, 2012). This chapter discusses how the framing of education for deaf students within a special education rather than bilingual education paradigm means that disability oppression intersects with language ideologies to produce inequities in education. This framing is reminiscent of Ruiz' (1984) language-as-problem orientation which is frequently linked to minority-language children. Ruiz' problem, right and resource orientations in language planning have frequently been employed as an analytical heuristic in deaf education (e.g. Nover, 1995; Reagan, 2011).

The United Nations Convention on the Rights of Persons with Disabilities (CRPD) calls on states parties to 'take appropriate measures to employ teachers, including teachers with disabilities, who are qualified in sign language' (Article 24 [4]). Article 24 also calls on states parties to facilitate the learning of sign language and promote the linguistic identity of the deaf community in the education system (3[b]). As of 2010, Canada has signed and ratified the CRPD in addition to ratifying the Optional Protocol in 2017 that allows individuals and groups to approach the CRPD committee if a country has violated CRPD provisions (Council of Canadians with Disabilities, 2016; Office of the High Commissioner on Human Rights, 2018). However, as Lo Bianco (2001: 42) observes, language rights derived from 'claims to apply locally the provisions of international conventions' are often constrained in the absence of adequate 'endogenous provisions'. In other words, language phenomena occur and interact in complex ways on macro and micro levels (Tollefson, 2015).

In Ontario, there has been a historical pattern of resistance by teacher education program providers to policy initiatives for establishing standards for teachers' sign language proficiency and the recruitment and licensure of signing deaf teacher candidates. The grassroots Deaf Ontario Now movement that began in 1988 called for more hiring of deaf teachers and the full implementation of American Sign Language (ASL) across the curriculum in schools with deaf students (Carbin, 1996). In 1989, the *Review of Ontario Education Programs for Deaf and Hard of Hearing Students* recommended that ASL become a language of instruction at the Ernest C. Drury School for the Deaf, Milton (Ontario Ministry of Education, 1989). Subsequently, the school became the site of a pilot bilingual bicultural project that led to the ratification of a policy statement on bilingual bicultural education for deaf children at all three Anglophone provincial schools for deaf students in Ontario (Carbin, 1996). Bilingual bicultural education of deaf students utilizes a native sign language of a deaf community as a language of instruction and study, and involves the learning of a majority spoken/written language (Czubek & Snoddon, 2016; Gibson *et al.*, 1997). In 1993, Bill 4 was incorporated into the Ontario Education Act, sanctioning the use of ASL and Langue des signes québécoise (LSQ) as languages of instruction in all schools for deaf students in Ontario. In 2007, the Ontario Ministry of Education announced that it was enacting a regulation to facilitate the provision of ASL and LSQ by school boards, which are local groups that have been delegated authority over aspects of education by the province, as well as provincial schools for the deaf. In Ontario, provincial schools for the deaf are virtually the only providers of an education in sign language. This regulation was to be accompanied by the Ontario College of Teachers' establishment of standards for teachers' ASL and LSQ proficiency (Steenkamp, 2007). These policy texts may be viewed through the lens of Ruiz' (1984) language-as-right orientation, as compensatory measures intended to counter a deficiency perspective on deaf learners that has been pervasive in deaf education (Komesaroff, 2008).

Despite this seeming progress at the policy level in sign language status and acquisition planning in Ontario deaf education, there has been a marked pattern of resistance to systemic change at levels of government and teacher accreditation, teacher of the deaf preparation programs, school boards and provincial school administration. This chapter outlines this history with regard to: the Teacher Education Centre at the Ontario School for the Deaf, Belleville, which operated from 1919 to 1991; the Deaf and Hard of Hearing Teacher Education Program at York University, Toronto that replaced it and continues to the present day; and surrounding deaf community activism and ensuing policy developments. In so doing, this chapter foregrounds a critical approach to language policy, which acknowledges the role that policies and policymakers play in maintaining systems of social inequality and promoting the interests of dominant groups (Tollefson, 2006). Frequently, resistance to sign language rights in education manifests as opposition to establishing standards for teacher sign language proficiency and to dismantling barriers to teacher education for deaf candidates, who are essential for enacting bilingual education programs since most deaf children lack access to proficient adult sign language models (Mahshie, 1995). This chapter outlines the trajectory of deaf community activism, policy change and subsequent resistance concerning teacher education and licensure that has worked against the implementation of plurilingual education for deaf students in Ontario.

Methodology

This chapter employs historical-structural analysis of policy texts and other primary sources related to the events discussed in this chapter. As Tollefson (1991: 32) writes, 'The major goal of policy research is to examine the historical basis of policies and to make explicit the mechanisms by which policy decisions serve or undermine particular political and economic interests'. Historical-structural analysis focuses on power and inequality in language policy and planning, and looks at how dominant groups often control historical processes of policymaking (Tollefson,

2015). In this chapter, structural factors in sign language planning relate to the stigmatization of deaf learners within special education models as 'individual pathological models of service delivery' (Slee & Allan, 2001: 174). In these models, the language practices of dominant, nondeaf groups are ideologically maintained as 'natural and commonsense' (Tollefson, 2015: 142), while the linguistic practices of deaf communities are cast as deviant. This chapter explores the roles of texts, actors and planning agents in resisting and perpetuating historical processes in sign language policy and planning.

This chapter is based on data including historic policy documents, reports and media texts as primary sources. Many of these documents were shared with me by Gary Malkowski, a key actor in sign language policy and planning in Ontario. As a deaf scholar and language activist, I also witnessed and participated in several 21st century events that are described below.

Background and History

Deaf children are almost always taught by hearing teachers who are not fluent in sign language (Hoffmeister, 2007); however, the matter of teachers' sign language proficiency is rarely made a direct focus of policy initiatives in deaf education. National standards for teachers of deaf students often do not require sign language proficiency (e.g. Council on Education of the Deaf, 2018), although these may exist at the state level (e.g. Massachusetts Department of Elementary and Secondary Education, 2013; Michigan Department of Education, 2017) or at the level of individual teacher education programs or schools for the deaf. However, the USA-based Council on Education of the Deaf requires teacher preparation programs that claim to prepare teachers for ASL educational environments to demonstrate how their graduates are proficient in ASL and provide their assessment instruments (Fischgrund, J., personal communication, 15 April 2018). The Canadian Association of Educators of the Deaf and Hard of Hearing (2016: 7) requires candidates to demonstrate only 'novice to advanced beginning teaching skills in appropriate contexts in using ASL'. This point illustrates how 'people who experience the consequences of language policy' may not 'have a major role in making policy decisions' (Tollefson, 2006: 45), and how deaf education has been dominated by nondeaf ways of learning. Instead, in keeping with a special education model, legal and policy instruments dealing with deaf students' educational rights focus largely on the matter of school placement in mainstream versus deaf schools (e.g. Ontario Human Rights Commission, 2004; US Department of Education, 2015).

Inclusive education advocates have often privileged placement in mainstream settings with nondeaf peers rather than deaf students' access to sign language and bilingual programs (e.g. Kayess & Green, 2017). As

Hult and Compton (2012: 615) observe, 'framing educational contexts for deaf students in policy instantiates a process of language planning whereby the languages to be taught and learned are determined by the context in which students are placed'. A focus on mainstreaming deaf students in regular schools without sign language despite the expressed concerns of deaf communities (World Federation of the Deaf, 2018) reflects special education's 'appropriation of inclusion in order to maintain unreconstructed notions of schooling and educational defectiveness' (Slee & Allan, 2001: 174). While provision of a sign language interpreter may be viewed as facilitating inclusion, an interpreter cannot provide a bilingual education or replace direct instruction in sign language or opportunities to study sign language as a school subject with signing teachers and peers (Kauppinen & Jokinen, 2014), which are part of the legislative intent of Article 24 of the CRPD (Murray *et al.*, 2020). Instead, an interpreter is 'a compensatory tool for accessing the dominant hearing classroom environments' (Hult & Compton, 2012: 612).

This policy focus on educational placement rather than language access persists despite bilingual education research that shows the role that instruction in ASL plays in deaf students' literacy and academic achievement (e.g. Chamberlain & Mayberry, 2008; Crume, 2013; Cummins, 2006; Mayberry *et al.*, 2011; Scott & Hoffmeister, 2017). Since 1985, when the Ontario government implemented Bill 82 of the Education Act regarding the integration of disabled children into regular schools, enrolment at K-12 provincial schools for the deaf has steadily declined. Bill 82 did not provide for accommodations for deaf students in regular schools in the form of sign language interpreters or ASL/LSQ instruction, and its drafters did not consult with deaf advocacy organizations (Legislative Assembly of Ontario, 1988). In 2016, the four provincial schools for deaf students in Ontario reported a total enrolment of 254 students (Malkowski, G., personal communication, 8 April 2018), while in 2013–2014, Ontario school boards reported a total enrolment of approximately 2000 deaf and hard-of-hearing students via the Identification, Placement, and Review Committee (IPRC) process that identifies exceptional pupils who require special education programs or services (Ontario Ministry of Education, 2018a, 2018b). In the IPRC process, a parent or guardian must make a written request to a school principal who refers the student in question to an IPRC. The IPRC then decides whether the student is an exceptional pupil and what type of educational placement is appropriate. However, statistics regarding the numbers of deaf students in school boards may be underestimated since boards may not always conduct an IPRC process. Instead, boards may issue an Individual Education Plan that on occasion misidentifies deaf students as having language impairments or intellectual disabilities (Lafrance, C., personal communication, 8 April 2018; Malkowski, 2005). This situation of misidentification of deaf students and lack of sign language access mirrors that of other contexts which report that mainstreaming and a lack of sign language teaching in education has led to a rapid loss of sign language fluency among deaf children and adults, as compared to the generations educated prior to mainstreaming (Compton, 2014; Holmström & Schönström, 2017; O'Neill, 2017). For example, Weber (2020) describes the loss of approximately two generations of deaf community participants and of standard ASL models since the 1991 closure of the R.J.D. Williams School for the Deaf in Saskatchewan, Canada. The sign language fluency of earlier generations persisted in spite of the oralist classroom environment at schools for the deaf for much of the 20th century. This is due to the congregation of deaf children in deaf schools and the flourishing of ASL in dormitories and other extracurricular spaces. The oralist paradigm in deaf education continued in the 1970s, supported by the creation of artificial systems for manually encoding spoken English.

In Ontario, professional training for teachers of the deaf was not initiated until after the ideology of oralism became dominant in the early 20th century. This phenomenon was mirrored by international developments in deaf education after 1880, the year of the International Congress for the Improvement of the Conditions of Deaf-Mutes in Milan. The outcome of this Congress was to terminate collaboration between hearing teachers of the deaf and sign language educators (Supalla & Clark, 2015) and resulted in a sharp rise in the numbers of deaf students taught in oralist classroom environments (Van Cleve & Crouch, 1989). Historically, the pedagogical knowledge of sign language educators has most often not been conveyed through professional training for teachers (Humphries, 2013). This point demonstrates the ideological power of dominant groups and how their linguistic practices appear as 'natural and commonsense' (Tollefson, 2015: 142). The reorganization of deaf education as special education focused on rehabilitative approaches reflects 'the cultural politics of knowledge formation' about deafness, language and disability (Slee & Allan, 2001: 175).

Prior to the establishment of formal teacher education, the province's first deaf school provided a sign language environment. When the Ontario Institution for the Education and Instruction of the Deaf and Dumb was founded in 1870, its first principal, Wesley Palmer, promoted the use of what was then known as 'the sign language' and required teachers to 'assemble for weekly practice in the sign language' (Carbin, 1996: 93). Deaf teachers were appointed from the school's first session onwards (Carbin, 1996). However, the second head of the school, Robert Mathison, left suddenly in 1906; Carbin speculates that he was forced out by Department of Education reports that were critical of the small amount of speech training provided. The third superintendent, Charles Coughlin, curtailed the hiring of deaf teachers, introduced a policy of oralism and established the Professional Training for Teachers of the Deaf department in 1919 at the renamed Ontario School for the Deaf.

As Carbin (1996) notes, not only was nearly every teacher of deaf children in the province trained by this department, which followed an oralist philosophy and employed only hearing teacher trainers, but also admission was limited to individuals already in possession of Ontario Teacher's Certificates that qualified these individuals to teach in elementary and secondary schools. This policy precluded the training of deaf teachers; none was hired in Ontario until 1975, when the Ministry of Education changed its teacher certification regulation so that deaf individuals with a college degree that qualified them for admission to a teacher's college could be admitted (Ontario Ministry of Education, 1989). This resulted in deaf teachers graduating with a Letter of Standing instead of an Ontario Teacher's Certificate, and until the 1990s they were not subsequently provided with opportunities to upgrade their credentials (Advisory Committee on Deaf Education, 1990; Ontario Ministry of Education, 1989). Moreover, deaf candidates reported being rejected for employment at the provincial schools in favor of hearing teachers (Van Coillie, 1990). This pattern of discrimination against deaf teachers reflects how in historical-structural analysis, 'language involves both the code and its use – the person's language and the person' (Tollefson, 1991: 36). In 1967, the department changed its name to the Teacher Education Centre, under the purview of the Ministry of Education that determined training content and admission standards (Ontario Ministry of Education, 1989). Between the years 1967 and 1988, 521 teachers graduated from the Teacher Education Centre, including 16 deaf teachers who were admitted after 1974 and 12 hearing Francophone teachers (Ontario Ministry of Education, 1989).

Initially, most graduates of the Teacher Education Centre secured employment in Ontario provincial schools for deaf students. These schools consist of the Ontario School for the Deaf, Belleville (later renamed the Sir James Whitney School for the Deaf), which was joined in 1963 by the Ontario School for the Deaf, Milton (renamed the Ernest C. Drury School for the Deaf), and in 1974 by the Robarts School for the Deaf, London. Also in 1974, Centre Jules-Léger opened as a University of Ottawa program for disabled Francophone students that later became a provider of bilingual education in LSQ and French (Carbin, 1996). In 1995, this school was transferred to the Special Education and Provincial Schools Branch (Lafrance, C., personal communication, 25 March 2018), thus becoming a provincial school.

In later years, more teachers graduating from the Teacher Education Centre were hired by school board programs (Ontario Ministry of Education, 1989). After oralism was supplemented by sign systems for manually encoding spoken English, training content included 30 hours of the Rochester Method, or 'Visible English', which requires fingerspelling every word as it is spoken and which was introduced as a teaching method at the Milton and Belleville schools in 1971 and 1972 (Carbin, 1996).

Training also included 30 hours of signed English, which was introduced at the provincial schools when the Total Communication movement that followed decades of oralist policies supplemented Visible English (Carbin, 1996). Branson and Miller (1993: 28) refer to the 'symbolic violence' of signed English, which 'has not only devalued native sign languages but has sought to assimilate the Deaf into the majority language and majority culture as overtly deficient participants'. Thus, the manualism that was introduced in the 1970s served to maintain the position of dominant groups in deaf education.

Deaf Ontario Now

Historically, deaf people have been shown to mobilize when denied a voice in their educational institutions (Christiansen & Barnartt, 1995). The Ontario Association of the Deaf (OAD) was formed in 1886 by two deaf teachers from the Ontario Institute for the Education and Instruction of the Deaf and Dumb; the OAD's early advocacy focused on issues related to employment before becoming more concerned in the 20th century with the oralist language policies and lack of deaf teachers at the Belleville school (Carbin, 1996). In 1986, the OAD formed an Education Task Force (ETF) that was led by then board member Gary Malkowski. Malkowski later stated that the ETF became inspired by the March 1988 Deaf President Now protest at Gallaudet University, Washington, DC, which drew international attention (Picard, 1988). The student-led protest at Gallaudet, the world's only university for deaf students, successfully called for a deaf president to be appointed and for a majority of the university board of trustees to be deaf persons (Christiansen & Barnartt, 1995).

In April 1988, Malkowski and fellow ETF member Patty Shores-Hermann approached Richard Johnston, then education critic for the provincial New Democratic Party (NDP), who on 5 May 1988 introduced a private member's bill in the Legislative Assembly of Ontario calling for a study of the needs of deaf students (Rebick, 1988). Johnston cited inferior standards in deaf education, the miniscule number of deaf teachers in the province, the nonuse of ASL as a language of instruction and the lack of French-language instruction for deaf students (Legislative Assembly of Ontario, 1988; Picard, 1988). The bill was approved unanimously (Picard, 1988). From 1988 to 1990, before and after Johnston introduced his bill, the OAD and affiliate deaf clubs held rallies across the province. This movement became known as Deaf Ontario Now. These protests were joined by other deaf community rallies across Canada and outside the Canadian embassy in Washington, DC (Carbin, 1996; Lalonde, 1989; Rebick, 1989). However, the Ontario Ministry of Education, which began its review on 1 November 1988, did not release its report until December 1989, after deaf community advocates staged an occupation of then Minister of Education Sean Conway's office at Queen's Park (French, 1989).

Review of Ontario Education Programs for Deaf and Hard-of-Hearing Students

The Ministry's report dealing with English-language education was prepared by internal and external review committees and contained internal and external reports. Separate reports and reviews by different committees dealing with French-language services were also commissioned, with a first report released in May 1990 and a second in in August 1992. The French-language reports recommended recognition of LSQ as a language of instruction in addition to structural changes to amend the inequitable funding and lack of resources for Franco-Ontarian deaf students, including the transfer of Centre Jules-Léger from the Special Education and Provincial Schools Branch to Francophone control under the Direction de l'Education en Langue Française (Bisson *et al.*, 1992; Bruley *et al.*, 1990). On 12 October 2017, the Ministry announced that in the following year, governance of Centre Jules-Léger would be transferred to a new consortium of French-language school boards in Ontario, but even though this results in governance 'by and for Francophones' (Ontario Ministry of Education, 2017), it remains to be seen what effect this change will have on LSQ provision for education for deaf students. Under the Education Act, French-language rights holder groups have been eligible to develop proposals related to the use of LSQ as a language of instruction (s. 294[2(e)]).

For the English-language report, the internal committee was composed of Ministry of Education, school board and Office for Disabled Persons representatives. The external committee was comprised of experts in deaf education, including faculty members from York University, the Ontario Institute for Studies in Education, the University of Alberta and Gallaudet University, in addition to deaf school and school board administrators (Ontario Ministry of Education, 1989). As part of the internal review report, a literature review was commissioned regarding the effects of instruction in sign language on majority language acquisition by deaf students (Israelite *et al.*, 1992; Ontario Ministry of Education, 1989). This literature review, like Johnson *et al.*'s (1989) working paper for the Gallaudet Research Institute, documented the failure of English-based sign systems used by hearing teachers in deaf education and the superior academic performance of native signing deaf children of deaf parents as compared to deaf children of hearing parents. Israelite *et al.*'s (1992) review drew on Jim Cummins' (1981) linguistic interdependence hypothesis to explain the role of native sign languages in providing deaf children with the underlying language proficiency to support acquisition of a written language. However, Cummins was cited in the review as stating that the most critical area for bilingual bicultural deaf education is the power relationships between dominant and subordinated groups that deny deaf communities a stake in deaf education and the subsequent effect of this disempowerment on deaf children's school performance (Israelite *et al.*, 1992).

As Israelite *et al.* (1992: 50) wrote, 'In most jurisdictions it is possible to become a professional in a deafness-related field without achieving a minimum level of competence in sign language. Sign-language classes are electives rather than requirements in many teacher-preparation programs'. Cummins' point regarding the role of power relations in deaf education has paradoxically been both illustrated and ignored by empirically unsubstantiated claims that deaf children's learning of sign languages does not support learning of written languages (e.g. Mayer, 2017).

Recommendations

The Ministry report included numerous recommendations across several categories by the internal review committee. With regard to teacher education, a main recommendation was that the provincial training program for teachers of deaf students be transferred to a university faculty of education (Ontario Ministry of Education, 1989: 137). The rationale for this transfer was described in the external committee's report as fostering a research perspective on deaf education and more cooperation with other education programs and disciplines. This was followed by recommendations that support services and affirmative action policies be instituted to enable more deaf people to acquire teacher certification on an equal basis with hearing candidates and for deaf teachers holding Letters of Standing to be able to upgrade their qualifications to an Ontario Teaching Certificate (Ontario Ministry of Education, 1989: 137–138). Funding was recommended for in-service training courses to enable teachers to upgrade their ASL skills, and it was also recommended that the Ministry of Education in cooperation with school board programs should establish standards for teacher ASL proficiency (Ontario Ministry of Education, 1989: 137).

With regard to communication methodologies, it was recommended that a pilot project be initiated where ASL was the language of instruction and that, separately, ASL be recognized as a heritage language in Ontario, enabling it to be taught as a heritage language class outside of regular day public schooling (Mycek, 2015). Heritage language classes in Ontario are linked to the federal government's 1971 Multiculturalism Policy which aimed to indicate a supportive attitude toward immigrant languages and cultural identities while maintaining an official language policy that recognizes only English and French (Mycek, 2015). However, heritage language classes do not replace bilingual programs for minority children who are at risk of school failure (Cummins, 1990). In fact, ASL did not become an available course offering under the provincial International Languages Elementary Program until 2016 (Hysen, L., personal communication, 9 February 2016). The inclusion of ASL as an extracurricular heritage language in Ontario raises the issue of whether the province may attempt to claim it is fulfilling the mandates of Article 24 of the CRPD, while failing to meet the educational needs of deaf learners. There are often far more extensive opportunities for nondeaf learners to study sign languages than there are for deaf children and their parents (McKee, 2017; Reagan, 2011). This paradox may be linked to the construction of deaf children as deficient learners rather than bilinguals. The internal committee also recommended that ASL courses be offered for credit in high schools, and that faculties of education establish additional teacher qualification ASL courses (Ontario Ministry of Education, 1989: 139).

The recommendations made by the external review committee went further in recommending that ASL be recognized as a language of instruction in Ontario schools, effective September 1991, and that the Ministry should begin work on curriculum development and programing (Ontario Ministry of Education, 1989: 161–162). The external committee also recommended that teachers be required to undertake a test of competence in ASL, but this was only to be for teachers in ASL programs (Ontario Ministry of Education, 1989: 172). This committee recommended that a university-based Centre for Deafness Studies in Ontario (CDSO) be established with a main goal being teacher preparation (Ontario Ministry of Education, 1989: 174). Half of the faculty at the envisioned CDSO were to be deaf (Ontario Ministry of Education, 1989: 177). In addition, citing 'little or no public process for policy development in respect of programs for deaf and hard-of-hearing students' due to the relatively small numbers of deaf students and their parents, the external committee recommended establishment of 'an Ontario Board of Deaf Education … to be responsible for administration of the provincial schools and Regional Centres' (Ontario Ministry of Education, 1989: 187–188). The Board was to be composed of 'deaf and hard-of-hearing adults, parents of deaf and hard-of-hearing children, professionals with specialized training in education of deaf and hard-of-hearing students, and representatives of various community service and volunteer organizations serving the deaf community' (Ontario Ministry of Education, 1989: 188). In recognizing the cultural capital of signers and sign languages, these recommendations illustrate not only Ruiz' (1984) compensatory language-as-right orientation but also his language-as-resource perspective, which is 'both descriptive and aspirational' (Hult & Hornberger, 2016: 38). However, in a January 1990 meeting with an advisory committee of consumer group representatives, then Minister of Education Sean Conway expressed opposition to this idea, citing lack of accountability to taxpayers since the board would not be elected (Cowan & Rebick, 1990). The Regional Centres, also called for in the external committee review report, were to be independent centers located throughout the province with the mandate of providing services and information to deaf students in school board programs (Ontario Ministry of Education, 1989: 180–182).

Implementation

Following the release of the Ministry's report, deaf communities continued to hold rallies across Ontario, and on 22 March 1990 Richard Johnston introduced Bill 112 in the Ontario Legislature, calling for recognition of ASL and LSQ as languages of instruction in Ontario schools. In the same month, the bill passed its first and second readings but was not made law. This was despite extensive media coverage and 4 May 1990 rallies held by the OAD and its affiliates in Windsor, London, Kitchener, Toronto, Thunder Bay, Sudbury, Belleville and Ottawa, in addition to another rally of Canadian Gallaudet students outside the Canadian Embassy in Washington, DC. On 13 June 1990, Minister of Education Sean Conway made a statement to the Ontario Legislature to announce that, beginning in September 1990, a pilot project where ASL was an optional language of instruction would be conducted at the Ernest C. Drury school and that the Ministry had begun steps to transfer teacher education from the Sir James Whitney school to a faculty of education by September 1991, with additional support promised for deaf teachers and provincial school resource centers. Similar promises of support were made with respect to French-language deaf education (Conway, 1990).

However, the OAD took this announcement as an 'insult' (Maychak, 1990). Protests were again held across Ontario, including one by Ernest C. Drury high school students. In June 1990, a group of deaf parents and students who attended the Robarts school occupied the London constituency office of then Premier David Peterson to express their frustration with the government's lack of commitment to Bill 112. Another occupation was held at a Member of Provincial Parliament's office in Kitchener, and later that month more demonstrations were held across Ontario.

On 30 July 1990, Peterson called a provincial election, in effect killing Bill 112. However, on 6 September the NDP swept to its first-ever Ontario majority government, and Malkowski, who had run for election following a suggestion from Johnston, was elected as Member of Provincial Parliament for York East. The OAD subsequently called for more rallies to urge Premier-elect Bob Rae to reintroduce Bill 112 and hire more deaf teachers and administrators. In response, on 27 November 1990 Minister of Education Marion Boyd announced that her government was committed to recognizing ASL and LSQ as optional languages of instruction and that in July of the following year, the training program for teachers of the deaf would be transferred to the Faculty of Education at York University (Boyd, 1990). In 1991, David Mason was hired as an assistant professor to coordinate the bilingual bicultural teacher education program at York (Carbin, 1993; Small & Mason, 2008). In May 1993, a policy statement on bilingual bicultural education at all three Anglophone provincial schools was ratified (Carbin, 1993). In July 1993, Bill 4 was passed into law recognizing the use of ASL and LSQ as languages of instruction by teachers (Carbin, 1993). By September 1993, the number of deaf teachers in the province had jumped from eight (from before May 1988) to 33, in addition to five deaf administrators hired by the Ministry (Carbin, 1993). In 1999, a team of deaf teachers at the three Anglophone provincial schools began implementation and field testing of an ASL language arts curriculum for first-language learners from nursery school to Grade 3; over successive years, the primary curriculum expanded to junior, intermediate and senior grades (Small & Mason, 2008).

Resistance to Sign Language Rights in Education

ASL/LSQ regulation

Despite the above advances, in the years since Deaf Ontario Now, initiatives for accommodating sign language rights in Ontario deaf education have the appearance of 'anti-policy' (Lo Bianco, 2001). This resistance to change illustrates how dominant groups have maintained control over sign language policymaking. With the passage of Bill 4, the Ontario Education Act authorized the development of regulations for the use of ASL and LSQ as languages of instruction (Malkowski, 2006). Bill 4's amendment to the Education Act of 1993 stated that 'a teacher or temporary teacher may use American Sign Language or Quebec Sign Language in accordance with the regulations' (s. 264[1.1)]). Such regulations can carry the weight of enforcement. Beginning in 1993, the NDP government circulated a draft regulation requiring mandatory ASL instruction for at least 50% of the day where a minimum of five pupils were enrolled in a grade or division in a school board program or provincial school for the deaf (Carbin et al., 1993). For LSQ instruction, the minimum enrolment was to be three pupils. However, the provincial schools' Office of Bilingual/Bicultural Education for Deaf Children compared the draft regulation's constraints on provision of ASL and LSQ with the sections of the Education Act dealing with French-language instruction which mandate that every French-speaking person has the right to receive instruction in French throughout the school day (Carbin et al., 1993).

In April 1994, a policy forum was scheduled to direct the development of the regulation, and in September 1994, the draft regulation was circulated to school boards and parent and professional associations. These procedures revealed foreseen and actual implementation concerns regarding the lack of support from parents of deaf students who feared ASL instruction hindering the learning of English, a lack of teachers proficient in ASL or LSQ and a lack of teacher training opportunities for improving ASL and LSQ proficiency (Jessen, 1994). Several school boards refused to support the draft regulation in principle as being contrary to inclusion and impractical to implement, and a greater number of boards preferred the provision of ASL and LSQ as optional rather than mandatory (Marchand,

1994). One of several options considered following this stage of the consultation process was to amend the draft regulation to eliminate mandatory provision of ASL and LSQ (Marchand, 1994). These conflicts illustrate a pervasive language-as-problem orientation in Ontario deaf education that stands in contrast to the aims of Deaf Ontario Now.

In 1994, an ASL Competency Evaluation Committee was struck under the leadership of the Office for Bilingual/Bicultural Education for Deaf Children. This committee recommended additional support for developing an ASL curriculum and assessments for teachers of deaf students, with minimum required proficiency levels for new teachers to be defined through the curriculum (Carbin, 1994). The teachers' union, FOPSAT, expressed concerns both with the requirement for ASL proficiency for teachers since this was not part of any regulation, and with the assessment of teachers' ASL proficiency at any stage (Carbin, 1994).

No further action was taken by the NDP government with regard to an ASL/LSQ regulation or establishing teacher proficiency standards for ASL and LSQ. The Progressive Conservative government that replaced the NDP in 1995 was presented with recommendations for regulations: mandatory endorsement of ASL and LSQ as languages of instruction to any deaf student benefiting from this instruction (Proulx, 2000d); mandatory pre-service and in-service ASL/LSQ teacher training and Additional Qualification courses (Proulx, 2000a); mandatory teacher evaluation for ASL and LSQ proficiency and training in ASL and LSQ linguistics (Proulx, 2000c); and ASL and LSQ curricula as mandatory policy documents for the provincial schools and school boards (Proulx, 2000b). However, there was no evident follow-up with these recommendations.

The Ontario Liberal government that came to power in 2003 under then Education Minister Kathleen Wynne also began a consultation process regarding drafting an ASL/LSQ regulation. The regulation proposed by Wynne in January 2006 and eventually passed in June 2007 made scant expansion to Bill 4's amendment to the Education Act of 1993. In 2007, Regulation 298 of the Education Act was amended to add a new section, as follows:

SIGN LANGUAGE
32.   Where it is practical to do so and if the pupil understands American Sign Language or Quebec Sign Language, as the case may be, a teacher or temporary teacher may use American Sign Language or Quebec Sign Language,
(a)   in the classroom; and
(b)   as a language of instruction and in communications in regard to discipline and management of the school.

The above legislation, with its emphasis on the contingent and voluntary, has the appearance of 'face value policy work' (Lo Bianco, 2001: 28). Referring to the marginal status of disabled children, Slee and Allan (2001: 180) note, 'Policy statements, legislation, and special education texts are littered with conditional statements'. As Lo Bianco (2001: 21) writes, 'An examination of the alternative ways that the policy could have been expressed, that is, what is silenced and not stated in the policy that perhaps should or could have been dealt with openly, reveals a considerable part of the policy authoring process'.

In the case of the ASL/LSQ regulation, what are silenced are recommendations by the OAD that encompassed mandatory enforcement of the right to education in sign language under provincial school and school board programs, mandatory ASL and LSQ curricula, and teacher sign language proficiency levels in addition to proficiency levels for interpreters and educational assistants (Jackson & Snoddon, 2006). Many of these recommendations were echoed in communications from the Canadian Hearing Society that called on the Minister of Education to provide the same treatment for ASL and LSQ as English and French in the Education Act (Malkowski, G., personal communications, 14 March 2005, 12 July 2007). Also silenced is the history of Deaf Ontario Now activism and the recommendations of the government's own 1989 *Review of Ontario Education Programs for Deaf and Hard-of-Hearing Students*.

The Ontario College of Teachers' standard-setting exercise

The Ministry of Education has indicated that the Ontario College of Teachers, which was established in 1997 as a certification body, is responsible for determining teacher ASL and LSQ proficiency standards (Levin, B., personal communication, 1 September 2006). Accordingly, when Regulation 298 of the Education Act was passed in July 2007, it was accompanied in the same month by Regulation 342/07 under the Ontario College of Teachers Act 1996, regarding qualification for teaching students who are deaf or hard of hearing. This regulation states that a prerequisite for admission to the Teaching Students who are Deaf or Hard of Hearing program is that a candidate:

(i) has successfully completed at least two courses in American Sign Language (ASL) or Langue des signes québécoise (LSQ) acceptable to the College, or

(ii) his or her proficiency in American Sign Language or Langue des signes québécoise is at least equivalent to the proficiency that would be achieved by completing two such courses. (s. 42.2[1(b)])

On 8 February 2008, the College convened a panel meeting for the purpose of eliciting recommendations for defining ASL proficiency standards for entrance to the deaf education program at York University. A separate French session for determining LSQ standards was held on 9 May 2008. A chief focus for the ASL meeting was determining which two courses were acceptable to the College (Ontario College of Teachers, 2008a).

While the College's (2008a) report recognized that 'it is often preferable for a standard to be established by experts who possess native-like fluency in the target language', as occurred with processes conducted by the College for establishing English proficiency requirements, in the case of the ASL and LSQ standards many of the panel invitees did not possess this proficiency. The deaf education program at York University maintains two separate streams for ASL and aural/oral communication (Faculty of Education, n.d.), and this streaming process, which constructs a binary opposition between oralism and bilingual approaches in deaf education, is upheld by Regulation 347/02 of the Ontario College of Teachers Act (s. 24.1[3]). As such, the College 'decided to assemble a very large panel to ensure that as many stakeholders as possible would have input to the standard-setting outcome' (Ontario College of Teachers, 2008a: 7).

Panel invitees were divided into two groups representing bilingual education and oralist education stakeholders to review first the ASL Proficiency Interview (ASLPI) as a standard-setting assessment tool and then the *Signing Naturally* curriculum that is widely used for teaching ASL (Gallaudet University, n.d.; Smith *et al.*, 2008). However, this process appeared to be dominated by the matter of some participants disagreeing 'that ASL proficiency was needed by practitioners choosing to follow the aural/oral stream' (Ontario College of Teachers, 2008a: 8). Although in the course of the day participants were 'given six opportunities to submit a recommendation' (Ontario College of Teachers, 2008a: 9), consensus was not achieved regarding a recommended minimum ASLPI score or level of *Signing Naturally* coursework required for entry to the deaf education program. However, the unpublished version of the College's (2008a) report on the standard-setting exercise found that a cumulative percentage of participants agreed that ASLPI Level 3 and *Signing Naturally* Level 203 or greater should be the prerequisite for entry regardless of whether the ASL or oral/aural stream was chosen. Since there is no standardized assessment instrument for LSQ that is similar to the ASLPI, the LSQ panel discussion focused mainly on coursework, with a majority recommending three LSQ courses (Ontario College of Teachers, 2008b). To date, however, the College has not implemented minimum ASL or LSQ proficiency requirements for teachers of the deaf (Malkowski, G., personal communication, 25 March 2018). This resistance to sign language rights for deaf learners reflects the 'symbolic violence' of professionalism that seeks to ward off any perceived threat 'to undermine the expertise of the hearing teacher of the Deaf' (Branson & Miller, 1993: 30).

York University's Deaf and Hard of Hearing Teacher Education program

Since replacing the former Teacher Education Centre in Belleville, the teacher-of-the-deaf education program at York University has not fulfilled the mandate it was given in the 1989 *Review* to establish support services and affirmative action policies for deaf teacher candidates with the aim of increasing the numbers of deaf teachers in Ontario. Beginning in 1991, during David Mason's tenure as professor and coordinator of the bilingual bicultural teacher education program, York University accepted between three and eight deaf teacher candidates per year, and this directly contributed to the increase in the hiring of deaf teachers and administrators at provincial schools and some school boards (Malkowski, 2005).

However, in 1997 Barry Denman, who had previously represented the Ontario Ministry of Education and Training on the program's advisory board, became coordinator of the deaf education program. At this time, York University ceased to follow the policy, first implemented by the Teacher Education Centre, of allowing deaf teacher candidates with undergraduate degrees but without Ontario College of Teachers licensure to enroll in the deaf education program (Malkowski, 2005). This practice has persisted (Faculty of Education, 2018) despite the enshrinement of this affirmative action principle in the Ontario College of Teachers Act (Ontario College of Teachers, 2006; Ontario Regulation 184/97: s. 19) and despite documentation of pervasive barriers to postsecondary education faced by deaf learners (Canadian Hearing Society, 2014). Accordingly, the numbers of deaf graduates of the York University teacher preparation program have been sharply reduced, and no deaf full-time faculty members have been retained by the program since Mason's departure in 2002. York University's professional use of mechanisms to hinder deaf individuals' acquisition of teaching certification demonstrates a nexus of state, ideological and discursive power to maintain the interests of dominant groups in deaf education (Tollefson, 2015).

Moreover, even though the 1989 *Review* and successive government communications (e.g. Ontario Ministry of Education, 2007) made substantive reference to the provision of ASL classes for pre-service and in-service teacher candidates, and despite the practice of providing such courses in previous years (Tancock, 2002), York University presently offers no ASL courses as part of its teacher preparation program (Faculty of Education, n.d.). A specialized course in ASL linguistics is offered as part of the ASL Communication stream (Faculty of Education, n.d.). This situation is in contrast to the case of Franco-Ontarian teacher-of-the-deaf education, where the University of Ottawa offers five levels of LSQ courses for teacher candidates, with completion of three courses in LSQ being a prerequisite for entry and completion of five courses required for graduation (University of Ottawa Faculty of Education, n.d.). Unlike the two separate streams at York University, the University of Ottawa program offers a single stream of courses for teachers of the deaf.

Despite this lack of support for candidates' learning of ASL, the York University program maintains an ASLPI score of 3.0 as a prerequisite for entry into the ASL Communication stream (Manktelow, S., personal communication, 9 April 2018). Without providing opportunities for teacher candidates to improve their ASL skills, and in the virtual absence of signing deaf candidates admitted to the program, this policy has the effect of shutting down ASL and English bilingual teacher training opportunities in Ontario, since York is the only Anglophone provider of a deaf education program in the province (Faculty of Education, 2018). As such, the discriminatory policies and practices of the former Teacher Education Centre are maintained in the present day.

Conclusion: Looking Forward

This chapter has attempted a historical-structural analysis of events in Ontario deaf education that shows how the progress of sign language policymaking has been impeded by state, ideological and discursive power (Tollefson, 2015) which perpetuates a deficiency, language-as-problem perspective on deaf people. Deaf learners are disabled in education systems that frame the former as in need of individualized interventions instead of a bilingual education through the medium of sign language. These systems also maintain the hegemony of teacher-of-the-deaf education following a special education model as a 'tactic to depoliticize school failure ... and legitimize the professional interest of special education workers' (Slee & Allan, 2001: 175). This hegemony reflects the intersection of ableism with ideologies surrounding ASL and other natural sign languages (Reagan, 2011).

The history of sign language planning and policy in Ontario illustrates Skutnabb-Kangas' (2002: 189–190) observation that deaf learners are 'more or less outside the rights system in most or all countries'. In its review of developments in sign language status and acquisition planning from 1989 to 2018, this chapter has described several instances when educational policy actors could have benefited deaf students in Ontario by facilitating an education in sign language but failed to do so. The chapter has also described how the province's publicly funded teacher-of-the-deaf education program could have recruited and trained more deaf and hearing candidates qualified in sign language to provide exemplary bilingual education models. These policies and practices are enshrined on a macro level in the UN CRPD but are largely absent from the micro level of classroom education of Ontario deaf children.

The lack of enforcement of deaf students' right to education in sign language has persisted despite the achievements and promise of Deaf Ontario Now. Over the past 30 years, the weakening of community institutions that nurture and sustain deaf communities and the impact of provincial austerity measures on deaf learners' access to postsecondary education have impacted the strength of deaf organizations in Ontario (Canadian Hearing Society, 2014). The implementation of universal neonatal hearing screening in Ontario and operational policy restrictions on deaf children's learning of ASL and LSQ when children receive cochlear implants has further entrenched systems of oralism (Snoddon, 2008) and led to schools acting as extensions of the cochlear implant clinic whereby teachers of the deaf are reclassified as auditory-verbal therapists (Mauldin, 2016).

It is generally acknowledged that legal recognition of sign languages has been ineffective in ensuring bilingual education rights for deaf children (De Meulder *et al.*, 2019; McKee, 2017). This is likely true in Canada, where in 2019 ASL, LSQ and Indigenous sign languages were recognized as primary languages for communication by deaf persons in the context of the Accessible Canada Act (Snoddon & Wilkinson, 2019). However, a human rights model of disability in the UN CRPD as a legal instrument that includes provision for sign language rights in education may strengthen the claims of deaf advocacy organizations (Murray *et al.*, 2018). This is in addition to endogenous claims made for the application of the *Canadian Charter of Rights and Freedoms* to uphold deaf children's right to learn sign language (Paul & Snoddon, 2017). At the same time, sign language teachers are better positioned to develop and implement rigorous curricula that can be specialized to meet the needs of educators of deaf children, as called for in the 1989 *Review* and the Office of Bilingual/Bicultural Education's recommendations (Carbin, 1994). This is seen in the continued development of the *Common European Framework of Reference for Languages* and its application to sign language teaching and learning (European Centre for Modern Languages, 2018; Oyserman & de Geus, this volume; Snoddon, 2015).

In terms of sign language policy in Ontario teacher education, it is clear that enforceable status planning instruments and adequate acquisition planning measures are still lacking. More collaborative relationships between teacher education providers and deaf communities may support both teachers' sign language proficiency and the provision of bilingual education for deaf students in Ontario. Development of these relationships may depend on reframing sign language as both a right and a resource and on deconstructing a special education model for deaf children in favor of one that supports bilingualism and inclusion.

Acknowledgments

Special thanks to Dr Robert Hoffmeister for his comments on an earlier version of this chapter.

References

Advisory Committee on Deaf Education (1990) *Meeting with Minister Sean Conway*, 23 January. Toronto, ON: Canadian Hearing Society.

Bisson, G. *et al.* (1992) *Second Report of the Comite Consultatif Ministeriel sur l'Éducation des Sourds Francophones: Francophone Equivalent to Provincial Schools*, August. Toronto, ON: Ontario Ministry of Education.

Boyd, M. (1990) *Statement to the Legislature on Deaf Education*, 27 November. Toronto, ON: Ontario Ministry of Education.

Branson, J. and Miller, D. (1993) Sign language, the deaf, and the epistemic violence of mainstreaming. *Language and Education* 7 (1), 21–41. doi:10.1080/09500789309541346

Bruley, L., Kipp, B. and Pelletier, I. (1990) *Enquête sur les programmes à l'intention des élèves sourds*. Toronto, ON: Ontario Ministry of Education.

Canadian Association of Educators of the Deaf and Hard of Hearing (2016) *Revised CAEDHH Certification Standards*, November. See https://www.caedhh.ca/certification (accessed 26 March 2018).

Canadian Hearing Society (2014) *Canadian Hearing Society's Position Paper on Challenges and Issues Affecting Access to Post-Secondary Education for Deaf and Hard of Hearing Students*. See https://www.chs.ca/sites/default/files/final_board_approved_chs_position_paper_on_post-secondary_education_nov_29_2014.pdf (accessed 11 April 2018).

Carbin, C. (1993) Ontario's new ASL/LSQ law: PAH! *Gallaudet Today* 24 (2), 15–17.

Carbin, C. (1994) *Memorandum re: Draft Recommendations for ASL Competency Evaluation Policies and Procedures for Teachers in the Provincial Schools for Deaf Students*. Toronto, ON: Ontario Ministry of Education.

Carbin, C. (1996) *Deaf Heritage in Canada*. Toronto, ON: McGraw-Hill Ryerson Ltd.

Carbin, C.F., Small, A.R. and Smith, D. (1993) *Memorandum re: Review of 'Regulation for Use of ASL as a Language of Instruction'*, 19 November. Toronto, ON: Ontario Ministry of Education.

Chamberlain, C. and Mayberry, R. (2008) American Sign Language syntactic and narrative comprehension in skilled and less skilled readers: Bilingual and bimodal evidence for the linguistic basis of reading. *Applied Psycholinguistics* 29 (3), 367–388. doi:10.1017/S014271640808017X

Christiansen, J.B. and Barnartt, S.N. (1995) *Deaf President Now!: The 1988 Revolution at Gallaudet University*. Washington, DC: Gallaudet University Press.

Compton, S.E. (2014) American Sign Language as a heritage language. In T.G. Wiley, J.K. Peyton, D. Christian, S.C.K. Moore and N. Liu (eds) *Handbook of Heritage, Community, and Native American Languages in the United States* (pp. 272–286). New York: Routledge.

Conway, S. (1990) *Statement to the Legislature by the Honourable Sean Conway, Minister of Education on Deaf Education*, 13 June. Toronto, ON: Ontario Ministry of Education.

Council of Canadians with Disabilities (2016) *Canada to Ratify CRPD's Optional Protocol*, 23 December. See http://www.ccdonline.ca/en/international/un/canada/CRPD-OP-23Dec2016 (accessed 14 February 2018).

Council on Education of the Deaf (2018) *CED Standards for Programs Preparing Teachers of Students Who are Deaf and Hard of Hearing*, February. See http://council-ondeafed.org/standards/ (accessed 26 March 2018).

Cowan, M.R. and Rebick, J. (1990) What's happening with the Ontario Education Review? *Vibrations*, September, 7–8.

Crume, P. (2013) Teachers' perceptions of promoting American Sign Language phonological awareness in an ASL/English bilingual program. *Journal of Deaf Studies and Deaf Education* 18 (4), 464–488. doi:10.1093/deafed/ent023

Cummins, J. (1981) The role of primary language development in promoting educational success for language minority students. In California State Department of Education (eds) *Schooling and Language Minority Students: A Theoretical Framework* (pp. 3–49). Los Angeles, CA: Evaluation, Dissemination and Assessment Center, California State University.

Cummins, J. (1990) Denial of voice: The suppression of deaf children's language in Canadian schools. In J. Cummins and M. Danesi (eds) *Heritage Languages: The*

Development and Denial of Canada's Linguistic Resources (pp. 81–97). Toronto, ON: Our Schools/Our Selves Education Foundation.

Cummins, J. (2006) *The Relationship Between American Sign Language Proficiency and English Academic Development: A Review of the Research.* See http://citeseerx.ist.psu.edu/viewdoc/download?doi=10.1.1.521.8612&rep=rep1&type=pdf (accessed 9 March 2018).

Czubek, T.A. and Snoddon, K. (2016) Bilingualism, philosophy and models of. In G. Gertz and P. Boudreault (eds) *The Deaf Studies Encyclopedia, Vol. I* (pp. 79–82). Thousand Oaks, CA: Sage Publications.

De Meulder, M., Murray, J.J. and McKee, R.L. (eds) (2019) *The Legal Recognition of Sign Languages: Advocacy and Outcomes Around the World.* Bristol: Multilingual Matters.

European Centre for Modern Languages (2018) *Sign Languages and the Common European Framework of Reference for Languages: Descriptors and Approaches to Assessment.* See https://www.ecml.at/ECML-Programme/Programme2012-2015/ProSign/PRO-Sign-referencelevels/tabid/1844/Default.aspx (accessed 11 April 2018).

Faculty of Education (2018) *Admission Requirements & Application: Residents of Ontario.* See http://edu.yorku.ca/academic-programs/deaf-hard-of-hearing-education/how-to-apply/ (accessed 11 April 2018).

Faculty of Education (n.d.) *Courses.* See http://edu.yorku.ca/academic-programs/deaf-hard-of-hearing-education/courses/ (accessed 10 April 2018).

French, O. (1989) Seeking better education for deaf, activists occupy Conway's office. *The Globe and Mail*, 16 December, p. A9.

Gallaudet University (n.d.) *American Sign Language Proficiency Interview (ASLPI).* See https://www.gallaudet.edu/the-american-sign-language-proficiency-interview/aslpi (accessed 9 April 2018).

Gibson, H., Small, A. and Mason, D. (1997) Deaf bilingual bicultural education. In J. Cummins and D. Corson (eds) *Encyclopedia of Language and Education, Vol. 5: Bilingual Education* (pp. 231–240). Dordrecht: Kluwer.

Hoffmeister, R. (2007) Language and the deaf world: Difference not disability. In M.E. Brisk (ed.) *Language, Culture, and Community in Teacher Education.* New York: Lawrence Erlbaum.

Holmström, I. and Schönström, K. (2017) Resources for deaf and hard-of-hearing students in mainstream schools in Sweden: A survey. *Deafness & Education International* 19 (1), 29–39. doi:10.1080/14643154.2017.1292670

Hult, F. and Compton, S. (2012) Deaf education policy as language policy: A comparative analysis of Sweden and the United States. *Sign Language Studies* 12 (4), 602–620. doi:10.1353/sls.2012.0014

Hult, F.M. and Hornberger, N.H. (2016) Re-visiting orientations to language planning: Problem, right, and resource as an analytical heuristic. *Bilingual Review* 33 (3), 30–49. See http://bilingualreview.utsa.edu/index.php/br/article/view/118

Humphries, T. (2013) Schooling in American Sign Language: A paradigm shift from a deficit model to a bilingual model in deaf education. *Berkeley Review of Education* 4 (1), 7–33. See https://escholarship.org/uc/item/4gz1b4r4.

Israelite, N., Ewoldt, C. and Hoffmeister, R. (1992) *Bilingual/Bicultural Education for Deaf and Hard-of-Hearing Students: A Review of the Literature on the Effects of Native Sign Language on Majority Language Acquisition.* Toronto, ON: Queen's Printer for Ontario.

Jackson, J. and Snoddon, K. (2006) Proposed regulations to *Bill 4: Amendment to the Education Act, 1993.* Presentation to the Ontario Ministry of Education, Toronto, ON, 16 January.

Jessen, L. (1994) *Memorandum: Development of a Regulation on the Use of ASL/LSQ*, 15 April. Toronto, ON: Ontario Ministry of Education and Training.

Johnson, R.E., Liddell, S.K. and Erting, C.J. (1989) *Unlocking the Curriculum: Principles for Achieving Access in Deaf Education*. Gallaudet Research Institute Working Paper No. 89-3. Washington, DC: Gallaudet University.

Johnston, T., Leigh, G. and Foreman, P. (2002) The implementation of the principles of sign bilingualism in a self-described sign bilingual program: Implications for the evaluation of language outcomes. *Australian Journal of Education of the Deaf* 8, 38–46.

Kauppinen, L. and Jokinen, M. (2014) Deaf culture and linguistic rights. In M. Sabatello and M. Schulze (eds) *Human Rights and Disability Advocacy* (pp. 131–145). Philadelphia, PA: University of Pennsylvania Press.

Kayess, R. and Green, J. (2017) Today's lesson is on diversity. In P.D. Blanck and E. Flynn (eds) *The Routledge Handbook of Disability Law and Human Rights* (pp. 53–71). New York: Routledge/Taylor & Francis.

Komesaroff, L. (2008) *Disabling Pedagogy: Power, Politics, and Deaf Education*. Washington, DC: Gallaudet University Press.

Lalonde, M. (1989) Deaf Canadians to march in dozen cities for American Sign Language in schools. *The Globe and Mail*, 11 May, p. A19.

Legislative Assembly of Ontario (1988) *Hansard*, 5 May. See https://www.ola.org/en/legislative-business/house-documents/parliament-34/session-1/1988-05-05/hansard (accessed 25 March 2018).

Lo Bianco, J. (2001) From policy to anti-policy: How fear of language rights took policy-making out of community hands. In J. Lo Bianco and R. Wickert (eds) *Australian Policy Activism in Language and Literacy* (pp. 13–44). Melbourne: Language Australia.

Mahshie, S.N. (1995) *Educating Deaf Children Bilingually: With Insights and Applications from Sweden and Denmark*. Washington, DC: Gallaudet University Press.

Malkowski, G. (2005) *Response of the Canadian Hearing Society to the Ontario College of Teachers' 'Preparing Teachers for Tomorrow Initial Teacher Education in Ontario'*, 29 April. Toronto, ON: Canadian Hearing Society.

Malkowski, G. (2006) *Submission to the Standing Committee on Social Policy with Respect to Bill 78: An Act to Amend the Education Act, the Ontario College of Teachers Act, 1996 and Certain Other Statutes Relating to Education*, 7 May. Toronto, ON: Canadian Hearing Society.

Marchand, M. (1994) *Memorandum: ASL/LSQ Teacher Certification*, 9 June. Toronto, ON: Ontario Ministry of Education and Training.

Massachusetts Department of Elementary and Secondary Education (2013) *ESE Announces Acceptable Test for the Deaf and Hard-of-Hearing: American Sign Language/Total Communication License*. See http://www.doe.mass.edu/news/news.aspx?id=7833 (accessed 7 April 2018).

Mauldin, L. (2016) *Made to Hear: Cochlear Implants and Raising Deaf Children*. Minneapolis, MN: University of Minnesota Press.

Mayberry, R., Del Giudice, A.A. and Lieberman, A. (2011) Reading achievement in relation to phonological coding and awareness in deaf readers: A meta-analysis. *Journal of Deaf Studies and Deaf Education* 16 (2), 164–188. doi:10.1093/deafed/enq049

Maychak, M. (1990) Deaf students insulted on schools, group says. *Toronto Star*, 14 June.

Mayer, C. (2017) Written forms of signed language: A route to literacy for deaf learners? *American Annals of the Deaf* 161 (5), 552–559. doi:10.1353/aad.2017.0005

McKee, R. (2017) Assessing the vitality of New Zealand Sign Language. *Sign Language Studies* 17 (3), 322–362. doi:10.1353/sls.2017.0008

Michigan Department of Education (2017) *American Sign Language*. See http://www.michigan.gov/documents/mde/American_Sign_Language_557246_7.pdf (accessed 7 April 2018).

Murray, J., De Meulder, M. and le Maire, D. (2018) An education in sign language as a human right? The sensory exception in the legislative history and on-going interpretation of Article 24 of the UN Convention on the Rights of Persons with Disabilities. *Human Rights Quarterly* 40 (1), 37–68. doi:10.1353/hrq.2018.0001

Murray, J.J., Snoddon, K., De Meulder, M. and Underwood, K. (2020) Intersectional inclusion for deaf learners: Moving beyond General Comment No. 4 on Article 24 of the UNCRPD. *International Journal of Inclusive Education* 24 (7), 691–705. doi:10.1080/13603116.2018.1482013

Mycek, A. (2015) International language teaching: An exploration of the successes and challenges of the International Language Elementary (ILE) program in Ontario. Master's thesis, Ontario Institute for Studies in Education, University of Toronto.

Nover, S. (1995) Politics and language: American Sign Language and English in deaf education. In C. Lucas (ed.) *Sociolinguistics in Deaf Communities* (pp. 109–161). Washington, DC: Gallaudet University Press.

Office of the High Commissioner on Human Rights (2018) *Optional Protocol to the Convention on the Rights of Persons with Disabilities.* See http://www.ohchr.org/EN/HRBodies/CRPD/Pages/OptionalProtocolRightsPersonsWithDisabilities.aspx (accessed 21 March 2018).

O'Neill, R. (2017) Bilingual deaf education: Language policies, linguistic approaches, and education models in Europe. In K. Reuter (ed.) *UNCRPD Implementation in Europe: A Deaf Perspective. Article 24: Education* (pp. 86–109). Brussels: European Union of the Deaf.

Ontario College of Teachers (2006) *Preparing Teachers for Tomorrow: The Final Report.* Toronto, ON: Ontario College of Teachers.

Ontario College of Teachers (2008a) Defining an ASL prerequisite for the Teaching Students who are Deaf or Hard of Hearing program. Unpublished report to the Ontario College of Teachers, Toronto, ON, 18 February.

Ontario College of Teachers (2008b) *Report to Council on ASL/LSQ Standard-Setting,* 25–26 September. Toronto, ON: Ontario College of Teachers.

Ontario Human Rights Commission (2004) *Guidelines on Accessible Education.* See http://www.ohrc.on.ca/sites/default/files/attachments/Guidelines_on_accessible_education.pdf (accessed 11 March 2018).

Ontario Ministry of Education (1989) *Review of Ontario Education Programs for Deaf and Hard-of-Hearing Students.* Toronto, ON: Program Implementation and Review Branch, Ministry of Education.

Ontario Ministry of Education (2007) *McGuinty Government Delivering More Support for Students Who are Deaf: Teachers Can Use American Sign Language in Ontario's Schools,* 12 October. Toronto, ON: Ontario Ministry of Education.

Ontario Ministry of Education (2017) Centre Jules-Léger to be governed by and for Francophones. *News Release,* 12 October. See https://news.ontario.ca/edu/en/2017/10/centre-jules-leger-to-be-governed-by-and-for-francophones.html (accessed 2 April 2018).

Ontario Ministry of Education (2018a) *The Identification, Placement, and Review Committee: Identifying the Needs of Exceptional Pupils.* See http://www.edu.gov.on.ca/eng/general/elemsec/speced/identifi.html (accessed 8 April 2018).

Ontario Ministry of Education (2018b) *Provincial and Demonstration Schools in Ontario: Moving Forward.* See http://www2.edu.gov.on.ca/eng/parents/robarts.html (accessed 9 April 2018).

Paul, J.J. and Snoddon, K. (2017) Framing deaf children's right to sign language in the *Canadian Charter of Rights and Freedoms. Canadian Journal of Disability Studies* 6 (1). See http://cjds.uwaterloo.ca/index.php/cjds/article/view/331/549

Picard, A. (1988) Deaf community hails education review bill. *The Globe and Mail,* 6 May, p. A10.

Proulx, M. (2000a) *Memorandum: Regulation Mandating that Teacher Training, in Service Training & Additional Qualifications on American Sign Language/Lingue des signes quebecois Curriculum Be Provided*, 30 November. Toronto, ON: Ontario Ministry of Education.

Proulx, M. (2000b) *Memorandum: Regulation on American Sign Language/Lingue des signes quebecois Curriculum as a Policy Document*, 4 December. Toronto, ON: Ontario Ministry of Education.

Proulx, M. (2000c) *Memorandum: Regulation Mandating ASL/LSQ Competency Staff Evaluation and Accompanying Teacher Training in ASL/LSQ Linguistics*, 9 December. Toronto, ON: Ontario Ministry of Education.

Proulx, M. (2000d) *Memorandum: Language of Instruction Regulations American Sign Language (ASL) and Langue des signes quebecois (LSQ)*, 18 December. Toronto, ON: Ontario Ministry of Education.

Reagan, T. (2011) Ideological barriers to American Sign Language: Unpacking linguistic resistance. *Sign Language Studies* 11 (4), 606–636. See www.jstor.org/stable/26190771

Rebick, J. (1988) Major overhaul needed. *Vibrations*, July, p. 5.

Rebick, J. (1989) *Deaf Education Review*: The waiting game. *Vibrations*, December, p. 15.

Ruiz, R. (1984) Orientations in language planning. *NABE Journal* 8 (2), 15–34. doi:10.1080/08855072.1984.10668464

Scott, J.A. and Hoffmeister, R.J. (2017) American Sign Language and academic English: Factors influencing the reading of bilingual secondary school deaf and hard of hearing students. *Journal of Deaf Studies and Deaf Education* 22 (1), 59–71. doi:10.1093/deafed/enw065

Skutnabb-Kangas, T. (2002) Marvelous human rights rhetoric and grim realities: Language rights in education. *Journal of Language, Identity, and Education* 1 (3), 179–205. doi:10.1207/S15327701JLIE0103_2

Slee, R. and Allan, J. (2001) Excluding the included: A reconsideration of inclusive education. *International Studies in Sociology of Education* 11 (2), 173–192. doi:10.1080/09620210100200073

Small, A. and Mason, D. (2008) American Sign Language (ASL) bilingual bicultural education. In J. Cummins and N. Hornberger (eds) *Encyclopedia of Language and Education, Vol. 5: Bilingual Education* (2nd edn) (pp. 133–149). Dordrecht: Springer.

Smith, C., Lentz, E.M. and Mikos, K. (2008) *Signing Naturally Units 1–6 Teacher's Curriculum*. San Diego, CA: Dawn Sign Press.

Snoddon, K. (2008) American Sign Language and early intervention. *The Canadian Modern Language Review* 64 (4), 581–604. doi:10.3138/cmlr.64.4.581

Snoddon, K. (2015) Using the *Common European Framework of Reference for Languages* to teach sign language to parents of deaf children. *The Canadian Modern Language Review* 71 (3), 270–287. doi:10.3138/cmlr.2602

Snoddon, K. and Wilkinson, E. (2019) Problematizing the legal recognition of sign languages in Canada. *The Canadian Modern Language Review* 75 (2) 128–144. doi:10.3138/cmlr.2018-0232

Steenkamp, P. (2007) *New ASL/LSQ Regulation*, 4 July. Toronto, ON: Ontario Ministry of Education. See http://www.edu.gov.on.ca/eng/policyfunding/memos/New ASLRegulations.pdf (accessed 9 March 2018).

Supalla, T. and Clark, P. (2015) *Sign Language Archaeology: Understanding the Historical Roots of American Sign Language*. Washington, DC: Gallaudet University Press.

Tancock, M. (2002) Getting a sound education. *York Communications* 32 (11), 23 January. See http://www.yorku.ca/yul/gazette/past/archive/2002/012302/issue.htm (accessed 11 April 2018).

Tollefson, J.W. (1991) *Planning Language, Planning Inequality: Language Policy in the Community*. New York: Longman.

Tollefson, J.W. (2006) Critical theory in language policy. In T. Ricento (ed.) *An Introduction to Language Policy: Theory and Method* (pp. 42–59). Malden, MA: Blackwell.

Tollefson, J.W. (2015) Historical-structural analysis. In F.M. Hult and D.C. Johnson (eds) *Research Methods in Language Policy and Planning: A Practical Guide* (pp. 140–151). Chichester: Wiley.

University of Ottawa Faculty of Education (n.d.) *Professional Development.* See https://education.uottawa.ca/en/lsq (accessed 12 April 2018).

US Department of Education (2015) *Deaf Students Education Services.* See https://www2.ed.gov/about/offices/list/ocr/docs/hq9806.html (accessed 11 March 2018).

Van Cleve, J.V. and Crouch, B.A. (1989) *A Place of Their Own: Creating the Deaf Community in America.* Washington, DC: Gallaudet University Press.

Van Coillie, D. (1990) Deaf teacher protests hiring at Robarts. *London Free Press,* 9 January.

Weber, J. (2020) Interrogating sign language ideologies in the Saskatchewan deaf community: An autoethnography. In A. Kusters, M. Green, E. Moriarty Harrelson and K. Snoddon (eds) *Sign Language Ideologies in Practice* (pp. 23–39). Berlin: Mouton de Gruyter.

World Federation of the Deaf (2018) *WFD Position Paper on Inclusive Education.* See https://wfdeaf.org/wp-content/uploads/2018/07/WFD-Position-Paper-on-Inclusive-Education-5-June-2018-FINAL-without-IS.pdf (accessed 29 July 2020).

3 Bourdieu, Plurilingualism and Sign Languages in the UK

Dai O'Brien

This chapter examines the history of deaf education in the UK, with particular attention paid to education policy through the lens of Bourdieusian theory. This lens lends a sociological grounding to the exploration of the (denied) possibilities of plurilingual education in the UK by using the concepts of linguistic capital, linguistic habitus and linguistic marketplace. Based on analysis of historic deaf education policy documents, reasons for the inhibition of plurilingual bimodal education environments are outlined, with a possible way forward based on the example of the revitalisation of the Welsh language by successive legislative and policy acts.

Introduction

Over the last few years, plurilingualism has enjoyed something of a day in the sun in the field of education studies, with many researchers in different fields such as TESOL and language teaching promoting it as a way of encouraging people to learn more languages and to challenge traditional notions of language learning (for example, see Mariani, 2008; Moore & Gajo, 2009; Taylor & Snoddon, 2013; Tupas, 2011). For the sake of this chapter, plurilingualism is defined following the Council of Europe's position on language learning, founded upon the notion of the language repertoire which 'is made up of different languages and language varieties at different levels of proficiency and includes different types of competences. It is dynamic and changes in its composition throughout an individual's life' (Council of Europe, n.d.). Plurilingualism is therefore considered as a way of understanding the range of different capabilities individuals have in different languages and modes and how they put these capabilities together, sometimes in creative ways, to make themselves understood and to understand others.

While some academics, language teachers and others have embraced this definition (see, for example, Swanwick, 2017) it has thus far failed to make much positive impact on education policy connected to deaf children and young people in the UK (O'Neill, 2017). Education policy in the UK still favours the monolingual approach, and deaf education policy still fails to officially recognise the specific importance that British Sign Language (BSL) could have for deaf young people in schools. The term BSL was only widely accepted in the 1980s, after the establishment of the field of signed language linguistics in the UK. In this chapter, when talking about signed languages in the UK prior to this time, I will use 'signed language'. References to signed language in the UK after this time will be made using the term 'BSL'.

This chapter will use a novel application of the sociological theory of Pierre Bourdieu with respect to historic UK deaf education policy documents to explore why plurilingualism has been neglected in deaf education in the UK. Bourdieu's work on linguistic habitus and capital will be used to understand why there has long been reluctance to recognise the benefits of plurilingualism relating to the field of deaf education in the UK and how this can be challenged.

What is Plurilingualism?

Plurilingualism is different from the notion of multilingualism, which focuses on competency in more than one separate language, treating each language as independent and usually seeing any 'leakage' between languages as a bad thing. The term multilingualism can also be used on a geographical scale. By this it is meant that an area that is rich in different languages could be called a multilingual neighbourhood, even if individuals who live in that area are each only familiar with a single language. Plurilingualism, rather, is the dynamic interaction and interrelation between different languages in a single person's repertoire.

It has been a traditional view of multilingualism in education that each language is separate, and the measure of competence in each language is the achievement of a level of native-like competency – in effect, becoming a fluent monolingual speaker of multiple languages with no seepage or feeding between them (see, for example, Cenoz & Gorter, 2013). In the field of Deaf Studies, rather than using the term multilingualism it is more common to see the term bilingualism being used. There has, in fact, been some debate about whether or not such linguistic transfer is actually possible between a signed language and a spoken/written one, because the modalities of each are so different, although there is growing evidence that such transfer does indeed happen (Menéndez, 2010; Swanwick, 2016).

To date, plurilingualism in deaf education has been little researched (see Swanwick, 2017; for exceptions, see Swanwick *et al.*, 2016), but there is a growing interest in deaf plurilingualism, which often also engages with the concept of translanguaging (see Kusters *et al.*, 2017; for more on translanguaging in education, see Canagarajah, 2011; García & Li Wei, 2014). One such example is the *Ishaare* project, in which a team of researchers explored the language use of deaf citizens of Mumbai, showing their ability to switch between Indian Sign Language, mime, gesture and spoken/written forms of language (Kusters & Sahasrabudhe, 2018). These rich language environments and skilful switches between languages, codes and modalities are everyday experiences for most signing deaf people, which matches the Council for Europe's pragmatic definition of plurilingualism very well.

Plurilingual Education Environments

Plurilingual education environments are increasingly being recognised in academic literature as beneficial for children. Benefits are not limited to the learning of other languages, but also accrue from lowering children's frustration in language learning by allowing use of both L1 and L2 in classrooms to encourage free and fluent expression of ideas and 'not dampen their excitement' (Lin, 2013: 535). Plurilingual learning environments also allow learners to use their 'discourse and pragmatic knowledge of other languages when writing ... or when formulating speech acts in a communicative situation' (Cenoz & Gorter, 2013: 597) or, in other words, to learn effective ways to use languages, and how these ways can be transferred between languages. As discussed below, this contributes to the development of richer resources of linguistic capital through understanding of the 'secret code' (Bourdieu, 1992: 51) of languages, how to use pauses and silences, understanding not just the vocabulary to use, but how to use it well. As Bourdieu points out, 'the Sophists used to say that what is important in learning a language is to learn the appropriate moment, Kairos, for saying the appropriate thing' (Bourdieu & Wacquant, 1992: 142).

Bourdieu's Concepts

Pierre Bourdieu's sociological work on language was often very critical of linguistics as a field, but his insights concerning the use of language as intrinsically interwoven with the social conditions of its use help us to understand how languages work. It is relatively recently that sustained engagement with his ideas about languages and linguistics has been made (see, for example, Hasan, 1998, and the subsequent discussion in the same journal by Chouliaraki & Fairclough, 2000; Collins, 2000; Corson, 2000; Grenfell, 2011; Hasan, 2000; Robbins, 2000). Until recently, within the field of Deaf Studies very little has been published regarding Bourdieu's work. However, his concepts provide effective and thought-provoking tools to analyse and understand the social context of language use and language power.

The key concepts that we will discuss in this chapter are habitus, field and capital. Habitus can be defined as:

> systems of durable, transposable dispositions, structured structures pre-disposed to function as structuring structures, that is, as principles which generate and organize practices and representations that can be objectively adapted to their outcomes without presupposing a conscious aiming at ends or an express mastery of the operations necessary in order to attain them. (Bourdieu, 1990: 53)

In this sense, habitus can be seen as a concept that helps us to understand how we structure our past and present circumstances and are structured by them in turn. Bourdieu conceptualised habitus as working unconsciously on us; we do not consciously make decisions, but are guided by the dispositions that the habitus engrains in us. These dispositions are durable – while they can be changed, to do so takes time. Furthermore, dispositions are transposable as they can be transferred to different social situations. As such, they structure what is and is not acceptable for a particular social agent to do in particular social situations.

Habitus cannot be understood as a concept by itself alone. All habitus exist in relation to field. The field, as defined by Bourdieu, is a particular social space within which different forms of capital, as discussed further below, are at stake. Social actors compete within the field for control of this capital, and to determine which form of capital is legitimate. A useful analogy would be one that Bourdieu himself uses on several occasions (Thomson, 2008: 68), that of a playing field. Each field has defined positions that are analogous to the positions of a team in a game, rules of what can and cannot be done, boundaries and stakes that can be won or lost. Within each field are the commonly held truths, or doxa, which are used to explain or justify the behaviours and beliefs of the field. The doxa 'misrecognises the logics of practice at work in the field' (Thomson, 2008: 70), which allows agents within the field to see their 'truths' as natural and unassailable. Examples of field that Bourdieu has used in his work are the field of the economy, of education, of higher education and of languages. Habitus and field are intrinsically intertwined; the one depends on the other.

Bourdieu uses the idea of linguistic marketplaces to show how language and language competence can cross many different fields. The metaphor of a marketplace illustrates that the only legitimate language is the one that bears value in a particular set of social circumstances. In order to exert any control over the market, or indeed to partake in the market, an agent will need to have sufficient capital in the legitimate language, and a habitus that is well suited to the field associated with that market (Grenfell, 2011).

Capital is the third concept of Bourdieu's that will be used in this chapter. Capital is not equivalent to monetary exchange but denotes symbolic values that can be staked or exchanged within or across fields. Symbolic capital, in this sense, illustrates how much influence, power and interest an agent can wield. Within different fields, agents can hold not only different types of capital (for example, social, cultural or linguistic), but also different forms of capital that are embodied, objectified or institutionalised. Embodied capital shows the agents' taste, their culture, their knowledge of the rules of the game and the ability to exploit those rules for personal gain through the ways in which they behave, act and physically carry themselves. Objectified capital is capital that is embedded in objects; for example, possession of an expensive painting or first edition, which shows an agent's ability to appreciate and understand the cultural value of an object. Institutionalised capital is capital that has been officially recognised and found worthy; for example, the award of a university degree, honorary award or similar bestowment of recognition by a respected institution.

For this chapter, we will consider these concepts from a linguistic perspective. I will discuss the linguistic habitus which is the prior and continuing experience agents have of languages and how that experience structures and is in turn structured by their social practices. Linguistic capital is the capability that agents hold in languages, not only their knowledge of vocabulary and grammar, but also their ability to use the language in meaningful ways and their understanding of the secret codes of the language. The multiple linguistic fields in which the agent lives are the marketplaces in which the agents can bring their linguistic capital to bear. It is only through the interplay of these three concepts that the full picture of the social experience of agents and their plurilingual and pluricultural competence can be understood. To illustrate, Bourdieu writes as follows:

> Any speech act or any discourse is a conjuncture, the product of the encounter between, on the one side, a linguistic habitus, that is, a set of socially constituted dispositions that imply a propensity to speak in certain ways and to utter determinate things (an expressive interest) as well as a competence to speak defined inseparably as the linguistic ability to engender an infinite array of discourses that are grammatically conforming, and as the social ability to adequately utilise this competence in a given situation; and on the other side, a linguistic market, i.e. a system of relations of force which impose themselves as a system of specific sanctions and specific censorship, and thereby help fashion linguistic production by determining the 'price' of linguistic products. (Bourdieu & Wacquant, 1992: 145)

Here, the concepts of habitus, field, market and capital are inextricably interwoven in determining the value or 'price', or indeed the very possibility of what is allowed to be said and which languages are permitted or considered to be legitimate. This is very important for the field of deaf education, where so much emotion, energy and ideology has been tied up in debates about which languages and modalities are most effective as a medium of education.

The Situation in the UK

A particularly useful aspect of Bourdieu's work is that he outlines why many nation-states are monolingual in policy, if not in practice (or vice versa)[1]:

> Thus, only when the making of the 'nation', an entirely abstract group based on law, created new usages and functions does it become indispensable to forge a standard language, impersonal and anonymous like the official uses it has to serve, and by the same token to undertake the work of normalizing the products of the linguistic habitus. (Bourdieu, 1992: 48)

The creation of the nation-state also creates a particular marketplace which values only one kind of capital. In order to work together, to impose and control the laws of the newly formed nation-state, the language must be controlled and standardised. Similarly, in order for standardisation, or normalisation, of linguistic habitus to occur, the way in which these habitus are produced must be controlled as much as possible.

Bourdieu claims that the grounding of the habitus, or the primary habitus, is formed in the family. The language-based and other experiences of a child as they grow up are largely centred around the family, and so the habitus is structured by what the child encounters. Subsequent refinement of this habitus occurs in the school, which according to Bourdieu is not really an educational institution, but rather a site of reinforcement of legitimate capital and habitus. In *Reproduction* (Bourdieu & Passeron, 1990), Bourdieu outlines the way in which the school is selective: rewarding and reinforcing those who already hold legitimate linguistic and cultural capital learned from their families, and punishing and excluding those who do not.

Each field has a legitimate language. For most of the UK, particularly in the educational field, this is Standard English. However, it is important to understand that this language is not pre-ordained but is dependent on various social and cultural factors. The hierarchising of minority and majority languages is dependent on 'very specific historical processes' (May, 2011: 151), which affect the taken-for-granted attitudes and approaches taken by people and policymakers to value certain languages over others. Bourdieu himself explored this in relation to his native Béarnais language and the relative status of French (see Bourdieu, 1992: 68). Indeed, it has been suggested that education has been '*the* key agency of linguistic standardization (some might call it linguistic genocide)' (May, 2011: 257, emphasis in original), and thus the establishment of a legitimate language in society often, but not always, comes at the expense of minority languages.

In order to understand the historical processes that have led to the pursuit of a monolingual approach in education for deaf children which disparages the role of signed languages, we need to take a diachronic approach to language policy (May, 2011). A historical understanding of where the dominance of English came from in UK deaf education is needed in order to understand more clearly why English (particularly in the spoken mode) is valued so much more than signed languages. While many who read this volume will be familiar with the decision of the Milan Congress in 1880 to pass resolutions which claimed the 'incontestable superiority of speech over signs' in deaf education, less may be known about how these resolutions specifically affected the education system in the UK for deaf children and young people. Below, I explore in more detail historic policy documents that outline the place of oralism and signed language deprivation in the UK education system.

The first legal document in the UK that explicitly dealt with the educational methods to be used for deaf children and young people was the 1889 *Report of the Royal Commission on the Blind, The Deaf and Dumb etc. of the United Kingdom*. This document illustrates the attitudes of its authors to deaf people, including disturbing references to views such as that deaf people should be 'strongly discouraged' from marrying one another to prevent the causation of 'a deaf variety of the human race' (Blind etc. Commission, 1889: xlviii). Alexander Graham Bell, the originator of this term, was one of the expert witnesses called by this Commission. Beside these troubling references to eugenics, the Report is also notable for the conflation of 'language' with 'speech'. Throughout the report, speech is consistently referred to as 'language', whereas signed languages are referred to as 'systems'. These are references that belittle the status of sign by denying it the possibility of being a language. There is also no record made in the report of the use of signed languages outside the school system. For example, in the UK, signed languages have been used in marriage ceremonies since at least 1576 (Cox, 1910), and community records of signing deaf people exist from 1602 (Carew, 1602). However, there is no mention of this in the report, nor is there any mention of potential linguistic markets for signed languages outside schools.

The implication here is that deaf children arrive at a school in a state of *tabula rasa*, with no language at all. This was a problem because it did not take into account the possible home language contexts and repertoires of deaf children, some of whom may have had deaf parents or siblings and who used either a 'home sign' system or a more widely used signed language. It is mentioned in the report that upon arrival at school, children might be able to express themselves using 'natural signs' or 'finger language' (Blind etc. Commission, 1889: lv), but there is no consideration of the home language environment of the child, or how the languages used in and outside school could complement each other. This lack of acknowledgement of the social context of language use and learning causes a misrecognition that such 'linguistic deprivation' is natural rather than socially constructed, and can be treated purely as a technical challenge, that is, through rote learning of speech (Grenfell, 2011: 53). This ignores wider considerations of the development of the deaf child's linguistic habitus from birth, and how the primary and secondary habitus are developed by the interaction between conditions at home and at the school (Bourdieu & Passeron, 1990: 43–45).

There are two further important points within this document. The first is that the summary of recommendations includes the point that 'sign or manual systems' of education must be reserved only for those deaf children who are 'physically or mentally disqualified' from learning under the 'pure oral system' (Blind etc. Commission, 1889: xc). This sets a clear hierarchical relationship between signed and spoken languages. Signed languages were relegated to use by 'failures' of the oral system. This is a clearly a case of socially constructed superiority within the education system. Despite evidence in the report that 'under the manual system a child can get a larger amount of knowledge in four years than under the oral system in the same time' (Blind etc. Commission, 1889: lviii) and that the oral system requires much more investment due to 'the necessity of a large number of teachers, fully one-third more than the manual system' (Blind etc. Commission, 1889: lxvi), it was decided that the pure oral system should be adopted in the UK. Again, this shows the greater value placed on speech. Policymakers were prepared to support the slower, less efficient and more expensive teaching method simply because of the greater prestige that speech held over sign.

The second point is the recommendation that 'all teachers should be in possession of all their faculties and have had previous experience in teaching hearing children' (Blind etc. Commission, 1889: xci). This point not only denies deaf adults the possibility of teaching in schools for deaf children, but also, by reference to the 'teaching of hearing children', implicitly denies the possibility of pedagogic signed language development. Preventing sign language people from teaching suppresses the development of the requisite vocabulary for pedagogic purposes, further devaluing signed languages. Indeed, this exclusion of deaf people from teaching carried on in the subsequent formation of colleges for training Teachers of the Deaf (ToD) in the UK (see Branson & Miller, 2002: 205–206). Upon the 1912 amalgamation of the different ToD training colleges, the name chosen for the new organisation was the National Association for the Oral Instruction of the Deaf (Branson & Miller, 1998). The inclusion of the word 'oral' in the name also illustrates the linguistic approach taken and the prestige placed on speech as the medium of instruction.

While some deaf people qualified both as teachers and as ToDs during these years (see Silo, 1991, for an account of the struggles it took to qualify), it was only much later in the 20th century, after the introduction of the Disability Discrimination Act which outlawed discrimination on the grounds of disability, that larger numbers of deaf people were able to become ToDs. Even then, deaf teachers were obliged to train in oral approaches under the British Association of Teachers of the Deaf (2017) which, while no longer an awarding body for ToD qualifications, still emphasises that any prospective ToD should be an 'effective spoken language communicator with clear lip patterns'. The commitment to 'acquire basic sign language skills' seemed to appear as an afterthought (Simpson, 2017) and the use of the adjectives 'effective' and 'basic' is indicative of the relative status the two modes of language held. Indeed, as of 2014 less than 9% of ToDs in the UK hold a BSL Level 3 or above (CRIDE, 2014). Level 2 BSL, which is the most widely held BSL qualification among ToDs (46.3%) (CRIDE, 2014) is considered to be equivalent to a GCSE Grade B. These restrictions on who was allowed to teach impacted the structure of the educational field, the linguistic marketplace existing within that field and the habitus of the deaf children being educated in that field. The dominant individuals within the school system were hearing, and they shaped the system in order to replicate their beliefs grounded in their own habitus and field. By banning both signed languages and deaf teachers, the education system in the UK removed any possible expansive influences these entities could have on the linguistic market within the field of deaf education.

In 1938, the UK Board of Education produced a report on 'problems relating to children with defective hearing' which proposed to classify children with 'defective hearing' into four grades depending only on their hearing levels, without considering their possible language repertoires. This report accepted that it was 'natural' for deaf children and young people to sign together after hours in school (Board of Education, 1938: 68), but still held that it was of the utmost importance that signing and fingerspelling must not be used in class for educational purposes.

While the 1944 *Education Act* encouraged the attendance of young disabled people in mainstream schools, most deaf children at this point in the UK were educated in residential schools which covered large geographical regions, as opposed to local mainstream schools close to the deaf children's homes (Borsay, 2005: 111). This was at least partly attributed to the relatively low incidence of deafness, which made provision of local support in mainstream schools difficult, and so 'the boarding school fills a necessary role' (Ministry of Education, 1946: 14). However, deaf students were placed in mainstream schools only on the premise that they 'develop and retain their spoken language to a degree commensurate with that reached by hearing children of similar age and intelligence' (Ministry of Education, 1946: 15). Otherwise, as oral failures, 'they should be sent to special schools' (Ministry of Education, 1946: 15), again emphasising the primacy in the government's eyes of speech over sign. Even so, the Ministry of Education felt obliged to warn that that 'the pupils' attainment of high academic standards must not be expected since nearly all the handicapped are to some extent backward' (Ministry of Education, 1946: 33).

These attitudes towards signed languages and deaf teachers continued throughout most of the early and middle 20th century. Some examples of the fetishisation of speech over language include Lack's (1955) *The*

Teaching of Language to Deaf Children, which is preoccupied with speech training and does not contain a single mention of signed languages. Similarly, Dale's (1967) *Deaf Children at Home and at School* emphasises that deaf children 'should be encouraged to try to speak rather than make signs', and that parents 'should put as little emphasis as possible on the use of the hands' to the extent that they should 'at all times resist temptation to point to things' (Dale, 1967: 52). Lynas *et al.* (1991) insisted that teachers had a '*moral* responsibility to enable deaf children to acquire the *dominant* language of our society as a first priority' (Lynas *et al.*, 1991: 127, emphasis in original). Again, the refusal to provide any space in the field for signed languages, or to recognise any kind of linguistic capital other than that of the dominant, spoken modality, is clear.

Language is both the medium and the subject of students' learning (Hardy, 2011: 172). However, if the balance is in favour of the learning of a language as a subject at the expense of the language being a medium of learning, this becomes a problem. The 'inculcation of correct oral attitudes from the infant stage throughout school ... and total immersion of speech teaching within and at every stage of language development' has for long been the order of the day in deaf education (McLaughlin, 1987: 107). Many deaf people who describe their experiences of education state that schools focused so rigidly on speech and listening that deaf learners left school with little or no academic success or knowledge of the world outside the school (Craddock, 1991; Fitzgerald, 2010; Mason, 1991). This all-consuming focus on speech is shown again in McLaughlin (1987: 121), who states about physical education in schools for deaf children, 'the gains in balance, good breath flow and rhythm were always to be placed at the service of speech and language'. This shows that it was not just that the linguistic capital of spoken English was revered above that of other languages and modalities, but that other forms of capital, including physical capital (see Edwards & Imrie, 2003; Shilling, 1991) were also to be considered subservient to the linguistic capital of speech.

The Lewis (1968) report investigated whether there was a role for fingerspelling and signing in the education of deaf children in the UK. While the report concluded that there was potential for both to be useful in the education of deaf children and young people, and thus eventually opened the door to the introduction of Total Communication in the 1970s (Ladd, 2003: 43), the way in which the report reached this conclusion is problematic. The report was particularly effusive in its praise of the artificial signing system developed by Paget and Gorman, which attempted to show English syntax and grammar on the hands, and praised it for 'having the characteristics of a language' (Lewis, 1968: 27). This suggests that the report's author considered similarity to English as the only marker of whether something should be thought a language or not, which makes one wonder what the author of the report thought of other spoken/written languages such as French or Spanish, each with their own syntax and grammar different from that of English, and how these would fit this particular definition of 'language'. While this report was published after the ground-breaking work of Stokoe *et al.* (1965), which proved that American Sign Language was indeed a language in its own right, this work was not yet common knowledge in the UK. The Lewis report's dismissal of signed languages as 'ungrammatical' and 'parasitic upon well-developed mastery of conventional language' (Lewis, 1968: 27) shows the widely held attitudes, or doxa (Deer, 2014), towards signed languages in schools in the UK at the time.

The Lewis (1968) report called on the views of many expert witnesses on the topic of whether signed languages and fingerspelling should be included in schools. It contained many professionals' viewpoints, including those of ToDs and trainers of ToDs, such as Sir Alexander Ewing, who was an avowed oralist. These people may be considered to have had an investment in maintaining the status quo. Submissions from deaf adults were treated more sceptically. The report's authors accepted that many deaf people would have difficulty in submitting written evidence due to linguistic barriers. However, it refused to include the many submissions from members of the British Deaf and Dumb Association which had created a pro forma template to circumvent those barriers (Lewis, 1968: 55–56, 79). This denied many deaf people the opportunity to contribute to a process which had immediate impact on the lives of deaf young people in the UK.

In 1979, Conrad's *The Deaf School Child* investigated the language skills of 600 deaf school leavers in England and Wales who were between the ages of 15 and 16 and a half. The report showed that deaf school leavers from a system which was almost solely oral in approach had an average reading age of a nine-year-old hearing child (Conrad, 1979: 154), no more skill in lip-reading than 'untrained and inexperienced hearing children' (Conrad, 1979: 189) and speech that was so unintelligible that Conrad concluded 'there can be no escape from the conclusion that speech communication between hearing and profoundly deaf people remains a problem of immense magnitude' (Conrad, 1979: 216). Conrad (1980) reiterated the findings of his report and called for signed languages to be given a place in the linguistic repertoire of deaf children. This damning indictment of pure oral education did not have an immediate impact on deaf education in the UK but remains a key reference for anyone researching deaf children's education or language acquisition in the UK.

Both the Warnock (1978) report, which preceded Conrad's publication of his research, and the Education Act which followed it in 1981, recommended that 'the majority of children with special educational needs will have to be … helped within the ordinary school' (Warnock, 1978: 95). Again, this shows the recognition of only a single linguistic market in UK schools, and the determination to try and integrate deaf children into that market, to try and construct habitus that would fit fields in which English is the only legitimate language. While there is no outright prohibition of signed language in the Warnock report (which makes occasional reference to 'techniques for communicating with profoundly deaf children', Warnock, 1978: 94), there is a suggestion that the number of children with specific special educational needs (SEN) within a particular school should be limited to prevent 'the formation of a separate sub-group' (Warnock, 1978: 103). By extension, this would lead to the suppression of opportunities for deaf children to socialise and learn from each other within the school and thereby prevent the establishment of a signing linguistic market among children.

The next major legislation affecting deaf children and young people was the *Special Educational Needs and Disability Code of Practice* (SEND COP), first published in 2001 and updated regularly in subsequent years, with the most recent version in 2015. The SEND COP defines who is eligible for support in schools and in what form. A child or young person is considered to have an SEN if they have 'a learning difficulty or disability which calls for special educational provision to be made for him or her' (DfE & DoH, 2015: 15). A child or young person is considered to be disabled if they have:

> a significantly greater difficulty in learning than the majority of others of the same age, or has a disability which prevents or hinders him or her from making use of facilities of a kind generally provided for others of the same age in mainstream schools or mainstream post-16 institutions. (DfE & DoH, 2015: 16)

Within this definition, young deaf people are considered to have an SEN if they are unable to make use of the same facilities as the hearing majority without support or intervention to make these facilities more accessible, whether this is through providing artificial hearing technology or through signed language. This short definition may finally allow for the re-entry of signed language support in schools and the creation of a plurilingual environment by allowing the use of signed language as a medium of education as a way to redress these 'difficulties' and 'hindrances'. The SEND COP (2015), however, states that 'difficulties related solely to learning English as an additional language are not SEN' (DfE & DoH, 2015: 85). To get support in schools, deaf young people and their families must therefore 'buy into' their framing as 'disabled', and their need for signed language then becomes framed as a way of supporting a disability, rather than signed languages being valued as languages in their own right. This further diminishes the status of signed languages within the language market, harkening back to the 1889 policy that sign is only for those who have failed under the oral approach. In fact, the SEND COP (2015) has no mention of signed language at all, but several mentions of speech and language therapy support for deaf or hard-of-hearing students. This reinforces that English is the legitimate language of the state and education system in the UK, and thus any habitus or fields that make use of signed languages are devalued.

Furthermore, while in theory the policy of informed choice has been pursued in the UK for several years in regard to parents making decisions about their deaf child's education, this promise of choice is somewhat empty. Only 3% of deaf children are currently educated in specialist deaf schools (CRIDE, 2019), and the number of specialist deaf schools in the UK has fallen from 75 in 1982 (Gregory, 2017) to just 21 in 2016 (CRIDE, 2016). In England, the most recent figures for fully qualified, registered interpreters employed in schools is only 9.6 full-time equivalent people over the whole country (CRIDE, 2019). It is clear that there are structural barriers to the implementation of any sort of informed choice for parents of deaf children who wish their child to access a BSL-medium education.

Thus, the implication is that when a student or family attempts to campaign for language access or for recognition of their linguistic capital in a signed language, they are not just fighting against a single teacher or school, but against the whole educational establishment and the weight of history. Bourdieu makes this point in connection to colonial languages:

> In this case the dominated speaks a broken language ... and his linguistic capital is more or less completely devalued. ... In short, if a French person talks to an Algerian, or a black American to a WASP, it is not two persons who speak to each other but, through them, the colonial history in its entirety, or the whole history of the economic, political, and cultural subjugation of blacks (or women, workers, minorities, etc.) in the U.S. (Bourdieu & Wacquant, 1992: 143)

Here, Bourdieu uses the term 'broken language' from the viewpoint of the colonial power or ruling class. This shows the difficulties that speakers and signers of oppressed or minority languages can face when trying to achieve recognition for their languages. They are not just challenging the current circumstances, but also the weight of history. For deaf young people and their families, the historic power of the oralist hegemony and the influence of the Milan Congress of 1880 are still present. This use of the term 'broken' does not only apply to languages. For Bourdieu, language and identity are inextricably linked (May, 2011). Linguistic habitus, or the dispositions of language use, is only part of the wider habitus of an individual. This habitus both structures and is structured by an individual's social identity and their position in and interaction with the world. To portray a language as 'broken' is also to portray the linguistic (and by association, the entire) habitus of an individual who uses that language as broken or deficient (see, for example, Bourdieu, 1992). This impacts the self-worth and self-esteem of a deaf child in possession of what is perceived as a 'broken' habitus, who is thus deemed an 'oral failure'. This is also evident in the literature authored by deaf people concerning childhood experiences in schools in the UK, their struggle with acquiring English and the denigration of the legitimacy of a 'deaf' habitus, which resulted in deaf people whose self-image was that of being 'stupid' (DEX, 2003; Ladd, 1991: 93).

The priority of these deficit discourses (Lamb, 2015) is to ensure that those who have a different language from the dominant language are made to 'fit' by trying to develop their capacity to use the language of the school. For children whose multilingualism includes capacities in languages that are not recognised by the school (such as deaf children who sign BSL), the discourse focuses more on 'their deficit in English than on their potential plurilingualism, as their languages are seen as a barrier to formal learning' (Lamb, 2015: 154). This is especially true of those whose 'deficiency' can also be linked to a physical or sensory disability, as it then becomes easy to conflate issues linked to language or culture with those of disability and reproduce ideologies regarding deaf children's signed language learning as a marker of a deficient social identity.

Plurilingual Signed Language Environments

How would one combat this view of signed languages? Bourdieu has been criticised in the past for being deterministic and not providing scope within his theoretical framework for resistance or change of the system. This is not a fair assessment. It is true that Bourdieu often emphasises how imbalanced the scales of social justice can be, but there is scope for resistance (see May, 2011; Yang, 2014). Habitus, while conservative, is not impervious to change. Recognition of plurilingualism and pluricultural competence in education is one such context in which change is possible. Bourdieu suggests that:

> It is for this reason that those who seek to defend a threatened linguistic capital … are obliged to wage a total struggle. One cannot save the value of a competence unless one saves the market, in other words, the whole set of political and social conditions of production of the producers/consumers. The defenders of Latin, or in other contexts, of French or Arabic, often talk as if it the language they favour could have some value outside the market, by intrinsic virtues such as its 'logical' qualities; but, in practice, they are defending the market. (Bourdieu, 1990: 57)

It is clear here that you cannot preserve a language or linguistic capital simply by demanding that it be taught in school. There must also be a market for it. It is not enough that signing deaf children may have a market for their language at home or within their community if it is not recognised by the educational establishment as a legitimate market. In order to promote a plurilingual approach to education for deaf young people, a plurilingual market needs to be created or maintained. Grenfell states that:

> Teaching knowledge is not the transfer of known things to unknowing subjects (pupils), but the transformation from unknown to known things in relationships with a pedagogic other. The extent this can happen depends on pupils' and teachers' habitus and their interplay within a field context. Pupils learn when they interpret and take control of knowledge, but this arises in relationships which are imbued with field and habitus specific generating structures. (Grenfell, 1998: 87)

According to the above, teaching and learning relies on interaction. If there is no interaction between the habitus of the pupil and teacher and the field, then learning does not occur. If there is no way for the pupil and teacher to fully interact, that is, if they cannot communicate with one another, learning cannot happen. If there is no way for the pupil to access the field of education (for example, through reading course books, accessing classroom discussion, incidental learning, understanding the value of specific forms of knowledge and behaviour), then again, learning cannot happen. So, there must be a demand for plurilingualism in BSL and English to allow for this interaction to occur. There cannot be a meaningful level of interaction of the sort outlined by Grenfell between a habitus that is solely or mainly a BSL habitus (the pupil) and a habitus and field that is monolingual in English (the teacher and the educational system). There is already some provision of communication support workers and BSL/English interpreters in schools to facilitate this interaction, but this is not standardised under any national policy guidance, and there is little or no evidence that these support workers are utilising plurilingual competencies in contrast to simply proceeding with a dual-monolingual model. Furthermore, there is no evidence one way or another to show that these support workers are enough to create a plurilingual environment, as they can simply be viewed as compensatory tools.

Of course, for many parents, maintaining this language market at home is a challenge in itself. If parents do not already sign fluently, they often struggle to access resources to help them learn. Hume (2019) points out that in the UK financial support for parents who wish to learn BSL is a 'postcode lottery', where whether you will receive funding depends on where you live. However, some have pointed out that exposure to fluent language models does not have to take place solely within the home (Humphries et al., 2019; Napoli et al., 2015). So long as the child has access to fluent BSL in different aspects of their lives – such as at school, by socialising with fluent signers or by consuming signed media – parents, while requiring competence in BSL, do not necessarily have to be fluent signers themselves. But again, this is about preserving the whole of the linguistic market, not preserving BSL in one aspect of a fractured linguistic field.

Some would argue that learning signed language is unnecessary for deaf children, since many deaf children now have good access to sound and speech through hearing technology. However, there is still an attainment gap between deaf and hearing children (NDCS, 2019), even for those deaf children who, thanks to technology, have 'good' access to spoken English. Deafness is not itself a learning disability, so why does this attainment gap persist? Hall et al. (2019), in a thorough review of the literature, show that although oral-only children attain stronger spoken language outcomes than deaf children who use a signed language, these oral-only children are still 'significantly delayed with respect to age expectations' (Hall et al., 2019: 372). Hall et al. (2019) also point out that even when 'children are able to acquire a spoken language via cochlear implants, the increased listening effort demanded of these DHH [deaf and hard-of-hearing] children relying on spoken language results in significant cognitive fatigue' (Hall *et al.*, 2019: 327). While some deaf children do have access to auditory information, this is not without effort or cost. Signed languages, on the other hand, are accessible to all deaf children (Hall, 2017; Humphries *et al.*, 2016, 2019; Napoli *et al.*, 2015), regardless of the level of sound they can perceive. It makes sense that signed languages should be valued and used equally to spoken languages in the education system to ensure that all deaf children have access to all information taught.

Ways Forward?

One of the key issues in ensuring that plurilingual sign habitus are valued is to ensure that there is a market for the linguistic capital that they produce. This requires that the value of BSL is recognised in schools and beyond as a practical, functional language which is used and is useful in everyday life. For instance, a recent UK parliament debate on 5 March 2018 considered whether BSL could be included in the UK National Curriculum as a GCSE subject (equivalent to CEFR A2/B1 level) (UK Parliament, 2018). The proposal was rejected by Nick Gibb, the Conservative Minister for School Standards. However, the proposal itself would not have succeeded in creating a plurilingual sign field within the school. BSL was only to be a single optional subject that students could elect to take at GCSE level, rather than a medium of education in its own right. In Scotland, the BSL Act Scotland of 2015 may provide an opportunity for invigoration of the market for BSL, rather than focusing simply on provision of BSL as an optional subject at GCSE level (Scottish Parliament, 2015). The Act requires that a National Plan be published by the Scottish government, followed by other public bodies publishing their Authority Plans, which should reflect the views and needs of the BSL community in Scotland and also what can realistically be delivered in terms of providing access to public services in BSL. It is hoped that this official recognition will reinvigorate the market for BSL, particularly if the plans refer to the need for more translation and interpretation of information into BSL and more access for young people and children who use BSL in school. In Bourdieu's terms, this will not just defend the threatened linguistic capital, but also the marketplace in which it is used.

An interesting parallel is with the Welsh language in Wales. The Welsh Language Act of 1993 stated that it is a legal requirement for public records and official documents to be presented throughout Wales in both Welsh and English (UK Government, 1993). Subsequent publication of Welsh language strategies, such as *Cymraeg 2050: A Million Welsh Speakers* (Welsh Government, 2017; as well as National Assembly for Wales, 2011; Welsh Assembly Government, 2010; Welsh Government,

2012, 2016), outline common themes of encouraging Welsh to be used every day as part of the general linguistic market of the country. This is well described in the 'Vision' of Cymraeg 2050:

> The year 2050: The Welsh language is thriving, the number of speakers has reached a million, and it is used in every aspect of life. Among those who do not speak Welsh there is goodwill and a sense of ownership towards the language and a recognition by all of its contribution to the culture, society and economy of Wales. (Welsh Government, 2017: 4)

This desire not only to foster increasing numbers of Welsh speakers, but also to ensure that Welsh is 'used in every aspect of life' is essential, if we use Bourdieu's framework, to maintaining a market for the language. The document also states an aim to 'create favourable conditions – infrastructure and context' for this vision (Welsh Government, 2017: 4). The growth in the marketplace for Welsh has resulted in an increase in the number of Welsh-English interpreters and translators. As more immigrants arriving in Wales are learning Welsh, those with Welsh language habitus have an advantage in the field. A similar respect and nurturing of BSL could see a reflection in the flourishing of a BSL market nationwide.

Using Bourdieu's concepts of habitus and capital to analyse the field of deaf education in the UK provides a useful way of looking at the historical influences that have shaped the current reluctance in the UK to contemplate a plurilingual school environment that values BSL as an equal to English, either as subject or medium of education. Bourdieu's concepts also point to possible means for instigating widespread, sustainable change in the field, a change which would not only be beneficial to deaf young people, but also to all members of society.

Note

(1)   Thanks to Dr Clare Cunningham for this useful insight.

References

Blind Etc. Commission (1889) *Report of the Royal Commission on the Blind, the Deaf and Dumb etc. of the United Kingdom*. London: Her Majesty's Stationary Office.

Board of Education (1938) *Report of the Committee of Inquiry into Problems Relating to Children with Defective Hearing*. London: His Majesty's Stationary Office.

Borsay, A. (2005) *Disability and Social Policy in Britain Since 1750*. Basingstoke: Palgrave MacMillan.

Bourdieu, P. (1990) *The Logic of Practice*. Cambridge: Polity Press.

Bourdieu, P. (1992) *Language and Symbolic Power*. Cambridge: Polity Press.

Bourdieu, P. and Passeron, J.-C. (1990) *Reproduction in Education, Society and Culture* (2nd edn). London: Sage.

Bourdieu, P. and Wacquant, L.J.D. (1992) *An Invitation to Reflexive Sociology*. Cambridge: Polity Press.

Branson, J. and Miller, D. (1998) Nationalism and the linguistic rights of Deaf communities: Linguistic imperialism and the recognition and development of sign languages. *Journal of Sociolinguistics* 2 (1), 2–24.

Branson, J. and Miller, D. (2002) *Damned for their Difference: The Cultural Construction of Deaf People as 'Disabled': A Sociological History*. Washington, DC: Gallaudet University Press.

British Association of Teachers of the Deaf (2017) Training as a teacher of the deaf. Retrieved September 27, 2018 from https://www.batod.org.uk/information/training-as-a-teacher-of-the-deaf/

Canagarajah, S. (2011) Translanguaging in the classroom: Emerging issues for research and pedagogy. *Applied Linguistics Review* 2, 1–28. doi:10.1515/9783110239331.1

Carew, R. (1602) *The Survey of Cornwall*. See http://www.gutenberg.org/ebooks/9878.

Cenoz, J. and Gorter, D. (2013) Towards a plurilingual approach in English language teaching: Softening the boundaries between languages. *TESOL Quarterly* 47 (3), 591–599. doi:10.1002/tesq.121

Chouliaraki, L. and Fairclough, N. (2000) Language and power in Bourdieu: On Hasan's 'The disempowerment game'. *Linguistics and Education* 10 (4), 399–409.

Collins, J. (2000) Comment on R. Hasan's 'The disempowerment game: Bourdieu and language in literacy'. *Linguistics and Education* 10 (4), 391–398.

Conrad, R. (1979) *The Deaf Schoolchild*. London: Harper & Row.

Conrad, R. (1980) Let the children choose. *International Journal of Pediatric Otorhinolaryngology* 1, 317–329.

Corson, D. (2000) Freeing literacy education from linguistic orthodoxies: A response to R. Hasan's 'The disempowerment game: Bourdieu and language in literacy'. *Linguistics and Education* 10 (4), 411–321.

Council of Europe (n.d.) *Education and Languages, Language Policy*. See https://www.coe.int/t/dg4/linguistic/Division_EN.asp (accessed 6 April 2020).

Cox, C.J. (1910) *The Parish Registers of England*. London: Methuen.

Craddock, E. (1991) Life at secondary school. In G. Taylor and J. Bishop (eds) *Being Deaf: The Experience of Deafness*. London: Pinter.

CRIDE (Consortium for Research in Deaf Education) (2014) *2014 UK-wide Summary: CRIDE Report on 2014 Survey on Educational Provision for Deaf Children*. See https://www.ndcs.org.uk/media/1845/cride_2014_uk_wide_summary.pdf (accessed 3 August 2020).

CRIDE (Consortium for Research in Deaf Education) *2016 UK-wide Summary: CRIDE Report on 2016 Survey on Educational Provision for Deaf Children*. See https://www.ndcs.org.uk/media/6502/cride-2016-england-report-finaldocx.pdf (accessed 3 August 2020).

CRIDE (Consortium for Research in Deaf Education) (2019) *2019 Report for England: CRIDE Report on 2018/19 Survey on Educational Provision for Deaf Children in England*. See https://www.ndcs.org.uk/media/6547/cride-2019-england-report-final.pdf (accessed 3 August 2020).

Dale, D.M.C. (1967) *Deaf Children at Home and at School*. London: University of London Press.

Deer, C. (2014) Doxa. In M. Grenfell (ed.) *Pierre Bourdieu: Key Concepts* (2nd edn). London: Routledge.

DEX (2003) *Between a Rock and a Hard Place*. Wakefield: Deaf Ex-Mainstreamers Group.

DfE & DoH (Department for Education and Department of Health) (2015) *Special Educational Needs and Disability Code of Practice: 0 to 25 Years*. See https://www.gov.uk/government/publications/send-code-of-practice-0-to-25.

Edwards, C. and Imrie, R. (2003) Disability and bodies as bearers of value. *Sociology* 37 (2), 239–256. doi:10.1177/0038038503037002002

Fitzgerald, K. (2010) *Deafness of the Mind: The Forgotten Children of Boston Spa*. Manchester: Kevin Fitzgerald.

García, O. and Li Wei (2014) *Translanguaging: Language, Bilingualism and Education*. Basingstoke: Palgrave MacMillan. doi:10.1057/9781137385765_5

Gregory, S. (2017) *Schools for the Deaf*. See https://www.batod.org.uk/information/schools-for-the-deaf/ (accessed 3 August 2020).

Grenfell, M. (1998) Language and the classroom. In M. Grenfell and D. James (eds) *Bourdieu and Education: Acts of Practical Theory* (pp. 72–88). London: Falmer Press.

Grenfell, M. (2011) *Bourdieu, Language and Linguistics*. London: Continuum.

Hall, M.L., Hall, W.C. and Caselli, N.K. (2019) Deaf children need language, not (just) speech. *First Language* 39 (4), 367–395.

Hall, W.C. (2017) What you don't know can hurt you: The risk of language deprivation by impairing sign language development in deaf children. *Maternal and Child Health Journal* 21 (5), 961–965. doi:10.1007/s10995-017-2287-y

Hardy, C. (2011) Language and education. In M. Grenfell (ed.) *Bourdieu, Language and Linguistics* (pp. 170–196). London: Continuum.

Hasan, R. (1998) The disempowerment game: Bourdieu and language in literacy. *Linguistics and Education* 10 (1), 25–88.

Hasan, R. (2000) Bourdieu on linguistics and language: A response to my commentators. *Linguistics and Education* 10 (4), 441–458.

Hume, C. (2019) Parents of deaf children face funding 'postcode lottery'. See https://www.bbc.co.uk/news/uk-wales-47070741 (accessed 3 August 2020).

Humphries, T., Kushalanagar, P., Mathur, G., Napoli, D.J., Padden, C., Rathmann, C. and Smith, S. (2016) Avoiding linguistic neglect of deaf children. *Social Service Review* 90 (4), 589–619.

Humphries, T., Kushalnagar, P., Mathur, G., Napoli, D.J., Rathmann, C. and Smith, S. (2019) Support for parents of deaf children: Common questions and informed, evidence-based answers. *International Journal of Pediatric Otorhinolaryngology* 118, 134–142. doi:10.1016/j.ijporl.2018.12.036

Kusters, A. and Sahasrabudhe, S. (2018) Language ideologies on the difference between gesture and sign. *Language and Communication* 60, 44–63. doi:10.1016/j.langcom.2018.01.008

Kusters, A., Spotti, M., Swanwick, R. and Tapio, E. (2017) Beyond languages, beyond modalities: Transforming the study of semiotic repertoires. *International Journal of Multilingualism* 14 (3), 219–232. doi:10.1080/14790718.2017.1321651

Lack, A. (1955) *The Teaching of Language to Deaf Children: Based on the Natural Development of the Child*. London: Oxford University Press.

Ladd, P. (1991) Making plans for Nigel: The erosion of identity by mainstreaming. In G. Taylor and J. Bishop (eds) *Being Deaf: The Experience of Deafness* (pp. 88–96). London: Pinter.

Ladd, P. (2003) *Understanding Deaf Culture: In Search of Deafhood*. Clevedon: Multilingual Matters.

Lamb, T. (2015) Towards a plurilingual habitus: Engendering interlinguality in urban spaces. *International Journal of Pedagogies and Learning* 10 (2), 151–165. doi:10.1080/22040552.2015.1113848

Lewis, M.M. (1968) *The Education of Deaf Children: The Possible Place of Finger Spelling and Signing*. London: Her Majesty's Stationary Office.

Lin, A. (2013) Toward paradigmatic change in TESOL methodologies: Building plurilingual pedagogies from the ground up. *TESOL Quarterly* 47 (3), 521–545.

Lynas, W., Huntington, A. and Tucker, I. (1991) A critical examination of different approaches to communication in the education of deaf children. In S. Gregory and G.M. Hartley (eds) *Constructing Deafness* (pp.125–130). London: Pinter.

Mariani, L. (2008) The challenge of plurilingual education: Promoting transfer across the language curriculum. *Perspectives* XXXV (1), 20–21.

Mason, C. (1991) School experiences. In G. Taylor and J. Bishop (eds) *Being Deaf: The Experience of Deafness* (pp. 84–87). London: Pinter.

May, S. (2011) Language policy. In M. Grenfell (ed.) *Bourdieu, Language and Linguistics* (pp. 147–169). London: Continuum.

McLaughlin, M.G. (1987) *A History of the Education of the Deaf in England*. Gosport: Ashford Colour Press.

Menéndez, B. (2010) Cross-modal bilingualism: Language contact as evidence of linguistic transfer in sign bilingual education. *International Journal of Bilingual Education and Bilingualism* 13 (2), 201–223. doi:10.1080/13670050903474101

Ministry of Education (1946) *Special Educational Treatment*. London: His Majesty's Stationary Office.

Moore, D. and Gajo, L. (2009) Introduction – French voices on plurilingualism and pluriculturalism: Theory, significance and perspectives. *International Journal of Multilingualism* 6 (2), 137–153. doi:10.1080/14790710902846707

Napoli, D.J., Mellon, N.P., Niparko, J.K. *et al.* (2015) Should all deaf children learn sign language? *Pediatrics* 136 (1), 170–176. doi:10.1542/peds.2014-1632

National Assembly for Wales (2011) *Welsh Language (Wales) Measure*. Norwich: TSO.

NDCS (National Deaf Children's Society) (2019) 'Lost generation' of deaf children falling a grade behind at GCSE. See https://www.ndcs.org.uk/about-us/news-and-media/latest-news/lost-generation-of-deaf-children-falling-a-grade-behind-at-gcse/ (accessed 3 August 2020).

O'Neill, R. (2017) Bilingual deaf education: Language policies, linguistic approaches and education models in Europe. In K. Reuter (ed.) *UNCRPD Implementation in Europe – A Deaf Perspective: Article 24: Education* (pp. 88–111). Brussels: European Union of the Deaf.

Robbins, D. (2000) Bourdieu on language and linguistics: A response to R. Hasan's 'The disempowerment game: Bourdieu and language in literacy'. *Linguistics and Education* 10 (4), 425–440.

Scottish Parliament (2015) *British Sign Language (Scotland) Act*. Norwich: TSO.

Shilling, C. (1991) Educating the body: Physical capital and the production of social inequalities. *Sociology* 25 (4), 653–672.

Silo, J. (1991) A deaf teacher: A personal odyssey. In G. Taylor and J. Bishop (eds) *Being Deaf: The Experience of Deafness* (pp. 147–155). London: Pinter.

Simpson, P. (2017) *Training as a Teacher of the Deaf*. See https://www.batod.org.uk/information/training-as-a-teacher-of-the-deaf/ (accessed 3 August 2020).

Stokoe, W., Casterline, D. and Croneberg, C. (1965) *A Dictionary of American Sign Language on Linguistic Principles*. Silver Spring, MD: Linstok Press.

Swanwick, R. (2016) Deaf children's bimodal bilingualism and education. *Language Teaching* 49 (1), 1–34. doi:10.1017/S0261444815000348

Swanwick, R. (2017) *Language and Languaging in Deaf Education: A Framework for Pedagogy*. Oxford: Oxford University Press.

Swanwick, R., Wright, S. and Salter, J. (2016) Investigating deaf children's plural and diverse use of sign and spoken languages in a super diverse context. *Applied Linguistics Review* 7 (2), 117–147. doi:10.1515/applirev-2016-0009

Taylor, S.K. and Snoddon, K. (2013) Plurilingualism in TESOL: Promising controversies. *TESOL Quarterly* 47 (3), 439–445.

Thomson, P. (2008) Field. In M. Grenfell (ed.) *Pierre Bourdieu: Key Concepts* (pp. 65–82). Durham: Acumen.

Tupas, T.R.F. (2011) English-knowing bilingualism in Singapore: Economic pragmatism, ethnic relations and class. In A. Feng (ed.) *English Language Education Across Greater China* (pp. 46–69). Bristol: Multilingual Matters.

UK Government (1993) *Welsh Language Act 1993*. London: TSO.

UK Parliament (2018) *Hansard*, 5 March. See https://hansard.parliament.uk/Commons/2018-03-05/debates/553511A4-468B-4B1E-9AD9-A55DCBF3ED06/BritishSignLanguageNationalCurriculum.

Warnock, M. (1978) *Special Educational Needs: Report of the Committee of Enquiry into the Education of Handicapped Children and Young People*. London: HMSO.

Welsh Assembly Government (2010) *Welsh-Medium Education Strategy*. See https://dera.ioe.ac.uk/4248/1/100420welshmediumstrategyen.pdf.

Welsh Government (2012) *A Living Language: A Language for Living – Welsh Language Strategy 2012 to 2017.* See https://gov.wales/sites/default/files/publications/2018-12/welsh-language-strategy-2012-to-2017-a-living-language-a-language-for-living.pdf.

Welsh Government (2016) *Taking Wales Forward 2016–2021.* See http://gov.wales/about/programme-for-government/?skip=1&lang=en.

Welsh Government (2017) *Cymraeg 2050: A Million Welsh Speakers.* See https://gov.wales/sites/default/files/publications/2017-08/taking-wales-forward.pdf.

Yang, Y. (2014) Bourdieu, practice and change: Beyond the criticism of determinism. *Education Philosophy and Theory* 46 (14), 1522–1540. doi:10.1080/00131857.2013.839375

4 Plurilingualism in Deaf Education in France: Language Policies, Ideologies and Practices for the Bimodal Bilingual Skills of Deaf Children

Saskia Mugnier

This chapter analyses language policies and bilingual deaf education in France. I argue that research on plurilingualism and language learning cannot be separated from an understanding of social practices and representations of deaf learners, which makes it possible to see deaf children's language competences in a new light that goes beyond the centuries-old conflict between those who reject and those who promote sign language pedagogy. Moreover, understanding the variety and richness of language practices used by deaf learners can help teachers to adapt their overall approach and specific methods, especially in classroom interactions with deaf children involving spoken and written French and LSF productions. To this end, the ethnographic study investigated the language practices of children and adults in plurilingual settings. The findings show the extent to which language policies related to deaf education in France are appropriate, if the stated goal is successful early plurilingual education. Policy changes are suggested based on these findings and on a broader analysis of the successes and setbacks that, within the social space, hinder or facilitate LSF's role in deaf plurilingualism. Furthermore, the findings support the idea that teachers who work within a plurilingual setting need to implement a pedagogy that considers the whole spectrum of deaf children's language practices.

Introduction

This chapter examines the construction, deconstruction and reconstruction of official models of bilingualism in the field of deaf education, and the intertwinement of public policies concerning education, health and languages. In fact, socio-educational aspects of deafness have always been profoundly impacted by ideology, resulting in the so-called war between manual and oral modes of communication that has raged in France for four centuries without ever coming to an armistice. The issue is identification with one group or another which, as Coste *et al.* (1997: 249) noted, involves 'separation and differentiation, the construction of symbolic boundaries'. It is about being deaf or Deaf, a distinction proposed by Woodward (1982) to differentiate between a medicalised view of hearing deficiency (deaf) and membership in a community and culture (Deaf) generally associated with sign language (in France, Langue des Signes Française [LSF]). However, in addition to the difficulty of dissociating physiological from symbolic and cultural aspects, recent research into the language practices of deaf adults and children (Estève & Mugnier, 2012; Millet *et al.*, 2008; Mugnier, 2006) has highlighted the importance of rejecting this division in order to focus on the ways language use and identity actually develop.

I begin by examining the historical construction of social representations of deafness in France, and then review the evolution of official policies on language learning and use, and special education for deaf children. I argue that a compartmentalised vision of languages, which feeds an idealistic definition of bilingualism that is partly based on the myths of *pure language* and *ideal native speaker* does not stand up when compared with real language practices that take a wide variety of forms. The final section draws on an exploratory classroom study of language use by deaf children to show the need to move away from the 'idealised bilingual model' towards a 'multi-modal plurilingual' model.

Deafness and Language Policy in France

The issues raised by plurilingualism tend to be complex because they involve a wide variety of historical, sociological, political, pedagogical and affective factors, and because responses to contact with other languages, plurilingual practices and attitudes towards languages are, as discussed below, largely governed by cultural and social representations. Although this complexity is characteristic of many sociolinguistic situations, deafness impacts the most fundamental dimensions of the language issue. For example, the fact that almost 95% of deaf children are born to hearing parents raises the question of first language acquisition when the environment does not provide a fully accessible language. This question is combined with the notion of a mother tongue or first language, another complex and highly symbolic issue that is profoundly associated with identity construction through transmission and filiation:

> The characteristics of identification are dependent on the parent's view of their child's impairment and the underlying educational-therapeutic choices they make. They may immediately choose to move towards the deaf community, but this is not easy to do. This community is often unknown, poorly understood and, most importantly, unrecognised as a linguistic minority. Sign language is a central value but in the eyes of hearing people it does not so much represent the culture as it represents deafness. (Dunant-Sauvin & Chavaillaz, 1993: 65)

In France, the histories of deaf education and of the social, cultural and linguistic recognition of deaf communities are closely interwoven. When discussing the history of education for deaf children, I share the view of Michel Poizat (2001: 107): 'the history of deaf education cannot be described as a linear progression – as is often done – but as a pendulum that has oscillated between periods dominated by the oralist tendency to periods when the manual tendency became dominant, before swinging back towards oralism, and so on.' Schooling for deaf children depends on the places where the language or languages are used, a parameter that is inextricably intertwined with representations of deafness. In fact, educational models are based on widely pervasive social representations, which in turn generate identity projections and attributions.

Throughout history, the representational *millefeuille* surrounding deafness has given rise to two main models of the deaf person. Generally, the place a society accords deaf people is conditioned by the way it regards the body and gesture. This situation is made even more complex by the fact that attitudes towards deaf people have fluctuated between fascination and repulsion, so deaf people have sometimes been allowed to take their rightful place in society and sometimes been considered pariahs. Thus, attitudes towards deafness and deaf people have varied across time and space, from one culture to another, ranging from shame to exclusion to benevolence.

This ideological debate truly began in the 18th century, with the first use of signs in teaching, and grew more intense during the 19th and 20th centuries. In France, this debate gave rise to the two idealised conceptions of deaf identity that are still present today – deaf people who sign and those who speak orally. The following sections retrace the serpentine history of these two conceptions.

The first anthropological bilingual model

Abbé de l'Épée's (1712–1789) pioneering work heralded what has often been called a *golden age* for the deaf community in France and around the world, as his student Laurent Clerc trained teachers from several different countries. For the first time in France, deafness was

considered from an anthropological perspective, leading to greater acceptance of deaf people and the blossoming of deaf culture and the deaf
community, both socially and intellectually. Deaf people and hearing
people worked together in education, although most deaf children
attended special boarding schools, a form of schooling that is commonly
considered the 'cradle of deaf culture' and perhaps even the birthplace of
the 'deaf world' (Delaporte, 2002: 369). This schooling contributed to the
spread of sign language, which was taught by deaf adults within the education system and used during conversations between students. It also,
through its transmission from generation to generation, helped to improve
and enrich sign language. Importantly, deaf adults played a direct part in
education, not only as teachers but also as school principals (e.g. Massieu
in Lille, Comberry in Saint-Étienne and Lyon, Bertrand in Limoges and
Plantin in Le Puy) (Lamothe, 2001). Despite these real advances, it is
important to revisit the idea of a 'golden age'. According to Sero-
Guillaume (1995), this period has too readily been described as idyllic.
For example, contrary to frequent claims, deaf experts in deafness 'have
never been, apart from one or two exceptions, teachers in the general
education system'; what is more, 'there were very few deaf adults in specialist institutions' (Sero-Guillaume, 1995: 32).

With the emergence of a community of 'deaf people', as they now
referred to themselves (Dethorre, 1997), primacy was given to sign language. This period also saw the development of the first bilingual education models designed to take into account the specific needs, culture and
identity of deaf people. Nevertheless, not everyone agreed with the
emphasis put on sign language, and supporters of an 'oralist' approach
based on speech, lip-reading and speech rehabilitation continued applying their methods during this 'golden age'. Hence, the debate was far
from settled and, as a result of changes in the sociohistorical context, it
was the oralists who would emerge victorious in the latter part of the
19th century.

The new oralist order: The imposition of a monolingual model

Several factors contributed to the oralists' victory, not least of which
were the education reforms introduced in the 1880s by the French
statesman Jules Ferry. Designed to promote equality and weaken the
church's hold over education, Ferry's reforms made primary education
mandatory, instituted a standard curriculum for the entire country and
banned all languages except French (a measure that sounded the death
knell for many minority languages). In France, as in many other countries during this period, language policy can be summed up by the equa-
tion 'one nation = one language'. Advances in science and medicine led
to the development of hearing aids and a more clinical approach to
deafness. New diagnostic methods and apparatus allowed doctors to

identify and classify different types of deafness and to measure the severity of a person's hearing loss. As a result, deafness, which had once been accepted as just a fact of life, began to be treated as an illness (Delaporte, 2002).

Small schools were the first to be affected by the oralist wave. In addition to the factors described above, a major reason for this was a shortage of sign language teachers. The surge of new schools created to provide every child with now-mandatory primary education meant there was not enough time to train the additional sign language teachers required by the increase in the number of deaf students. Consequently, many schools had no choice but to adopt oral methods (Dubreuil, 2001).

The turning point for larger institutions came in 1880, with the International Congress on the Education of the Deaf in Milan that gave almost unequivocal support to the oralist method. Despite the importance of the Congress's decisions for deaf people everywhere, only one of the 164 delegates was deaf, and most of them were churchmen. The following extract from a speech given at the Milan Congress in 1880 reveals prevailing ideologies, in which 'mimicry' was decried because gestures were viewed as physiological manifestations of the body:

> Speech is the only force that can reignite the light God bestowed on man when, on giving him a soul in an earthly body, He also gave him the means to understand, think and express himself [...]. Where, on the one hand, signs and expressions are not enough to fully express thoughts, on the other hand, they favour and glorify the imagination and all the faculties of this sense [...]. The fantasies of sign language exalt the senses and enflame passions, whereas speech elevates the spirit with calmness, prudence and truth, and avoids the risk of exaggerating the sentiments expressed and of spawning nocuous mental impressions. (Abbé Tarra, quoted in Ministry of Education, 1994: 25)

Although the Congress's first resolution did not designate a chosen method, it stated that 'articulation' was a clear objective for education. Hence, speech, which had formerly been one means of communication among others, became an end in itself and the sole goal of education of the deaf (Mottez, [1977, 1984] 2006). In many countries, the Milan Congress was followed by a major turnaround in the situation of the deaf community and by a wave of scientism to normalise deaf people. In a break with the naturalist philosophy of the Enlightenment, positivist thinking consigned gestures and signs to the register of 'inarticulate expression and to that of a still animal sensuality' and tried 'to "scientifically" establish the primacy of the phonic and articulated essence of speech over gestural language' (Virole, 2000: 31). At this time, experiments on deaf people, such as trepanation, took place to try to make them hear and to better understand how audition works (Cuxac, 1983). The increase in understanding of the biological aspects of language that was gained by clinical experiments promoted the belief that the absence of speech in deaf people was a pathology.

The turning point of the 1960s: The 'réveil sourd' and the emergence of the deaf community

The civil rights movement that emerged in the 1960s in the United States benefited many minority groups, including deaf people, who began asserting their right to be different and to have their own language and culture. At this time, the American linguist William Stokoe began conducting the first modern research into sign language.

In France, the social unrest of May 1968 helped raise awareness of the country's minority languages and cultures, especially Breton and Basque. Deaf people, too, began portraying themselves as a linguistic minority with the right to learn and use their own language. The term '*réveil sourd*' (deaf awakening) was coined to describe this period of great change in LSF (Delaporte, 2002: 24). However, official recognition for LSF would be a long time coming.

The World Federation of the Deaf (WFD) held its sixth World Congress in Paris in 1971. Despite the oralist context, some professionals in the field of deaf education were starting to realise the richness and effectiveness of sign language, and the issue of reintegrating LSF into education timidly began to raise its head. This process was greatly advanced four years later at the WFD's seventh World Congress in Washington, DC, where French participants became aware of new methods devised in the United States (such as sign systems for manually encoding spoken language, Total Communication and American Sign Language) and the impact they were having. In America, sign language contributed to the social and intellectual development of the deaf community, and the provision of resources such as professional interpreters facilitated integration.

On their return to France, some of these participants set up an association to promote a new vision for teaching deaf children. Nationally, the movement was supported by an active community who wished to be included in the process of drawing up proposals and solutions for deaf education, and whose overall objective was to give deaf people an official status and public voice. Most notably, these activists showed that the education system for the deaf was at best mediocre and at worst a failure.

In the early 1970s, new representations of deaf people provided the foundation for cultural and social initiatives, including: the International Visual Theatre (a cultural centre for deaf people in Vincennes); the French Sign Language Academy (ALSF) in Paris; centres for social advancement catering to deaf people's continuing educational and professional needs; and new training courses in LSF. In terms of education, parents began demanding high-quality teaching that met their deaf children's needs, while the '2 Languages for One Education' (2LPE) movement demanded the reintroduction of LSF in state schools for deaf students. Danièle Bouvet (1989), in conjunction with a deaf teacher named Marie-Thérèse Abbou, opened the first bilingual class in 1982, and with support from the Ministry of Health, the first bilingual early learning centre opened its doors. In conjunction with these events and with support from sociologists (Markowicz, 1980; Mottez, [1976] 2006) and linguists (Cuxac, 1983), in the mid-1970s France's Deaf community began to be considered as a linguistic minority in its own right. As such, they became part of the prevailing sociolinguistic paradigm under which contact between languages inevitably resulted in conflict between communities and languages.

Hence, at the very moment when France began to embrace an educational policy that gave deaf children the opportunity – the right – to study in ordinary state schools, a large proportion of deaf adults and professionals began campaigning for the right to be different, including the right to use a different language in education. This stance was in line with the contemporary sociological view of linguistic minorities in France (Vermes, 1988). At the same time, deaf people rejected both the medical approach that had been prevalent for almost a century and its associated social representations of deaf people as disabled. In France, sign language transmission and deaf children's congregation emerged thanks to the first special school supported by the Ministry of Health. While almost all deaf schools under this Ministry support a medical model of disability, since the late 1980s some of the schools paradoxically included signing in mainly signed French and very rarely LSF.

The Language(s) Issue: The Winding Road of Language and Education Policies

As indicated in the preceding section, deaf children were historically mainly educated in special schools under the Ministry of Health and outside the state school system which was under the Ministry of Education. In 1975, a new education act gave deaf children the right to be educated within schools run by the Ministry of Education. However, they could also attend schools run by the Ministry of Health, the traditional guardians of deaf education, and it was left to parents to choose which option they preferred for their child. This lack of decisiveness by the public authorities over who should be responsible for the education of deaf children is not without symbolic importance. Historically, these two ministries have overseen two forms of schooling, with the Ministry of Health and Social Affairs supervising special schools for deaf children, including public schools such as the National Institute for Young Deaf People and private schools such as the Institution for Young Deaf People. At the same time, the Ministry of Education has educated a very small number of deaf students in ordinary state schools; under legislation passed in 1975, these schools must educate all children, either within ordinary classes or by creating special classes. The general tendency was to marginalise deaf education in separate schools, where sign language transmission and deaf children's congregation emerged.

These two ministries each established two parallel but separate models of education: oralist or bilingual. An educational model which fully includes LSF is still uncommon in France, and is mainly available via groups of teachers rather than a certain type of school. Theoretically, bilingual classroom are present in both mainstream and special schools.

The following analysis of Ministry of Education texts sheds light on official policy regarding the management and organisation of language learning by deaf students, which has a direct impact on the way deaf students are taught in schools. A more specific aim of this analysis was to determine the relative importance attributed to sign language and other communication modes and techniques, that is, to show what the Ministry of Education's circulars and programmes have prescribed and proscribed.

From the (re)-introduction of LSF to its official recognition

The first official reference to LSF by the Ministry of Education since the Milan Congress in 1881 was in a circular published in 1987. Nevertheless, the wording of this circular highlights the slowness of the general educational establishment in modifying its position towards LSF, as the circular continues to insist on the primacy of oral French. In other words, the Ministry was still suspicious of sign language.

> Whatever the place given to sign language, speech and auditory teaching must remain a central preoccupation. [...] But teaching to young children may also include a signed contribution, French sign language or signed French [...], without abandoning the requirement for oralisation. [...] Thus, speech training and teaching oral language skills to all deaf children are, more than ever, absolute teaching imperatives.[1]

Hence, the circular's main focus was rehabilitation or speech training, and LSF was to be used only as a tool for attaining this objective. The circular recognised the coexistence of bilingual and so-called 'modernised oral' methods, although it did not use these actual terms. The latter methods may include manual codes, such as cued speech, which involves producing signs next to the mouth in order to differentiate between sounds that look identical on the lips, or other visual or corporeal tools for supplementing oralism. However, even in the 'bilingual' method, which by definition involves two languages, the circular stressed that the focus had to be on 'spoken and written' French. In other words, the education ministry's position at this time remained firmly anchored in a monolingual French model, and the terms bilingual and bilingualism were not used when referring to pedagogical practices.

It was not until the 1991 Fabius Act that the question of French/LSF bilingualism was addressed explicitly. This Act, which was intended to 'alleviate the conflict between the two pedagogical currents', recognised the right of 'young deaf people and their families to choose freely between bilingual communication – sign language and French – and oral communication' (Act 91-73 [title III], Article 33, of 18 January 1991). Thus, for the first time, LSF was officially mentioned in law. A decree (no. 92-1132, 8 October 1992)[2] set the conditions under which this choice could be made, as well as the measures schools and special education services had to take to ensure these choices could be honoured. However, the decree did not lay out any training plan that would enable deaf people to become teachers or provide hearing teachers with the skills required to teach bilingually. In addition, the text left it to teaching teams to determine the place of oral and signed modes of communication, the time given to teaching each of the two languages, and each language's role during lessons, other school periods and family time. The overly general content of the government's decree betrayed the government's lack of commitment to the issue and, inevitably, led to disparities in the way it was implemented across the country.

The final piece of legislation considered in this brief summary is the Participation and Citizenship of Disabled People – Equal Rights and Opportunities Act of 11 February 2005, which gave official recognition to sign language:

> French sign language is recognised as a separate language. Every student affected must be able to receive training in French sign language. The National Council for Education will promote the teaching of this language. It will receive regular updates on conditions for its evaluation. It can be chosen as an optional examination subject, including in vocational training examinations. Its use in administrative services will be facilitated. (Article L. 312-9-1)

Given the long hesitation and innumerable debates over the place of LSF in education, this Act represented a major step forward. Nevertheless, it is a shame that it only covered the use of LSF in education rather than plurilingual education. What is more, although it allowed for the teaching *of* sign language on equal terms with foreign languages, it did not allow for teaching *in* LSF for both deaf and hearing pupils. Provisions covering teaching in LSF were included in initial drafts of the bill but removed from the final version. French was still the official teaching language for all students at state schools. With respect to the way deaf children communicate, Article 19 of the 2005 Act reaffirmed the right to choose that was present in the 1991 Act: 'In the education and careers of young deaf people, the freedom to choose between bilingual communication, sign language and French, and to communicate in French is a right.'

Therefore, the new legislative context created by the 2005 Act's recognition of LSF, with the social implications this had for accessibility, was undeniably an encouraging move towards a more inclusive society. As proof of this recognition and regarding the need to support parents of deaf children, in 2009 the National Authority for Health (HAS) published a guide to be given to parents as soon as a child's deafness was identified and before he or she started school.

Shifting boundaries and strengthening ideologies: The HAS's recommendations to parents and the circular of 2017

Even though the HAS's (2009) recommendations about meeting the needs of deaf children prior to three years of age were produced by professionals from the health sector, the publication of this guide shows a change in the way deafness is perceived. This document can be used to promote the development of plurilingualism combining LSF and French. However, as Table 4.1 shows, society appears incapable of conceiving a truly multi-modal plurilingualism based on deaf children's potential language resources in both written and oral French and LSF.

The typology set out in this table shows the antagonistic relationship between French and LSF. The hierarchisation and compartmentalisation of languages have resulted in the emergence of two additional forms of bilingualism available to deaf people besides French-LSF bilingualism.

Table 4.1 Choice of early-learning programmes available to parents as a function of their educational wishes for their child

Education project	'Communication in French' education		'Bilingual communication, LSF and French' education	
Objective	Acquisition of French		Acquisition of two languages: LSF and French[a]	
First language(s) provided prior to 3 years of age	Spoken French		Spoken French and LSF	LSF
Principal means of verbal communication used before 3 years of age	Interactions in spoken French ± LPC code[b]	Interactions in signed French[c]	Interactions in spoken French and LSF alternately	Interactions in LSF
Types of early intervention programmes	Programme with LPC	Programme in signed French	Audiophonic programme with LSF	Visuo-gestural programme
	Audiophonic approach			Visuo-gestural approach
Implementation principle	To stimulate the auditory pathways			To stimulate the visual pathways

Notes: [a]French is provided with the two modalities (spoken and written) within the framework of an audiophonic approach, whereas in a visuo-gestural approach French is addressed mainly by written French.
[b]LPC: French cued speech.
[c]Signed French: spoken French simultaneously accompanied by isolated signs from LSF (equivalent to Signed English).

These additional forms of bilingualism are 'audiophonic' bilingualism (*Audiophonic programme with LSF*), which seems to banish the visual and gestural dimensions that are such an intrinsic part of LSF, and 'visuo-gestural' bilingualism, which seems to banish spoken French. This raises the question of when a true plurilingualism will emerge that takes into account all language resources in visuo-gestural and audiophonic modalities.

Finally, the latest Ministry of Education circular[3] published in February 2017 covers 'the implementation of the teaching programme for young deaf people' and sets out the conditions governing a family's choice of modes of communication, the modalities of schooling for young deaf children and the different courses provided by teaching centres for young deaf people (PEJS). This circular reiterates the HAS's proposals and lays out a framework for modes of communication and modalities of schooling for deaf children, which gives parents of deaf children a choice between two types of programme:

- A *written French/LSF bilingual programme*. In this programme, LSF is one of the languages taught and the language used for teaching. This is a big step forward, but by placing spoken French and LSF in competition by removing the oral dimension of language, the ministry has imposed a truncated vision of bilingualism, giving the idea that spoken French and LSF cannot cohabit in this context.
- A *French language programme* divided into two sub-programmes, one involving *French supported by cued speech* and one involving *French supported by LSF*. The term bilingual is never used in association with this second sub-programme, despite the presence of two languages and all the modalities. This programme includes LSF, but it is viewed as a tool or crutch of the same order as cued speech, rather than as a separate language with all the linguistic, cultural and identity dimensions that implies.

As noted in a previous article (Mugnier, 2016), this division between educational choices is consistent with the circular of 2008 that lays out an initial language-based socialisation within the existing education system. However, this division imposes on parents, 95% of whom are hearing, a difficult choice between programmes with crucial outcomes for identity, linguistic, social and cognitive development. The programmes are explained to parents in a way that I believe is far from impartial.

Consequently, although the general orientation of legislation and policies shows a desire for change, the official texts and positions presented here appear to be based on a medical view, which regards deafness as an affliction requiring a therapeutic approach. Neither the results of research carried out in France or other European countries, nor anthropological arguments demonstrating the possibilities offered by sign language, have yet found resonance in official discourse in France.

When Children's Language Practices Undermine Institutional Models: An Exploratory Classroom Study

This section explains why the compartmentalised vision of languages, which feeds an idealistic definition of bilingualism that is partly based on the myths of *pure language* and *ideal native speaker*, does not stand up when compared with real language practices. This is especially true in the case of deaf people who are bimodal plurilinguals.

Theoretical and methodological bases

Individual bilingualism, plurilingualism and bimodality

In recent decades, the growing body of research on contact between languages, individual bilingualism and the definitions of bilingualism now incorporates the pragmatic and functional dimensions of languages. Grosjean's (1982) book was a turning point in this respect because it presented bilingualism not as the ideal sum of two monolinguals but as an ensemble of original skills that are combined in different ways according to the communication situations in which bilingual people find themselves. Viewed from this dynamic perspective, 'bilingual speech' is considered an original and specific entity, as Lüdi and Py (1986/2002) explained:

> It must be understood that it is not enough to add together two separate languages or two schemas of reality to characterise the bilingual-bicultural competence. Through contact with each other, they modify each other to such an extent that the result is something original, something new [...]. (Lüdi & Py, 1986/2002: 54)

Hence, it is time to reject as a myth the idea of 'perfect acquisition' of language and to view second-language learning as 'the continuous extension of a multiple repertoire' (Lüdi, 2000). Over the last 15 years, researchers in the field of didactics have preferred the terms 'plurilingual' and 'plurilingualism' to 'bilingual' and 'bilingualism' (see, among others, Castellotti, 2001; Coste, 2001; Moore, 2006; Py, 2000). As Coste *et al.* (1997: 11) noted, the prefix 'bi' 'summons up images of balance or imbalance, community or difference, dialogue or opposition'. This didactic notion of plurilingualism is the 'main foundation' of European language education policies (Beacco & Byram, 2002; Coste *et al.*, 1997), as reflected in the *Common European Framework of Reference for Languages* which defines plurilingual and pluricultural skills as follows:

> Plurilingual and pluricultural competence refers to the ability to use languages for the purposes of communication and to take part in intercultural interaction, where a person, viewed as a social actor, has proficiency, of varying degrees, in several languages and experience of several cultures. This is not seen as the superposition or juxtaposition of distinct competences, but rather as the existence of a complex or even composite competence on which the social actor may draw. (Coste *et al.*, 1997: 11)

This approach has spread a new conception of languages and language learning by placing at its heart the notion of *verbal repertoire* (or 'language repertoire'), defending a vision that embraces *variation*, and describing a *plurilingual competence* (Billiez, 2005; Coste, 2001; Coste *et al.*, 1997; Dabène, 1994). These changes in terminology have not been without complications, as everyday usage and social representations often still follow a traditional vision of ideal bilingualism or even monolingualism, especially within schools (Lambert, 2005). I believe this perspective opens up new ways for understanding plurilingualism in deaf people.

At the same time, it is necessary to adopt a wider conception of *language*, in line with McNeill's (1992: 2) realisation that 'gestures are an integral part of language as much as are words, phrases, and sentences – gesture and language are one system'. All humans communicate bimodally, but deafness imposes a new shape on this bimodality because the languages deaf people use involve different channels. French, for example, is centred around the audio-vocal modality, whereas LSF uses the visual-gestural modality. For most deaf people, speech and gesture modalities can support verbal and non-verbal communication. These theoretical premises provide a variety of tools for observing and analysing the way in which deaf people deploy their bimodal bi-plurilingual language resources in their language practices.

Study methodology

In this exploratory study, I used observations and recordings to analyse the productions of seven deaf children during a series of classroom episodes. These children (labelled S1 to S7 in the following analysis of the data) were part of a CE2 or elementary-level inclusive education class in a regular school that also included an eighth student who was not hearing impaired, but who had been placed in this class due to other impairments. Most children in CE2 are eight years old, but the children in the study sample were aged between eight and ten years. S2 had a moderate hearing loss with other impairments; S1, S3 and S4 were profoundly deaf; S5 had a moderate hearing loss; and S6 and S7 were severely deaf.

The resulting data, collected in agreement with the school's teaching team, were built around two variables: 'language' and 'type of text'. My hypothesis was that LSF can help deaf children learn French, as in a bilingual language dynamic, LSF can be used to overcome certain difficulties linked to understanding.

For the 'type of text' variable, I decided to study teaching sessions that focused on two texts of different styles and difficulties. The first text (Everyday Story), written in standard conversational French, related a simple story; the second text (Literary Tale) was a tale written in more academic French (which included simple past tense, more specialist vocabulary and more formal structures), and which called upon the reader to use their imagination.

In order to analyse the 'language' variable, I chose teaching sessions based on the texts that gave rise to exchanges with the teachers in French (with or without cued speech) and/or in sign language. The sign language teacher was a deaf person employed by SSEFIS (Family Education and School Integration Support Service), which was set up by the Department of Health to help deaf children and young people carry out their schooling close to home in a standard school. SSEFIS teachers provide teaching support in different schools within a French *département*. Only the teachers were restricted to one means of communication; the children were free to choose whichever language(s) they preferred.

The students studied each of the texts in three stages:

- In *Stage 1*, the students studied the first part of each of the texts with the class's regular teacher who did not use LSF;
- In *Stage 2*, the students studied the first and second parts of the full texts with a deaf sign language teacher using LSF;
- In *Stage 3*, the students studied only the second part of the text, this time with the regular teacher and in French and/or LSF.

Table 4.2 summarises this protocol.

One part of the analysis was a quantitative non-experimental study in which the filmed interactions were studied to examine the language environments that took shape during each teaching session and to determine a language profile for each child.

A variety of language profiles

Whether in sessions with the deaf teacher or the hearing teacher, very few of the children's productions involved a single language, whether French or LSF. The students used fingerspelling during discussions about how a word is spelled. Table 4.3 shows the heterogeneity of the students' language practices.

For example, S4 used LSF in 36.5% of his interactions, never used cued speech, used Spoken French in 41.3% of interactions, and mixed LSF

Table 4.2 Teaching protocols followed during the study

Organisation		Literary Tale 'LitTal'	Everyday Story 'EveryDStory'
Regular teacher Stage 1	First part of the text	In French (+ cued speech) without LSF 'LitTal-Stage1'	In French (+ cued speech) without LSF 'EveryDStory-Stage1'
Deaf teacher Stage 2	Review first part and study second part	In LSF 'LitTal-Stage2'	In LSF 'EveryDStory-Stage2'
Regular teacher Stage 3	Second part of the text	In French (+ cued speech) LSF permitted 'LitTal-Stage3'	In French (+ cued speech) LSF permitted 'EveryDStory-Stage3'

Table 4.3 Distribution of interaction types for each pupil per choice of language

(% lines)	LSF	Cued speech	Spoken French	Mixed LSF/French	Fingerspelling
S1	37.7		23.7	38.6	
S2	15.2		63.6	18.2	3
S3	58.7	2.2	12	23.9	3.3
S4	36.5		41.3	22.2	
S5	28.8		46.2	23.1	1.9
S6	24.5	1.9	60.4	11.3	1.9
S7	2.9		95.7	1.4	
Total	31.6	0.6	43.1	23.3	1.4

and spoken French in 22.2% of interactions. In fact, detailed examination of the distribution of the languages used shows that there is no dichotomy in language practices, with some of the children favouring one language and the other children favouring another language. The table also shows the importance of bimodal practices, which in some children account for as many productions as LSF alone or French alone. This is the case for S1, who used a mix of languages in 38.6% of his interactions, LSF for 37.7% and French for 23.7%. Each of the pupils, to different degrees, used all of the language resources at their disposal. This can be shown by placing them on a continuum ranging from practices oriented towards French ('+ French' pole) to practices oriented towards LSF ('+ LSF' pole). Each student's position on the continuum was determined using data for all their language practices. Hence, if two children showed similar percentages for LSF, but one used French alone more frequently and the other used a mixture of languages more frequently, the second was positioned closer to the '+ LSF' pole even if that student's percentage of LSF use was slightly lower than that of the first student.

Figure 4.1 shows the result for the full corpus of all interactions. For example, student S2 uses LSF more in his interaction than S3, who tends to use more French.

Individual analyses of the students for each of the sessions with the regular teacher (Figure 4.2) or the sign language teacher (Figure 4.3) revealed great variation between their language profiles, for which it is difficult to extract precise rules. Grouping together the continuum diagrams for each session provides a dynamic representation of the students' profiles.

Analysis of the quantitative data for all the sessions revealed three distinct 'language profiles':

- Two students – S1 and S3 – consistently favoured LSF;
- Two students – S2 and S7 – consistently favoured French;
- Three students – S4, S5 and S6 – exhibited very fluid language practices.

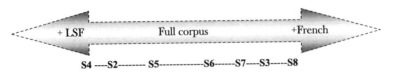

Figure 4.1 Full corpus – continuum of students' language practices

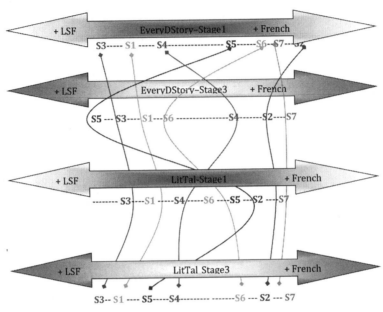

Figure 4.2 Continuum of students' language practices with the regular teacher

Combinations of the children's bilingual and bimodal resources

The children's language practices were related to the language resources that they personally or contextually had at their disposal. They used these resources differently with each of the two regular and sign language teachers and, perhaps most importantly, depending on the nature of the task and the difficulty of the text. The individual variations observed during the sessions may, to a certain extent, be related to degrees

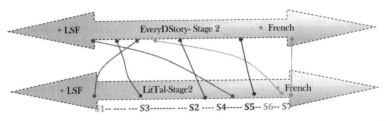

Figure 4.3 Continuum of students' language practices with the sign language teacher

of deafness, but this cannot be the entire explanation, as children with the same degree of deafness sometimes used different resources. Our data were also compared to parents' responses to a pre-intervention questionnaire. This shed new light on the degree to which each pupil – and particularly each family – accepted each language.

Students who tended towards the '+ LSF' pole of the continuum

S1 stands out from the other students because he mixed languages much more frequently than his classmates. In addition, he used mostly mixed languages with the regular teacher. Nevertheless, following the sessions with the sign language teacher, he mixed languages less and used LSF more, and he participated more in the sessions. These features of S1's practices suggest that the sessions with the sign language teacher left him feeling more secure, confident, and comfortable with using LSF. His parents' responses to a questionnaire show that they are wary of LSF, which they considered to be in direct competition with French. Hence, mixing languages was a way for S1 to satisfy his parents' expectations while making the best use of his own abilities. Thus, he mostly used LSF with the deaf teacher. His participation in the sessions varied greatly in that he participated a lot in the Everyday Story sessions but very little in the Literary Tale sessions. This difference may have been due, at least in part, to the difficulty of the literary tale. Hence, S1's language practices varied, but in a methodical way.

S3 was the other profoundly deaf child in the class. Unlike S1, neither of his parents is deaf. His mother has only recently accepted LSF. S3 was the child who used LSF the most in almost all of the sessions. He made little use of mixing languages. He participated more in the sessions with the sign language teacher when these sessions followed LSF sessions, which also increased his use of standard LSF. In addition, he actively participated in the sessions with the sign language teacher, and he was one of the rare students who participated more in the Literary Tale session than in the Everyday Story – Stage 3 session. It is likely that the LSF sessions helped him improve his abilities in LSF. He felt less insecure than S2 in his choice of using LSF alone.

'Fluid' students on the continuum

S5, who had a moderate hearing loss and could access French relatively easily, sometimes predominantly used LSF. Overall, she used the different languages more or less equally, adapting the language to the hearing status of the teacher. Hence, S5 moved along the continuum and felt secure and confident in using her entire repertoire. The fact that her family did not appear to have any negative preconceptions of LSF meant she felt free to use it, even though her ability to express herself in spoken French was in line with normative monolingual criteria that meant that she was perceived as not needing to use sign language.

In general, S4 (who was moderately to severely deaf) preferred using French only with the regular teacher. In fact, S4 was one of the only students to use French more than LSF during the Everyday Story – Stage 3 session. Furthermore, she participated more following the sessions with the sign language teacher, during which she used mostly LSF. She also adapted the language she used to the teacher.

S6 was a very unobtrusive student who did not stand out in either her degree of participation or her language practices. Of all the students, she was the most consistent in the degree to which she participated in the different sessions. In terms of her language use, she favoured French in all of the sessions except Everyday Story – Stage 3 and Everyday Story – Stage 2. This may be because she was uncertain of her mastery of LSF, in which case the fact that she did not use LSF during the Literary Tale – Stage 2 session may have been due to her lack of confidence in this language.

Students who tended towards the '+ French' pole of the continuum

S2 (who was hard of hearing with other impairments) participated very little in any of the sessions, which makes it difficult to pinpoint his language practices. Nevertheless, he never used LSF alone with the regular teacher (ten interventions), preferring French or a mix of languages. With the sign language teacher (nine interventions) he used either LSF, French alone or a mixture of languages. His parents considered LSF to be an important complement to French, but they wanted French to be the main language used in class.

S7's language profile was uniform across all sessions, as she used mostly French, even with the deaf teacher (100% of interactions). The only session in which she used LSF was Everyday Story – Stage 1 (5.9% of interactions). Her preference for French is probably due to the fact that she had been in contact with sign language for only two months. She was a recent arrival at this school, having previously been in a mainstream class. During the sessions led by the regular teacher, she participated more in the Everyday Story sessions than in the Literary Tale sessions. For example, she was the student who participated the least in the Literary Tale – Stage 1 session, probably due at least in part to the difficulty of the text. In addition, she rarely participated in the LSF sessions (one intervention in Everyday Story – Stage 2; seven interventions in the Literary Tale – Stage 2).

Upon observing these deaf children's language practices and backgrounds, it becomes clear that despite prevailing social representations and the identity constructions and assignations they engender, the children deploy their language resources in an extremely dynamic way. French alone does not allow the children to express all their competences and knowledge. In fact, this monolingualism promotes a sort of circularity in the content of exchanges. A monolingual LSF environment is not the solution either, as the goal is to build bridges between languages. Deaf children construct a variety of forms of bilingualism which can possibly be supported by gesture, signing and speech for verbal and non-verbal communication. Consequently, a deaf child's bilingualism should not be considered a 'stabilised situation' but 'an ensemble of language practices' (Lüdi & Py, 1986/2002: 107), and the classroom should be viewed as a potentially bilingual space with teachers who demonstrate a truly open attitude in order to encourage children's bilingual practices and enable them to construct skills in each language.

However, adopting a relatively wide definition of bilingualism and opting for the recognition of 'bilingual expression' in no way signifies acceptance of a bimodal mixture of languages. In fact, this mixture of languages and codes does not make use of all language facilities (Alegria & Charlier, 1996) and, as Johnson *et al.* (1989) showed, such practices by teachers, whose use of sign language is often far from perfect, give profoundly deaf people an almost incomprehensible sign language. In short, mixing languages and codes in this way is useful only to people who have residual hearing and who can make do with (incomplete) information provided via a vocal language.

It is also crucial to determine the degree to which language practices are the result of natural interactions or teaching methods, so a more didactic approach can be taken to the teaching of the different languages and modes (Castellotti, 1997). This can be done only by providing teachers, who are at the heart of the process, with appropriate practical training aimed at modifying their language practices and representations. As Moore (2003: 75) noted, 'bi/plurilingualism in itself is not necessarily a sufficient factor, but schoolwork to support and bring together these skills is essential in order to turn plurilingualism into an advantage'.

Several earlier qualitative studies of language practices produced similar observations. Millet *et al.* (2008) collected qualitative data on the language repertoires of young deaf adults who adapted the way they used gestural and vocal modalities, and French and LSF, according to the context: some people favoured bilingual bimodal practices (e.g. oral French and LSF); other people favoured monolingual bimodal practices (e.g. oral French and gestures). In other words, these young adults dynamically applied the languages and modalities in their repertoire. What is more, this feature of their language practices was independent of the schooling choices made by their parents (deaf or hearing). In another study examining the language abilities of deaf children, Estève (2011) showed that children, just like adults, use all available verbal and non-verbal resources to communicate, whatever the language choice into which the child is propelled.

These observations of deaf people's language practices show that the current preschool and school systems impose a ideological stereotypical model that excludes bimodal bilingualism. Hence, rather than making parents choose between programmes that focus on one or another mode of communication, it is time that deaf children were given the possibility to learn and use different forms of plurilingualism, which means more support for standard LSF in teacher training.

In Lieu of a Conclusion ... the Need to Take into Account Children's Bimodal Language Practices

The history of deafness and the deaf community is multidimensional and reflects the often conflicting relations between deaf and hearing people (Delaporte, 2002). People's positions on issues pertaining to deafness, which are underlain by value systems and representations, take on a special dimension with respect to communication because deafness raises issues of the Other and of difference. Consequently, questions relating to education have resulted in debates driven by relations of power where philosophical, ideological and symbolic dimensions intertwine.

Although more research into signed languages and deafness, the higher profile of sign language in the media and via LSF courses, and many other factors have improved this situation, the social representations surrounding deafness enable certain marks of the past to persist. Why is there such resistance towards deaf people and their language? The difficulty in gaining recognition for LSF is, I believe, a perfect illustration of this resistance, first at an official level, then among the general public and finally among deaf people themselves. Because this history has not yet been consigned to the past, it continues to weigh heavily on debates about the education of deaf children, where the oralist and bilingual positions remain separate movements and forces that at best progress in parallel and at worst descend into war, and where progress in one is seen as a defeat for the other.

The preceding review of laws and policies governing the education of deaf children and the pathways available to them shows the urgent need to abandon centuries-old ideologies and the identity stereotypes they generate. For deaf people, as for hearing people, identity construction as fluid and in flux should be facilitated and not hindered, by providing an unrestricted right to learn a variety of languages (French, LSF) and modes (vocal/gestural, oral/written).

These choices of languages and modes are not subject to change as a function of context, desires or abilities; they evolve continuously throughout the identity construction process. It is only by removing the obstacles created by archaic, antagonistic and divisive points of view which differentiate between the gestural/manual deaf and the oral/speaking deaf that the social sphere can allow this complex, diverse and ever-evolving symbolic construction of a multi-faceted deaf identity to be freed from enduring and divisive social representations.

To achieve what still appears to be a utopian dream, it is necessary to bring together every strand of society in order to give all deaf people, starting with young children, the means they need to dynamically construct their language repertoires including, in an entirely natural form of plurilingualism, vocal languages, gestural languages and a range of non-verbal resources.

Notes

(1) Circular EN no. 87-273 and 87-08 of 7 September 1987; Ministry of Education Bulletin (BOEN) no. 32 of 17 September 1987.
(2) Decree no. 92-1132 of 8 October 1992 related to the education of young deaf people and set application conditions for Article 33 of Act no. 91-73 of 18 January 1991 pertaining to the dispositions relating to public health and social insurance.
(3) Circular no. 2017-011 of 3-2-2017.

References

Alegria, J. and Charlier, B. (1996) L'éducation de l'enfant sourd au seuil du 3ème millénaire: Base pour un bilinguisme articulé. *Actes du colloque: Perception, Cognition, Handicap, Recherche en défectologie*, Lyon, Université Lumière – Lyon 2, 53–62.

Beacco, J.-C. and Byram, M. (2002) *Guide d'Elaboration des Politiques Linguistiques Educatives en Europe. De la Diversité Linguistique à l'Education Plurilingue.* Strasbourg: Editions du Conseil de l'Europe: Division des politiques linguistiques.

Biliez, J. (2005) Répertoires et parlers plurilingues. Déplacements à opérer et pistes à parcourir à l'école. In L.F Prudent, F. Tupin and S. Wharton (eds) *Du Plurilinguisme à l'Ecole. Vers une Gestion Coordonnée des Langues en Contextes Educatifs Sensibles* (pp. 323–340). Bern: Peter Lang.

Bouvet, D. (1989) *La Parole de l'Elève Sourd: Pour Une Education Bilingue de l'Enfant Sourd.* Paris: Presses Universitaires de France.

Castellotti, V. (1997) Langues étrangères et français en milieu scolaire: didactiser l'alternance ? *Etudes de Linguistique Appliquée* 108, 401–410.

Castellotti, V. (2001) *La langue maternelle en classe de langue étrangère.* Paris: CLE International.

Coste, D. (2001) La notion de compétences plurilingues et ses implications possibles. In *L'Enseignement des Langues Vivantes, Perspectives* (pp. 29–38). CRDP Versailles: Direction de l'enseignement scolaire.

Coste, D. (ed.) (2012) *Les Langues au Cœur de l'Education: Principes, Pratiques, Propositions.* Brussels: EME éditions.

Coste, D., Moore, D. and Zarate, G. (1997) *Compétence plurilingue et pluriculturelle. Langues vivantes. Vers un cadre européen commun de référence pour l'enseignement et l'apprentissage des langues vivantes. Etudes préparatoires.* Strasbourg: Conseil de l'Europe.

Cuxac, C. (1983) *Le Langage des Sourds.* Paris: Payot.

Dabène, L. (1994) *Repères Sociolinguistiques pour l'Enseignement des Langues.* Paris: Hachette.

Delaporte, Y. (2002) *Les Sourds C'est Comme* ça. Paris: Editions de la Maison des Sciences de l'Homme.

Dethorre, M. (1997) Histoire de surdité. Réflexions psychanalytiques et anthropologiques sur les représentations de la surdité et ses effets. *Handicaps Inadapt – Cah CTNERHI* 74, 15–33.

Dubreuil, B. (2001) L'intégration: Moyens ou finalités? Intégration ou réintégration. *Communautés Éducatives Surdité Co-Éducation* 117, 6–19.

Dunant-Sauvin, C. and Chavaillaz, J.-F. (1993) Un bilinguisme particulier: français/langue des signes. *Tranel* 19, 61–79.

Estève, I. (2011) Approche bilingue et multimodale de l'oralité chez l'enfant sourd: Outils d'analyses, socialisation, développement. Thèse de doctorat, Université de Grenoble.

Estève, I. and Mugnier, S. (2012) Tensions identitaires et réalités langagières chez les enfants sourds, construction identitaire et langagière à l'école. In J. Sauvage and F. Demougin (eds) *La Construction Identitaire à l'Ecole – Perspectives Linguistiques et Plurielles* (pp. 79–91). Paris: L'Harmattan.

Grosjean, F. (1982) *Life With Two Languages: An Introduction to Bilingualism.* Cambridge, MA: Harvard University Press.

HAS (Haute Autorité de Santé) (2009) *Surdité de l'enfant: Accompagnement des familles et suivi de l'enfant de 0 à 6 ans.* See https://www.has-sante.fr/portail/upload/docs/application/pdf/2010-09/children_deafness_-_0_to_6_years_-_quick_reference_guide.pdf.

Johnson, R., Liddell, S. and Erting, C. (1989) *Unlocking the Curriculum: Principles for Achieving Access in Deaf Education.* Washington DC: Gallaudet University.

Lambert, P. (2005) *Les répertoires plurilectaux de jeunes filles d'un lycée professionnel. Une approche sociolinguistique ethnographique,* Thèse de doctorat de sciences du langage sous la direction de J. Billiez, Université Stendhal-Grenoble 3.

Lamothe, M. (2001) De l'instruction du sourd-muet, à l'intégration de l'élève handicapé à l'école. *Communautés Éducatives Surdité Co-Éducation* 117, 39–51.

Lüdi, G. (2000) Synthèse: construire des répertoires pluriels dans l'interaction »In *La notion de contacts de langues en didactique,* NeQ 4, S. 179–189.

Lüdi, G. and Py, B. (1986/2002) *Etre Bilingue.* Bern: Peter Lang.

Markowicz, H. (1980) La communauté des sourds en tant que minorité linguistique. *Coup d'oeil,* 24. Paris: CEMS – École des Hautes Études en Sciences Sociales.

McNeill, D. (1992) *Hand and Mind: What Gestures Reveals About Thought.* Chicago, IL: University of Chicago Press.

Millet, A., Estève, I. and Guigas, L. (2008) Pratiques communicatives d'un groupe de jeunes sourds adultes. See https://halshs.archives-ouvertes.fr/halshs-00419204/document (accessed 23 January 2018).

Ministry of Education (1994) L'intégration d'élèves sourds dans l'enseignement secondaire. National training course, Collège des Buclos, Meylan, France, 7–11 February.

Moore, D. (2006) *Plurilinguismes et école.* Paris: Collection LAL, Didier.

Mottez, B. (2006) *Les Sourds Existent-Ils?* Paris: L'Harmattan.

Mugnier, S. (2006) Surdités, plurilinguisme et Ecole Approches sociolinguistiques et sociodidactiques des bilinguismes d'enfants sourds de CE2. Thèse de doctorat, Université de Grenoble.

Mugnier, S. (2016) Succès et revers dans l'élaboration de modèles de plurilinguisme en contexte de surdité. In G. Lane Mercier, D. Merkel and J. Koustas (eds) *Plurilinguisme et Pluriculturalisme. Des Modèles Officiels dans le Monde* (pp. 139–155). Montréal: Press Universitaire Montréal.

Poizat, M. (2001) La société face à la surdité. In F. Pellion (ed.) *Surdité et Souffrance psychique* (pp. 26–34). Paris: Ellipses.

Py, B. La construction interactive de la norme comme pratique et comme représentation, In *Acquisition et interaction en langue étrangère* [En ligne], 12 | 2000, http://journals.openedition.org/aile/1464; https://doi.org/ 10.4000/aile.1464

Sero-Guillaume, Ph. (1995) Langue des signes et culture, *Le Courrier de Suresnes* n°63 (pp. 29–33), Surenes.

Vermes, G. (1988) *Vingt-cinq Communautés Linguistiques de la France. I. Langues Régionales et Langues Non Territorialisées, II. Les Langues Immigrées.* Paris: L'Harmattan.

Virole, B. (2000) *Psychologie de la Surdité.* Brussels: De Boeck Université.

Woodward, J. (1982) *How You Gonna Get to Heaven if You Can't Talk to Jesus: On Depathologizing Deafness.* Silver Spring, MD: T.J. Publishers.

5 Plurilingualism and Policy in Deaf Education

Joanne C. Weber

The polarization of language choices for deaf children and youth – that is, spoken English or American Sign Language (ASL) – encourages competition in deaf education for resources, personnel and spaces. This chapter examines a plurilingual frame towards a contemporary policy document concerning language pedagogy for deaf children. I analyze two historic Saskatchewan Ministry of Education documents which contain language planning discourses that subscribe to the cognitive-imperialist ideological frame concerning language acquisition in deaf children. In 2016, the Saskatchewan Human Rights Commission Report and the theatre play, Deaf Crows, *in referring to direct experiences of deaf children and their parents, challenged the cognitive-imperialist discourses that appeared in the historic reports. An examination of* Deaf Crows *further reveals the multiple semiotic resources that contribute to plurilingualism. Consideration of available linguistic, material, cultural and social resources contributes to a plurilingual frame for language planning and may provide more expansive guiding principles for deaf children's language access and acquisition.*

Introduction

In Saskatchewan, Canada, plurilingualism has yet to make its way into policy documents concerning language acquisition in deaf children and youth. Competition for educational resources continues between two factions: professionals (educators, audiologists, speech and language pathologists) who promote an oralist philosophy which relies on the exclusive use of cochlear implants, augmentative listening devices and speech therapy, and those who promote a bimodal bilingual approach (ASL and English) (SHRC, 2016a). Within the bimodal bilingual approach, ASL and English are presented as languages to be learned and used to access the K-12 curriculum designated by the Ministry of Education. Preference for the oralist approach was indicated in two historic reports produced in 1989 and 1990. There is no contemporary official policy document on the education of the deaf.

There are only three government-issued documents specifically addressing deaf education in this province. The issuance of these documents is widely spaced over a period of nearly 30 years (1989–2016). These documents are as follows:

(1) The Saskatchewan Task Force on Deaf Education (1989) report, which collected feedback from stakeholders including parents, teachers, professionals and students and made initial recommendations regarding the provision of educational programs and services to deaf children and youth.
(2) The Deaf Education Advisory Forum or DEAF report. This group was established in 1990 with the mandate to expand the recommendations made by the Task Force Committee and to oversee the implementation of those recommendations.
(3) The third document, produced by the Saskatchewan Human Rights Commission (SHRC), collected and reported on feedback from stakeholder groups (similar to the groups that participated in the original Task Force report) and included recommendations with which to address systemic inequality that impinges on the rights of deaf and hard-of-hearing individuals.

I will argue that these reports draw upon certain assumptions about deaf people and their educational opportunities that work to maintain the status quo of deaf education in this province. The presence of continued language deprivation in Saskatchewan suggests that not all needs of deaf children are currently being met (SHRC, 2016a). Plurilingualism may be a way out of the stalemate between the two educational approaches to language acquisition in deaf children and youth.

Specifically, I examine the discourses in two historic reports on deaf education in Saskatchewan (Saskatchewan Deaf Education Advisory Forum, 1990; Saskatchewan Task Force Report on Deaf Education, 1989) about deaf children, their parents and educational placements. I also examine how two contemporary texts produced in 2016 challenge the discourses in the historic reports. The contemporary texts are the SHRC report entitled *Access and Equality for Deaf, deaf, and Hard of Hearing People: A Report to Stakeholders* (hereafter known as the SHRC report), and a theatre script for the play *Deaf Crows* (Ells *et al.*, 2016), which was produced by the Deaf Crows Collective. Finally, I explore the movement towards plurilingualism in the *Deaf Crows* theatre script and its contribution to future policy development pertaining to educational services for deaf children and youth in Saskatchewan. The next section further defines the concept of plurilingualism.

Plurilingualism, Posthumanism and Language Deprivation

Plurilingualism refers to 'functional competence in partial languages', thus placing emphasis on individual linguistic repertoires (Canagarajah, 2013: 6). The increasing diversity of languages and cultures brought about by shifting patterns of globalization has resulted in the blurring of boundaries between languages and cultures (Canagarajah, 2013). García *et al.* (2015) suggest that languages are not bounded according to political or ethnic divisions or scripted according to standard forms of usage. Rather, individual repertoires containing multiple and partial linguistic competences include the diverse ways in which individuals use their knowledge of language and culture to facilitate communication (Swanwick, 2017). For instance, Kusters (2015) produced an ethnographic video, *Ishaare*, exploring signs and gestures employed between hearing and deaf interlocutors in the marketplace in Mumbai. The intra-actions in this video between the material, spatial, bodies, written texts and multiple spoken and signed languages attest to the interplay between languages and semiotic resources, suggesting that there are no strict distinctions made by participants who negotiate meanings with the resources afforded by their individual linguistic repertoires. When focusing on what people do with languages, it becomes clear that grammatical forms of language are co-constructed within a variety of contexts, social networks, ecologies and material objects (Canagarajah, 2017). These intra-actions reveal a post-humanist onto-epistemology.

Plurilingualism in posthumanist onto-epistemology

In response to the devastating effects of human domination on this planet, posthumanism proposes a flattened onto-epistemology in which the actions, decisions and forces exerted by non-human actors such as plants, animals, earth and machines are presented as worthy of equal consideration. Posthumanism also suggests alternative research paradigms, particularly the construction of cartographies that highlight the performative elements of an assemblage. A cartography is a mapping of the associations, connections and responses made between human and non-human actors. An assemblage is a collection of human, animal, machine and earth elements that are continually in motion, producing and being produced by each other (Deleuze & Guattari, 1987). An assemblage often appears as a random assortment of human and non-human actors but, upon closer scrutiny, reveals intricate performative linkages as they intra-act with each other, producing and being produced by the other as they move throughout the assemblage. In later sections of this chapter, I reveal an assemblage within the performance space of *Deaf Crows*. Within the anthropocentric frame, forms of humanism abound which seek to imprint the will and desire of human beings to control, form, shape and use resources without constraint or consideration of the ecology in which human beings take part (Braidotti, 2013). Languages are hierarchized towards this end; dominant languages are inextricably tied to the claim that human beings and, particularly, certain human beings are selected to be masters of the planet's destiny (Pennycook, 2018).

Cognition and language, therefore, are distributed throughout the assemblage rather than located in the individual and are embedded within the performative intra-actions in which human and non-human actors produce and are produced by each other. Plurilingualism placed within a posthumanist frame allows for the consideration of multiple semiotic resources that contribute to plurilingual language acquisition. More recent theoretical models of language acquisition explore the spatiotemporal dimensions of language learning (Canagarajah, 2017; Pennycook, 2012). Canagarajah (2017) explains that structuralist approaches to teaching language ignore the spatiotemporal entities associated with communication. The context for language acquisition is often presented as an afterthought, with a view to establishing distinctions between bounded languages as if there were no other considerations concerning diverse linguistic populations and spatial and material resources that are used to communicate (Canagarajah, 2017).

Languages in the assemblage are not the function of innate cognitive processes within the human individual or decisions made by particular communities. Rather, languages are distributed throughout the assemblage and are shaped by and shaping intra-actions between humans, animals, machines and earth. Here, language is 'embodied, embedded and distributed across people, places and time' (Pennycook, 2018: 51). Applied posthuman linguistics suggests that languages within an assemblage are performative; that is, languages take on multiple, shifting, partial and negotiated meanings while drawing upon material, spatial, cultural and social semiotic resources (Pennycook, 2018).

Language deprivation

Thirty years after the production of the historic reports issued by the government of Saskatchewan, the two contemporary texts of the SHRC report and the *Deaf Crows* theatre script were developed in response to reported claims about the presence of language deprivation in many deaf children and youth in Saskatchewan. The *Deaf Crows* play was created in the tradition of research-based popular theatre (Beck *et al.*, 2011; Weber, 2018) and was developed from a participatory action research project which highlighted actual experiences of deaf students who struggle with language deprivation in the context of their schooling experiences in Saskatchewan. Language deprivation syndrome is a neurodevelopmental disorder with sociocultural origins (Hall *et al.*, 2017). Glickman and Hall (2019: 2) define language deprivation as the outcome of 'growing up without any quality exposure to any accessible language'. Access to language may be circumscribed in part by the limitations of hearing technologies such as cochlear implants, which are reported to have variable results (Conway *et al.*, 2014) and by poor sign language models in the home, family and school environments (Glickman & Hall, 2019). Gulati (2019) observes that geography presents challenges to language access as well. Many children born in remote and rural areas often do not have access to services for learning sign language. Lack of access to a sign language occasioned by geographic isolation and lack of educational opportunities and social services make for a mismatch in the deaf child's habitus (see O'Brien, this volume). The consequences of language deprivation involve lifelong challenges, including: cognitive deficits; language, academic achievement and social-emotional developmental delays; and reduced opportunities for postsecondary education and employment (Glickman & Hall, 2019).

While it is indisputable that cognitive deficits arise from linguistic neglect of deaf children (Davenport *et al.*, 2016; Gulati, 2019; Hall *et al.*, 2017; Humphries *et al.*, 2012, 2016; Mayberry *et al.*, 2011; Peterson *et al.*, 2010), I suggest that cognitive deficits can best be ameliorated with pedagogy and practices that support plurilingualism, founded upon co-constructed meanings and partial, truncated linguistic repertoires (Blommaert *et al.*, 2005; Canagarajah, 2013; Swanwick, 2017). Furthermore, I suggest that cognitive imperialism is the impetus for language deprivation.

Cognitive Imperialism

Slee (2004) suggests that we understand disability from a distance and through ideological frameworks held by educators, administrators, policymakers and medical professionals. Moreover, special needs of learners are framed as originating from deficits within their neurological, psychological or sensory capacities (Slee, 2004). Matthews (2017) reports that the methodological shift from sign language to oral language in deaf education pedagogy represented the establishment of a medical model of deafness. The need to ameliorate the effects of hearing loss and to assimilate deaf children into the hearing world became the dominant discourse in the 18th century and was the driving force behind the decision at the Milan International Congress on Education of the Deaf to restrict the use of sign language and to promote the use of oral language in the education of the deaf (Lane, 1984; Matthews, 2017). The subsequent removal of deaf children from deaf schools resulted in the dominance of prescribed early interventions by hearing medical professionals for deaf children at birth, including assimilation into inclusive education environments. Medical discourses are hegemonic, buttressed by the medical profession's reliance on scientific classifications in the 18th century, which described how the body deviated from norms established by European white males (Davis, 1995; Foucault, 1973). This hegemonic discourse also allied with cognitive imperialism discourses advanced by the Age of Enlightenment which served to position the Eurocentric, male, white, able-bodied person at the forefront of all humanity.

Cognitive imperialism supports the notion of the individual as the primary site of learning and cognition (Battiste, 2013) and draws upon the Enlightenment's hegemonic themes of universality, freedom and autonomy of the individual regardless of context. Cognitive imperialism ascribes deviance or the failure to learn as emanating from the individual. Deficits in learning are attributed to inferior cognitive abilities as established by the norm and instituted through Eurocentrism. With cognitive imperialism, the striving for universality promotes Eurocentric knowledge, experiences, cultures and languages to the exclusion of other, non-European languages and cultures (Battiste, 2011). Efforts are expended to enforce these norms without consideration of cultures, languages, contexts and social organizations in which the individual may be immersed (Battiste, 2013; Davis, 1995).

Cognitive imperialism, originally defined to describe the oppression of First Nations through the suppression of language and culture, is also an epistemology applicable to non-Western Indigenous cultures (Wu et al., 2018). While some Deaf Studies scholars eschew the use of postcolonial metaphors to describe the linguistic oppression of deaf people (O'Brien, 2017), there is a documented confluence of racism and ableism within Canadian government policies (Peers, 2015). Cognitive imperialism's long reach into the education system is manifested in public schooling's intended production of white, skilled Canadian nationals and the differentiation and exclusion of populations known as the 'other' (Peers, 2015). Cognitive imperialism also imposes English as the dominant language upon Indigenous and marginalized populations (Pennycook, 1998, 2018).

Cognitive imperialism reinforces the conception of deaf children as in need of a cure in order to approximate the efforts of white, abled-bodied citizens (Graham & Slee, 2008; Mauldin, 2016). In such discourses, sign language is often given passing reference, while the focus of many deaf education policies is on acquiring spoken and written forms of the dominant language (see Snoddon, this volume). Cognitive imperialism ascribes the failure to approximate the monolingual and monocultural norms to 'cultural and racial origins rather than the power relations that create inequality in a capitalistic economy' (Battiste, 2013: 161). For instance, cognitive-imperialistic discourses on deafness indicate that the failure of cochlear implants is the result of a lack of parental compliance in following the instructions of cochlear implant clinics (Mauldin, 2016). Mauldin (2016) notes that most perceived failures of cochlear implants occur in minoritized and racialized populations. In short, cognitive imperialism favors white, middle-class families (Battiste, 2013; Mauldin, 2016).

The next sections of this chapter outline the timeline of texts and how they challenge or reinforce plurilingualism and cognitive imperialism.

Timeline

In 1989, the Saskatchewan Task Force on Deaf Education was formed to address the issue of dwindling enrolment at the provincial school for the deaf and the increasing emphasis by parents, professionals and administrative policymakers on the promise of cochlear implants and placement in mainstream educational environments in home communities. The Task Force Committee solicited opinions from several stakeholder groups in order to determine the best way forward for deaf education in the province. The Task Force Committee consisted of: two Ministry of Education officials, Merv Houghton and Robert Livingston; the principal of the R.J.D. Williams School for the Deaf, Bill Lockert; and Patti Trofimenkoff, a deaf teacher and parent of two deaf children. The committee became divided between two ideological positions: one that favored oralism and mainstreaming, and another that favored the use of sign language and placement in congregated programs. Lockert and Trofimenkoff (1989) filed their own dissenting report (known as the Minority Report) after the Task Force Report was completed. The Minority Report reaffirmed the importance of congregated settings and the use of ASL, and recommended that the school for the deaf remain open (Lockert & Trofimenkoff, 1989). The Minority Report was overruled, and the Ministry of Education accepted the Task Force Report.

After the Task Force on Deaf Education had fulfilled its mandate, the Deaf Education Advisory Forum was immediately organized to take over the implementation of the recommendations of the Task Force and to develop further recommendations that supported the conclusions of the Task Force Committee. The DEAF committee implemented the recommendation to close the school for deaf and coordinated the dispersal of the current students back to their own home communities or to the Alberta or Manitoba schools for the deaf.

In 1991, 25 years after the closure of the school for the deaf in Saskatchewan and the issuance of the DEAF report, the SHRC investigated human rights claims made by deaf individuals and their families. The resulting report, *Access and Equality for Deaf, deaf, and Hard of Hearing People: A Report to Stakeholders*, is 'part of a longer-term, systemic advocacy process. Systemic advocacy address differential treatment, policies, and rules that can unfairly disadvantage a group of people' (SHRC, 2016a: 2). The report compiles data gathered in 2015 from community consultations in four centers in the province. The Commission also received reports, presentations and reflections upon public services designed to meet the needs of deaf people. The highlights of the report included the need for universal newborn screening, linking diagnosis to intervention information and options, including sign language training. Other issues include the limited availability of interpretation services and assistive technology in the education system, in healthcare settings and in the receipt of public services (SHRC, 2016a). In summary, the SHRC report concerning deaf people crosses multiple disciplines, including education, health care and justice systems, and aims to support the goals of the Saskatchewan Disability Strategy, a document that focuses on addressing the needs of people with disabilities in this province.

In 2016, members of the Regina deaf community established the Deaf Crows Collective, a deaf arts and theatre non-profit organization, and initiated several arts-based initiatives designed to address the plurilingual development of deaf youth who were not consistently exposed to ASL or spoken English during their early school years. One of their plays, *Deaf Crows*, is a text addressing the experiences of deaf students who are not fluent in spoken English or ASL. The play features intra-actions with material, spatial and embodied semiotic resources that enable the students to convey their experiences growing up in environments that were bewildering and oppressive.

Deaf Crows is a critical artistic text developed to address the cognitive-imperialist epistemological assumptions concerning monolingual discourses driving language acquisition in deaf children and youth. Artist-activists often challenge dominant discourses through material, social and cultural means embedded within art, theatre and performance to point to alternative discourses that might level the playing field for other people (Hickey-Moody & Page, 2016). The information in *Deaf Crows* is presented as contextualized, jargon free and with little reference to abstract concepts, although the information is similar in content to the SHRC report. The report contains transcriptions of complaints from actual stakeholders (SHRC, 2016a). In *Deaf Crows*, the audience's emotions and engagement are solicited as possible responses to the theme of social and cultural challenges to the language acquisition of the deaf child. The adolescent and adult deaf actors of *Deaf Crows* use cochlear implants and hearing aids, and are diverse in terms of race and class. They tell of their own experiences of language deprivation without recourse to the cultural script afforded by the signing deaf community of Saskatchewan. The creation of the play was a deliberate response to the two reports issued 25 years ago and an attempt to provoke critical awareness about discourses reinforcing cognitive imperialism.

Analysis of the Historic Reports

Analysis of the documents discussed in this section reveals certain beliefs, theories and assumptions about deaf children and youth. Often theory, rather than research findings, shapes educational practice and pedagogies (Cummins, 2000). The theoretical positioning of language acquisition frequently braids observations and practices into a cohesive whole, which in turn generates discourses that maintain certain practices and pedagogies (Cummins, 2000). Fairclough (2010) outlines strategies often used to maintain hegemonic practices. Hegemonic practices include the favoring of a monolingual language policy (such as English in Saskatchewan) and the maintenance of educational institutions and programs that support monolingualism (Canagarajah, 2013). In this section, I will analyze discourses that work together to maintain selected beliefs or assumptions about deaf children, their parents and educational placements.

Establishing dominance of a discourse over other discourses often requires strategic maneuvers to obtain stakeholder consent (Fairclough, 2010). Hegemonic struggle persists in the form of combining and recombining contradictory ideological positions to obtain stakeholder consent and to establish an equilibrium in which dominant discourses can remain dominant and consent is won from dissenting voices (Fairclough, 2010). Hegemonic struggle

> requires a degree of integration of local and semi-autonomous institutions and power relations, so that the latter are partially shaped by hegemonic relations. This directs attention to links across institutions, and links and movement between institutional orders of discourse. (Fairclough, 2010: 64)

The dominant institution employs many strategies to maintain the equilibrium which may at any moment be undermined by other groups (Fairclough, 2010). At stake is the maintenance of cognitive imperialism, an ontological position reinforced by the government through practices such as market research (opinion polls, surveys and focus groups), which dominate the content of stakeholder reports (Fairclough, 2010).

The scope of my analysis will begin with the examination of the historic documents (Task Force Report, 1989, and the DEAF report, 1990). I then analyze two contemporary texts: the SHRC report and the *Deaf Crows* theatre play. The analysis of *Deaf Crows* will identify new discourses that support the inclusion of plurilingualism in future policy development.

Recommendations of the historic reports

The first recommendation of the Task Force Commission was to establish a Deaf Education Advisory Forum. In its rationale for the DEAF committee, the Task Force committee described the 'unhealthy competition among programs which in turn has diminished efforts of parents and professionals to work together to provide quality education for the deaf' (Saskatchewan Task Force on Deaf Education, 1989: 3).

The admonishment to professionals to work together is presented as a moral imperative: 'It is timely that the parents and professionals involved unite and solidify their efforts to better serve the deaf children of Saskatchewan' (Saskatchewan Task Force on Deaf Education, 1989: 3). Within this text, elements in discourses are viewed as related or different and not entirely separate from each other (Fairclough, 2010). The Task Force report framed the polarization between camps (oralism versus bilingualism) as an educational placement issue, or one of integration versus segregation, with little reference to linguistic choices, needs or contexts. Subsuming the language debate under educational placement issues serves to sidestep language acquisition needs and seemingly unites the disparate linguistic camps. This attempt to bypass the language debates (i.e. the use of either ASL or spoken English in fostering deaf children's language acquisition) continues to frame the polarization as an educational placement issue. Here, language acquisition by deaf children is under erasure within 'social relations, power, institutions, beliefs and cultural values' (Fairclough, 2010: 230).

In the following year, the DEAF document provided guiding principles as to how quality education for the deaf is to be achieved regardless of the 'child's level of hearing loss or geographical location' (Saskatchewan Deaf Education Advisory Forum, 1990: 3). The use of moral imperatives initiated by the Task Force document continues in the preamble to the principles in the DEAF document. The appeal to moral imperatives is an attempt to increase consciousness of obligations and duties imposed by cultural and moral expectations which in turn support the interests of the hegemonic class (Fairclough, 2010). Here, the moral imperative exhorts the polarized factions to work together, without considering the needs of the deaf child. The blatant disregard for language acquisition needs only serves to avoid the issue at hand, that is, how best to meet the needs of all deaf children. The recommendation to close the school for the deaf (as stated in Section IV of the DEAF report) sets the stage for the increasing focus on providing educational services to deaf children in their home communities. The influence of cognitive imperialism in the reinforcement of monolingualism echoes the Enlightenment's hegemonic theme of universality, freedom and autonomy of the individual regardless of context.

The first two principles emphasize parental choice and individual self-fulfillment: 'Based on the provision of information, the ultimate responsibility and right to choose an educational program for a child remains with his or her parents. As a child matures, he or she shares in that responsibility' (Saskatchewan Deaf Education Advisory Forum, 1990: 3). This suggests that the parents can make freely formed and independent decisions concerning language choices and educational placements for their deaf children. Second, the child is presented as a free and autonomous individual who can then take on the responsibility for their education. This is visible in the corollary principle: 'Each child is an individual and should be encouraged to reach his or her full potential' (Saskatchewan Deaf Education Advisory Forum, 1990: 3). By extension, as the child matures, they are free to decide about their own language and communication choices. This reinforces the Enlightenment cognitive imperialism concerning the individual as rational, free, autonomous and fully conscious (Mansfield, 2000).

The third principle focuses on the equity of educational opportunities and says, 'programs and services should be provided for each student regardless of level of hearing loss or geographical location' (Saskatchewan Deaf Education Advisory Forum, 1990: 3). This assurance of equity is another moral imperative that places linguistic resources under erasure. Again, in emphasizing placement, the exhortation to provide a complete array of programs and services fails to attend to the restraints imposed by geography, levels of hearing loss and available linguistic, cultural and social resources (Gulati, 2019). Thus, the conditions are created for depriving deaf children of an accessible language. In short, the principles concerning the freedom of parents and children to make choices independent of available linguistic, cultural, social, economic and material resources promotes a false consensus towards cognitive imperialism.

The fourth principle urges consideration of the needs of the whole child. Language deprivation is a condition that affects cognitive development, academic achievement, social and emotional development and post-secondary education and employment outcomes (Glickman & Hall, 2019). The fourth principle states that students' 'safety and well-being, must be recognized for an educational program to be effective' (Saskatchewan Deaf Education Advisory Forum, 1990: 4). This is an oblique reference to the holistic development of a child but glaringly omits the domino effects of language deprivation on various aspects of human development. Fairclough (2010) identifies this discursive strategy as linking ideas in discourses as related or different and not entirely separate from each other. What is whole and what is normal in deaf people is aligned with Enlightenment norms (Davis, 1995). Cognitive imperialism, in this case, refers to the hegemonic practice of determining what is acceptable in terms of human development (Mansfield, 2000).

The fifth principle in the DEAF report makes the observation that 'deafness is unlike any other disability and must be recognized as such. As a result, the hearing-impaired child should be equipped to take part in both a hearing society and the deaf world to the extent the child chooses to do so' (Saskatchewan Deaf Education Advisory Forum, 1990: 4). This is an attempt to integrate the medical and cultural approaches towards deafness. The implication that a deaf child is free to align himself with their habitus, which may or may not be fully accessible, is problematic because there continues to be a wide variability in the success rates of cochlear implants (Humphries *et al.*, 2012, 2016). There is also precarity in the availability of trained and qualified interpreters within the school environments (see Russell, this volume). The mention of a hearing society and the deaf world in this principle should be noted as a strategy to integrate two opposing worlds while ignoring the issue of language deprivation. Moreover, the expectation that the deaf child will pick up attitudes, practices and perceptions through inculcation into the hearing world during early childhood (Emery & O'Brien, 2014) leads to the desire that the deaf child's habitus, supported by mainstream educational placements, will align itself with corresponding fields, that is, through relationships with specific social contexts (Bourdieu, 1991; Emery & O'Brien, 2014). Such alignments with social and cultural fields will culminate in social, economic, cultural and linguistic capital of the dominant culture (Bourdieu, 1991).

The final principle refers to the excellence of standards to be reached by deaf students. The DEAF report says: 'The quality of education should be such that deaf and hard-of-hearing students reach the standard achieved by their hearing counterparts to the best of their ability' (Saskatchewan Deaf Education Advisory Forum, 1990: 4). The phrase 'to the best of their ability' suggests that successful language development relies on innate cognitive abilities within the deaf child and the child's ability to approximate the monolingual culture within Saskatchewan. Cognitive imperialism ascribes the failure to reach monolingual and monocultural norms to 'cultural and racial origins rather than the power relations that create inequality in a capitalistic economy' (Battiste, 2013: 161). I suggest that this insight be equally applied to deaf children and youth. Medicalized discourses on deafness indicate that the failure of cochlear implants is the result of a lack of compliance in minoritized and racialized parents in following the prescriptions provided by the cochlear implant clinics (Mauldin, 2016).

Furthermore, the ability of the child and the parents to be compliant with the prescriptions concerning language acquisition issued by cochlear implant clinics (Mauldin, 2016) is often presented as a moral imperative (Lee, 2016). Yet a large percentage of implanted children continue to lag several years behind their hearing peers (Humphries *et al.*, 2012, 2016), and cognitive deficits have even been found in what are deemed to be successful implanted children (Humphries *et al.*, 2012).

The cognitive imperialism discourses in the historic reports pertaining to education of deaf children continue in the contemporary documents, the SHRC report and the *Deaf Crows* theatre play. I will examine how cognitive imperialism is maintained in the SHRC report and how *Deaf Crows* challenges cognitive imperialist discourses, therefore making way for plurilingualism.

Challenges to the Historic Reports: SHRC and Deaf Crows

Saskatchewan Human Rights Commission Report, 2016

Twenty-five years after the closure of the school for the deaf and the issuance of the DEAF report in 1990, the SHRC investigated human rights claims made by deaf individuals and their families. Several sections of the report echo the DEAF report produced in 1990 and use similar discursive strategies to maintain monolingual dominance. The SHRC report provides a summary of the continued polarization over language choices in the province. The report describes the conflict as the pitting of the cultural approach (i.e. deaf culture) against the medical approach which includes the use of cochlear implants and hearing aids and which has repercussions for early identification, treatment and education services. The report also includes testimonials from parents who claim that they were not provided with adequate and accurate information concerning the medical and cultural approaches.

The SHRC report also provides a short commentary on the role of the Saskatchewan Pediatric Rehabilitation Centre (SPARC), located at the University of Saskatchewan in Saskatoon. SPARC serves as a resource to the University of Saskatchewan medical school, to the Ministry of Education and to school divisions (SPARC, n.d.). SPARC personnel are part of the multidisciplinary team working under the auspices of the Cochlear Implant Program which provides counselling to parents, mapping services, and monitoring the progress of cochlear implant recipients. SPARC also provides follow-up services to deaf school-aged children in school divisions. To this day, SPARC describes itself as an 'early detection, assessment and (re)habilitation program with hearing loss in the Province of Saskatchewan' (SPARC, n.d.). As SPARC does not provide ASL service referrals, their message is unequivocally clear: the clinic provides support for the development of oral English in deaf children. The report attests to how dominant monolingual discourses promulgated by SPARC continue to shape education and health services in Saskatchewan. The SHRC report (2016a) directly links complaints about early childhood intervention programs to SPARC in one paragraph:

> Parents reported that they had requested American Sign Language (ASL) instruction for their families upon their children's diagnosis. Many of these parents, along with other participants, reported being told by health professionals that ASL instruction is not preferable or available for deaf children or their parents. Some parents of deaf children reported feeling that the dearth of ASL services in early childhood is related to an ideology in the healthcare system that favours the use of aural and oral (i.e., hearing and speaking) means of communication with the assistance of cochlear implants or hearing aids and lip-reading. Some parents believe that the current healthcare system also favours the use of hearing assistive devices and that this impedes early language acquisition. However,

multiple parents said audiologists and speech pathologists at SPARC discouraged the use of ASL with young deaf children on the premise that this would impede their aural and oral communication (and even if they were awaiting cochlear implants). (SHRC, 2016a: 5–6)

A counter discourse is presented by Saskatchewan Deaf and Hard of Hearing Services, a non-profit service agency, and some school boards and parent groups who present both cochlear implants and ASL as desirable and not mutually exclusive (SHRC, 2016a).

Cognitive imperialism depends upon the promotion and maintenance of monolingual language policies which position deaf children as in need of a cure in order to approximate the efforts of white, abled-bodied citizens (Graham & Slee, 2008; Mauldin, 2016). In such discourses, sign language is given passing reference, while the focus of many deaf education policies is on acquiring spoken and written forms of the dominant language (see Snoddon, this volume). Some parents in Saskatchewan are beginning to articulate the desire for plurilingualism for their deaf children and are interested in a bilingual bimodal education for their deaf child (Grodecki, M., personal communication). Yet this desire is compromised by the persistence of the cognitive-imperialist positioning of spoken language as superior to signed languages.

Deaf Crows, 2016

By fostering plurilingualism among deaf children and youth and disrupting cognitive-imperialist approaches to language development in deaf education, *Deaf Crows* is a radical departure from the three government reports. In this section, I will explore how the play used material, spatial, social, cultural, linguistic and semiotic resources to facilitate plurilingualism in deaf children and youth.

The performance space of *Deaf Crows* features three worlds (see Figure 5.1):

(1) To the left of the stage is the world of medicalized discourses, occupied by an audiologist, a parent and her seven-year-old deaf child. The audiologist and parent are locked in bitter dialogue about whether to use sign language, as the window for language acquisition is nearly closed. The area is denoted by a rectangular shape on the stage.

(2) The center stage is a bleak landscape consisting of scattered *Deaf Crows* trying to navigate their way through elementary school, the playground and the hearing world with their own linguistic repertoires and semiotic resources.

(3) The right of the stage is the world occupied by a Deaf elder and storyteller who reminisces about his days at the school for the deaf.

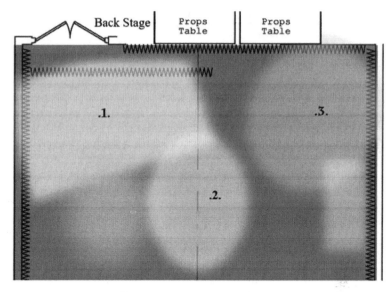

Figure 5.1 Stage layout of key areas within the *Deaf Crows* play

The play incorporates the viewpoint of a Deaf elder who is bilingual, having acquired ASL at the former school for the deaf in Saskatchewan. With his appearance as a storyteller and with his help in *Deaf Crows*, plurilingual discourses begin to make their way into the public space, outside of policy and planning documents pertaining to deaf education. The following sections explore the scenes developed by the deaf students through participation in several workshops exploring their deaf experiences.

Jade

According to cognitive imperialist discourses and the neoliberal values originating in the European Age of Enlightenment that have guided deaf education policy, each student is presented as an atomistic subject, autonomous, free and agentic, unshackled by the demands of family, community and society (Mansfield, 2000). As the play progresses, we see how the students are abandoned by teachers, adults and play-mates, left to wander in a barren landscape devoid of meaningful interactions with humans, animals, earth or machines. In the lives and stories of the individual Deaf Crows, the toll of inappropriate interventions for deaf children becomes apparent. In the first story, we are introduced to Jade, a young deaf child who attends school for the first time. Uncomprehending, surrounded by her hearing classmates who snicker when she does not do what is expected of her, she is confronted by a teacher who ineffectively uses material and semiotic resources to teach a large classroom. The following is an excerpt from the play (all excerpts in this chapter are from Ells *et al.*, 2016):

SCENE II: JADE

TEACHER (*mouthing*): Come sit down. Sit down.
> *Teacher crosses to Jade and taps her on the shoulder. Jade looks up at the teacher.*

TEACHER (*mouthing*): Sit down.
> *Jade does not respond. The teacher points at the chair.*

TEACHER (*mouthing*): Sit down.
> *Jade slowly goes to the chair and sits down. The students giggle at Jade. The teacher crosses back to the front of the class.*

TEACHER (*mouthing*): Get out your books.
> *The hearing students all lean down to the floor and pick up books. Jade swings her feet and looks around. The teacher turns her back on the class and draws a map on the board. She does not look at the students.*

TEACHER (*mouthing*): This is North America. This is South America. Here is Canada up here. Now where is Saskatchewan?
> *The teacher turns to look at the class. All the students are taking notes.*

THOMAS (*mouthing and pointing*): In the middle.

TEACHER (*mouthing*): Very good.
> *The teacher turns back to draw Alberta on the board, and Jade gets up and crosses to her old spot downstage right.*

TEACHER (*mouthing*): Now here is the next province over. What is it called?
> *The teacher turns around. Emma holds up her hand and points at Jade. The students giggle. The teacher crosses to Jade, taps her on the shoulder again, and points at the chair.*

TEACHER (*mouthing*): Sit in your chair!
> *All the hearing children get up and run out, taking their chairs.*

TEACHER (*mouthing to Jade*): You stay in your chair through recess.

The teacher fully asserts her authority in this scene. Jade is never introduced to the other students, and the material objects such as the blackboard, pointer, chalk and chairs are not to be moved or touched. The teacher continues to misread Jade's inability to participate in the classroom as acts of defiance and therefore being unable to learn. Such continued misinterpretations often lead to the culture of low expectations (O'Brien & Placier, 2015) in which teachers and other auxiliary professionals develop a deficit perspective (Gay, 2010) towards the deaf student as cognitively flawed and therefore unable to access the cultural and social capital within the dominant society (see O'Brien, this volume). The withholding of and control over material and semiotic resources such as books, the pointer and the blackboard prompt Jade to return repeatedly to what she knows: her chair and her own gaze. Her longing for something meaningful is focused elsewhere. She is looking to something else, perhaps to her own potential as to what she could become.

The Deaf elder, who finds Jade after the class has dispersed, tries to connect with her. Finding that she is not able to respond to his signing, he presents her with a crow feather. She takes this feather in a matter-of-fact manner, without acknowledging this gift or its meaning, and walks off the stage. Here, for the first time, a deaf space has been created by the Deaf elder, and the feather now encapsulates Jade's encounter with the Deaf elder. The Deaf elder creates the deaf space by extending a crow feather to Jade. The feather is potent in that it opens the way to her future intra-actions with deaf people and provides an embodied memory beyond language itself. Here, the feather is a semiotic resource which extends beyond the construct of languages as bounded systems and comes into intra-actions with other material resources in a deaf space. The question posed through this action is not what does the feather represent, but what does it do to Jade and what will Jade do with the feather?

Oliver

The following scene addresses the social-cultural bias against sign language.

Immediately in the next scene, a mother of a deaf child is in a heated conversation about the language deprivation that her child is experiencing:

SCENE AS VOICED

AUDIOLOGIST: Come on in, Maureen. Hi, Oliver.

MOTHER: Hello.

AUDIOLOGIST (*She points to her clipboard to which Oliver's audiogram is fastened*): So, the results are back from Oliver's hearing test. His hearing is stable. That means he will be able to speak more and hear more.

MOTHER: But he can say only fifty words and he is seven years old! You don't think that he needs to learn sign language?

AUDIOLOGIST: I've been telling you for 7 years, he must learn to speak to function in the hearing world. Just keep it up. He will eventually learn to speak. And whatever you do, DON'T use sign language.

MOTHER: But how will he learn if he can't hear? He is so frustrated. I can't understand him, and he can't understand me. Maybe if he learned sign--

AUDIOLOGIST (*interrupting*): If he doesn't learn to use his ears, he will be stuck with Deaf people. If you sign to him, he will not learn to speak. He belongs to the hearing world and he will eventually learn to speak. Just keep up the hard work. See you again in six months.

MOTHER: If I come back …

AUDIOLOGIST (*She faces Oliver and shouts*): Bye Oliver! (*She opens the door and ushers them out; the three of them leave.*)

The clipboard containing the audiogram in the hand of the audiologist is an agentic material resource to which both adults refer. The audiogram is the point of entry into services for deaf children and, ironically, the deaf community as well (Brueggeman, 2009). The power of the audiogram lies in its ability to predict the future of the deaf child and to establish teleological goals (the what-goals that are future oriented) that will eventually come to pass if one works hard enough for them. This scene depicts two women arguing, the authority of the audiogram, and the deaf child looking about in bewilderment while holding his mother's hand. Bodily movements, facial expressions, and a piece of paper that emits an agentic, virtual, unseen, almost ghostly presence become collapsed in a sparring match between the mother and the audiologist who, in the end, shouts out a farewell in a condescending manner to the deaf child.

Mauldin (2016) suggests that the choices available to parents concerning language pedagogy are too stark and narrow; parents, deaf children and deaf adults may be reforming the medicalization and anti-medicalization discourses into their own ambivalent discourses by dropping or picking up various aspects of these discourses. Ambivalent discourses suggest that parents are provided with a script to follow in securing their child's future and, at the same time, these discourses provide relief when some aspects of that script are dropped or replaced with a script from the anti-medicalization discourses. The mother's last response to the audiologist ('If I come back') indicates ambivalence about the value of continuing with the audiology appointments. The mother does not want to close the door on medicalization discourses but is not willing to accept the prescriptions offered by the audiologist. The family is the 'key social site where meanings of deafness and disability are assigned but also perhaps rewritten' (Mauldin, 2016: 24). The mother in *Deaf Crows* leaves to puzzle out what is happening to her child in terms of his language development and to seek resources that will protect her child from language deprivation. In the play, it is not clear if she ever is successful in her quest.

Blossom

The Deaf elder encounters another deaf child, Blossom, on the school playground. Blossom has been abandoned by her playmates despite her desperate attempts to join in with her peers' game of hide and seek. The Deaf elder teaches the child the signs for 'I', 'me', 'you' and 'sad'. After Blossom struggles to learn the signs, the Deaf elder gives Blossom the second crow feather (Jade received the first one). Blossom seizes the feather and examines it carefully. The Deaf elder waits with his hand outstretched until Blossom realizes the feather is not hers. Reluctantly, she returns the feather to the elder, and he models signing, 'Thank you'. Then he gives the feather back to Blossom, and she makes the sign for 'Thank you'. The feather is agentic in that it evokes a sequence of exchanges where dignity is restored to Blossom and accorded to the Deaf elder who is well versed in deaf community life and able to support the development of her individual linguistic repertoire. Furthermore, Blossom is fascinated by the feather, pondering what it means and sensing that the feather is communicating something beyond language.

While the feathers continues to morph, stretch and project different agentic actions upon the deaf students, additional material resources begin to crop up in the rest of the play, exerting their own agency. A ball in the hands of a child abandoned by his frustrated teacher, who tells him to play by himself on the playground during class time because she cannot teach him, becomes a teaching tool in the hands of the Deaf elder, who discovers the child on his way back from grocery shopping. Bully masks and placards bearing denigrating terms such as 'retard', 'dumb' and 'deaf' obscure the true identities of the bullies and their own fear and anger with which they attack two vulnerable deaf students and prompt one of them to begin bullying the other. The Deaf elder, by then having a group of deaf children with him, confronts the deaf student-turned-bully and instructs the deaf children to break the placards and put them in a garbage bag. He makes an impassioned plea to the audience:

> It doesn't matter if deaf people can speak or sign or both. There are so few of us. We need to work together, to support each other. We are not hearing people or copies of hearing people. We are Deaf!

The masks, placards and garbage bag provide additional semiotic and material resources in the scene, which culminates in the presentation of a feather to the two vulnerable deaf students. One student gratefully accepts the feather, and the other vulnerable student-turned-bully dashes the feather to the floor in his refusal to accept the invitation. The students and the Deaf elder leave the stage sadly, while the bully stoops to the ground, pondering the feather before determinedly walking off the stage without it. The feather on the ground has claimed the stage and therefore produces a deaf space.

Oliver Redux

At the end of the play, language appears in the social, material, cultural and personal intra-actions engaging the young deaf students who ponder their future. The group of actors is now settled in a new pattern of intra-actions. The feather abandoned by the deaf bully exerts a mysterious force upon the oldest deaf student, who is about to graduate and to go out into the wide world. She picks up the feather, which prompts her to ask, 'How?' Her fellow deaf classmates also ask each other, 'How?' while exploring their dreams and hopes. The question moves from fixed goals in the future (what will I do, what will I accomplish, what will I become?) to which all deaf children must aspire, towards a performative question: 'How will I continue to move through an assemblage of material, social, and cultural resources and entities which continue to produce me and which I exert influence upon?' Questions concerning 'how' are questions concerning agency within an assemblage of human and nonhuman actors and are performative in nature. The scene concludes with the entrance of the Deaf elder, who is carrying a book containing a history of the Canadian deaf community. The book is presented to the older student in response to her question about how she will navigate the future.

In turn, the graduating deaf teen presents a feather to Oliver, which now represents initial contact with the cultural, social and linguistic knowledge possessed by the Deaf community. The last interaction is between the audiologist and Oliver, the deaf child. Oliver takes the feather, scrambles down off the stage, runs to the audiologist's door and knocks. She opens the door.

AUDIOLOGIST: Well hello, Oliver.
Oliver hands her the feather and looks at her.
AUDIOLOGIST (*puzzled but ponders the feather and signs*): Thank you.
OLIVER (*signing*): You're welcome. Bye!
Audiologist closes the door.

Oliver is confident that the feather will lead the audiologist to search out others in pursuit of the questions brought forth by her own clientele, who insist that the deaf community and sign language are viable resources and have a significant role within the assemblage. He invites the audiologist to consider her role within an assemblage of human and material semiotic resources. Here, Oliver is comfortably situated between both worlds and can mediate the opposing camps by offering the mysterious crow feather, a material resource provoking reflection on the part of the audiologist.

Discussion and Conclusion

Plurilingualism is context dependent in that bodily, material, spatial, linguistic, cultural, social and even historical semiotic resources determine what is possible in terms of co-constructed meaning with the use of individual linguistic repertoires (Blommaert *et al.*, 2005). Here, the negotiation of material, linguistic, social, spatial, visual and cultural resources provokes new understandings of language acquisition in deaf children. For instance, Oliver's feather provides a material resource, a potent challenge to the audiologist who then pauses and expresses gratitude in a non-condescending manner. The audiologist is now prompted to think about other ways of approaching Oliver's language needs, which in turn lead to the development of plurilingual policies and pedagogies.

A plurilingual language policy may build upon what people do with language and how they use their linguistic repertoires to achieve tasks at hand. This may furthermore facilitate linguistic, social, spatial, visual and cultural resources including animals (the crow) and machines (the audiogram), and material resources such as the ball, book, shopping bags, placards, masks and feather. The Deaf elder never contests or rejects the presence of hearing actors throughout the play; rather, during several intervals in the play, he encourages the audience to learn signs from him. The entire stage, initially separated into three worlds, becomes a cohesive assemblage of hearing, deaf and non-living actors, each morphing, exerting influence on and being influenced by each other, suggesting that language acquisition is performative rather than cognitively based. Spatiality becomes a critical aspect of language acquisition, and the provision of deaf spaces becomes a valuable contribution to language acquisition as performative. Canagarajah (2017) suggests that changes in spatial environments impose different linguistic requirements and semiotic resources that may be beyond language and yet contribute to the distribution of language as a function of a whole assemblage (Pennycook, 2018).

In responding to language planning policy debates, *Deaf Crows* is an attempt to address cognitive imperialism by proposing a way out of the binarization of sign language and spoken language. The presence of performative discourses, capitalizing on multiple semiotic resources, eschews the highly polarized state of deaf education in Saskatchewan. Furthermore, the intra-actions of material, linguistic, social, spatial, visual and cultural resources, made visible through a posthumanist lens, refocus on protection from language deprivation and steer discourses away from debates over educational placements. These discourses can then move towards a more expansive understanding of language acquisition as context-dependent, paying attention to multiple semiotic resources negotiated between intra-actions between humans, animals, machines and earth.

Performative discourses addressing the actions of humans, animals, earth and machines may provide a more nuanced description of what deaf children do with their individual repertoires within their home, school and community environments. A plurilingual language policy for deaf children and youth in Saskatchewan would consider the availability of linguistic, cultural, social and material resources as essential factors in the prevention of language deprivation.

References

Battiste, M. (2011) Cognitive imperialism and decolonizing research: Modes of transformation. In L.K. Chehayl, M.M. McDermott, C. Reilly and L.K. Russell (eds) *Surveying Borders, Boundaries, and Contested Spaces in Curriculum and Pedagogy* (pp. xv-xxviii). Charlotte, NC: Information Age Publishing.

Battiste, M. (2013) *Decolonizing Education: Nourishing the Learning Spirit*. Saskatoon, SK: Purich Publishing.

Beck, J.L., Belliveau, G., Lea, G.W. and Wager, A. (2011) Delineating a spectrum of research-based theatre. *Qualitative Inquiry* 17 (8), 687–700.

Blommaert, J., Collins, J. and Slembrouck, S. (2005) Spaces of multilingualism. *Language and Communication* 25, 197–216.

Bourdieu, P. (1991) *Language and Symbolic Power*. Cambridge, MA: Harvard University Press.

Braidotti, R. (2013) *The Posthuman*. Cambridge: Polity Press.

Brueggeman, B. (2009) *Deaf Subjects: Between Identities and Places*. New York: New York University Press.

Canagarajah, S. (2013) *Translingual Practice: Global Englishes and Cosmopolitan Relations*. New York: Routledge.

Canagarajah, S. (2017) Translingual practice as spatial repertoires: Expanding the paradigm beyond structuralist orientations. *Applied Linguistics* 39 (1), 31–54. doi:10.1093/applin/amx041

Conway, C., Deocampo, J., Walk, A., Anaya, E. and Pisoni, D. (2014) Deaf children with cochlear implants do not appear to use sentence context to help recognize spoken words. *Journal of Speech, Language and Hearing Research* 57 (6), 2174–2190. doi:10.1044/2014_JSLHR-L-13-0236

Cummins, J. (2000) *Language, Power and Pedagogy: Bilingual Children in the Crossfire*. Clevedon: Multilingual Matters.

Davenport, T., Halgren, E., Leonard, M., Mayberry, R., Ramirez, N. and Torres, C. (2016) Neural language processing in adolescent first-language learners: Longitudinal case studies in American Sign Language. *Cerebral Cortex* 26 (3), 1015–1026. doi:10.1093/cercor/bhu273

Davis, L. (1995) *Enforcing Normalcy: Disability, Deafness and the Body*. London: Verso, New Left Books.

Deleuze, G. and Guattari, F. (1987) *Thousand Plateaus: Capitalism and Schizophrenia*. Minneapolis, MN: University of Minnesota Press.

Ells, C., Hi, B. and Weber, J. (directors) (2016) *Deaf Crows* (World Premiere). Artesian Theatre, Regina, SK, Canada, 19 & 21 June. See https://www.deafcrowscollective.ca/.

Emery, S. and O'Brien, D. (2014) The role of the intellectual in minority group studies: Reflections on deaf studies in social and political contexts. *Qualitative Inquiry* 20 (1), 27–36. doi:10.1177/1077800413508533

Fairclough, N. (2010) *Critical Discourse Analysis: The Critical Study of Language*. London: Routledge.

Foucault, M. (1973) *The Birth of the Clinic*. New York: Pantheon Books.

García, O., Otheguy, R. and Reid, W. (2015) Clarifying translanguaging and deconstructing named languages: A perspective from linguistics. *Applied Linguistics Review* 6 (3), 281–307. doi:10.1515/applirev-2015-0014

Gay, G. (2010) *Culturally Responsive Teaching: Theory, Research and Practice*. New York: Teachers College.

Glickman, N.S. and Hall, W.C. (2019) *Language Deprivation and Deaf Mental Health*. New York: Routledge.

Graham, L. and Slee, R. (2008) An illusory interiority: Interrogating the discourses of inclusion. *Educational Philosophy and Theory* 40 (2), 277–293. doi:10.1111/j.1469-5812.2007.00331.x

Gulati, S. (2019) Language deprivation syndrome. In N.S. Glickman and W.C. Hall (eds) *Language Deprivation and Deaf Mental Health*. New York: Routledge

Hall, W., Levin, L. and Anderson, M. (2017) Language deprivation syndrome: A possible neurodevelopmental disorder with sociocultural origins. *Social Psychiatry and Psychiatric Epidemiology* 21 (5), 961–977. doi:10.1007/s00127-017-1351-7

Hickey-Moody, A. and Page, T. (2016) *Arts, Pedagogy and Cultural Resistance: New Materialisms*. London: Rowan & Littlefield.

Humphries, T., Kushalnagar, P., Mathur, G., Napoli, D., Padden, C., Rathmann, C. and Smith, S. (2012) Language acquisition for deaf children: Reducing the harms of zero tolerance to the use of alternative approaches. *Harm Reduction Journal* 9 (1), 16. doi:10.1186/1477-7517-9-16

Humphries, T., Kushalnagar, P., Mathur, G., Napoli, D., Padden, C., Rathmann, C. and Smith, S. (2016) Avoiding linguistic neglect of deaf children. *Social Service Review* 90 (4), 589–619. doi:10.1086/689543

Kusters, A. (director) (2015) *Ishaare. Gestures and Signs in Mumbai* [Motion picture]. See https://vimeo.com/142245339 (accessed 21 July 2018).

Lane, H. (1984) *When the Mind Hears: A History of the Deaf.* New York: Random House.

Lee, J. (2016) Cochlear implantation, enhancements, transhumanism and posthumanism: Some human questions. *Science and Engineering Ethics* 22, 67–92. doi:10.1007/s11948-015-9640-6

Lockert, W. and Trofimenkoff, P. (1989) *Minority Report – Task Force on Education of the Deaf.* Regina, SK: Saskatchewan Department of Education.

Mansfield, N. (2000) *Subjectivity: Theories of the Self from Freud to Haraway.* St Leonards, NSW: Allen & Unwin.

Mathews, E.S. (2017) *Language, Power, and Resistance: Mainstreaming Deaf Education.* Washington, DC: Gallaudet University Press.

Mauldin, L. (2016) *Made to Hear.* Minneapolis, MN: University of Minnesota Press.

Mayberry, R., Chen, J., Witcher, P. and Klein, D. (2011) Age of acquisition effects on the functional organization of language in the adult brain. *Brain and Language* 119 (1), 16–29. doi:10.1016/j.bandl.2011.05.007

O'Brien, C. and Placier, P. (2015) Deaf culture and competing discourses in a residential school for the deaf: 'Can do' versus 'can't do'. *Equity and Excellence in Education* 48 (2), 320–338. doi:10.1080/10665684.2015.1025253

O'Brien, D. (2017) Deaf-led deaf studies: Using Kaupapa Maori principles to guide the development of deaf research practices. In A. Kusters, M. De Meulder and D. O'Brien (eds) *Innovations in Deaf Studies: The Role of Deaf Scholars* (pp. 57–76). New York: Oxford University Press.

Peers, D. (2015) From eugenics to Paralympics: Inspirational disability, physical fitness and the White Canadian nation. Unpublished doctoral dissertation, University of Alberta.

Pennycook, A. (1998) *English and the Discourses of Colonialism.* New York: Routledge.

Pennycook, A. (2012) What might translingual education look like? *Babel* 47 (1), 4.

Pennycook, A. (2018) *Posthumanist Applied Linguistics.* New York: Routledge.

Peterson, N., Pisoni, D. and Miyamoto, R. (2010) Cochlear implants and spoken language processing abilities: Review and assessment of the literature. *Restorative Neurology and Neuroscience* 28, 237–250. doi:10.3233/RNN-2010-0535

Saskatchewan Deaf Education Advisory Forum (1990) *Preliminary Report on Deaf Education to the Honorable Ray Meiklejohn, Minister of Education.* Regina, SK: Saskatchewan Ministry of Education.

Saskatchewan Task Force Committee on Deaf Education (1989) *Report of the Task Force on the Education of the Deaf.* Regina, SK: Saskatchewan Ministry of Education.

SHRC (Saskatchewan Human Rights Commission) (2016a) *Access and Equality for Deaf, deaf, and Hard of Hearing People: A Report to Stakeholders.* Saskatoon, SK: Ministry of Justice.

SHRC (Saskatchewan Human Rights Commission) (2016b) SHRC releases Deaf and Hard of Hearing Stakeholder Consultations Summary Report. *Media release*, 12 May. See https://saskatchewanhumanrights.ca/media_release/shrc-releases-deaf-and-hard-of-hearing-stakeholder-consultations-summary-report/.

Slee, R. (2004) Meaning in the service of power. In L. Ware (ed.) *Ideology & the Politics of (In)Exclusion* (pp. 46–60). New York: Peter Lang.

SPARC (Saskatchewan Pediatric Auditory Rehabilitation Center) (n.d.) *Services.* See http://healthsciences.usask.ca/sparc/what_we_do/index.php.

Swanwick, R. (2017) *Languages and Languaging in Deaf Education: A Framework for Pedagogy* (Kindle edn). New York: Oxford University Press.

Weber, J. (2018) Becoming Deaf in the posthumanist era: Posthumanism, arts-based research and Deaf education. Unpublished doctoral dissertation, University of Regina.

Wu, J., Eaton, P., Robinson-Morris, D., Wallace, M. and Han, S. (2018) Perturbing possibilities in the postqualitative turn: Lessons from Taoism and Ubuntu. *Journal of Qualitative Studies in Education* 31 (6), 504–519. doi:10.1080/09518398.2017.1422289

Part 2

Plurilingual Education Practices and Models

6 Sign Bilingualism as Semiotic Resource in Science Education: What Does It Mean?

Camilla Lindahl

Developing a scientific dialogue with students in the sign bilingual science classroom presents some challenges. The aim of this chapter is to illustrate how Swedish Sign Language and Swedish in written form contribute to joint meaning-making in science education. This sign bilingualism, together with other modalities in the science classroom such as tables, charts, test tubes and Bunsen burners, was analyzed from a multimodal social semiotic perspective. This chapter discusses how translanguaging as a pedagogical tool is used along with other social semiotic resources to communicate scientific concepts in relation to terms, concepts and models in the written majority language. The development of instructional strategies in the linguistically complex teaching environment supports deaf students' ability to develop their knowledge in science, including the use of scientific language in both sign language and spoken/written language.

Sign Bilingualism and Sign Bilingual Education

It is possible for sign language users to master one or more languages, and therefore these individuals are *plurilingual*. On the other hand, deaf schools in Sweden teach in Swedish Sign Language, *Svenskt teckenspråk* (STS), and Swedish in written form (and also in spoken form for some pupils). For this reason, the concept *sign bilingualism* (commonly referred to as bimodal bilingualism in Canada and the United States) is used in the chapter. This model of bilingualism is not called simply bilingualism because the term sign bilingualism suggests two modalities, therefore clarifying that sign language is one of the languages. The visual and gestural modalities of sign language contribute other aspects to this model of bilingualism as compared to other languages in written or spoken form.

Thus, with plurilingualism as a basis, I will discuss bilingualism as a linguistic ability that honors individual linguistic repertoires, and translanguaging as a pedagogical tool in a teaching model that uses both languages. In other words, teaching a class of bilingual students is not equivalent to bilingual education. The teacher may have a linguistic competence in some languages, but he or she also needs to employ a teaching framework that uses both languages as resources. However, the didactic knowledge in sign bilingualism needs to be developed, according to experienced teachers (Schönström & Holmström, this volume).

In Sweden, the National Agency for Special Needs Education and Schools (SPSM) is responsible for special schools for deaf students. In accordance with the curriculum at the special schools, the schools should develop deaf students' sign bilingualism. Accordingly, SPSM has formulated a language plan (Specialpedagogiska skolmyndigheten, 2017) with clear guidelines for what sign bilingualism means and how the special schools should meet the goal of the curriculum, which states that students leave school with sign bilingualism that increases their opportunities for further studies and participation in society. This means that teaching should help students develop language competence that enables a creative, innovative and critical use of all of the students' available languages in many different contexts in society.

Sign bilingualism is initially discussed within the framework of social semiotics, multimodality and translanguaging. The chapter also discusses what it means to learn science through dialogic education in a sign bilingual classroom. Thereafter, some examples from a larger study, previously presented in Lindahl (2015), are used to illustrate what sign bilingualism as a semiotic resource in science education might mean. Sign bilingualism, together with other modalities in the science classroom such as tables, charts, test tubes and Bunsen burners, is used as a resource in science education in Sweden. In conclusion, the chapter discusses conditions for teaching development in sign bilingual education.

Sign Bilingualism in Terms of Multimodal Social Semiotic and Translanguaging

Within the framework of *social semiotics*, the focus is on the dynamics of language use (van Leeuwen, 2005) in different *communities of practice* (Lave & Wenger, 1991) with different phraseologies. Different social practices have developed their own language usages with specific terminologies. The dynamic use of language, dependent on social practices and contexts, often shows a meaning-making potential that achieves a specific aim in communicating with other people within the same social practices. As an example, the word *power* in terms of energy, watt and work is used in different ways from the word *power* in terms of authority, hierarchy within an organization and control over other people. Thus, the meaning of communicative symbols, such as single words or signs, cannot be studied in isolation or beyond their context.

Different modalities, such as spoken language, written language, gestures, pictures and sign language, use different communicative symbols. In *multimodality*, meaning-making is considered as a process and product of the use of multiple modalities in interaction with other individuals within specific contexts (Kress, 2010). If we study the usage of multiple modalities in combination, in context and in current social practice, then we can understand what meaning-making potential they can offer. We can also understand how different modalities contribute or not to meaning-making. Thus, the term *multimodal social semiotic* assumes that languages and modalities constitute potentially mediating resources or affordances (Kress *et al.*, 2001). Kress *et al.* (2001) argue that the use of such resources contributes to more innovative meaning-making in interaction with other individuals.

The modality of sign language can also contribute to meaning-making in various multimodal environments. However, in order to understand sign bilingual learning in a multimodal environment, we need more detailed study of to what extent sign language contributes, or not, to meaning-making in different contexts. Since sign language and spoken/written language are both modalities and intertwined linguistic resources, we also need to manage the plurilingual perspective in the argument about a multimodal social semiotic.

In recent years, an increasing number of studies have presented plurilingual individuals' usage of their entire language repertoire in interaction with others (see, for instance, Ash, 2004; García & Sylvan, 2011). The use of the entire linguistic repertoire means not only that individuals switch between different languages in different situations and for different purposes, but also that the languages interact in the individuals' communication. The concept of *translanguaging*, which describes the dynamic use of the broad linguistic repertoire, allows us to consider plurilingualism as a single and integrated linguistic competence. García and Li Wei (2014) argue that the integrated linguistic competence affords more than the individual languages together. They claim that language proficiency in several languages provides greater communicative skills, as Cummins (1991) claims regarding *the common underlying proficiency* across languages. Access to several languages also increases understanding of language structure and meaning-making. It is rare that any language can be translated into another language word for word. Understanding is required not only for a language's syntax but also for the meaning potential of different words. Within the framework of translanguaging, Li Wei (2011) also states that access to different languages contributes to a creative and critical acquisition of an entire linguistic repertoire. Through the use of different languages, a more nuanced reasoning is enabled when the meanings of different concepts are surveyed and the learner's understanding of these concepts is refined and deepened.

Furthermore, Li Wei (2011) claims that translanguaging includes multiple modes such as gestures, writing and reading. With access to various languages and multiple modes, a *translanguaging space* is created (Li Wei, 2011). Van Lier (2004) calls this *action potential*. Together, the languages and the modalities form a broad repertoire of various potential resources for meaning-making, which can inspire a more insightful and critical use of these resources. The translanguaging space enriches communication on a variety of levels. For example, the translanguaging space affords the addition of new expressions to individual languages. Thus, translanguaging is complex because there is a tension between the common language proficiency and competence in the individual languages and the emphasis that everything is interconnected; one language strengthens the other language and the common language proficiency becomes greater than the individual languages together.

Translanguaging does not mean that different languages are mixed, in the sense that the language user does not have a sufficient understanding of the grammar and structure of the individual languages. Instead, it is about the language user's ability to choose the expression in the language that is best suited to a particular social context. Consequently, it does not imply a language use in which one language only functions as a support for the other language, i.e. *sign-supported spoken Swedish* (Schönström & Holmström, this volume).

For sign bilingual individuals, this means that they do not sign and speak at the same time. Instead, it means that language proficiency in sign language strengthens language proficiency in spoken/written language and that one language helps to enrich the second language, with more possible meanings for different terms. It also means a critical approach to how sign language and spoken/written language are related to one another. In Swedish, the word *skala* (which means scale, gradation or peel) is spelled in the same way regardless of context, but in STS there are different signs for the Swedish word. The context determines which sign is most appropriate; for instance, the sign to peel an orange is not the same as the sign to peel a potato.

From the perspective of translanguaging, the status of the different languages as first or second languages is of secondary importance to the affordances of each language for the individual. However, for many deaf students, sign language is a prerequisite for learning. There is simply no other reasonable option for these students to communicate naturally with others. This makes it extra important for deaf people in this group to be given sign language as their first language. The status of sign language as a first language can also contribute to the sign bilingual person's identity development.

In this chapter, however, the theoretical framework concerning the affordances of the multimodal social semiotic resources and plurilingualism is not limited to consideration of sign language as first language. Sign bilingual individuals may have a spoken/written language as their strongest language. The framework considers sign language as one of the languages in the bilingual environment and studies its contribution to language development and learning and to translanguaging, as the number of didactic studies focused on translanguaging in sign bilingual education is limited. We need more knowledge about how translanguaging in sign bilingual education leads to sign bilingual language development. Conversely, knowledge in sign bilingualism can contribute to the development of the theoretical concept of translanguaging (García & Cole, 2014). This form of plurilingualism is characterized by the fact that sign language is visual, spatial and simultaneous, and the other language is auditory and sequential. This is evident in how plurilingual students use these linguistic resources in joint meaning-making with others.

The basic premise of translanguaging is that access to different languages offers a wider opportunity than monolingualism for creative and critical meaning-making in interaction with others. Several scholars show that plurilingual individuals use their broad linguistic repertoire in teaching and learning (see, for instance, Baker & Wright, 2017; Creese & Blackledge, 2010). Using translanguaging in teaching enables languages to evolve. This happens when one language can serve as support, reinforcement or inspiration for other languages, and this form of teaching is a powerful tool in scaffolding students' language development. Thus, translanguaging can be perceived as a pedagogical tool emphasizing process rather than results (Lewis *et al.*, 2012). Within the didactic perspective it means that the interest lies in how the different languages are used as resources, i.e. the process itself, in different contexts in the teaching in order to develop skills in the languages or knowledge in the current school subject. Thus, the main interest is not in measuring the language skills of the individual languages, although it can be considered as a consequence of the process. This pedagogical tool is applicable in sign bilingual education.

Translanguaging as a Sign Bilingual Pedagogical Tool

The first step in a didactic study of translanguaging as a pedagogical tool in sign bilingual education should be to identify and visualize the language shifts taking place in sign language dialogues and show what is included in the spectrum of translanguaging in sign language. Lindahl (2015) shows the use of sign language in the classroom on a spectrum that ranges from depicting signs to fingerspelling and so-called signed Swedish. Depicting signs, also called productive signs, is a linguistic category in sign language that visually illustrates different events and experiences, or shapes and sizes of different objects. Often, an object's shape and size can be illustrated while describing its location in an event. Fingerspelling is a natural part of sign language but, depending on context, this category also constitutes a kind of bridge to the written language. Signed Swedish is not a natural part of STS, but in the above-mentioned study there are some situations in which the written Swedish language needed to be visualized word by word in STS.

The reasoning about the shifts between written Swedish and STS could be conducted within the framework of the concept of *chaining* (e.g. Humphries & MacDougall, 1999; Tapio, 2019). Within the framework of chaining, situations are captured and described when the different languages and modalities are linked to each other. However, the emphasis in this chapter is on joint meaning-making through the use of the different languages and modalities. Thus, the concept of translanguaging, together with the theoretical perspective of multimodal social semiotics, operates as a significant starting point.

Regarding translanguaging as an educational tool, the central didactic issue concerns the contribution of translanguaging to learning in science. Before discussing the study results, I will discuss what learning in science through sign bilingual dialogic teaching might entail.

Scientific Meaning-Making Through Sign Dialogue

Science is a social practice with physical and linguistic resources (Lave & Wenger, 1991), in which knowledge is perceived through a collective meaning-making process. Scientific language is constructed over time by experienced people and contains not only science specific terms and definitions but also everyday language and metaphors with the purpose of describing our world. For instance, in school students are introduced to the scientific method for observing our environment. They also gradually develop an understanding and use of scientific language. One example is how students develop understanding of a scientific explanation for sunrises and sunsets in terms of the earth's rotation in our solar system. Another example is how students are able to differentiate 'work' as an everyday or scientific concept. Thus, isolated concepts without context add no function to joint meaning-making. In addition, students should be able to describe, explain, formulate questions, investigate and draw conclusions. This means that they also will learn to discuss, argue and compare different concepts, phenomena and processes. Thus, science learning is a dynamic process in which dialogue and language are powerful tools.

Dialogue can be spontaneous and without specific purpose in everyday interaction with others (Bakhtin, 1981, 1986). In the educational context, Alexander (2006) discusses dialogue as a purpose-oriented tool. He describes dialogic teaching as a process in which argumentation, questioning and words with different possible meanings are given space for joint review. With the support of the teacher, the student's learning in science takes place through the development of language use and thus increased participation in joint meaning-making. Mercer (2000, 2008) describes the meaning-making process as a long conversation in which new statements are often based on previous ones. Hence, language use over time is a fundamental factor for learning. This perspective on learning is based on Vygotsky's theories where language is seen as a prerequisite for thinking (Vygotsky, 1999). The ability to develop language use occurs in interaction with other individuals, and language is an important mediating tool in the learning process. Since interpersonal languaging contributes to intrapersonal learning, meaning-making through dialogue can be regarded as a linguistic act.

It is often a challenge for students to understand and make use of scientific language. For plurilingual students, this may be an additional challenge as they often learn the subject in a language they do not speak every day – for example, with their family. The challenge is further expanded when the learning process takes place in a bilingual education environment. This means that students are expected to develop the ability to switch between an everyday and a scientific approach to the world in both languages.

Challenges in the Sign Bilingual Science Classroom

In order to develop, define and refine scientific language in sign language, a critical mass of sign bilingual people with a focus in the field of science is required. Sign bilingual deaf people are a minority; consequently, the number of scientists in the group is limited. The small number of sign bilingual deaf scientists are linguistic models. Competent teachers who are sign bilinguals make an important contribution to our knowledge of science education in sign bilingual classrooms. However, as previously mentioned, sign bilingual individuals do not automatically make their teaching sign bilingual.

The classroom languages constitute a powerful resource. The students' language development is encouraged by allowing them unlimited access to languages. Language development for sign bilinguals is about the development of both languages in parallel. In practice, the prerequisite for language development in both languages is that the students have access to teaching in sign language and the opportunity to discuss subject content in sign language with teachers and peers.

From a plurilingual social semiotic perspective, it is imperative that the teacher does not only identify the different languages, but also develops an understanding of the languages' meaning potential within a specific subject. Sign language as a modality helps teachers and students to visualize different concepts, and adds a different dimension to meaning-making. Doing so requires linguistic skills in both languages and pedagogical awareness of how to promote language development in both languages within the subject field. With high levels of language proficiency, a broad spectrum of semiotic resources is available to push the dialogue forward. Linguistic acts regarding processes and relationships between languages become available.

The Study: A Sign Bilingual Science Classroom

This chapter features examples from a larger study (Lindahl, 2015) about how the visual, gestural and spatial features of STS contribute to science learning in a context where general education is based on the Swedish language. One of the study's research questions examines what characterizes language shifts in a sign bilingual science classroom. Another question is whether translanguaging as a pedagogical tool is used in this specific teaching environment. A total of 17 lessons were filmed during a period of two months. The collected data were analyzed using a multimodal social semiotic perspective. The participant group consists of two deaf science teachers and eight students between the ages of 13 and 15 years. All of the students are deaf and have been sign bilingual since early childhood. All participants have parents who learned STS when the participants were young, and the participants attended sign bilingual preschools.

Schönström and Holmström (this volume) describe a changing group of deaf and hard-of-hearing students in Sweden. Fewer of these students learn STS at an early stage, which affects the bilingual teaching in the deaf schools. At the same time, as previously mentioned, the authors state that the interviewed teachers have a desire for an increased knowledge of how sign bilingualism can be used in teaching. To understand how STS and Swedish can interact in science education, it is therefore important to have a group of students with age-appropriate language skills in both languages as a starting point.

In this chapter, the teachers are called Lars and Lisa (with the initial letter L as in *Lärare*, which means 'teacher' in Swedish). The students are also given pseudonyms.

From dialogue in sign language to transcript

In this study, the focus is on the content of and identification of translanguaging in the STS dialogue. Thus, instead of a word-for-word transcription, an interpretation and translation into English is necessary. In order to visualize sequences in the sign language dialogue that illustrate meaning-making or translanguaging, a transcription system is used, sometimes with figures illustrating the signs. For example, FISH means a single, lexical sign, while SHELL^FISH means a compound sign. **Text in bold** is a translation from depicting signs to English. Fingerspelling is transcribed as F-I-N-G-E-R-S-P-E-L-L-I-N-G.

Illustrating Sign Bilingualism as Semiotic Resource in Science Education

This section illustrates how translanguaging can be identified in sign language dialogue and how it is used as a pedagogical tool. How the participants use their linguistic resource in a creative and critical manner is also illustrated. The examples below demonstrate the need for metalinguistic dialogue and show that depicting signs have a greater significance in this dialogue than what are perceived to be correct signs for scientific concepts.

Creative use of multimodality and linguistic resources

In the lesson described here, the teacher, Lars, introduces the concepts of energy of position, kinetic energy and elastic energy. Initially, he points to the words on the digital board, fingerspells the words and shows how they are signed. He also gives a description of the potential meaning of the concept of energy of position and compares it with the concept of a plateau. In his presentation about the three concepts, he switches between depicting signs, lexical signs and fingerspelling. On a few occasions, he uses 'signed Swedish' to, for example, stress the scientific definition that energy never disappears but is constantly transformed into other forms. Lars illustrates energy transformations with various examples, including a football bouncing on the classroom floor.

To temporarily use fingerspelling or signed Swedish can be considered as a loan from the Swedish language. As we can see, the possibility of switching between sign language and fingerspelling or signed Swedish is used as a resource to create links between the languages. This example thus shows how translanguaging in sign language communication can be identified as a potential mediating resource. The seamless language shifting between depicting signs, lexical signs, fingerspelling and signed Swedish can be regarded as purposeful. Translanguaging is thus also an educational tool.

The lesson continues with the same theme. The group has discussed the three energy forms and tried to identify them when the ball bounces on the floor. Lars explains that energy of position is the moment when the ball is at the highest point of the trajectory. A student, Robin, wants to summarize and uses depicting signs to describe how to find the energy of position.

Robin: The fact is that **when the ball goes down like this it is pointing downward, the ball bounces up and then it's pointing upwards. When the ball reaches up here** (*slowing down the movement*) **it's turning horizontally. Right here, just before it turns down again, when it points horizontally, it is right here.** (See Figure 6.1.)

Robin creatively depicts the ball's trajectory. The index finger represents the direction of movement of the ball, indicating the position energy takes when the motion of direction points horizontally.

From a multimodal perspective, this example shows how the modality of STS, together with the artifact of the football and the scientific

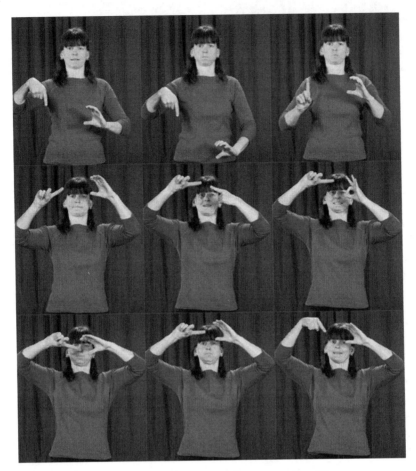

Figure 6.1 Robin uses depicting signs to describe energy of position

definition in Swedish, contributes to meaning-making. It also shows that Robin has mastered a language competence that gives him the ability to comprehend the scientific definition, which is based on Swedish, and to transform it into STS.

Lars listens to Robin and confirms his conclusion by using the same depicting signs. He adds a concept in his response:

Lars: **Right there that it points horizontally, it is** ENERGY OF P-O-S-I-T-I-O-N **That is right.** [...] (See Figure 6.2.)

Lars's linguistic and scientific skills enabled him to determine whether Robin's reasoning is accurate. With Lars's confirmation, they jointly created meaning with depicting signs as semiotic resources in relation to the scientific definition in Swedish.

Figure 6.2 Lars' response to Robin about the energy of position using the same depicting sign that Robin suggested: (1) **Right there that it points horizontally**; (2) and (3) ENERGY OF P-O-S-I-T-I-O-N (in STS); (4) **That is right**

Critical use of multimodality and linguistic repertoire

We continue with the same lesson as above. The group has repeated the activities and discussed different examples of these concepts. Meanwhile, the lexical sign for elastic energy (see Figure 6.3) has been formulated by the depicting sign where the ball is compressed and bounces back up (see Figure 6.4). Over time, the depicting sign developed into a lexical sign by Lars. For example, when Lars mentions the concept of

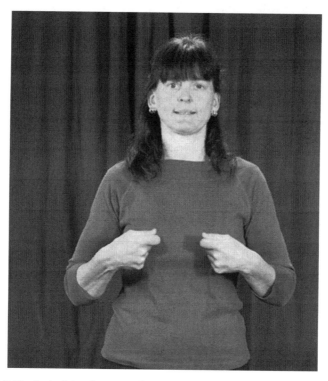

Figure 6.3 The lexical sign for ELASTIC (energy) in STS

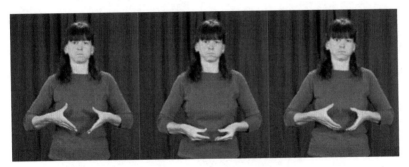

Figure 6.4 Depicting sign for how the ball **compresses and bounces back**

elastic energy, the sign COMPRESS AND BOUNCES BACK is used as a lexical sign for the term. None of the students objects to this, and they continue to discuss the subject in common.

Towards the end of the lesson, Robin again wants to summarize. He uses the same depicting signs as last time, but this time he uses a stone as an example instead of the ball. This provides a detail that Lars apparently does not perceive at first.

Lars: Yes, exactly (*nods*), it is position, kinetic, COMPRESS AND BOUNCES
          BACK, kinetic, position, up and down again and again.
Erika: It bounces.
Robin: There is no **elasticity** in a stone?

When Lars confirms the trajectory of energy, he uses signs in which elastic energy is signed as if it is a ball compressed flat and then bouncing back into shape. Erika and Robin react to this. In the statement 'There is no **elasticity** in a stone', Robin uses the depicting sign for elasticity, as in Figure 6.4. Subsequent discussion is about where elastic energy actually takes place. Is it inside the bouncing object or in the space between the object and the substrate? Unfortunately, Lars and his students do not reach any clarity on the issue, but the question has nevertheless been awakened by the visually oriented sign language. This form of discussion would not have taken place unless triggered by discussion in the visual sign language. The ability to question statements or language use can be interpreted as an important resource in the development of knowledge and language skills. Misunderstandings, or occasions where languages seem contradictory, can be used as a resource and trigger for further discussion, argumentation or investigation.

Metalinguistic discussion and the 'right' sign

The lesson described here is about inertia, a physics term. In STS there is no established sign for the term, which is why Lars is fingerspelling the term. He suggests, however, that the group eventually agree on a sign. But first he wants the students to understand the meaning of the term:

Lars: Let's imagine I-N-E-R-T-I-A, then the sign ... we start by understanding the concept, then maybe we can agree on a sign. Okay, we imagine we're in a bus, it's one of the examples shown in the book, it's a train, bus or other (*picks up the textbook and points to one page*). Say we're in a bus, it has not begun to go yet, and I'm standing inside the bus and holding the strap from the ceiling. The bus starts to go, it increases speed, what happens to my body?

Following Lars' introduction, the group discusses different examples that can represent the concept of inertia. The dialogue is characterized by active participation as both teachers and students respond to one another's statements and base their arguments on previous statements.

After several turns, Lars asks if they could agree on a sign for inertia. Lars proposes two options. The first sign (see Figure 6.5) resembles the sign for gravity. The other, which Lars prefers, corresponds to the idea of friction (see Figure 6.6). He argues that the second suggestion could be interpreted as 'slowly slipping forward'. Two students, Erika and Katrin, instead suggest a compound sign (see Figure 6.7). In Swedish, inertia is spelled *tröghet*. The word *trög* means 'dull' or 'sluggish'. Erika's and Katrin's suggestion, TRÖG^H-E-T, can, loosely translated, mean dullness. Lars reacts to this:

Lars: Dull? Well, it means dull, that's right but with (the spelling) -het, how should we sign it? What do you say?

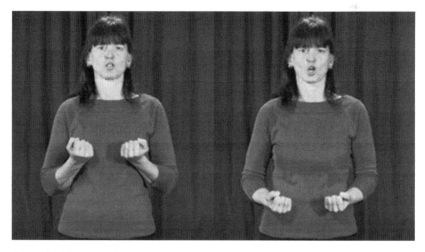

Figure 6.5 Suggested sign for INERTIA #1

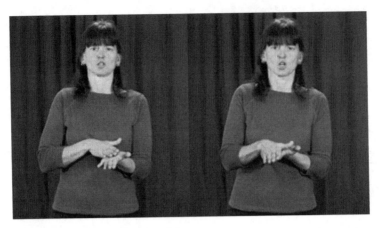

Figure 6.6 Suggested sign for INERTIA #2

Figure 6.7 Suggested sign for INERTIA #3 [in STS: TRÖG^H-E-T]

Despite Lars' attempts to argue that his proposal is better, the students feel that his idea is less important. Katrin, eventually, agrees with him:

Katrin: Yes but take INERTIA #3, we still understand.
Lars: INERTIA #2, can we agree?
Katrin: Mm okay then …

After deciding on the sign for inertia, the group returns to discussing the definition of the term and give different examples, many from students' own experiences. Several turns later, Katrin wants to contribute another example of inertia:

Katrin: Now I am talking! Okay, everyone knows that I-N-E-R-T… Well, I know that I-N-E-R-T-I-A is signed INERTIA #2 but we know what it's like … but in any case, when you go behind a horse then [...] That's it. It's the same with INERTIA #3.

Katrin announces that she is aware that Lars prefers the sign for INERTIA # 2, but emphasizes that because 'we know what it's like', it does not matter how the term is signed. Students note that there may be some alternative signs, but prefer to discuss the meaning of the term. In their reasoning, depicting signs are used to a great extent. Thus, the 'right' sign for scientific terms is subordinate to the depicting signs. Lars' reasoning about the relationship between the term inertia in Swedish and the sign for the term from a scientific perspective indicates the need to handle possible language collisions. Meaning-making through dialogue also means being able to discuss languages at the meta-level (Mercer, 2000). Metalinguistic discussion is apparently a valuable tool in dialogic teaching in this sign bilingual classroom, which aims at giving the students space to use languages in interaction with each other, thereby developing both their knowledge and language skills, both in STS and Swedish.

Dynamic Sign Languaging is a Powerful Tool for Learning in Science

Because in a multimodal, plurilingual dialogue, different modalities and languages are closely intertwined, it is not possible to illustrate them separately. However, we can consider the same situation from different perspectives of multimodality, translanguaging and dialogic teaching. Across these perspectives, we can see how communicative resources contribute to joint meaning-making. In this section, I discuss what the different examples above illustrate in relation to these perspectives and to what extent they contribute to the learning of science in sign bilingual education.

Multimodality

Although multimodality is included in the concept of translanguaging, we can discuss this concept in a somewhat isolated way. In the above episodes, there are significant characteristics of multimodality that indicate the meaning-making potential of sign language.

While sign language is generally considered a modality that features the visual and gestural, the examples in this chapter show how a particular category in sign language is distinguished. Depicting signs appear to have a prominent role in classroom dialogue about different scientific phenomena, processes and concepts. Robin's description of energy of position, which contains a simultaneous depiction of both the ball and its direction of movement, is creative and advanced. The teacher, Lars, introduced the sign for energy of position, but it is clear that the description of the concept with depicting signs contributes to understanding scientific meaning in the dialogue.

In the classroom dialogue about the scientific phenomenon of inertia, the group lacked a lexical sign for the word, but this did not prevent them from discussing their own experiences of inertia using depicting signs. Despite the group's attempt to create a lexical sign for the word, the group further discussed this concept using mainly depicting signs.

It is obvious that depicting signs are a driving factor that pushes the dialogue forward, but there are also situations where depicting signs risk becoming an obstacle. The introduced sign of elastic energy, based on how a ball compresses and bounces back, became a problem when a stone was used instead of the ball as an example of energy transformations and their trajectory. If the visual and gestural description is misleading, this may lead to misunderstandings and present an obstacle to continued meaning-making. However, students in this group demonstrated good language skills and they handled the situation critically. The incorrect sign in this context instead triggered a deeper discussion of the concept of elastic energy.

These data demonstrate that depicting signs are a significant category in sign language, even if they may be misleading. Classroom dialogue was shown to be a powerful tool to overcome these possible obstacles. I will return to this perspective below.

Translanguaging

The classroom dialogue shows a pattern of dynamic language use in a multimodal plurilingual environment, which is the definition of translanguaging. Both teachers and students switch seamlessly between depicting signs, lexical signs, fingerspelling and 'signed Swedish' in their reasoning with each other, thus utilizing their entire linguistic repertoire.

These dynamic language shifts seem to be a natural part of sign bilingual dialogue in the classroom and succeed as an educational tool. When Lars switches to the definition of energy transformations in Swedish, signing word for word, the purpose is very likely to strategically instruct students in the scientific perspective on energy. In the context of the scientific perspective, Lars uses a broad linguistic resource and switches back and forth in a continuum ranging from depicting signs to 'signed Swedish'. The students also use both languages in their reasoning; they both sign and fingerspell terms and concepts in a manner similar to the teacher's and seem comfortable doing this.

Participants' dynamic use of available languages and active participation in classroom dialogue show that multiple language resources create a larger space to examine potential meanings for different terms in different languages. The form of language use leads to creative and critical reasoning, which appears in the dialogue about the inelastic stone or how the term inertia 'should be' signed. These examples present translanguaging as a pedagogical tool for promoting students' bilingual language development in science. But, as in the case of the teacher and the students being unable to agree on a sign, translanguaging cannot be seen as a complete solution for sign bilingual language development.

The different languages provide different words, signs and definitions, which may contribute to misunderstandings. As with the above examples in the section titled 'Multimodality', these potential misunderstandings do not always have to be seen as an obstacle, but can be a driving force for continued dialogue. Instead of continuing the discussion about the correct sign for inertia, the group stops and discusses the concept of inactivity and inertia. Lars points out the similarity between *tröghet* (inertia) and *trög* (dull) with regard to the spelling and redirects the discussion to focus on the scientific concept. Thus, translanguaging as a pedagogical tool needs to be combined with other pedagogical tools, such as metalinguistic dialogue, where the potential meanings in different languages are explicitly discussed.

Dialogic teaching

Due to the use of dialogic teaching, the students in this study group have the opportunity to test their reasoning and to develop their use of scientific language in collaboration with others. In this process, in which the students describe, argue and draw conclusions, they also develop their language proficiency. Since both modalities and languages are allowed to interplay and interact in the sign dialogue, it becomes clear that they constitute an important resource for students' knowledge and language development. The dialogue becomes significantly nuanced.

Robin is given the opportunity to test his perception of the concept of energy of position when he summarizes Lars' descriptions. Lars has linguistic proficiency that enables him to follow Robin's reasoning. For instance, the depicting sign indicating how a ball compresses and bounces back over time develops into being a lexical sign denoting the concept of elastic energy.

The ensuing classroom dialogue becomes a long conversation resulting in an evolution of representations. In the dialogic progress, signs are introduced, reused, adjusted or refined. The dialogue can be redirected when there is ambiguous meaning of a word in Swedish or a sign in STS, or different connotations in one language or the other. This became evident when the new sign for elastic energy was used in the context of a stone bumping on the ground. This resulted in the lesson plan being put aside to allow the group to deepen their reasoning around the concept. Such asides are necessary because they contribute to the development of the nuances in scientific reasoning and to discussion of the deeper meaning of concepts. But if this development is really to take place, and when such situations arise, students need to be given space and support from the teacher through the facilitation of metalinguistic dialogue.

Through dialogue, Lars is able to negotiate the sign for inertia with students and assess how well the students understand the concept. While Lars reacts to the students' suggestion to use a sign that can be associated with the concept of dullness, the students think that they understand the scientific concept enough that the (incorrect) sign is of secondary importance. They are more interested in discussing their personal experiences with the concept. This example, together with the example with the new sign for elastic energy, also shows that individual signs for scientific concepts cannot develop scientific language use, either in Swedish or in STS. Instead, such language use requires the dynamic, creative and critical use of the entire language repertoire. The examples also show that teachers need a clear vision of how language proficiency and subject competence can be utilized in a dynamic bilingual education classroom and in turn require that teachers have the linguistic proficiency necessary to teach at this level. As shown in this chapter, sign bilingual teaching in a science classroom involves the linguistic complexity of joint meaning-making with others.

Conclusion

As noted above, there is no word-for-sign relationship with regard to scientific terms. However, the findings in this chapter show that it is not possible to assume that this is a shortcoming for either Swedish or STS. While there are no signs for some scientific terms, there are also no real counterparts in Swedish for depicting signs, which describe, among other things, natural science phenomena and processes. However, from a pedagogical perspective we can discuss areas for development in sign bilingual scientific teaching.

This chapter shows that depicting signs are of greater importance for knowledge and language development in science as compared to lexical signs, and that lexical signs often end up in the periphery of classroom dialogue. This means that we should pay attention to the overriding meaning of different scientific concepts, instead of a list of lexical signs for these concepts. A dynamic sign dialogue in a bilingual environment is of greater importance for building understanding of concepts. This does not mean that lexical signs are to be seen as redundant, but rather that language usage should be studied in its complexity.

From a didactic perspective, teachers need support in the development of instructional strategies and understanding of the dynamic linguistic process. This development and understanding involves an active effort to explicitly link modalities, languages and scientific concepts, as well as to discuss the potential meanings they can mediate.

Using linguistic repertoires in the sign bilingual classroom dialogue can be a challenge for many students. The participant group in this chapter demonstrated advanced sign language proficiency, very likely due to the very early availability of sign language for all members of the group.

Students who have access to sign language at a later stage in their language development may need additional linguistic support. These students may have more varied experiences with previous language development and schooling (see Schönström & Holmström, this volume). The main conclusion of this chapter is that we need to further increase knowledge in the area of sign bilingualism as a semiotic resource in order to provide a better foundation for students' ability to develop linguistic freedom in which they slide seamlessly along a continuum of both everyday and scientific language use in both languages.

References

Alexander, R. (2006) *Towards Dialogic Teaching: Rethinking Classroom Talk*. York: Dialogos

Ash, D. (2004) Reflective scientific sense-making dialogue in two languages: The science in the dialogue and the dialogue in the science. *Science Education* 88 (6), 855–884.

Baker, C. and Wright, W.E. (2017) *Foundations of Bilingual Education and Bilingualism* (6th edn). Bristol: Multilingual Matters.

Bakhtin, M.M. (1981) *The Dialogic Imagination: Four Essays*. Austin, TX: University of Texas Press.

Bakhtin, M.M. (1986) *Speech Genres and Other Late Essays*. Austin, TX: University of Texas Press.

Creese, A. and Blackledge, A. (2010) Translanguaging in the bilingual classroom: A pedagogy for learning and teaching? *The Modern Language Journal* 94 (1), 103–115.

Cummins, J. (1991) Interdependence of first- and second-language proficiency in bilingual children. In E. Bialystok (ed.) *Language Processing in Bilingual Children* (pp. 70–89). New York: Cambridge University Press.

García, O. and Cole, D. (2014) Deaf gains in the study of bilingualism and bilingual education. In J.J. Murray and H. Bauman (eds) *Deaf Gain: Raising the Stakes for Human Diversity* (pp. 95–111). Minneapolis, MN: University of Minnesota Press.

García, O. and Li Wei (2014) *Translanguaging: Language, Bilingualism and Education*. Basingstoke: Palgrave Macmillan.

García, O. and Sylvan, C. (2011) Pedagogies and practices in multilingual classrooms: Singularities in pluralities. *The Modern Language Journal* 95 (3), 385–400.

Humphries, T. and MacDougall, F. (1999) 'Chaining' and other links: Making connections between American Sign Language and English in two types of school settings. *Visual Anthropology Review* 15 (2), 84–94.

Kress, G. (2010) *Multimodality: A Social Semiotic Approach to Contemporary Communication*. New York: Routledge.

Kress, G., Jewitt, C., Ogborn, J. and Tsatsarelis, C. (2001) *Multimodal Teaching and Learning: The Rhetorics of the Science Classroom*. London: Continuum.

Lave, J. and Wenger, E. (1991) *Situated Learning: Legitimate Peripheral Participation*. Cambridge: Cambridge University Press.

Lewis, G., Jones, B. and Baker, C. (2012) Translanguaging: Developing its conceptualisation and contextualisation. *Educational Research and Evaluation* 18 (7), 655–670.

Li Wei (2011) Moment analysis and translanguaging space: Discursive construction of identities by multilingual Chinese youth in Britain. *Journal of Pragmatics* 43 (5), 1222–1235.

Lindahl, C. (2015) Tecken av betydelse: En studie av dialog i ett multimodalt, teckenspråkigt tvåspråkigt NO-klassrum. [Signs of significance: A study of dialogue in a multimodal, sign bilingual science classroom]. PhD thesis, Stockholm University.

Mercer, N. (2000) *Words and Minds: How We Use Language to Think Together*. London: Routledge.

Mercer, N. (2008) The seeds of time: Why classroom dialogue needs a temporal analysis. *Journal of the Learning Sciences* 17 (1), 33–59.

Specialpedagogiska skolmyndigheten (2017) *Språkplan för specialpedagogiska skolmyndigheten* [*Language Plan for the Swedish National Agency for Education*]. See https://www.spsm.se/globalassets/specialskolorna/sprakplan.pdf.

Tapio, E. (2019) The patterned ways of interlinking linguistic and multimodal elements in visually oriented communities. *Deafness & Education International* 21 (2–3), 133–150.

van Leeuwen, T. (2005) *Introducing Social Semiotics*. London: Routledge.

van Lier, L. (2004) *The Ecology and Semiotics of Language Learning: A Sociocultural Perspective*. Boston, MA: Kluwer Academic.

Vygotsky, L.S. (1999) *Tänkande och språk* (K. Öberg, trans.). Göteborg: Daidalos (original work *Thought and Language* published 1934).

7 Bimodal Bilingual Programming at a Canadian School for the Deaf

Charlotte Enns, Karen Priestley and
Shauna Arbuckle

Bimodal-bilingual or co-enrollment programs are emerging as one way to meet broader needs and provide expanded language, educational and social-emotional opportunities for students who are deaf and hard of hearing. However, there is limited research on students' spoken language development, signed language growth, academic outcomes or the social and emotional factors associated with children attending these multimodal and plurilingual programs. The purpose of this chapter is to discuss the first four years of implementing a bimodal-bilingual (American Sign Language and spoken English) program within an ASL milieu at a small Canadian school for the deaf. The considerations for language separation, access and teaching, the decisions regarding teaching personnel and learning support, and the analysis of formal and informal student outcomes are shared. In addition, staff and parent perceptions of the program are highlighted. The study found that bimodal-bilingual programming is complex and there are many aspects to consider when incorporating a spoken language component into a school for the deaf. The ever-evolving and increasingly variable deaf and hard-of-hearing student population means that exploration and development must continue in order to provide programming that meets the needs of all students.

Introduction

In the last several decades, education of deaf and hard-of-hearing (DHH) students throughout developed countries has shifted from the majority of students being educated in schools for the deaf to the majority of students being educated in mainstream or regular classrooms (Marschark *et al.*, 2014). The transition of DHH students into regular classrooms has been impacted by early diagnosis of hearing loss coupled with the development of advanced technology (Cole & Flexer, 2015). Powerful hearing aids and cochlear implants are providing better access to speaking and listening as a viable option for DHH students. Families often want access to spoken language opportunities for their DHH children (Paludnevicience & Leigh, 2011; Spencer & Oleson, 2008). As a result, many DHH students, typically using hearing aids or cochlear implants, are able to attend schools with their hearing peers in regular classrooms with various individualized supports, such as speech therapy, tutoring, acoustic modifications, computerized notetaking or interpreting/signed language (US Department of Education, 2006). The students are educated in spoken language environments with supports that help maximize access to auditory information.

Some DHH students, approximately 25% in the United States, still attend schools for the deaf, which largely provide sign bilingual programming within specialized settings (Antia, 2013; US Department of Education, 2006). Typically, bilingual programming at schools for the deaf in Canada and the United States means that instruction and communication occurs in ASL and that English is primarily taught and accessed in a visual mode, through reading and writing. Students are also immersed in both Deaf and hearing cultures and norms. The goal of bilingual programming is twofold: to provide full, visual access to language and communication (curriculum, instruction, peer interactions), and to instill a positive sense of identity as a Deaf individual.

Although academic outcomes for students who are in the mainstream and at schools for the deaf have improved over the past several decades, outcomes for the DHH population, even with early diagnosis and cochlear implants, are typically not at age-appropriate levels of hearing English-speaking peers (Antia et al., 2009; Marschark et al., 2015; Qi & Mitchell, 2012). There does not seem to be one ideal learning environment for this very diverse group of students. Schools for the deaf and mainstream environments are expanding and exploring programming to meet the needs of a new DHH student demographic that may have more access to audition and developing spoken language but continue to recognize the benefits of early exposure to a signed language.

At schools for the deaf where ASL is the language of instruction, providing more access to spoken English often requires a shift in programming from individualized speech therapy sessions to using spoken English in the classroom. With over 95% of DHH children being born into hearing families and having better access than ever to hearing technology, development of spoken language is often a priority for families (Yiu & Tang, 2014). Some Deaf children of Deaf parents are also receiving cochlear implants so that spoken language is a viable option for their children. Mitchiner and Sass-Lehrer (2011) studied the experiences of a group of Deaf families who chose to have their children use cochlear implants and learn spoken English as well as ASL. They found that these Deaf parents clearly wanted their children to be 'part of both worlds – hearing and Deaf' (Mitchiner & Sass-Lehrer, 2011: 80) and to 'be fluent in both languages' (Mitchiner & Sass-Lehrer, 2011: 86), which is becoming a viable goal for all DHH children and their families.

In mainstream environments, families with DHH students who benefit from a signed language also need equitable options and full language access. Providing interpreters and individual signed language programming often leaves DHH students who use ASL unable to communicate freely with teachers and peers. Even with current access to spoken language through their implants or hearing aids, these students can and do feel isolated and segregated in a mainstream environment (Moog *et al.*, 2011). They may require signed language to access information, but they also want to be included in classroom activities and discussions.

The more equitable use of both ASL and spoken English, with the benefits of positive identity development in both languages, has recently been discussed by various researchers regarding viable educational programming options for DHH students with cochlear implants at schools for the deaf and in mainstream schools (Christensen, 2010; Knoors & Marschark, 2012; Paludneviciene & Leigh, 2011; Spencer & Marschark, 2010; Yiu & Tang, 2014). This type of discussion supports the global trend towards bilingual programming and the advantages of knowing more than one language and culture. For DHH students, potential advantages also include improved access to language, better learning potential, understanding Deaf cultural values to facilitate identity (Deaf, hearing, bilingual) development, and the ability to move between the Deaf and the hearing worlds. The goal is to enrich the total educational experience of DHH students and for them to 'have it all'.

There are different definitions, but basically this emerging type of bilingual programming involves students using two modes of communication – speaking and signing – in an extensive and inclusive manner, with the goal of developing proficiency in both languages. It is important to clarify several terms, including: (a) bimodal – input and output in two modes (signed and spoken); (b) bilingual – the understanding and use of two languages, such as ASL and English; and (c) co-enrollment – including both DHH and hearing learners in the same class. Although all three components may be present in one program, this is not always the case and can cause confusion in the literature. All programs use spoken and signed languages, but they may use them differently: some programs follow an English-based approach by speaking with sign support (such as Total Communication, also known as Sign Supported Speech) while others divide the use of both a natural signed language (such as ASL) and spoken language throughout the day or in different activities. It is the second type, where two separate and distinct languages are used, which we refer to as bimodal-bilingual programs. The school-wide learning environment and culture also varies, with spoken language typically being prominent in mainstream schools and signed language being prominent in schools for the deaf. Regardless of the school environment, the goal is to broaden the learning potential, improve outcomes and expand opportunities for DHH students to function optimally within Deaf and hearing environments.

Arguably, one of the biggest concerns of learning both a signed and a spoken language is that use of one language will impede development of the other. The relationship between signed and spoken language is complex; however, similar to bilingual abilities in other children, with early exposure and clear modelling of standard varieties of ASL and English by parents and teachers the use of signed language does not decrease or impede speech attainment across DHH children (Knoors & Marschark, 2012; Spencer & Marschark, 2010; Wilbur, 2000; Yoshinaga-Itano, 2006). In fact, spoken English outcomes 'appear to be more strongly related to many of the factors that may affect performance rather than the use of ASL' (Nussbaum & Scott, 2011: 183). These factors may be specific to the child and family, such as hearing level, benefits from assistive technology, cognition, social interaction, parental involvement and education, and access to support services. However, factors outside the family also influence spoken English outcomes. The power differential between ASL and English, where ASL is a minority language and not known to most parents of DHH children, influences opportunities and priorities for language learning experiences available to parents of DHH children. Individual studies have contradictory results and methodological inconsistencies that make comparisons challenging. Some studies have shown that signing supports spoken language development (Davidson *et al.*, 2014; Hassanzadeh, 2012; Yoshinaga-Itano, 2006; Yoshinaga-Itano & Sedey, 2000), while other studies find that auditory verbal programs with no signing result in better spoken language outcomes (Geers, 2006; Nicholas & Geers, 2007). This again highlights the complexity of the relationship, but further emphasizes that signing or signed language is *not* the primary determining factor in spoken language outcomes.

Co-enrollment Programs

Marschark *et al.* (2014) note that co-enrollment programs vary greatly, but they typically involve several DHH students learning within a mainstream classroom that is co-taught by a specialist in DHH education and a regular teacher. All classroom members develop skills in both languages to the best of their ability and learn curricular material together:

> the common philosophy behind the co-enrollment programs is the avoidance of both the academic segregation of DHH students and their integration into classes with hearing students without appropriate support services or modifications of instructional methods and materials. Rather, it seeks to give DHH learners the best of both educational worlds. (Marschark *et al.*, 2014: 450)

It is acknowledged that creating an appropriate balance between the two languages is difficult and that the best balance may differ among different students and different programs (Martin *et al.*, 2014).

All of the co-enrollment programs where research is available have been conducted with young, school-aged children (approximately kindergarten to Grade 6 levels). Hermans *et al.* (2014) discuss a co-enrollment program in the Netherlands called the Twinschool. Twinschool was established to provide both signed language and specialized instruction, as well as spoken language, within an environment enriched with broad peer support. They found that the DHH students felt supported by having similar peers in the classroom. The students' language levels remained 'above average in comparison to deaf peers' and 'the DHH children, hearing children and their parents had a positive view of the Twinschool' (Hermans *et al.*, 2014: 420).

Antia and Metz (2014) reviewed seven research studies on co-enrollment programs in the United States and found the following common benefits: (a) DHH students being part of the classroom community; (b) increased social interaction among all students; and (c) advantages of co-teaching (one hearing and one Deaf teacher in a classroom). The authors also presented findings regarding academic achievement and concluded that 'co-enrollment appears to benefit DHH students academically' (Antia & Metz, 2014: 431). Further research is needed to determine the extent of these benefits.

Finally, a study on co-enrollment education in Madrid was conducted by Martin *et al.* (2014). The program was initiated by the collaboration of three schools for the deaf with community schools, where the schools for the deaf opened their doors to hearing students in order to create a 'more diverse and rich educational context' (Martin *et al.*, 2014: 370). The programs gradually moved from having primarily DHH students in classrooms to a co-enrollment model with 15–20 hearing and five to six DHH students in a classroom. They tested their DHH students in the co-enrollment programs and found 'good development of language, even within normal ranges; however, this is coupled with much variability between children and also between aspects of language evaluated' (Martin *et al.*, 2014: 386).

It is evident that programming involving the use of spoken/written and signed languages for students who are DHH is emerging in new ways and that schools for the deaf are part of this trend. Spoken language options are being sought and are appropriate for many of today's DHH students (Christensen, 2010; Knoors & Marschark, 2012). Therefore, 'if traditional schools for deaf students are to survive, they must adapt' (Paludneviciene & Harris, 2011: 12) to meet the needs of and provide the most appropriate educational programming for current and future DHH students. Programs at schools for the deaf have begun to include modified auditory-verbal approaches, particularly with the increased prevalence of early cochlear implantation, combined with an emphasis on early acquisition of natural signed language to support bilingual language development (Moores, 2011; Spencer & Marschark, 2010). This need to expand programming and incorporate both spoken/written and signed languages was also the motivation for change within the small school for the deaf that is the focus of the current study.

School Background

Over two decades ago, the school for the deaf in this study transitioned from using a Total Communication approach to becoming a bilingual-bicultural school teaching students through ASL. In this model, students develop fluency in both ASL and English and use ASL to support their learning of English (primarily in written form). Teachers and students engage in the standard provincial curriculum but access learning through ASL and within a Deaf cultural environment. Spoken English opportunities are available for students, as desired, on an individual therapy basis.

Several years ago, three families with young DHH children approached the school with a dilemma. They were struggling to find appropriate educational programming for their children who were using both spoken English and ASL. Due to the limited opportunity for ASL development and communication, these parents did not want their DHH children to be placed in their home schools. Nor did they want their children placed in the school for the deaf with limited opportunity for spoken language development and communication. They wanted to know if the school for the deaf could provide a program with both a strong ASL component and a strong spoken language component. Essentially, they wanted bimodal-bilingual programming for their children. Parent advocacy for new programming, which is often the impetus for change, resulted in a review of current practices and further exploration of the latest research.

The motivation to explore a new type of program was triggered by the need to provide families with DHH children with more options, but was also focused on the potential educational benefits for all students. The addition of a significant spoken language programming option to the school for the deaf was a strategy to revive enrollment and, more importantly, to better meet the needs of the full range of the DHH student population. Similar to other schools for the deaf in Canada, the population at this school consisted of students with late diagnoses, students with identified disabilities or learning challenges unrelated to their hearing loss, and students from ethnic minorities, as well as students with early exposure to ASL from Deaf parents. In other words, this was a highly variable population that subsequently required differentiated instruction for optimal learning (Jones & Jones, 2006), including a range of options along the linguistic continuum between spoken English and ASL. Programming options should be available to accommodate the full range of student learning needs, as every option is effective in some cases but 'no one approach is appropriate for all' (Spencer & Marschark, 2010: 188).

In addition to recognizing the need to provide the option of spoken language, it was critical to maintain a strong ASL learning environment at the school. The school for the deaf provided the only opportunity in the region for DHH students to learn through ASL. Some DHH students cannot use amplification technology and require ASL to learn, while others simply prefer to learn through ASL. Still other DHH students may want or need ASL at different points in their academic lives. Hence, the goal was to provide both ASL and English opportunities for three specific junior kindergarten (JK) students but also for future DHH students (including students with cochlear implants) who may benefit from such programming options.

Based on research and existing educational priorities, it was determined that the bimodal-bilingual program would include the following: (a) at least a half day using ASL and being exposed to native ASL users (i.e. Deaf teachers) and peers, and (b) at least a half day using spoken English and exposure to native English speakers and peers. Exposure to native Deaf signers and clear modelling of spoken and signed languages provide appropriate language exposure and help children establish a clear understanding of the two different languages. Because as the program began there were no peers to provide spoken language models in the school, hearing children were admitted into the program. These hearing students were children of Deaf parents who could use both spoken English and ASL. It was important to school staff that ASL and Deaf culture be respected in the lives of students in the bimodal-bilingual program.

The bimodal-bilingual program admitted approximately equal numbers of DHH and hearing students each year, for a total of five to seven students per class. There were several criteria for entry into the program that were the same for both DHH and hearing students and included the following: (a) age (four to five years of age for JK), (b) family desire to have bimodal-bilingual instruction, and (c) the use of both ASL and spoken English, to some extent. In terms of the final point, for hearing students it was essential that they had at least one Deaf parent who was exposing them to ASL and that they were developing age-appropriate language (both spoken and signed). This was to ensure that the hearing children could serve as language models in the program. Even with these strict criteria, there was no difficulty recruiting hearing children for the program, indicating strong support from Deaf parents. It is important to clarify that due to low enrollment, the bimodal-bilingual program was the only option available to students entering our school at the JK level. In fact, by opening up the school to hearing students, enrollment increased from two to three students per year to five to seven students per year. The decision to initiate bimodal-bilingual programming with the JK class marked the start of a school-wide change, as bimodal-bilingual programming continued as the students moved up through the grade levels. These changes introduced a significant increase in the amount and quality of spoken English, as well as a corresponding decrease in the amount of ASL exposure that the students received throughout the school day. Written English (reading and writing exposure and instruction) remained a significant focus of the students' educational programming. The study was initiated to monitor the students' language development and to determine whether the students received enough of each language to make sufficient gains.

Study Overview

In order to contribute to the evidence-based research on bimodal-bilingual programming at schools for the deaf and because, according to the research literature, the proposed bimodal-bilingual program was unique by virtue of being implemented within a school for the deaf, parental permission was obtained to collect and share data regarding the children's progress in the early years classrooms. It was important to record the development and acceptance of the program within the school, as it marked a shift to include spoken English as a language of instruction in school programming. Hence, staff and parents were surveyed for their impressions of and reactions to the bimodal-bilingual program. The information is still preliminary but contributes to a broader understanding of bimodal-bilingual programming for students who are DHH.

Bimodal-bilingual classroom context

A key aspect of the bimodal-bilingual program was the modelling and use of two languages. For this reason, the staff included both Deaf and hearing qualified and experienced teachers of the DHH, and educational assistants (EAs). All staff were fluent in ASL. Two experienced speech/language clinicians were also regularly involved in the program and, with a Deaf teacher, conducted the annual assessments. The school social worker, audiologist and program supervisor also supported the program. In Years 1 and 2, language modelling was organized around time of day: mornings were in English and taught by a hearing teacher and EA, whereas afternoons were in ASL and taught by a Deaf teacher and EA. Students had access to ASL as needed throughout the morning, with either (hearing) teachers or EAs repeating English instruction in ASL to the whole class during the lesson, or with individual students following the lesson. Some individual instruction in spoken English by an additional hearing staff member also occurred in a similar manner in the afternoons for students who were not able to follow the lesson in ASL. The intent was to deliver balanced instruction in both languages, and also to ensure that everyone had language access. Additional staff such as hearing and/or Deaf EAs, clinicians and specialists were often scheduled into both the morning and afternoon classes to support specific students, lessons and activities. These staff included the speech/language clinicians and ASL specialist working with individuals or small groups for specific language development and enrichment.

Program planning was undertaken by the hearing and Deaf teaching teams with input from clinicians and language specialists. Provincial curriculum guides were used to identify subject-area instructional goals, which were adapted as needed for individual students. Typically, the academic goals that were taught in the mornings in English were reinforced through ASL in the afternoons so that the students experienced them in both languages. For example, size concepts might be taught in the morning in English with a follow-up storybook reading of *Goldilocks and the Three Bears*. Those same concepts would be reinforced in ASL in the afternoon, with perhaps the students acting out the story of *Goldilocks and the Three Bears*. Written English was incorporated in both the morning and the afternoon as appropriate.

In Year 3, as the students moved to Grade 1, the half-day language separation became impractical for subject-specific instruction. At this point, the students had a clear understanding of the two languages and could appropriately maintain their separation. Students were grouped into larger, multi-age classrooms, and language use was based on the subjects being taught and the teacher (Deaf or hearing) assigned to the subject. Each teacher planned and implemented her own subject-area lessons, although collaborative team planning for overall themes, goals and group activities continued. The program followed a multi-grade team-teaching model where ASL and English were no longer strictly separated by half-days but one language was used for specific subjects. For example, with the Grade 1 class, math was taught through ASL by a Deaf teacher and social studies through English by a hearing teacher. Teaching assignments were rotated among teachers for different grade levels and over academic years to ensure each subject was taught in both languages. Large-group instruction, which typically occurred at the beginning of the day, reflected both languages so students could learn through the language of their choice. If a teacher used one language, interpreting by another teacher would be provided so that full access to information was available for all staff and students. During subject-specific instruction, the teacher would teach in ASL or English, and the alternate language was provided to individual students as needed. Moving the students into a larger multi-grade group allowed for more flexible use of programming options and staff.

Students

Although each year both DHH and hearing students were admitted into the bimodal-bilingual program, the focus of this chapter will be the progress of the initial group of students over the first three years of programming. This class included five DHH students and two hearing students. The five DHH students (A, B, C, D, E) all had hearing parents and congenital hearing losses, and used binaural hearing aids and classroom FM systems (none had a cochlear implant). One hearing student (F) had a Deaf single mother and the other hearing student (G) had two Deaf parents as well as a Deaf uncle and grandparents. All parents of hearing children were active in the Deaf community. All seven students started the program at the JK level when they were four or five years of age and were followed for three years, until they were seven or eight years old and completing Grade 1. All of the children appeared to have normal cognitive abilities with no major secondary disabilities.

Student assessment

Student outcomes were based on three years of standardized assessments, report cards and informal classroom observations. Although both DHH and hearing students were assessed using a variety of formal and informal measures, only the results from the following four measures are reported here because they represent standardized measures that were administered with all students over three years. The tests were selected to report on students' development of speech skills, English vocabulary and ASL development. We did not include a formal measure of written English abilities, as the focus of the study was the introduction of spoken language in the classroom; however, written English continued to be an important part of classroom instruction and activities and was included in report cards. Testing was conducted towards the end of each school year (March or April) when the students were completing JK (Year 1) and Grade 1 (Year 3).

(a) Spoken English skills – *Goldman–Fristoe Test of Articulation* (GF) (Goldman & Fristoe, 2000) The GF requires the student to name pictures that target specific speech sounds in order to assess speech articulation skills at the word level. The GF assesses speech skills only, not English-language skills. Scores are reported as a standard score with a mean of 100 ($SD = 15$).

(b) Spoken English vocabulary – *Peabody Picture Vocabulary Test, 4th edition* (PPVT4) (Dunn & Dunn, 2007) The PPVT4 assesses receptive vocabulary by requiring the child to match a word to the appropriate picture from a choice of four items. The test was administered in spoken English. ASL was used when the child did not know the spoken word; however, only the English results were recorded and converted into standard scores (mean of 100 and $SD = 15$).

(c) ASL concept development – *Test of Relational Concepts* (TRC) (Edmondston & Thane, 1999) The TRC assesses concept development, including understanding the relationships between locations (front/back), sizes (big/little) and time (first/last). It is administered in ASL and normed for DHH students. Scores are reported as standard scores with a mean of 50 (SD = 10). However, for the purposes of comparison with the other tests listed here, we have doubled all the students' standard scores on this test to reflect a mean of 100.

(d) ASL grammar – *American Sign Language: Receptive Skills Test* (ASL-RST) (Enns *et al.*, 2013) The ASL-RST measures children's understanding of ASL grammatical structures by matching a videotaped ASL sentence/phrase to the correct picture from a choice of four. Scores are reported as standard scores with a mean of 100 (SD = 15). Due to the limited normative data and wide range of scores within the average range for children under the age of five, the ASL-RST tends to overestimate the abilities of young children (Enns & Herman, 2011). However, as no other formal measure of ASL is currently available, the decision was made to continue using this test.

School report cards incorporating classroom teachers' assessment of students' skills were completed three times over each school year in the areas of language foundations, reading/writing, mathematics, social development and fine and gross motor skills. Annual report cards for the students were reviewed to augment descriptions of progress indicated by the formal assessments.

Staff/parent survey

Staff and parents completed a written survey during the fourth year of implementing the bimodal-bilingual program at the school. The survey was intended to gather staff and parent impressions of the students' academic progress and identity development within the bimodal-bilingual program. Parents and staff also responded to questions about the general advantages and disadvantages of the program. Open-ended questions were provided so that any additional information could be included.

Student Outcomes

Speech skills

The students' results in the area of speech skills are demonstrated by comparing their initial and final year scores on the GF. The scores of the seven students are presented numerically in Table 7.1.

These scores indicate that all five DHH students showed increases in their speech skills, although Student D made minimal gains, due to the fact that she was already within the normal range at the point of initial testing. Specifically, Student A progressed from a score of 48, representing a severe delay, to a score of 99 which is within the normal range. Similarly, Student E moved into the normal range by the final year, when his initial score was 73, representing a mildly delay. Although two students, B and C, did not achieve scores within the normal range by the final year, they

Table 7.1 Comparison of initial and final *Goldman–Fristoe Test of Articulation* scores

	GF-I	GF-F
Student A	48	99
Student B	16	66
Student C	44	75
Student D	99	101
Student E	73	99
Student F	105	107
Student G	117	115

did demonstrate significant gains over the three years of the project, moving from severely delayed scores (16 and 44, respectively) to moderately delayed (66) for Student B and mildly delayed (75) for Student C by Year 3. The hearing students (F and G) were within the normal range for speech development at initial testing and continued to be so at the time of final testing.

This overview illustrates that of the five DHH students, three of them had speech skills at the word level within the normal range by their third year in the program, and the other two were moderately and mildly delayed. In the case of three students, this represents a significant gain from initial skills that were severely delayed.

English vocabulary

A similar pattern of improvement was noted in the students' receptive English vocabulary skills as assessed by the PPVT4, although two DHH students (D and E) and the two hearing students (F and G) had initial scores that were already in the normal range. The initial and final PPVT4 scores of all seven students are presented numerically in Table 7.2.

Overall, the gains the students made in their PPVT4 scores were not as significant as the gains made in their speech skills. It is clear that only

Table 7.2 Comparison of initial and final PPVT4 scores

	PPVT4-I	PPVT4-F
Student A	52	78
Student B	53	55
Student C	57	75
Student D	88	95
Student E	88	96
Student F	105	110
Student G	130	128

four of the seven students (D, E, F and G) had PPVT4 scores in the normal range at the end of the third year, and these same students started the program with normal English vocabulary scores. Students A and C showed the most growth by moving from severely delayed scores (52 and 57, respectively) to scores in the mildly delayed range (71 and 75) by the end of Year 3.

Report cards

The results from formal testing of speech skills were supported with anecdotal evidence gathered from the students' report cards. Teachers initially described the DHH students' spoken English skills as being at the pre-language level, indicating that they were beginning to 'attend to the speaker' or 'gaining confidence in initiating conversations'. At the point of final assessment, all DHH students were described as effectively pronouncing written words and using spoken phonics to help with spelling and writing. Student B required consistent support in her spoken English when she began the program, and although she was still struggling with specific speech sounds (i.e. word ending blends) after two years in the program, along with several other students she was showing decreased frustration in sounding out words and reading. Student D, who entered with strong spoken English skills, shifted from enjoying listening to group stories to developing a love of reading independently.

ASL skills

As with the measures of English abilities, between the initial and final year of the project all the students improved their scores on the measures of ASL. Figure 7.1 shows the seven students' scores across the TRC and the ASL-RST. All seven students showed greater improvements on the TRC than the ASL-RST, suggesting growth in their conceptual skills that exceeded the accompanying growth of their understanding of ASL grammar. In particular, Student A showed a significant improvement in his initial TRC score of 10 (severely delayed) to his Year 3 score of 104, which put him in the average range for his age. Some of this change in scores may also reflect a better understanding of the test task; however, Student A was noted to make significant gains in all areas of language functioning over his three years in the program.

By the final year, all seven students were functioning in the average range as measured by both the TRC and the ASL-RST. Six students had receptive ASL skills within the average range when they started the program, although Student D was assessed at the lower end of this range (standard score of 88). Student E did not know enough of the 20 ASL-RST vocabulary items to proceed with initial testing, indicating his very limited knowledge and use of ASL when he entered the bimodal-bilingual

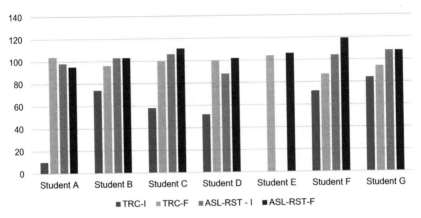

Figure 7.1 Comparison of initial and final ASL skills (TRC and ASL-RST)

program; however, he scored well within the average range at final testing. At the start of the program, none of the students had scores within the average range for relational concepts in ASL, but by the end of the third year all seven students scored within or above average on this measure.

Report cards

The teachers' initial comments described the students as having very basic ASL skills, such as counting, naming colors and expressing some wants and needs. The final comments reported that students were able to understand ASL stories, discuss family and community events and effectively use creative expression in ASL. Students D and E, who entered the program with minimal exposure to ASL, were described at the final assessment period as 'participating fully in class' and able to 'stay on task and join in class discussions'.

Parent/Staff Survey Outcomes

In the final year of the study, a one-page survey with four broad, open-ended questions (one with three parts) and an area for comments was sent to parents and staff near the end of the school year (see Appendix A). The survey was sent to all 25 parents with children in the bimodal-bilingual program, and a total of 13 were completed and returned (one survey was incomplete, and it was not used). Parents responding to the survey had been involved with the program for between one and four years. Two of the parent responders were Deaf and 11 were hearing. The staff survey was sent to 20 educational staff, and nine responses were received, including four from Deaf staff. The staff had between 10 and 35 years of experience at the school. Overall, for both parents and staff, the response rate was almost 50%. The survey data were compiled and analyzed, and several themes emerged, including student progress, Deaf identity and program benefits and challenges. Separate from these broad themes, it is important to note that the general survey question, 'How do you feel about the bimodal-bilingual program?', elicited strong emotional responses from parents. Comments included 'The program has changed my daughter' and 'this is the ideal place for my son', as well as the following descriptors: 'awesome', 'excellent', 'valuable' and 'wonderful'. One family described the program as 'life-changing' in terms of learning to appreciate two languages and cultures and recognizing their child's potential. Each of the survey themes is discussed below.

Student academic/language progress

Respondents noted variability in student progress both in individual students and across the group. Most staff members were not sure of the specific academic or linguistic progress of students and indicated 'N/A' for this item. One staff member indicated that DHH students 'are learning wonderfully in this environment ... [and] readily switch to ASL in order to include Deaf students who can't access spoken English'.

Parents were 'pleased' and saw their children as doing 'well' and 'making progress'. Some saw 'huge gains' and 'major improvements', and thought their children's performance was 'excellent' in various academic areas. Two said they felt their children were 'reading to their full potential' and this would not be the case if they did not have access to both spoken English and ASL. Four parents noted that their children had delayed skills but were 'making steady progress' and that they 'would not blame the bimodal-bilingual program for that at all'. In specific responses about linguistic progress, parents were very positive, describing 'dramatic', 'major', 'big' and 'a lot of' improvements. Several noted the growth and 'fluency in both languages'. Many discussed their individual child's preference or 'first choice' for one language over the other, but emphasized the need for both languages. One parent said that the bimodal-bilingual program was 'the perfect environment to continually grow and expand [her child's] language base', while others talked about the privilege of being able to 'choose' which language to use.

Development of Deaf identity

There were varied staff responses to the question about children's identity development as Deaf individuals. One Deaf staff member indicated that development was 'excellent', but three of the four Deaf respondents indicated some concern, such as: 'most students are proud of themselves, but not all students understand Deaf culture or respect the language'. One Deaf respondent said that some of the hearing students continue to use spoken English in front of Deaf staff; hence, 'we have not succeeded in creating a culture of respect where ASL is the primary mode of communication when we are with Deaf people'. Other staff were positive in their responses but stated that there was 'some confusion' regarding the use of spoken or signed language and being a hearing or Deaf individual. These comments suggest that students within the bimodal-bilingual program may be challenging the traditional processes and concepts of identity formation and moving away from 'either/or' categories of Deaf and hearing.

When parents discussed their child's progress as a Deaf individual, they talked about their 'great appreciation' of both languages and how 'we can coexist nicely'. They especially focused on becoming 'comfortable' with ASL, 'identifying with and learning about Deaf culture' and being 'respectful around our Deaf friends'. Several parents discussed their children as belonging, 'developing connections' and 'feeling included'. One parent noted that Deaf identity was 'something I'm so grateful [the school] has helped him to harness. He identifies as Deaf/HH and knows he has a place in the community'.

Bimodal-bilingual program benefits

When asked what is most beneficial about the bimodal-bilingual program, staff mentioned both languages 'providing access' to learning and the opportunity for 'some hearing students to develop ASL and some Deaf students to switch to spoken English'. They mentioned the 'language-rich environment', 'sense of community', 'sense of culture' and 'meeting the needs of students'. Teachers also liked the multi-year classroom and the opportunity for 'greater variety in peer group options'. Parent responses indicated that having their child learn both ASL and spoken English was very positive in their lives. They discussed it as 'a privilege', 'useful' and 'important' to have both languages. Some parents focused on English as the primary language and discussed using ASL 'to augment learning while maintaining spoken English skills' and as enhancing the 'ability to comprehend English'. One parent expanded on this, saying that 'the learning of this second language [ASL] is not in isolation, but has played an integral role in his English development'. Others talked about the bimodal-bilingual program as giving their children the 'best of both worlds'.

Challenges of the bimodal-bilingual program

Staff consistently responded that the biggest challenge is the fact that there is spoken language in the building and the school is not 'fully accessible to all staff and students at all times'. One teacher noted that 'the main issue is still the use of English language in the public areas', and another staff member said 'keeping communication accessible' was critical. There was concern that Deaf students and staff 'feel left out when students use voice anywhere'. These comments highlight the importance of establishing policies or common understandings of language use within the school, to ensure that equal access and respect for both languages is maintained.

Parents had limited responses to the question regarding the challenges of the bimodal-bilingual program. A couple of parents were concerned about 'grammar' or the tendency to 'speak ASL' and spoken English phrases being 'misunderstood' as a consequence. These concerns are valid, but they may also reflect normal emergent bilingual behavior typical of any child learning two languages. Another parent was concerned about developing friendships in the community when her child attended a specialized school for the Deaf. Parents discussed their children attending a 'smaller school' with a 'smaller group of peers', and requiring 'more sports' and broader opportunities in the future. A couple of parents also mentioned that transportation was difficult as the school was located 'quite a distance from home'.

The findings from both the student assessments and the staff/parent surveys provided objective and responsive data about the implementation of the bimodal-bilingual program within the school.

Discussion

In the first instance, the findings support the language learning benefits of educating DHH students within a bimodal-bilingual context incorporating spoken and signed languages. All students, regardless of hearing loss and entry language level, made positive gains in both spoken English and ASL. In some cases these gains were significant. In fact, the most significant area of improvement overall was the DHH students' production of speech sounds – perhaps not what would be expected when half the day was spent in an ASL environment. These findings support the view that signed language use may support, rather than interfere with, spoken language development for DHH learners.

The assessment scores showed that students who entered the program with strong ASL abilities continued to develop in this area, as well as improve their spoken English skills. Similarly, students who entered the program with strong spoken English skills continued to develop and maintain these skills, and effectively learned ASL. These findings reinforce the theory that bilingualism in signed and spoken languages follows similar principles to those of spoken language bilingualism in that knowledge and abilities gained in one language can have a beneficial impact on both languages (Cummins, 2000).

In a discussion of the language learning gains observed in the students attending the bimodal-bilingual program, it should be noted that all assessment scores were reported as standard scores. Therefore, the gains reported are not simply an increase in the number of correct items scored on the tests, but rather represent an increase in comparison to the norms – how these children are performing relative to other children their age. The findings demonstrate that within a few short years, several DHH children had achieved age-appropriate language abilities in some areas.

Although all of the students made significant language gains, there was considerable variability among the scores. Some students made more gains in one language or the other, and some made significantly more gains in one aspect of language than other areas of development. This variability can be partially attributed to the fact that the DHH students entered school with scores significantly below average for both spoken English and ASL, and their abilities were more variable than those typical for nondeaf students. Parents recognized that their DHH children had 'delayed skills' upon entry to the program. Since language development is the area most affected by hearing loss (Spencer & Marschark, 2010), it would be expected that the language scores of the DHH students were typically lower than their chronological age peers, especially for students with a later diagnosis of hearing loss.

Our students' variable language results may also be partially explained by looking at the results of hearing bilingual children. Bilingual children demonstrate variable rates of language development, at least in the first few years (Morere, 2011). As the students in this study were in the acquisition phase of becoming bilingual, some variability was expected. Additionally, 'bilingualism can impede clinical and educational assessment because resulting profiles rarely are accurately captured by monolingual norms' (Knoors & Marschark, 2012: 292). Assessments often focus on one language and specific components of that language, and therefore may not reflect bilingual children's overall language proficiency. Variability in language skills across children is typical for DHH students (Christensen, 2010; Spencer & Marschark, 2010). Although our DHH student scores continued to be variable, and in some cases below the norms for nondeaf students, it is important to note that all of the students made individual gains in their language and academic development.

Another important finding was that the benefits of the bimodal-bilingual program extended beyond language learning, including both cognitive and social-emotional development. Although not specifically a measure of cognitive development, growth in understanding spatial and temporal concepts was particularly evident in the significant gains all students made on the TRC. This finding is consistent with other research that suggests that students using both spoken and signed languages show improved aspects of thinking and nonverbal functioning (Knoors & Marschark, 2012). When students improve their thinking skills, metalinguistic awareness and ability to conceptualize, it has important benefits and implications for literacy learning (McBride-Chang, 2004).

Both staff and parents unanimously felt that the students were positively developing as learners who could fit within both the hearing and the Deaf worlds. Survey results further indicated that when students identified with both communities, it positively influenced the development of their self-concept. The psychological and social-emotional advantages of connecting with both the hearing and the Deaf cultures are often noted in the literature (Christiansen & Leigh, 2011; Lauderdale, 2010; Mitchiner & Sass-Lehrer, 2011). Leigh and Maxwell-McCaw (2011) noted that DHH student identities are positively influenced by participation in both hearing and Deaf communities because these opportunities allow them to acquire an affirmative image of their unique identity and build positive self-esteem. The positive self-concept and sense of belonging to both the hearing and Deaf world were important considerations for the parents of students in our study.

As identified by survey results and informal observations and discussions, the biggest challenge in moving forward with the bimodal-bilingual program was how to respectfully and sensitively incorporate the use of signed and spoken languages. The survey responses mention students using spoken language and not respecting Deaf staff and culture. Additionally, comments indicate sensitivity to the general use and potentially increased use of spoken English in our bilingual-bicultural school for the Deaf. It may feel threatening for staff to see spoken English being used at the school because it instigates concerns regarding the erosion of ASL as a core value of the school. It may also be that promoting spoken English fluency is not what is truly (altruistically) desired by our staff, but what they feel has to be done in order to increase the student population and/or meet the needs of families. Since ASL is a minority language, it is valid that Deaf staff were concerned about its protection and preservation. In addition to increasing the student population there is also a need to continue to prepare and retain qualified Deaf teachers.

During the spoken-language periods in the bimodal-bilingual classrooms, signs were frequently used as needed by teachers and students to facilitate comprehension. This fluid use of resources across languages and modalities has recently been described as 'translanguaging', or shifting along the continuum of signed and spoken languages to maximize students' access to meaning (Swanwick, 2017). The teachers incorporated a variety of strategies to link spoken, written and signed forms of language, including the well-established method of chaining, where written words are sequentially connected to their fingerspelled letters and signed meaning (Quinto-Pozos & Reynolds, 2012). Such strategies emphasize equivalencies between languages and foster metalinguistic awareness. As a result, translanguaging was not perceived as problematic by the staff and could well be appropriate given specific student needs. However, some aspects of 'mixing languages' challenged the current ideology held by many staff members of promoting standard ASL in the school. Although there was significant effort made to keep the two languages separate, in reality both languages were frequently present in the classrooms and one language was often used to clarify meaning in the other. The results from this study suggest that code-switching between languages does not necessarily denigrate either language. In fact, the use of strategic translanguaging (chaining, interpreting while reading aloud, fingerspelling written words, etc.) provided an integrated form of meaning-making between deaf and hearing students and teachers. It was critical to maintain effective modelling of standard varieties of ASL and English throughout the school day. It can also be argued that initially establishing a strong ASL language base is necessary prior to the introduction and effective use of translanguaging with spoken English.

The intent of the language modelling and providing space for the program within the broader ASL milieu was to ensure consistent development of ASL and also to incorporate Deaf culture into the lives of these young children. All of the DHH students in this study were from hearing families and therefore benefitted from rich ASL instruction to establish a solid language foundation and to understand typical (albeit perhaps evolving) behavior in Deaf culture.

In addition to the observed benefits for language growth, dual language use within a bimodal-bilingual program presents many challenges and raises numerous questions. How is the core language of ASL maintained while supporting spoken English? Should bimodal programming be limited to elementary school years or extend into high school? The ever-evolving and increasingly variable DHH student population means that exploration and development must continue in order to provide programming that meets the needs of all students. This may mean using ASL and spoken/written English in different ways and combinations to facilitate acquisition of a solid language base and optimal learning opportunities. Much more evidence-based research will help support the development of programs and practices that provide the best outcomes and benefits for the full range of DHH students.

One of the key reasons for providing a new bimodal-bilingual option at this school for the Deaf was to meet the needs of a broader range of DHH students. This also appears to be one of the reasons why bimodal classrooms are emerging in other educational settings, both mainstream schools and schools for the Deaf. The current study found that bimodal-bilingual programming is complex and there are many aspects to consider when incorporating a spoken language component into a school for the deaf with an ASL milieu. It cannot be stated with certainty that the bimodal-bilingual program provides enough of either language for students, but it did have positive implications for students and their families. All of the students made significant individual language development gains and demonstrated understanding of both Deaf and hearing cultures. Challenges as to where, when and how much spoken language should be used continue to exist and require further discussion.

Appendix A

---

*COMPLETION OF THIS BIMODAL/BILINGUAL SURVEY IS VOLUNTARY –
Information provided is confidential and anonymous.

BIMODAL PARENT SURVEY

My Child is	☐ Deaf	☐ Hearing	☐ Hard of Hearing
I am	☐ Deaf	☐ Hearing	☐ Hard of Hearing
My Child is in	☐ Jr. Kindergarten	☐ Kindergarten	☐ Grade 1/2/3

1. How do you feel about the bimodal/bilingual program?

2. How do you feel your child is progressing
   a.   Academically?

   b.   Linguistically (language development)?

   c.   As Deaf individuals (Deaf identity)?

3. What do you see as the most beneficial things about the bimodal/
   bilingual program (for your child and/or for [school name])?

4. What do you think are the most challenging things about the
   bimodal/bilingual program (for your child and/or for [school
   name])?

References

Antia, S. (2013) Deaf and hard of hearing students in the mainstream. *Raising and Educating Deaf Children: Foundations for Policies, Practice, and Outcomes. E-Bulletin post*, 23 February. See http://www.raisingandeducatingdeafchildren. org/2014/01/01/deaf-and-hard-of-hearing-students-in-the-mainstream/#.

Antia, S. and Metz, K. (2014) Co-enrollment in the United States: A critical analysis of benefits and challenges. In M. Marschark, G. Tang and H. Knoors (eds) *Bilingualism and Bilingual Deaf Education* (pp. 424–444). New York: Oxford University Press.

Antia, S., Jones, P. and Reed, S. (2009) Academic status and progress of deaf and hard-of-hearing students in general education classrooms. *Journal of Deaf Studies and Deaf Education* 14 (3), 293–311. doi:10.1093/deafed/enp009

Christensen, K.M. (ed.) (2010) *Ethical Considerations in Educating Children who are Deaf or Hard of Hearing*. Washington, DC: Gallaudet University Press.

Christiansen, J. and Leigh, I. (2011) Cochlear implants and deaf community. In R. Paludneviciene and I. Leigh (eds) *Cochlear Implants Evolving Perspectives*. Washington, DC: Gallaudet University Press.

Cole, E. and Flexer, C. (2015) *Children with Hearing Loss: Developing Listening and Talking* (3rd edn). San Diego, CA: Plural Publishing.

Cummins, J. (2000) *Language, Power and Pedagogy: Bilingual Children in the Crossfire*. Clevedon: Multilingual Matters.

Davidson, K., Lillo-Martin, D. and Chen Pichler, D. (2014) Spoken English language development among native signing children with cochlear implants. *Journal of Deaf Studies and Deaf Education* 19 (2), 238–250.

Dunn, L.M. and Dunn, D.M. (2007) *Peabody Picture Vocabulary Test Fourth Edition (PPVT4) Form B*. Bloomington, MN: Pearson.

Edmondston, B.B. and Thane, N. (1999) *Test of Relational Concepts (TRC)*. Washington, DC: Pre-College National Mission Programs.

Enns, C. and Herman, R. (2011) Adapting the Assessing British Sign Language Development: Receptive Skills Test into American Sign Language. *Journal of Deaf Studies and Deaf Education* 16 (3), 362–374.

Enns, C., Zimmer, K., Boudreault, P., Rabu, S. and Broszeit, C. (2013) *American Sign Language: Receptive Skills Test*. Winnipeg, MB: Northern Signs Research.

Geers, A.E. (2006) Factors influencing spoken language outcomes in children following early cochlear implantation. Advances in oto-rhino-laryngology 64, 50–65. https:// doi.org/10.1159/000094644.

Goldman, R. and Fristoe, M. (2000) *Goldman Fristoe 2 Test of Articulation*. Minneapolis, MN: Pearson.

Hassanzadeh, S. (2012) Outcomes of cochlear implantation in deaf children of deaf parents: Comparative study. *Journal of Laryngology and Otology* 126 (10), 989–994.

Hermans, D., Wauters, L., Klerk, A. and Knoors, H. (2014) Quality of instruction in bilingual schools for Deaf children: Through the children's eyes and the camera's lens. In M. Marschark, G. Tang and H. Knoors (eds) *Bilingualism and Bilingual Deaf Education* (pp. 272–292). New York: Oxford University Press.

Jones, T. and Jones, J. (2006) Educating young children with multiple disabilities. In B. Bodner-Johnson and M. Sass-Lehrer (eds) *The Young Deaf and Hard of Hearing Child* (pp. 297–329). Baltimore, MD: Brookes.

Knoors, H. and Marschark, M. (2012) Language planning for the 21st century: Revisiting bilingual language policy for deaf children. *Journal of Deaf Studies and Deaf Education* 17 (3), 291–304.

Lauderdale, M. (2010) Looking at residential schools for deaf students: Seeing a viable option. In K.M. Christensen (ed.) *Ethical Considerations in Educating Children who are Deaf or Hard of Hearing*. Washington, DC: Gallaudet University Press.

Leigh, I. and Maxwell-McCaw, D. (2011) Cochlear implants: Implications for Deaf identities. In R. Paludneviciene and I. Leigh (eds) *Cochlear Implants Evolving Perspectives*. Washington, DC: Gallaudet University Press.

Marschark, M., Tang, G. and Knoors, H. (eds) (2014) *Bilingualism and Bilingual Deaf Education*. New York: Oxford University Press.

Marschark, M., Shaver, D.M., Nagle, K.M. and Newman, L.A. (2015) Predicting the academic achievement of deaf and hard-of-hearing students from individual, household, communication, and educational factors. *Exceptional Children* 81 (3), 350–369. doi:10.1177/0014402914563700

Martin, M., Balanzategui, M. and Morgan, G. (2014) Sign bilingual and co-enrollment education for children with cochlear implants in Madrid, Spain. In M. Marschark, G. Tang and H. Knoors (eds) *Bilingualism and Bilingual Deaf Education* (pp. 368–396). New York: Oxford University Press.

McBride-Chang, C. (2004) *Children's Literacy Development*. London: Routledge.

Mitchiner, J.C. and Sass-Lehrer, M. (2011) My child can have more choices: Reflections of deaf mothers on cochlear implants for their children. In R. Paludneviciene and I. Leigh (eds) *Cochlear Implants Evolving Perspectives* (pp. 71–95). Washington, DC: Gallaudet University Press.

Moog, J.S., Geers, A.E., Gustus, C. and Brenner, C. (2011) Psychosocial adjustment in adolescents who have used cochlear implants since preschool. *Ear and Hearing* 32 (Suppl. 1), 75S–83S. doi:10.1097/AUD.0b013e3182014c76

Moores, D. (ed.) (2011) *Partners in Education Issues and Trends from the 21st International Congress on the Education of the Deaf*. Washington, DC: Gallaudet University Press.

Morere, D.A. (2011) Bimodal processing of language for cochlear implant users. In R. Paludneviciene and I. Leigh (eds) *Cochlear Implants Evolving Perspectives* (pp. 113–141). Washington, DC: Gallaudet University Press.

Nicholas, J. and Geers, A. (2007) Will they catch up? The role of cochlear implantation in the spoken language development of children with severe to profound hearing loss. *Journal of Speech Language and Hearing Research* 40, 1314–1327.

Nussbaum, D. and Scott, S. (2011) The cochlear implant education center: Perspectives on effective educational practices. In R. Paludnevicience and I. Leigh (eds) *Cochlear Implants Evolving Perspectives* (pp. 175–205). Washington, DC: Gallaudet University Press.

Paludneviciene, R. and Harris, R. (2011) Impact of cochlear implants on the deaf community. In R. Paludnevicience and I. Leigh (eds) *Cochlear Implants Evolving Perspectives* (pp. 3–19). Washington, DC: Gallaudet University Press.

Paludneviciene, R. and Leigh, I. (eds) (2011) *Cochlear Implants Evolving Perspectives*. Washington, DC: Gallaudet University Press.

Qi, S. and Mitchell, R. (2012) Large-scale academic achievement testing of deaf and hard-of-hearing students: Past, present, and future. *Journal of Deaf Studies and Deaf Education* 17 (1), 1–18. doi:10.1093/deafed/enr028

Quinto-Pozos, D. and Reynolds, W. (2012) ASL discourse strategies: Chaining and connecting-explaining across audiences. *Sign Language Studies* 12 (2), 211–235.

Spencer, L. and Oleson, J. (2008) Early listening and speaking skills predict later reading proficiency in pediatric cochlear implant users. *Ear and Hearing* 29, 270–280.

Spencer, P. and Marschark, M. (eds) (2010) *Evidence-based Practice in Educating Deaf and Hard-of-Hearing Students*. New York: Oxford University Press.

Swanwick, R. (2017) Translanguaging, learning and teaching in deaf education. *International Journal of Multilingualism* 14 (3), 233–249.

US Department of Education (2006) *A National Profile of Students with Hearing Impairments in Elementary and Middle School: A Special Topic Report from the Special Education Elementary Longitudinal Study*. Menlo Park, CA: SRI International.

Wilbur, R. (2000) The use of ASL to support the development of English and literacy. *Journal of Deaf Studies and Deaf Education* 5, 81–104.

Yiu, K.C. and Tang, G. (2014) Social integration of deaf and hard-of-hearing students in a sign bilingual and co-enrollment environment. In M. Marschark, G. Tang and H. Knoors (eds) *Bilingualism and Bilingual Deaf Education* (pp. 342–368). New York: Oxford University Press.

Yoshinaga-Itano, C. (2006) Early identification, communication modality, and the development of speech and spoken language skills: Patterns and considerations. In P. Spencer and M. Marschark (eds) *Advances in the Spoken Language Development of Deaf and Hard of Hearing Children* (pp. 298–327). New York: Oxford University Press.

Yoshinaga-Itano, C. and Sedey, A. (2000) Speech development of deaf and hard of hearing children in early childhood: Interrelationships with language and hearing. *Volta Review* 100, 181–212.

8 Implementing a New Design in Parent Sign Language Teaching: The *Common European Framework of Reference for Languages*

Joni Oyserman and Mathilde de Geus

This chapter focuses on the plurilingual needs of parents of deaf/hard-of-hearing children in the Netherlands and the availability of sign language courses. The parents in our study learned Sign Language of the Netherlands (SLN) to communicate with their deaf children, who were born between 1999 and 2014. All of the deaf children in the study use cochlear implants. The parents indicated that the old parent course system described in this chapter inadequately supported their own plurilingual needs and thus those of their children. They requested revised and extended SLN courses set to a higher language level. The parents aimed to sign fluently, that is, to use SLN as much as possible without hesitation. Parents' requests for more advanced courses were rejected by family service agencies and deaf schools with the rationale that professionals working at these agencies and schools were committed to providing courses in Sign Supported Dutch (SSD) instead of SLN. SLN has been regarded as being too difficult for parents of deaf children to learn to an advanced level. Because professionals did not meet their request, the parents in this study asked the authors of this chapter to design advanced parent course modules. This request prompted: (1) the provision of a discursive understanding of how parents' communicative and plurilingual needs can be aligned with a comprehensive language framework, in this case the Common European Framework of Reference for Languages (CEFR) for A (Basic User), B (Independent User) and C (Proficient User); and (2) the foregrounding of the importance of teaching SLN to parents so they are able to become

173

independent users, exercising autonomy in parent-child communication. This chapter summarizes the historical background of Dutch parents' experiences with SLN courses and presents a sample of data collected from the newly developed WeSign4 course, including teacher assessments, the CEFR self-assessment grid, and an evaluation survey completed by signing hearing parent participants. The results showed that supporting parents' development of communicative competence in SLN has significant implications for meeting their deaf children's communicative needs. Parents reported that they were learning SLN in the same way they had learned other spoken second languages. This study is the first to investigate the correlation between applying the CEFR to parents' bimodal needs and the development of parent courses.

Introduction

Parenting a deaf or hard-of-hearing child will introduce doubts concerning expectations for communication and language skills. Parents of deaf and hard-of-hearing children experience higher levels of stress (Humphries *et al.*, 2012) because they have to make critical language choices, facilitate communication and consider whether the language at home will be bimodal or monolingual (Schermer, 2012). Many parents request advice and support from professionals because they want to make the best choices for their child. The opinions of professionals, especially during the early years of language acquisition, are highly influential (Humphries *et al.*, 2015). However, information from professionals is not always consistent with what is observed in deaf children's language acquisition at school.

In the Fall of 2011, six mothers based in The Hague area contacted the authors of this chapter for two reasons. First, these mothers observed that other children receiving bilingual education in Sign Language of the Netherlands (henceforth abbreviated as SLN) and spoken Dutch seemed to have higher learning results compared to their children. Second, some time before the initial contact with the authors, these mothers made a day visit to one of the schools run by Kentalis, which is one of four educational organizations in the Netherlands for deaf, hard-of-hearing and deafblind children. They noticed that both the deaf and hearing teachers working together as a collaborative team in a specific class they visited always used a high level of SLN with the pupils. Another observation was that the deaf pupils in this class received lessons at the same level as their hearing peers. These parental observations reinforce Humphries *et al.*'s (2014) and Nilsson and Schönström's (2014) arguments for providing instruction in sign language to ensure optimal access to the school curriculum.

The parents' observations suggest that the education of deaf children can be optimized by creating equal access through the use of SLN in the classroom. The mothers were both relieved and concerned by this idea. They were relieved because they knew that the autonomy they desired was possible as parents educating and raising their deaf child. They were also concerned that they would not progress in their signing to the level exhibited by the teachers in the classroom they observed. Since the parent-child relationship is lifelong, it is very important that sustained and in-depth interaction can take place to ensure the quality of this relationship. Therefore, achieving a high level of SLN proficiency is crucial. As one mother pointed out:

> Schools for deaf children should provide support so that we parents can communicate with our children independently. Parents themselves make languages choices because they are primarily responsible for their deaf children. It is not the professionals who decide. They are not parents. Being able to communicate independently with a deaf child requires skills, including a high level of SLN proficiency. Deaf schools fulfil their task, which is delegated by the government when they help parents become skilled in educating and raising a deaf child so that parents no longer lack expertise and can help their children better integrate into society. The fear of parents becoming skilled in SLN so that they are in a position to assess the knowledge and services of deaf schools is totally unjustified. It bears witness to dated thinking and policy. (Personal communication, authors' translation from Dutch, October 2011)

Another mother added, 'It is time for a holistic approach where parents of deaf children can act as autonomously as possible thanks to having more skills, including SLN fluency' (Personal communication, authors' translation from SLN, October 2011).

These mothers sought an action-oriented, holistic approach to sign language acquisition. Their search led us to consider plurilingualism. The Council of Europe (2018) defines 'plurilingualism in the interrelatedness of holistic strategy and plurilingual repertoire' and thereby proposes an action-oriented direction. In this context, plurilingualism creates space for the dynamic and developing linguistic repertoire of an individual user/learner. This creative process in turn supports increased motivation on the learner's part.

The parents in this study were motivated to acquire SLN to communicate with their deaf children (Prinzi, 2007). Because they had already completed the beginner-level parent courses 1–3 that were provided by the Dutch Sign Centre (1994, 1995, 1997) and had waited for additional opportunities to develop their signing skills, they requested that the authors design new, advanced courses (Oyserman & de Geus, 2013). These parents did not wish to repeat information from older parent courses. Mainly, they wanted to use a well-founded linguistic framework to learn SLN as a second language (L2). The researchers also considered how the results of this pilot study could then be applied to the revision of the old beginner-level courses for parents with newborn deaf children.

The Level 1–3 courses were paid for by the national health insurance system in coordination with the Dutch deaf schools. The parents assumed that the local deaf school Kentalis Zoetermeer would provide additional courses, but their requests were repeatedly denied. The prevailing view at Kentalis Zoetermeer seemed to be that more advanced courses were not necessary and would be futile, since it was perceived to be too difficult for parents of deaf children to learn SLN to an advanced level (Knoors, 2011, 2016; Knoors & Marschark, 2012; Mayer & Leigh, 2010). The parents then asked the authors of this study whether sign language was indeed too difficult for them to learn or if perhaps there were other possibilities.

In preparation for this pilot study, we focused on two main questions in our literature review:

(1) why parents as L2 learners of sign language are different from other groups of learners in acquiring fluency in SLN;
(2) what SLN proficiency level is required to parent a deaf child as a skilled, autonomous SLN user.

We will answer these main questions based on a study (see Data and Methodology section below) in which we evaluate a newly developed course using three related questions. With the results obtained here, we can return to the main questions.

In reference to the first question, there are significant differences between parents of deaf children and other L2 learners, such as SLN interpreters. Parents' first need is to establish optimal communication with their young deaf children, whereas interpreters-in-training have professional or occupational needs for sign language learning (Harder & Meijer, 1994). A second difference concerns kinds of responsibility. The interpreter's responsibility can be viewed as temporary and time limited, whereas parents are everyday caregivers of deaf children. Third, interpreters generally work with adult signers who are not family members (Napier et al., 2007), whereas parents need to continuously nurture their relationship with their child.

The main difference between parents of deaf children and hearing parents of hearing children relates to the assumption that child language acquisition will naturally occur in the family. Based on information provided by professionals, some parents are not fully assured that their deaf children will acquire spoken and written language comparable to that of their hearing peers. Some parents assume it will be easier to use their own first, spoken language with their child (Knoors, 2011, 2016; Knoors & Marschark, 2012). However, facilitating deaf children's language acquisition in only spoken and written language may be difficult. The input that a deaf child receives in the critical phase for language learning is both decisive and precarious. Grosjean (2001) identified that the effects of inadequate monolingual input can be permanent if the deaf child does not demonstrate expected spoken language development. However, Calderon (2000) reported that deaf children of hearing parents with optimal early sign language intervention demonstrate better language development overall.

The second main question, pertaining to the SLN proficiency level needed to become a skilled, autonomous SLN user, is difficult to parse. An extensive review of previous studies of sign language acquisition by parents indicates that there are no clear descriptors of language proficiency that demonstrate how parents can act as effective communicators with their deaf children. In her study, Young (1997) concluded that, for parents, the aim is not native-like proficiency but to sign fluently as much as possible, without hesitation. Parents of deaf children often search for answers as to how to do this (Bruin & Nevøy, 2014; Dirks *et al.*, 2013; Hoiting, 2010). Like Snoddon (2014, 2015), we found that existing initiatives for teaching parents SLN may be inadequate in terms of supporting new signers or second modality (M2) learners (De Meulder, 2019; Rosen, 2011) in developing language proficiency.

Without clear descriptors to guide parents, we felt it was necessary to examine the SLN courses currently offered in the Netherlands and, in cooperation with the six original mothers who participated in this study, investigate how to optimally support parental SLN learning. In the next section, a historical overview of SLN courses for parents will be presented. This is followed by a section outlining the exchange of thoughts about a new, parent-focused pedagogy.

Sign Language Courses for Parents in The Netherlands

First steps in SLN parents' courses (1979–1994)

In the Netherlands, interest in sign language instruction was influenced by trends in the United States. The research of William Stokoe and colleagues (1965) proved that American Sign Language (ASL) had fundamental language elements, thereby raising the status of ASL from a so-called gestural system to a true and natural language. Dutch parents of deaf children followed these developments with much interest (De Geus, M.L.C. & De Geus, D.T.M., personal communication, July 2018). After several visits to the United States and attending an international conference in Copenhagen, Denmark, in 1979 which featured highly educated deaf people presenting lectures in different sign languages (Harder & Meijer, 1994), Amsterdam parents of deaf children requested parent courses in Total Communication (TC). The TC courses were aligned with elements of SLN and were developed by the Dutch Foundation for Deaf and Hard-of-Hearing Children (NSDSK) and Ben Tervoort, a professor in linguistics at the University of Amsterdam and a pioneer in researching SLN. In Fall 1981, an experimental parent course was held, led by the Paedologic Audiologic Institute, a department of NSDSK. Only parents living in the Amsterdam area could access these courses, which were designed by hearing professionals and taught by deaf teachers. Evaluation of course outcomes compared this experimental group to a control group participating in spoken-language NSDSK training programs. This comparison showed significant differences in the quality of parent-child communication (Tervoort, 1983).

As a result, in cooperation with Folk College Allardsoog-Hunneschans in Bakkeveen, family sessions in SLN were established (Van der Linde & Frieswijk, 2013: 255). Dutch schools for the deaf slowly adopted the use of SLN in their school language policies. From 1980 to 1995, most schools used TC or Sign Supported Dutch (SSD). Despite what was taught in some of NSDSK's nationally funded parent guidance programs, SSD was insufficient in terms of supporting parents' ability to communicate and children's language development (Harder & Meijer, 1994; Schermer, 2012; Ter Linden & Harder, 1997). Recognizing this insufficiency, a new shift began towards parent programs offering instruction in SLN. The development of the first courses built upon efforts of the NSDSK in cooperation with Guyot Deaf School in Groningen (Harder & Meijer, 1994; Koninklijk Effatha Guyot Groep, 1997; Schermer, 2012; Ter Linden & Harder, 1997). At this time, participating parents articulated their hope to reach their desired level of SLN (Koninklijk Effatha Guyot Groep, 1997). However, this goal was not clearly defined. The VISTA 'Signing Naturally' program for teaching ASL (Lentz *et al.*, 1988; Smith, 1988) provided a source of inspiration but could not replace the need for a different language framework for parents of deaf children.

Developments in parent SLN courses (1995–2011)

Starting in 1995, parents could choose courses in either or both SSD and SLN that were provided by NSDSK and deaf schools. Deaf people were trained as SLN instructors by the Dutch Sign Centre (Schermer, 2012). Level 1 of the parent SLN course consisted of six biweekly classes of two hours, each based on a theme such as 'school' or 'a day out'. Levels 1–3 did not have assessment components because professionals wished to avoid evaluating parents' SLN competencies (Harder & Meijer, 1994; Ter Linden & Harder, 1997). The long-term goal was to increase parents' SLN proficiency beyond the introductory level. To date, only Levels 1–4 have been developed, with no major or substantive changes to these courses.

Policy statements also indicate the status of the two languages. In 2003, the Policy Nota was developed by Koninklijk Effatha Guyot Group (KEGG), a predecessor of Kentalis. This policy was linked to school language choices and noted the importance of presenting spoken Dutch and SLN as equal in status. Also stated in the policy is that parents have the final responsibility in both raising and educating their deaf child. Furthermore, the policy emphasizes the importance of providing parents with unbiased information, conducting more research for optimizing language input, neutralizing the longstanding oralism-versus-manualism debate in teaching methods, and starting an open dialogue with parents concerning their needs (KEGG, 2003). In the Policy Nota, there are no further notifications, comments or actions related to parents' courses (KEGG, 2003). In Spring 2011, in communication with the six mothers, we concluded that, so far, no comprehensive, updated language framework had been implemented in the courses.

Exchange of Thoughts with Parents who Initiated our Study

The six original parents were surprised to discover that an updated language framework was not available. They felt that learning SLN should be as established as and similar to learning English as an L2. After learning several sign vocabulary lists in the old parent courses, the parent participants began to understand that they had barely learned the syntactical, semantic and morphological features of SLN. They started to contest Knoors' (2011) view that SLN was too difficult to acquire by pointing out that the lack of a clear sign language pedagogical framework had resulted in a pedagogy that overemphasized vocabulary learning. At the same time, a discussion about language status started: if no clear language teaching methodology is offered, does this mean that SLN as a language is withheld from parents, resulting in a regression to SSD courses?

The parents in this study requested that the advanced courses include an appropriate language framework comparable to other L2 courses in spoken/written languages. Moreover, in using communicative language pedagogical approaches, parents would be empowered as autonomous, independent language users and therefore better enabled to parent their deaf children. These approaches included, for example, how to: discuss; explain options; use listening behaviors and techniques; learn question-reply and turn-taking exchanges; provide an overview; and deal with, explain and manage conflicts with siblings. These approaches also included ways of supporting deaf children in their own continuous bimodal (SLN and Dutch) language acquisition. The acquisition of SLN should enable parents not only to communicate with their deaf child but also to achieve parent-child pedagogical communication skills to the fullest extent possible.

Overall, seeing parents as plurilingual and pluricultural beings meant allowing them to use all their linguistic resources and encouraging them to see similarities and regularities as well as differences between languages and cultures (Council of Europe, 2018: 27). A purposeful, pragmatic and action-oriented approach framework seemed to match their needs.

After an in-depth investigation of various language frameworks, the *Common European Framework of Reference for Languages* (CEFR) seemed to provide the best support for the parents of deaf children. The Council of Europe's ideas for developing a CEFR have existed since 1991. The CEFR was officially launched in 2001 and is now available in 40

European and non-European languages (Council of Europe, 2001). In the period from 2008 to 2013, a research team called ATERK NGT (2013), based in the Netherlands, worked on applying the CEFR to sign languages. An English version of the CEFR for Sign Languages can be found on the European Centre for Modern Languages website (Leeson *et al.*, 2016). It is important to note that this version was developed for professional purposes, that is, for sign language interpreters. One of the designers of the new parent courses was a consortium member of ATERK NGT. Thus, the developmental team could rely on this experience in developing new parent courses.

New System: Mapping the CEFR for Sign Languages

The CEFR and its benchmarks hold much promise for innovation in L2 teaching and learning, as they are rooted in the concept of a language learner as a social agent who develops long-term communicative competences while achieving everyday goals (Council of Europe, 2001). The CEFR makes the following provisions:

> The Common European Framework provides a common basis for the elaboration of language syllabuses, curriculum guidelines, examinations, textbooks, etc. across Europe. It describes in a comprehensive way what language learners have to learn to do in order to use a language for communication and what knowledge and skills they have to develop so as to be able to act effectively. The description also covers the cultural context in which language is set. The Framework also defines levels of proficiency which allow learners' progress to be measured at each stage of learning and on a life-long basis. (Council of Europe, 2001: 1)

This framework presents a comprehensive descriptive scheme of language proficiency (two fundamental proficiency aspects are mentioned: what the learner can do and how well they perform), and a set of common reference levels. The CEFR sets out to ensure that there is harmony between its components: (i) identification of needs; (ii) determination of objects; (iii) definition of content; (iv) selection or creation of material; (v) establishment of teaching/learning programs; (vi) the teaching and learning methods employed; and (vii) evaluation, testing and assessment (Council of Europe, 2001, 2018).

Sign language learners can develop various levels of proficiency (see Figure 8.1). The CEFR describes this as a ladder consisting of three general levels: the Beginner Level A for Basic User, the Intermediate Level B for Independent User and the Advanced Level C for Proficient User.

Within each level, the learner participates in sign language acquisition exercises in three sub-areas: (1) production, (2) understanding and (3) interaction (ATERK NGT, 2013; Leeson *et al.*, 2016). A fourth sub-area dealing with mediation has since been added (Council of Europe, 2018).

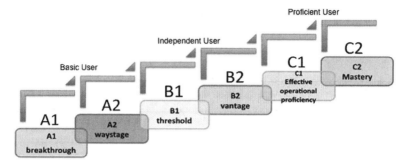

Figure 8.1 The language acquisition level ladder

Additionally, ATERK NGT pointed out that 'the learner engages with native signers and the success of that is evaluated by how successful this interaction is' (ATERK NGT, 2013: 10). The ongoing practice hours in these sub-areas focus on grammatical correctness, articulation, coherence, vocabulary and fluency, which are important for advancing up the CEFR staircase. The learner develops communication skills that are subsequently tested with the teacher as a native signer who provides directed support in the learning process. The CEFR tasks are described as can-do statements in the above-mentioned three sub-areas: what you can do in or with the target language, and knowing how to do it correctly (see Leeson *et al.*, 2016, for examples of can-do statements for sign languages). Through these can-do statements, the learner acquires SLN competences in a series of smaller steps. With this list of competences, parents are assured that the guiding principles of the curriculum are based on plurilingual pedagogical practices. Being plurilingual and having pluricultural competencies are described by the Council of Europe (2001: 168) thus: '[plurilingualism] refers to the ability to use languages for the purpose of communication and to take part in intercultural interaction, where a person, viewed as a social agent has proficiency, of varying degrees, in several languages and experience of several cultures'.

Plurilingualism is presented in the CEFR as a confluence of uneven and changing competences in which the user/learner's resources in one language or variety may be very different from linguistic repertories held by other users/learners. The CEFR posits that plurilinguals have a *single*, interrelated linguistic repertoire that they combine with their general competences and use of various strategies in order to accomplish tasks (Council of Europe, 2018: 28). Thus, learning language enables one to communicate with others through performing everyday linguistic tasks. Purposeful action in learning language is therefore central (North, 2017). The CEFR is action oriented in its approach. Tasks must therefore have a relevant context. In carrying out the task, the parent must have a goal (not just a language goal). There must be a desired outcome for this goal and support for the development of learner competences by performing real-life tasks. The CEFR system is flexible, dynamic, freely interpreted, easily applied and adaptable to any parent's needs. For parents as everyday care-givers of deaf children, there is continuity in undertaking courses developed within the CEFR framework. The numbers of guided learning hours, as stated by the Association of Language Testers in Europe (ALTE) guidelines, allows for more practice in acquiring language (see Cambridge English, n.d.). In progressing from beginner CEFR levels to Level B2, or Independent User, a learner needs a minimum number of guided learning hours to progress. For the English language, according to ALTE guidelines, this is approximately 500–600 hours (Cambridge English, n.d.). The number of hours for the acquisition of sign languages is not yet described within the CEFR. The number of guided learning hours needed for a sign language learner to reach all B2 level can-do statements remains an open question.

It is furthermore important to note here that deaf schools in the Netherlands are already familiar with the CEFR because Kentalis was a consortium member of ATERK NGT. The CEFR is used for assessing the SLN proficiency levels of professionals working at deaf schools. Courses such as Breakthrough (*Doorbraak*) and Waystage 1 and 2 (*Tussenstap 1 en 2*) were established, with A2 as the last level to be achieved. Recent inquiries indicate that no substantive major changes have been made to implement the CEFR in parent courses from Levels 1–3.

The next section will describe the methodology used to collect data from parent participants.

Data and Methodology

To our knowledge, no previous study has investigated correlations between sign language pedagogy and the development of CEFR-based courses. These correlations were addressed in the current study following three selected regional groups undertaking a CEFR-aligned course, WeSign4, that was developed by the authors of this chapter.

Our focus was on measuring outcomes associated with WeSign4 to make sure it worked for all parents regardless of geographical region. Not all groups who completed the first Level 4 course received access to the additional three follow-up courses (WeSign5–7). Thus, comparing results for WeSign5–7 was impossible. Due to extended waiting times after taking Levels 1–3 of the old parent courses (see Figure 8.4), we could not determine a uniform CEFR level for individual participants prior to taking WeSign4. Consequently, we decided to start with the hypothesis that participants would become familiar with a new language learning framework. This familiarity can be measured at the end of the WeSign4 course, thus indicating the validity of this framework for parents' learning. The completion of WeSign4 is insufficient for parents to reach CEFR Level B2, or Independent User. WeSign4 is only the start of a continuous learning trajectory to reach B2 level that includes WeSign 5–6–7 courses.

This empirical mixed-methods study was guided by the following questions:

(1) Which SLN level do parents achieve after they have finished an advanced SLN course (WeSign4) designed according to the CEFR and based on the action-oriented approach of supporting communicative competences?
(2) Upon completion of the course, what do parents report concerning their communications with their deaf children in the home?
(3) What learning needs did the participants express during the course?

Procedure and materials

In order to investigate these questions, multiple forms of data collection took place using the following: (1) a WeSign4 outcome assessment of parents' learning by teachers; (2) a CEFR self-assessment grid filled out by parent participants; and (3) an overall course evaluation form filled out by parent participants. These assessments were administered during the last session of WeSign4 for the first group of six parent participants. This procedure was repeated for the second and third groups who participated in this course. Data concerning waiting time between participants' completion of Level 3 of the old parent course system and the start of WeSign4 are included in addition to the number of dropouts.

The first group in Zoetermeer started with a 15-week WeSign4 course. Classes met once a week for 2.5 hours per session in the Fall and Winter of 2012. This was taught by a team of two qualified deaf native signer teachers, one of whom is a SLN teacher and linguist and the other a pedagogy specialist. This procedure was identical for the second and third groups that respectively met in Rotterdam and Utrecht. After finishing WeSign4, the participants could continue with WeSign5, 6 and 7. Parents were recruited by the six initial mothers from within their support networks using a snowball sampling method via a Facebook group for parents of deaf children (Stichting InfoDeSK, 2017) where WeSign4 information was posted. Parents were also recruited via a social network at deaf schools and through deaf children's activities.

Each new course in the series WeSign4–7 was developed according to the CEFR. Themes for classes were selected and disseminated throughout WeSign4–7. Parents practiced language learning activities at home on a daily basis. This made it possible for them to reflect on the can-do statements and whether they had achieved their individual goals. To this end, teachers' emphasis during class sessions on parenting communicative tools encouraged the parents to practice using vocabulary and sentences in the context of their daily linguistic environments. As discussed above, the content of each session was designed to meet the goal-oriented approach of the learners.

Table 8.1 Participant rates

	Zoetermeer $n = 11$	Rotterdam $n = 10$	Utrecht $n = 13$	Total $n = 34$
Started WeSign4	11 (100%)	10 (100%)	13 (100%)	34 (100%)
Dropouts	1 (9%)	3 (30%)	6 (46%)	10 (30%)
Finished WeSign4	10 (91%)	7 (70%)	7 (44%)	24 (70%)

Participants

The parents who completed the WeSign4 course were divided into three groups ($n = 24$) based on geographical location. As shown in Table 8.1, originally 34 parent participants enrolled, and 10 dropped out. During WeSign4, 30% of participants dropped out between the first and fifth sessions. The dropout rate was highest in the Utrecht area at 46%, or six out of 13 parents, followed by three out of 10 (30%) in Rotterdam and one out of 11 (9%) in Zoetermeer. The reasons for discontinuation of the courses are reported in the section below regarding parents' experiences and learning needs.

Children of the participants

Twenty-one children (eight boys and 13 girls, all with cochlear implants) may have been affected by their parents' SLN learning. Eight children attended mainstream schools, nine were in a deaf school and four were enrolled in deaf school programs for deaf children with additional disabilities (see Table 8.2). Parents' decisions to learn SLN appear not to be directly correlated with the type of educational program where their deaf children are enrolled.

In the next three sections of this chapter, we will describe how the assessment instruments were administered and the resulting data.

Step 1: Teacher assessments

The teachers assessed the progress of the parents following the six levels of the CEFR using Low, Medium and High sub-ratings, which

Table 8.2 Numbers of deaf children attending types of program per region

Program type	Zoetermeer $n = 11$	Rotterdam $n = 4$	Utrecht $n = 6$
Mainstream	4 (36%)	0 (0%)	4 (67%)
Deaf school	4 (36%)	4 (100%)	1 (17%)
Deaf school for children with additional disabilities	3 (27%)	0 (0%)	1 (17%)

allowed for scoring in 18 subcategories. The scores were then averaged to provide parents' achieved level. A descriptive CEFR-level rating was preferred instead of a numeric assessment, which can appear more static. One of the problems with the old parent courses was that they did not include assessments because professionals did not want to pressure parents concerning their SLN competencies (Harder & Meijer, 1994; Ter Linden & Harder, 1997). This is solved by using descriptive evaluative statements within these 18 subcategories within CEFR proficiency levels that provide a more qualitative assessment of learning progress and needs.

The parents' CEFR proficiency levels can be measured by checking the total number of can-do descriptors for each CEFR level we adapted, first from ATERK NGT (2013) and later from Leeson (2008) and Leeson *et al.* (2016) in the areas of production, comprehension and interaction. The 15th session of WeSign4 focused on the final assessment. Parents were divided into pairs and were assessed for approximately 40 minutes. Each assessment task was first explained in SLN, then in written Dutch so that they were able to check their understanding of the required task. Table 8.3 shows an overview of the assessment tasks. The production and interaction tasks were recorded with a video camera for later assessment.

Step 2: Self-assessment grid

During the 15th session of WeSign4, parents received a self-assessment grid with common reference levels as described in ATERK NGT (2013: 21–28). Each CEFR level from A1 to C2 has an associated scale with the competences of production (live and recorded), comprehension (live and recorded) and interaction (live). The parent participants' task was to individually complete this grid during the last 20 minutes of the 15th session, without consulting each other or their teacher. For each area, they were required to indicate their perceptions of what they had achieved. When reviewing the categories presented, they were asked to indicate which level

Table 8.3 WeSign4 assessment tasks

No.	Competence	Task description
1	Comprehension: 2-minute narrative	Participant is twice shown a short narrative film. Participant responds in writing to questions about the narrative.
2	Production: narrative	Participant creates a story using vocabulary from the course. Recorded on camera.
3	Comprehension vocabulary	Participant is shown a list of vocabulary items twice on video and responds to questions in writing.
4	Interaction in pairs	Participants receive different kinds of tasks, including role-play scenarios with pretend parent/child dyads. Each participant has to complete this task twice, once as a parent and once as a child. Recorded on camera.

(Low, Medium, High) they felt they had reached. Afterwards, their level was calculated through an average of the parents' self-assessments. This grid allows one to indicate their achievement of the can-do statements. For example, a self-assessment of High A2 means that a participant believes that they have reached the upper level of A2 but have not yet made the transition to Low B1.

Step 3: Evaluation form

To assess the content and quality of WeSign4, all parents were asked to fill out an evaluation form presented as a 5-point Likert scale. This form asked parents to indicate their level of agreement, with 1 = I do not agree; 2 = neutral; 3 = I agree; 4 = I totally agree; 5 = not filled in/user missing (Likert, 1932). The evaluation form consisted of 26 questions, including: 'I'm confident that I can apply what I've learned in the course'; 'I'm more confident in communicating with my child'; 'The CEFR course WeSign4 was very helpful for me'; 'This course is very different from earlier courses'; and three open-ended questions. To avoid bias, all participants were required to fill out the form without consulting one another or the teacher. This form did not request personal information.

The questions were organized into the following eight categories:

(1) Learning process, including questions about communication, vocabulary and application of what was learned in class.
(2) Evaluating the degree of difficulty of WeSign4 content.
(3) Satisfaction with the classroom facilities.
(4) Satisfaction with the teacher's role and quality of instruction.
(5) Satisfaction with online video content.
(6) Comparisons between the old parent courses and WeSign4.
(7) Suggestions for the content of WeSign4.
(8) Suitability of WeSign4 for other parents of deaf children.

Hereafter, the parents were asked to respond to three open-ended questions concerning their overall perception of the WeSign4 course: (1) positive aspects, (2) constructive criticism and (3) additional comments. Some of the responses to the 26 questions in this evaluation in the Zoetermeer, Rotterdam and Utrecht regions are highlighted in the next section.

Results

Step 1: Teacher assessments

The results of the assessment as displayed in Figure 8.2 show that most parents ($n = 13$) who completed WeSign4 achieved the High A2 level representing the upper end of the A2 level. This performance represents a strong Waystage performance for a Basic (A1–A2) User of SLN, but not

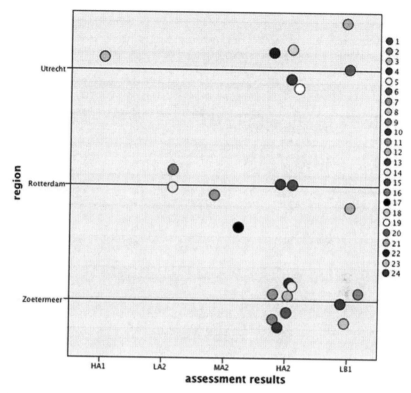

Figure 8.2 WeSign4 teacher assessment level (n = 24)

yet an Independent User (B1). The Low B1 level, which six participants achieved, reflects the Threshold level, which can be seen as the start of being an Independent User. Others who achieved High A1 (Breakthrough), Low A2 and Medium A2 (Waystage) levels are all Basic Users.

Step 2: Self-assessment grid

We collected self-assessment grids from 20 out of 24 parents. Four Zoetermeer-based parents did not hand in their forms. For this first group in Zoetermeer, we decided that completion of the self-assessment grid was voluntary. Figure 8.3 shows nine parents whom the teachers assessed as being High A2 level; one indicated in their self-assessment that they had reached High A2. Others rated themselves as having achieved higher levels: Low B1 (one), Medium B1 (four), High B1 (two) and High B2 (one). These are the Threshold and Vantage levels for Independent User. When analyzing the Low B1 assessments, we found there were six participants whose scores varied significantly.

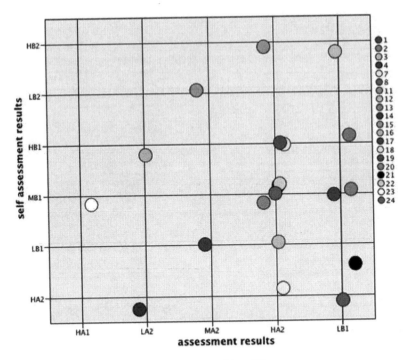

Figure 8.3 Results of the self-assessment grid (n = 20)

Looking at the distribution of scores, some discrepancy is visible between the parents' self-reporting of their acquired skills and evaluation of those skills by their teachers. Most parents self-evaluated their SLN competencies as being higher than the teachers' assessments. WeSign4 appeared to increase parents' confidence, as they stated they felt comfortable with the CEFR alignment of WeSign4. We noted that use of the self-assessment grid appeared to increase parents' confidence with their SLN skills.

Step 3: Evaluation form results

We collected completed evaluation forms from 22 out of 24 parents. Two parents did not hand in the form. Of the 22 evaluations, when asked to indicate their agreement with the statement 'I'm satisfied with the WeSign4 course', four parents checked 'Agree' and 17 selected 'Totally agree'. The remaining parent indicated a neutral response. Eleven respondents indicated that they agreed with the statement, 'I feel more able to communicate in-depth with my child'. Eleven additional parent participants selected 'Totally agree' as a response to this statement. Regarding the statement, 'This course is very different from earlier courses', eight parents selected 'Agree' and 14 parents chose 'Totally agree'. These results, which also answer the first of the three questions of the mixed-methods study (see Data and Methodology section) provide important insights into the second and third questions regarding specific experiences and learning needs of parents. These will be further outlined in the next section.

What are the parents' experiences and learning needs during the CEFR-aligned courses?

The parents described four key experiences during the WeSign4 course. First, they stated in the evaluation form that WeSign4 was fundamentally different from the sign language courses they had taken previously. Learning SLN in WeSign4 was more holistic because it was not focused on only learning vocabulary lists of signs. Second, in conversations with the teachers, all parent participants stated that after attending four or five sessions of WeSign4, they became aware of how to apply pedagogical strategies learned in class during interactions with their deaf children. They reported that old courses did not allow for this pedagogical awareness and attributed this difference to the application of the CEFR. For instance, this application enabled some key components in understanding their child's world: communication strategies, language use, language modelling, language tuition and information sharing.

Third, the parent participants stated that the problem-solving approach to their acquisition of SLN for use with their deaf children enabled the parents to be more creative and open to taking risks. Upon completion of WeSign4, parents verbally reported higher levels of motivation to complete their homework assignments, as they felt empowered through the application of pedagogical practices in communication with their deaf children. As teachers, we found that we needed to structure lessons to empower parents in applying their new knowledge when interacting with their children.

Finally, conversations with parents who dropped out of the course revealed four reasons for their decision: (1) an extended waiting time following completion of old parent courses (see Figure 8.4); (2) the lack of a unified system for continuous language learning in the old courses and the new course; (3) the feeling that they were too late in learning SLN because they were so used to learning isolated signs in the old course system, and WeSign4 felt very new and disorienting; and (4) the feeling of being too late in choosing to learn SLN, and thus SLN input for their deaf child was irrelevant because their child hardly signed at home but used speech only.

Concerning their learning needs, parents discussed several areas. First, it is important to learn a language according to a system that offers recognition of the sign language learning process, applicability to parents' situations and accessibility for parents. For example, in learning English, there is a profusion of learning materials available through

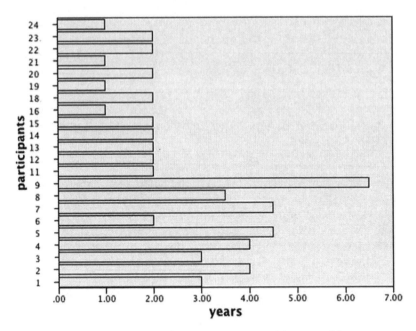

Figure 8.4 Waiting times as an influence in parent participant attrition

publishing companies, English as an additional language classes and the internet. For learning SLN, learning resources were limited. The implementation of the CEFR in the new parents' courses offered a clear structure and applicability to parents' situations. Related to accessibility, parents stated there still is a great need to develop these courses with additional printed, tangible learning materials, as well as more digital SLN resources for practicing. Second, parent participants expressed that they had come to understand that they were not only learning a second language but, more importantly, a second modality. This must be stated and included in sign language teaching. Third, it is important for parents of deaf children to reach the level of an autonomous, independent (B1–B2) sign language user.

The issues raised in this section confirm the urgency of establishing a solid and consistent language learning framework that matches the specific learning and communicative needs of parents.

Conclusion

The testing of the WeSign4 course revealed that if parents are offered a clear structure and CEFR action-oriented learning goals, obtaining the level of the Independent User (B2; see Figure 8.1) is possible. It is important to realize that parents are and remain L2 learners of SLN, so typical

L2 characteristics and occasional small errors will appear. Given these points, our hypothesis that parents would become familiar with and benefit from a new language learning framework through the WeSign4 course turned out to be justified.

Plurilingualism is the key to language learning, especially for parents of deaf children. Before the courses, participating parents repeatedly confirmed that they wanted to see SLN acquisition on an equivalent footing with the acquisition of any other language. The concept of plurilingualism sees sign language as contributing to the child's own identity and also to parents' identities. The parents in our classes argued that the broadening of the 'individual language spectrum' should be a choice made available to them. The CEFR as a language learning framework emphasizes a plurilingual repertoire and action-oriented language learning and therefore fits well with this target group.

Parents argue that recognition of the sign language learning process, accessibility of parent SLN courses and applicability of their learning to their individual situations are important links in the chain of their acquisition of a new language. While parent participants may have varied individually in learning pace and level, the CEFR can-do statements presented in each class made their learning progress visible while at the same time giving new insights and guidance concerning the building of linguistic repertoires. An indispensable insight related to the recognizability of the sign language learning process was parents' appreciation of a new modality involved in SLN learning. Incorporating the new modality as an essential component is different from simply naming it. It allows parents to better understand the nature of their deaf child's language repertoire. This positively influences parents' motivation to learn SLN. Sign language learning remains a challenge, but parents now understand that the extra 'layer' of challenge comes from this second modality. The WeSign4 courses' focus on supporting fluency turns out to be valuable for parents. The applicability of parents' learning becomes concrete through instruction provided in the classes followed by further practice in home environments.

We make the recommendations that future parents' sign language courses should be situated within a clear language learning framework, that the unique learning needs of parents as L2 learners be considered when designing such courses and that the challenges in using a second modality are recognized.

For future directions, more research must be directed towards the profile of parents of deaf children as a unique target group in L2 sign language learning. The development of a concrete profile can lead to better meeting the specific learning needs of parents. It is important that the worldwide deaf community works closely together with these hearing new signers as a means for the preservation of sign languages.

Acknowledgements

The authors wish to extend their gratitude towards all parents who participated. Without the support of the mentioned six initiating mothers, the 'WeSign' project would not be possible. Special thanks go to our cooperation partner Kristin Snoddon for her efforts for Canadian parents and her warm support. This study was not supported by any direct research grant.

References

ATERK NGT (2013) Het Europees Referentiekader voor Talen: Gebarentalen. Manuscript. See https://www.academia.edu/3748474/ATERK_NGT_2013_Europees_Referentiekader_voor_Talen_Gebarentalen_CEFR_CEFR_for_Sign_Languages_Dutch_version (accessed 30 March 2018).

Bruin, M. and Nevøy, A. (2014) Exploring the discourse on communication modality after cochlear implantation: A Foucauldian analysis of parents' narratives. *Journal of Deaf Studies and Deaf Education* 19 (3), 385–399.

Calderon, R. (2000) Parental involvement in deaf children's education programs as a predictor of child's language, early reading, and social-emotional development. *Journal of Deaf Studies and Deaf Education* 5 (2), 140–155.

Cambridge English (n.d.) *Guided Learning Hours.* See https://support.cambridgeenglish.org/hc/en-gb/articles/202838506-Guided-learning-hours (accessed 27 April 2020).

Council of Europe (2001) *Common European Framework of Reference for Languages: Learning, Teaching, Assessment.* Strasbourg: Language Policy Unit. See http://www.coe.int/t/dg4/linguistic/source/framework_en.pdf (accessed 15 November 2017).

Council of Europe (2018) *Common European Framework of Reference for Languages: Learning, teaching, assessment. Companion Volume with new descriptors.* Strasbourg: Language Policy Unit. See https://rm.coe.int/cefr-companion-volume-with-new-descriptors-2018/1680787989 (accessed 5 August 2019).

De Meulder, M. (2019) 'So, why do you sign?' Deaf and hearing new signers, their motivation, and revitalization policies for sign languages. *Applied Linguistics Review* 10 (4), 705–724. doi:10.1515/applirev-2017-0100

Dirks, E., Vermeij, B., Uilenberg, N. and Bogaers, I. (2013) Taalbeleid binnen de gezinsbegeleiding voor kinderen met een auditieve beperking. *Van Horen Zeggen* 4, 10–18.

Dutch Sign Centre (1994) *NGT-cursus voor ouders van dove kinderen, module1.* Amsterdam: NGc.

Dutch Sign Centre (1995) *NGT-cursus voor ouders van dove kinderen, module2.* Amsterdam: NGc.

Dutch Sign Centre (1997) *NGT-cursus voor ouders van dove kinderen, module3.* Amsterdam: NGc.

Dutch Sign Centre (1998) *NGT-cursus voor ouders van dove kinderen, module4.* Amsterdam: NGc.

Grosjean, F. (2001) The right of the deaf child to grow up bilingual. *Sign Language Studies* 1 (2), 110–114.

Harder, R. and Meijer, E. (1994) Sign language courses for hearing parents of Deaf children in the Netherlands. In H. Bos and T. Schermer (eds) *Sign Language Research 1994: Proceedings of the Fourth European Congress on Sign Language Research, Munich, September 1–3* (pp. 273–283). Hamburg: Signum.

Hoiting, N. (2010) Communicatie en taal maken deel uit van een heel mensenleven. *Van Horen Zeggen* 2, 8–9.

Humphries, T., Kushalnagar, P., Mathur, G., Napoli, D.J., Padden, C., Rathmann, C. and Smith, S.R. (2012) Language acquisition for deaf children: Reducing the harms of zero tolerance to the use of alternative approaches. *Harm Reduction Journal* 9 (16), 2–9. doi:10.1186/1477-7517-9-16

Humphries, T., Kushalnagar, P., Mathur, G., Napoli, D.J., Padden, C. and Rathmann, C. (2014) Ensuring language acquisition for deaf children: What linguists can do. Linguistic Society of America. *Language* 90 (2), 31–52.

Humphries, T., Kushalnagar, P., Mathur, G., Napoli, D.J., Padden, C., Rathmann, C. and Smith, S.R. (2015) Language choices for deaf infants: Advice for parents regarding sign languages. *Clinical Pediatrics* 55 (6), 513–517.

Knoors, H. (2011) Herijkt taalbeleid voor dove kinderen. *Van Horen Zeggen* 52 (4), 10–19.

Knoors, H. and Marschark, M. (2012) Language planning for the 21st century: Revisiting bilingual language policy for deaf children. *Journal for Deaf Studies and Deaf Education* 17 (3), 291–305.

Knoors, H.E.T. (2016) Foundations for language development in deaf children and the consequences for communication choices. In M. Marschark and P.E. Spencer (eds) *The Oxford Handbook of Deaf Studies in Language* (pp. 19–31). Oxford: Oxford University Press. See http://dx.doi.org/10.1093/oxfordhb/9780190241414.013.2.

KEGG (Koninklijk Effatha Guyot Groep) (1997) *Project Invoering Tweetaligheid.* Blauwdruk Notitie. Groningen: Koninklijk Instituut voor Doven H.D. Guyot.

Koninklijk Effatha Guyot Groep (2003) *Zorg en Onderwijs aan Dove kinderen met een Cochleair Implantaat.* Beleidsnota. Groningen: KEGG.

Leeson, L. (2008) *Note on the Adjustments Required for the Inclusion of Irish Sign Language into the Common European Reference Framework for Language.* Dublin: Trinity College.

Leeson, L., van den Bogaerde, B., Rathmann, C. and Haug, T. (2016) *Sign Languages and the Common European Framework of References for Languages. Common Reference Level Descriptors.* Graz: ECML. See http://www.ecml.at/Portals/1/mtp4/pro-sign/documents/Common-Reference-Level-Descriptors-EN.pdf (accessed 15 November 2017).

Lentz, E.M., Mikos, K. and Smith, C. (1988) *Sign Naturally.* Vista American Sign Language series. San Diego, CA: Dawn Sign Press.

Likert, R. (1932) A technique for the measurement of attitudes. *Archives of Psychology* 140, 1–55.

Mayer, C. and Leigh, G. (2010) The changing context for sign bilingual education programs: Issues in language and the development of literacy. *International Journal of Bilingual Education and Bilingualism* 13 (2), 175–186.

Napier, J., Leigh, G. and Nann, S. (2007) Teaching sign language to hearing parents of deaf children: An action research process. *Deafness & Education International* 9 (2), 83–100. doi:10.1179/146431507790560020

Nilsson, A. and Schönström, K. (2014) Development and impacts of sign language teaching. In D. McKee, R.S. Rosen and R. McKee (eds) *Teaching and Learning Signed Languages: International Perspectives and Practices* (pp. 11–34). Basingstoke: Palgrave MacMillan.

North, B. (2017) The CEFR: Innovative aspects and new developments. Presentation at the Lesico International Conference of Sign Language Teachers, Basel, Switzerland.

Oyserman, J. and de Geus, M.D. (2013) Hearing L2 parents and the fluency in sign language communication. Poster presented at the TISLR 11: Eleventh International Conference on Theoretical Issues in Sign Language Research, University College London. doi:10.13140/RG.2.2.31011.55848

Prinzi, L. (2007) Motivation and second language learning: Implications for ASL. Thesis, Rochester Institute of Technology.

Rosen, R.S. (2011) Modality and language in the second language acquisition of American Sign Language. In G. Mathur and D.J. Napoli (eds) *Deaf Around the World: The Impact of Language* (pp. 1–7). Oxford Scholarship Online. doi:10.1093/acprof:oso/9780199732548.001.0001

Schermer, T. (2012) Sign language planning in the Netherlands between 1980 and 2010. *Sign Language Studies* 12 (4), 467–493.

Smith, C. (1988) Sign naturally: Notes on the development of ASL Curriculum Project at Vista College. *Sign Language Studies* 59, 171–182. doi:10.1353/sls.1988.0001

Snoddon, K. (2014) Hearing parents as plurilingual learners of ASL. In D. McKee, R.S. Rosen and R. McKee (eds) *Teaching and Learning Signed Languages: International Perspectives and Practices* (pp. 175–196). Basingstoke: Palgrave MacMillan.

Snoddon, K. (2015) Using the Common European Framework of Reference for Languages to teach sign language to parents of deaf children. *The Canadian Modern Language Review/La Revue Canadienne des Langues vivantes* 71 (3), 270–287.

Stichting Infodesk (2017) *Informatiecentrum over Dove en Slechthorende Kinderen*. See https://stichtinginfodesk.nl/ (accessed 15 April 2018).

Stokoe, W., Croneberg, C. and Casterline, D. (1965) *A Dictionary of American Sign Language on Linguistic Principles*. Washington, DC: Gallaudet University Press.

Ter Linden, R. and Harder, R. (1997) Ontwikkeling en evaluatie van cursussen Nederlandse Gebarentaal aan ouders en leerkrachten van dove kinderen. In M. Hoefnagel and H. van der Neut (eds) *WAP Symposium, Taal, communicatie, gehoor* (pp. 93–112). Dordrecht: ICG Printing.

Tervoort, B.T. (1983) *Hand over Hand: Nieuwe inzichten in de communicatie van doven*. Muiderberg: Coutinho.

Van der Linde, M. and Frieswijk, J. (2013) *De Volkshogeschool in Nederland, 1925–2010* (pp. 251–256). Hilversum: Verloren.

Young, A.M. (1997) *Conceptualizing Parents' Sign Language Use in Bilingual Early Intervention*. Oxford: Oxford University Press.

9 Family Language Policy and Planning: Families with Deaf Children

Julie Mitchiner and Christi Batamula

This chapter discusses a Family Language Policy (FLP) and planning framework in relation to families' language practices, language beliefs and attitudes, and language management with their young Deaf children. Family members are the key participants who create plans as well as policies for language practices within the family setting. Therefore, families play a critical role in facilitating children's language development. The chapter discusses potential factors influencing families' decisions and language choices for Deaf and hard-of-hearing children. The authors also share steps for collaborating with families in developing language plans to foster plurilingual development. In order for the family language plan to be successful and to better understand families' beliefs, perspectives and attitudes about language, professionals must learn about the family, including their experiences acquiring and learning language. The family language plan is a tool that can be used to help families support their children's plurilingual development in sign language and written and/or spoken (when appropriate) languages.

Introduction

Early hearing detection services in hospitals and doctors' offices have led to early identification of children as Deaf or hard of hearing (JCIH, 2007). The term 'Deaf' refers to a person who is Deaf or hard of hearing, and the 'capitalization of Deaf brings within it the true recognition that all Deaf and hard-of-hearing children have a birthright to ASL, Deaf culture, healthy identity and being a part of the Deaf community' (Miller, 2015: Slide 64). Early identification is critical because the sooner the child is identified, the sooner the child can be provided with an accessible language. This process works well for families who are Deaf or who are fluent in sign language; however, statistics confirm that 90–95% of Deaf or hard-of-hearing children are born to hearing families (Karchmer &

Mitchell, 2004). For many of these families, their Deaf or hard-of-hearing child is the first Deaf person they have ever met. This has vast and critical implications for the language development of a young child. Without an understanding of what it means to be Deaf, families may hold a framework of being Deaf as a loss, which is affirmed through medical language such as 'hearing loss' (Snoddon, 2008). With this mindset, there is a push to help the child access spoken language to correct the perceived disability (Hehir, 2002; Hintermair, 2006). From an alternate point of view, Deaf-gain is a positive framework, recognizing the benefits that come with being Deaf (Bauman & Murray, 2014). Early identification is critical because it allows families and professionals to immediately provide accessible language to the Deaf child. With early language access, Deaf children have the same opportunities as their hearing peers to develop language skills and an understanding of the world around them.

After early identification, families face unique challenges, such as going through an adjustment process and especially deciding among language and communication opportunities. These decisions rely on various factors, including political and sociocultural pressures and parents' own experiences, attitudes and beliefs regarding languages. Families, often faced with concerns and feelings of uncertainty, turn to professionals for advice and direction (Young, 2010). Families with Deaf children frequently receive information and suggestions from professionals about deafness and language choices that are predominantly from a deficit view of deafness instead of from a cultural and social perspective (Hyde & Power, 2006; Li et al., 2003; Young et al., 2006). This means the information shared with families is typically based on the biased beliefs and attitudes of professionals, educators and specialists who work with Deaf children and their families (Li et al., 2003). As a result, families often receive recommendations for auditory-verbal approaches, especially for children with cochlear implants, and signed language is viewed as a last resort (Hintermair & Albertini, 2005; Knoors & Marschark, 2012). This means that if children are not successful in developing spoken language during their early years, they may experience language deprivation (Hall et al., 2017, 2019). When children are not provided with accessible language during the critical period of learning, their cognitive, linguistic and social development may be compromised (Mayberry, 2007). There is a concern that families who choose to use only spoken language with their Deaf child may increase the risks of language deprivation (Humphries et al., 2012; Kushalnagar et al., 2010; Murray et al., 2020). Spoken language, even with technological assistance, is often not fully accessible. In contrast, when a Deaf child has full access to sign language, they are not deprived of language but rather given a gift that will empower them to thrive linguistically, socially and academically.

There are conflicting perspectives on what it means to be Deaf between and within the Deaf community and the dominant culture. These perspectives, as well as beliefs about being Deaf and about language, impact how Deaf children acquire language and view themselves as Deaf individuals. In addition, there are a wide range of individuals who are Deaf with diverse backgrounds, auditory access and ways of being Deaf. This adds another level of complexity in decision making. These issues have made it difficult for families with Deaf children to navigate the often complicated and controversial world of early intervention and Deaf education. A Family Language Policy (FLP) framework (King et al., 2008) can provide an enhanced understanding of how families with Deaf children come to have their own beliefs and perspectives and, alternatively, a policy framework can invite families to examine and potentially transform their own language ideologies.

It is imperative for professionals to be ready to step in and provide direction that will give the Deaf child immediate and full access to language. However, simply telling a family how to support their child's language development is not sufficient. In making decisions, the families need to be dynamically involved in partnership with the professional. Each family needs guidance with developing an FLP. It is important to remember that each family has their own 'funds of knowledge', or a wealth of background knowledge and experience, culture and community practices that influence the child's identity and development (Moll et al., 1992). An important step for the professional is to learn and integrate the family's funds of knowledge as they develop a language plan for their child. This plan also needs to be tailored to the specific needs and goals of the family in order to be successful. For example, simply saying that the goal is plurilingualism does not mean that the child or family members will become plurilingual. Having a plan ensures that the families have a better understanding of how to raise a plurilingual child in a way that is comfortable and natural. Having a positive, Deaf-gain framework of the Deaf child as having unique gifts and skills that come with being Deaf, as well as a plan to provide a plurilingual, accessible environment for the child, will empower both Deaf children and their families. In this chapter, we will discuss our FLP framework and the potential factors influencing family decisions and language choices for Deaf and hard-of-hearing children. The term 'families' is used to refer to the adults who are responsible for contributing to the care and wellbeing of and making educational decisions for the child. It is intended to be inclusive of diverse family units and could include parents in the traditional sense, guardians, and extended family members such as aunts, uncles, grandparents or others.

FLP Framework

The FLP framework stems from studies of language acquisition and language policy within hearing families (King & Fogle, 2013). It explores language use patterns and literacy practices in the home environment with immediate and extended family members. The FLP framework examines: (1) family language ideologies, (2) family language practice and (3) language management within the family (King & Fogle, 2013; Schwartz *et al.*, 2010; Spolsky, 2012). Families' ideologies about languages include beliefs, goals, perspectives and attitudes concerning language use and development. These beliefs and perspectives influence language choices. Language management addresses how families regulate language use and language development in a way that will either intervene in or influence language behaviors in the family (Curdt-Christansen, 2009). The FLP is made either explicitly or implicitly (King *et al.*, 2008; Spolsky & Shohamy, 1999). Some families are conscious of language use and management in their homes and are vocal about when a particular language is to be used. Conversely, some families' choices for communication are unplanned, and families do not make explicit decisions about what language their children will receive and in which contexts.

Family members are the key participants that create policies for their language practices within families (Spolsky, 2012). De Houwer (1999) suggests there is a relationship between parental beliefs and attitudes towards bilingualism, parental linguistic choices and interaction strategies, and children's language development. Therefore, families and caregivers play a critical role in facilitating their children's language development. Recent FLP studies have explored how families navigate and manage multiple languages (Curdt-Christansen, 2009; Kang, 2015; King & Fogle, 2013; Kopeliovich, 2010; Liu, 2018; Piller & Gerber, 2018; Schwartz *et al.*, 2010; Smith-Christmas, 2014).

Curdt-Christansen (2009) indicates that the formation of an FLP is influenced by macro- and micro-level factors. On a macro level, the political, sociocultural, economic and sociolinguistic environment impacts the FLP. This environment may include political beliefs within the community, government or schools. In a study by Edwards and Newcombe (2005) on language transmission within families in Wales, families were urged to bring up their children bilingually with language planning undertaken with the support of health professionals, the community and organizations. This context is a unique situation where bilingualism is valued, since many immigrant families experience external pressures not to maintain their home languages or to practice bilingualism (Wong-Fillmore, 1991). Curdt-Christanen (2009) studied the FLP of 10 Chinese immigrant families in Montreal, where the families demonstrated that they placed high value on maintaining their home language. However, the families often experienced external pressure from schools and the dominant community not to use the home language. Immigrant families are often told by members of the dominant society, such as teachers, not to use their own language with their children due to concerns that it will not support the children's ability to learn the majority language or academic skills (Smith-Christmas, 2014).

Piller and Gerber (2018) provided another example of the dominance of English monolingualism influencing families to have concerns about fostering bilingualism within their families. Piller and Gerber (2018) collected responses from families regarding bilingual parenting through Australia's largest parenting online forum. While bilingualism was seen by many families as an asset that conferred academic and economic benefits, the families had concerns about potential issues with language delays and confusion. Families were concerned that learning a language other than English might have potential negative effects on English development. Families also did not have a full understanding about what bilingualism means, which led to some misconceptions and misunderstandings about bilingual parenting practices. One example of misconceptions was that families did not recognize the potential sociocultural benefits of being bilingual. The authors argued that this was due to a lack of or limited advocacy and outreach efforts, especially from schools and institutions, to foster multilingualism, particularly due to the dominance of English in Australian society.

Micro-level factors that influence the FLP include the home literacy environment, families' expectations, families' education and language experience, and knowledge of bilingualism. Families' ideologies can reflect societal attitudes and perspectives about languages (King et al., 2008). In countries where bilingualism or multilingualism are not valued, the push for monolingualism is evident when policies eradicate bilingual education programs. Some families who immigrate to the United States or who are multilingual defy macro-level constraints and maintain their heritage language (Fishman, 1991). For instance, Korean-American families in Kang's (2015) study valued additive bilingualism and biliteracy in English and Korean for their children's academic development. However, in this study there were inconsistencies in families' attitudes towards language management. Some families did not enroll their children in bilingual schools and only used Korean in their homes. Schwartz and colleagues (2010) studied immigrant bilingual families who speak Russian and Hebrew, and families' motivation and attitudes towards their children's preschool bilingual development. The authors compared two groups of families who sent their children to either a bilingual or a monolingual preschool. Both groups had similar sociocultural and linguistic profiles. The significant differences between the groups were their family language ideologies and practices. The bilingual group valued bilingual education more highly than the monolingual group. The bilingual group was more successful than the monolingual group in controlling their family language practices to facilitate the children's bilingual development.

Kopeliovich (2010) studied a Hebrew-Russian family living in Israel with eight children and their journey towards becoming bilingual. Perspectives on FLP were compared between the parents and their children. The parents valued maintaining their Russian language within the family in a Hebrew-dominant environment in order to have access to the Russian literary heritage and to be able to communicate with the children's grandparents. However, due to pressure and competing demands to use Hebrew, it proved to be challenging for the children to maintain Russian within their families. The study explored how the parents negotiated with their children in unsuccessful and successful ways to encourage bilingual proficiency.

A case study on the west coast of the United States explored a 1.5-generation Chinese immigrant family's FLP, focusing on their language practices, language ideology and language management (Liu, 2018). The study gave an example of micro-level factors that influenced the family to maintain their heritage language. The family believed it was natural to maintain their heritage language, Mandarin Chinese, with their two-year-old child, especially given that both parents' first language was Chinese. They also immersed themselves in a Chinese community. The family recognized the benefits of bilingualism due to its instrumental, familial, communal and developmental value. The study also explored how the family practiced bilingualism and managed both languages at home. The family was explicit about their language choices and chose to use Mandarin Chinese as their dominant language at home, but they chose to send their child to an English-based daycare to support language acquisition in English. The author cautioned that families may experience challenges as children grow older and are more exposed to English as a majority language.

These studies indicate the complexities of children's and parents' language ideologies and perspectives on language management, and how these factors impact language maintenance. Bilingual families in these studies parallel families who have Deaf children in navigating language and communication choices based on competing ideologies and values surrounding majority and minority languages.

Families with Deaf Children

The FLP framework can be applied to families who have Deaf children. As we mentioned in the introduction to our chapter, families with Deaf children are often faced with decisions regarding languages for their children, such as whether to adopt an aural-oral approach or a bimodal bilingual approach. Parents' and caregivers' decisions rely on many factors, and these factors involve families' beliefs, attitudes, ideologies and behaviors regarding what it means to be Deaf as well as regarding signed and spoken languages (Nover, 1995; Reagan, 2011). Past studies explored families' decisions in regard to language choices but did not employ a FLP framework (Crowe et al., 2014; Eleweke & Rodda, 2000; Li et al., 2003; Meadow-Orleans et al., 2003; Scarinci et al., 2018; Young & Tattersall, 2007; Young et al., 2006). Another set of studies explored hearing and Deaf families' decisions about language choices for their child prior to and after cochlear implantation (Huttunen & Välimaa, 2010; Hyde *et al.*, 2010; McKee & Vale, 2014; Mitchiner, 2015; Watson *et al.*, 2006, 2008; Wheeler *et al.*, 2009). A majority of the families in these studies chose to use spoken language only with their Deaf child. Most of the studies indicated that families are often influenced by the information they receive from professionals regarding communication options, and these professionals frequently recommend spoken language and only include sign language as an alternative means for communication. Several families with Deaf children in these studies chose sign language, but this was seen as a temporary communication option until children fully transitioned to spoken language. Families' decisions are also guided by their children's hearing levels, linguistic and cognitive abilities and type of amplification.

Bilingual Families who Use Sign Language

Recent studies investigated bilingual/multilingual families using sign language and a majority language that is spoken and/or written (Batamula, 2016; Kanto *et al.*, 2013; Kite, 2020; Mitchiner, 2015; Pizer *et al.*, 2013; Siran & Dettman, 2018). These studies explore families' ideologies about their language choices and language use with their children. The common theme among the families was that they valued sign language as well as bilingualism in their lives and felt bilingualism was beneficial for their children. Pizer *et al.* (2013) studied Deaf parents with hearing children who are bimodal and bilingual in English and ASL; the parents had the goal of balanced bilingualism for their hearing children. However, children of Deaf adults experienced external pressures to use spoken English. The hearing children's dominant language was English due to constant exposure to a spoken English environment in the school and in the community. As a result, they did not become highly fluent in ASL as adults. While most of these hearing adults with Deaf parents did not sign fluently, they were able to communicate with their parents in their own way. A similar goal for bilingualism in spoken and signed languages was evident in a study about Deaf Finnish parents with hearing children (Kanto *et al.*, 2013). The families valued bilingualism in Finnish Sign Language and Finnish as they considered it to be advantageous and they set a goal for their children to be bilingual in both languages. The study showed a strong relationship between the linguistic environment at home and the children's early bilingual language development. It indicated that ample exposure to sign language will support hearing children's sign language development.

Kite (2020) interviewed eight hearing families with Deaf children regarding their FLP. The families in the study valued bilingualism even though they were pressured by medical professionals to choose one language for their Deaf child and not to consider both ASL and English. All of the families in the study, except for one family that already knew ASL, experienced challenges in learning a new language. They viewed facilitating bilingualism as a good parenting strategy. Many of the families benefited from interactions with Deaf adults through Deaf mentoring programs.

Mitchiner (2015) surveyed 17 Deaf families with children who have cochlear implants and conducted follow-up interviews with eight families regarding their beliefs, attitudes and perspectives about bimodal bilingualism in ASL and English. All of the families in the study had positive beliefs and attitudes towards bilingualism in ASL and English. The common reason for providing their children with cochlear implants was to facilitate the children's spoken language skills. The families felt it was crucial for their children to develop spoken English skills along with learning ASL so their children could thrive in life. These families felt that as English is the majority language in the United States, it is mandatory for their children to develop spoken and written English skills. ASL was also highly valuable to the families as they believed that ASL was critical for their children's literacy and cognitive development, was part of their children's home culture and was the primary language in their homes.

A study by Siran and Dettman (2018) explored 34 families' perspectives regarding a bilingual-bicultural (Bi-Bi) approach using Australian sign language (Auslan) and English with their children who have cochlear implants. The families included Auslan as they recognized the benefits of using the Bi-Bi approach and aimed to broaden their children's options for communication. The parents and caregivers believed children who had access to both languages had the ability to be part of two cultures and two languages (oral-aural and signed), which supported the children's social and personal development. The parents and caregivers also recognized that using Auslan helped develop receptive language and speech, and believed that Auslan did not impede their children's spoken language skills.

While these studies address a diverse set of parents, it is important to specifically look at the parenting and decision-making experiences of immigrant families. This is because these families are often multilingual households and, in addition to parenting a Deaf child, are also adjusting to the language and culture within their new host country and in their child's school. In a study of immigrant families with young Deaf children, Batamula (2016) found that there were similarities in how they navigated language choices for their families and their Deaf children. While these families were influenced by professionals, they also sought advice from others in their community, referred to as gatekeepers. The immigrant families in this study were very much connected to communities of other people from the same country or region. Many of the families in the study learned about school programs and services for their Deaf children after being put in contact with other families with a Deaf child who were from the same country or region of origin. These gatekeepers had already navigated language choices with their Deaf children and could offer advice

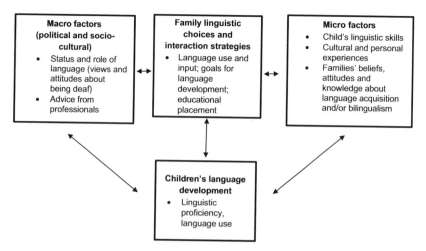

Figure 9.1 Family Language Policy framework for families with Deaf children
Source: Adapted from Curdt-Christiansen (2009).

and reassurance. All of the families in the study had chosen to raise their children plurilingually and bimodally, but nearly all of them said that they were unsure of how to use languages in their homes to support this goal.

It is very important to understand each family's experiences and goals, but it is also important to learn about the unique strengths and traits of the family. Using the FLP and funds of knowledge frameworks, existing studies identify macro and micro factors that influence families with Deaf children and their decisions, perspectives and attitudes about language choices. These factors can help to better understand the underlying issues families face when making decisions about Deaf children's language opportunities. See Figure 9.1, which outlines both types of factors.

Macro Factors

Political and sociocultural factors

Societal forces are a potential influence on family language policy and planning. Medical professionals often recommend that families with Deaf children withhold sign language except as the last resort, and some of these professionals require families to sign contracts promising not to sign with their Deaf children who have cochlear implants (Humphries *et al.*, 2012). This ties in with the role and status of ASL and English in the United States and how the languages are perceived, therefore impacting families' perspectives and attitudes towards language choices. In the United States, English is valued as the language of power. Therefore, English has a higher status than ASL, and ASL is seen as a minority language. The role and status of a language are discussed using Ruiz' (1984) proposed language orientations: language as a problem, language as a right and language as a resource. The language-as-a-problem orientation indicates that the language is a barrier to success in life. Sign language is typically viewed from the language-as-a-problem orientation because there are misconceptions that sign language will disrupt spoken language development or because sign language is not a majority language in our society (Nover, 1995; Reagan, 2011). Negative perspectives on being Deaf, or audism (Humphries, 1975), are also tied to negative perspectives on sign language. McKee and Smiler (2017) shared similar findings in their studies of FLP for deaf children in New Zealand, examining how the macro-level of status planning impacts the micro-level. Families with deaf children are informed about NZSL and Deaf culture, but they do not receive enough support or resources for sign language development or becoming bilingual in both NZSL and English. More focus tends to be on supporting Deaf children's spoken language development and the advancement of CI technology. Families were often advised against the use of sign language. This is a direct reflection of how sign language is not highly valued and supported. The language-as-a-right orientation argues for children's human right to have an accessible language. Advocates for Deaf children's right to sign language have declared that denying them access to sign language is a violation of the child's birthright (Humphries *et al.*, 2014; Skutnabb-Kangas, 2016). From the language-as-a-resource orientation, linguists and educators have presented evidence that sign language supports written language development. Ironically, teaching hearing babies sign language is seen as an asset for early communication and social development. Pizer *et al.* (2007) explored hearing families' decisions to use sign language with their hearing babies. Families' decisions were based on ideologies about early language and communication development and child rearing, and were not based on wanting to communicate with the Deaf community. These families hoped learning sign language with their babies would help improve parent-child communication by helping children to be better able to express their feelings, needs and thoughts. Sign language was seen as a temporary tool until the children were able to fully express themselves in spoken language.

Research on language development, language acquisition and bilingualism also supports families in making educated decisions about language opportunities. Many studies show the cognitive and linguistic benefits of bilingualism (e.g. Bialystok, 2001; Nicoladis & Genesee, 1996). Recent studies indicate positive outcomes for a bimodal and bilingual approach for Deaf children who use sign language and spoken English at an early age (Davidson *et al.*, 2013; Hassanzadeh, 2012; Rinaldi & Caselli, 2014).

It is also possible that families are influenced by social media about topics related to Deaf education. For example, in 2016 the California Association for the Deaf (CAD) and the American Society for Deaf Children (ASDC) launched a 48-hour social media campaign titled

'#WhyISign'. This campaign was initiated by Stacy Abrams, a Deaf early childhood advocate. In this campaign, over 100 individuals, including Deaf people, Deaf parents with Deaf children, hearing families with Deaf children, interpreters and ASL students shared their narratives on social media about why they sign, in order to advocate for access to sign language for Deaf children with hearing parents (#WhyISign, 2016). To this day, individuals continue to contribute their stories about why they sign.

Micro Factors

Beliefs, ideologies and attitudes about languages

Families' language choices and decisions are shaped by their beliefs and attitudes towards languages. Families often make decisions based on their goals for their child. Families may ask questions such as, 'What is the best communication option for my Deaf child?' and 'Which option is the easiest for the family?' Some families may have strong beliefs regarding learning sign language, but these may not be reflected in their practices. Possible reasons for this include limited resources for families to learn sign language and societal pressures for monolingualism.

Families' own language experiences and identities

Individual language experiences are what families are readily familiar with in regard to language acquisition and learning. Therefore, in making decisions for their Deaf child, families will rely on what they already know. Quite often, the first Deaf person hearing families will meet is their own Deaf child. More than 95% of Deaf children are born to hearing families, and these children do not share the same linguistic experiences as their family members. For many hearing families, sign language and Deaf culture appear foreign. Therefore, hearing parents opt for language choices that are familiar to them; it is common to choose an oral approach (without signs) in order for their Deaf child to develop spoken language skills. This is typically a deficit perspective; however, hearing families with Deaf children are often not aware of the benefits of being Deaf and therefore may benefit from learning through Deaf mentoring programs about educational practices and approaches for Deaf children. The remaining 5% of Deaf children are born to Deaf families. Deaf families include parents or family members who are Deaf, and these families also apply their own experiences of learning to speak or to sign when making decisions for their Deaf children. These families may choose to support their children in becoming bilingual in signed, written and/or spoken language. Families' cultural values and identities also influence language planning (McKee & Smiler, 2017). Hearing families who chose spoken language often expressed the value of being able to include their deaf children in their families and being able to communicate with their child (McKee & Smiler, 2017). Deaf and hearing families express the value of maintaining sign language with their families in order to build their children's Deaf identity and pride, as well as a sense of belonging within the Deaf community (Kite, 2020; Mitchiner, 2015).

Deaf children's linguistic and listening abilities

Families' language choices for their Deaf children are greatly guided by the children's listening and linguistic abilities, as well as access to listening technologies such as hearing aids and cochlear implants. In many cases, hearing families with Deaf children choose to use spoken language and will include sign language only when their children have difficulties in communicating orally and typically as a last resort. Families' goals for cochlear implantation are to facilitate their Deaf children's development of spoken language; therefore, these parents will opt for spoken language in their FLP. However, sometimes a Deaf child has additional disabilities, and this influences families' FLP. In a study by Crowe *et al.* (2014), Deaf children with additional disabilities benefited from using sign language. However, some decisions are based on assumptions about children's hearing and speaking abilities. Sign language advocates and researchers argue that sign language is fully accessible and that all Deaf children, including individuals who have cochlear implants, will benefit from access to sign language. A bimodal bilingual approach facilitates bilingual development in signed and spoken languages and social-emotional growth. This allows children to have access to both Deaf and hearing worlds as well as positive identity formation as a Deaf person (Bat-Chava, 2000; Chapman & Dammeyer, 2017; Hintermair, 2008). Deaf individuals who claim a bicultural identity typically have higher self-esteem than those who identify themselves as hearing or as having a marginal identity where they do not themselves identify with either Deaf or hearing cultures.

Family Language Plans

Many factors influence families' decisions about language goals for their family. Once families have chosen plurilingualism, they will then need to consider how their family will use each language in the home. There can be a tendency to set a goal without exploring the details of planning for how it will be met. Families are often not aware of the importance of family language planning. The process of developing an FLP can be complicated and overwhelming or, conversely, overly simplistic if not conducted with guidance and support from the early intervention team.

Families and professionals can share a common goal of the child developing bilingually in both sign language and the other language(s) of the home and community. However, simply having the goal of raising a bilingual child does not mean the child will indeed become bilingual. Without a clear plan, it is unlikely that there will be a balance of language exposure and use with the child throughout the day.

The FLP plan is not intended to be distributed to families to complete and follow on their own. Rather, it is meant to be developed in collaboration with early childhood specialists which can include the teacher, sign language specialist, early intervention service provider, Deaf mentors and/or the speech-language therapist. The FLP plan is a tool that will help families and professionals intentionally expose the child to purposeful and natural language throughout the day in sign language, printed language and, where and when appropriate, spoken language.

The FLP planning form is a guide that allows for customized adaptation for both daily routines and incorporation of as many languages as the family chooses. This allows for natural planning of language use throughout the typical day for each family. Families and professionals should consider daily routines from waking up to going to sleep and list each one. Then, they should discuss when it is most natural to use the target language during the day. For example, a family choosing to use spoken language with their child may use spoken language in the morning when the assistive listening devices have been put on and turned on. This will also help to test the batteries and ensure the devices are working. In some homes, dinner time is a time to come together and share news about the day. This may be a good time to use sign language to ensure that each family member has full access to the conversation. The key is that language use for each part of the day should be natural and intentional. When there are multiple languages used, it is also important to consider who will be with the child during that time and which language this individual can provide. For example, some families may have one family member who uses one language with the child. A mother may be fluent in Spanish and wish to pass that language on to her child. As the sole parent fluent in Spanish, it would be her primary responsibility to provide that language.

Steps in Planning with Families

When collaborating with families to develop the family language plan, it is important to consider each part of the process. Professionals bring their own beliefs and assumptions about the process and the role of the families. However, because all families are diverse and have their own understanding of what is best for their family, it is important for professionals to reflect on their own biases and assumptions, and work towards eliminating them and empowering families to take the lead in designing the best plan for their family.

(1) Select a time to meet. Selecting a mutually agreed upon time is important in reinforcing the partnership and collaboration between the professional(s) and the family. Although professionals typically work during daytime business hours, this may not be feasible for all families, so offering an evening or weekend meeting may allow for more family members to be present without the potential strain of having to miss work or other daytime responsibilities.

(2) Select a location for the meeting. The professional(s) working with the family should establish a meeting location, preferably a home visit, to present, review and complete the family language plan. Although some families may be hesitant about meeting in their homes, this should be presented as the optimal choice. This is because an important part of ensuring the success of the family language plan is making sure it is natural and fits the family's needs. Ideally, the professional will meet the family in their home. However, it is important to remember that not all families are comfortable with this arrangement. In this case, the professional can ask the family to describe or draw a map of their home to help them get a sense of where various routines and activities tend to happen. It is also important to create a schedule of daily routines and of who is with the child at various times in the schedule. Choosing a language can relate to an activity, a person or a place, or can be more complex or changeable in order for the child to experience different people, places or activities in all languages.

If the meeting with the family cannot happen in the home, meeting in a public space that the family frequents, such as a park or library, is another good choice. Meeting at a school or the office of the professional should be the last choice. This is because although the office or school is a comfortable place for the professional, meeting there may lead to the family, intentionally or not, deferring to the recommendations of the professional(s) and holding back some of their own thoughts and ideas.

(3) Before the meeting, share the FLP form with the family, translated into the language of their preference, so the family has time to think about their daily routines and the languages they may wish to use for each activity. In this way, when the meeting occurs, the family has a starting point for discussion and asking questions about designing a plan that is best for their child's language development. Both the professional(s) and the family should also list the child's current language use and strengths. This will help to frame the FLP plan on the day of the meeting.

(4) Preparing for the meeting. Before arriving, professional(s) should take some time to learn about the family and prepare to enter their home. Families represent various cultures and religions, and it is important that professional(s) familiarize themselves with important norms within the home so as not to offend the family and to show respect for

the family. This is best done through a conversation with the family. Professionals can ask the family if there is anything they should be aware of in terms of what to wear or other expectations. Talking with other culturally sensitive professionals who have been in the home is also helpful. Some families, although they practice certain customs that differ from those of some professionals, will not ask visitors to comply with their customs, while others prefer that a visitor does comply. Also, as necessary and in advance of the meeting, be sure to reserve language interpreters or translators so there are fewer language barriers.

(5) Arriving at the meeting. The professional(s) can start by sitting and talking with the family in a relaxed and informal conversation. The professional(s) can first ask about the family's goals and values, and the ways in which they support their child at home, at school and in the community. The professional(s) can use this time to introduce the FLP plan and share background information about family language planning in a family-friendly manner. The professional(s) may then introduce several blank printed copies of the family language plan (see Figure 9.2). They should review the form and complete the five initial prompts based on the family's responses. The professional(s) can review the rest of the form as they prepare to tour the home and ask the family to think about their daily routines in a typical day (both weekdays and weekends). The activities listed in the FLP form should be activities that are part of the family's natural routine.

(6) It is critical for families to examine their own beliefs, experiences and perspectives about language learning and acquisition before moving forward with language planning. Through this process, families can identify possible factors that influence their own beliefs and perspectives. Questions for families to consider can include: What were the family members' experiences of learning languages? What do they know and believe about learning multiple languages? What are their beliefs and perspectives about signed, spoken and written language? Answering these questions will help families identify their attitudes and beliefs about sign language and spoken and written language, including their home language when appropriate. Also, it is essential to identify families' strengths and funds of knowledge (González *et al.*, 2005). For instance, families may value home literacy practices, and this can be reinforced to support children's literacy development.

(7) The professional(s) can ask the family for a tour of the home as they explain their daily routines; for example, after the children wake and dress, do they typically have some play time before school? Where does that happen? As the professional(s) walk through the home, each adult should bring the form and a clipboard to take notes as they are reminded of daily routines or areas of the home that should be assigned for both the current language and desired language for that routine or area.

Family Language Plan

Family beliefs about languages used at home:

Purposes of using these languages:

Language goals for your child:

Language goals for your family:

Your child's abilities and interests:

Resources:

Activity	Current Language	New Language Plan
Morning		
Afternoon		
Evening		
Bedtime		

Figure 9.2 Family language plan
Source: Batamula *et al.* (2015).

(8) After the tour, the professional(s) and family can sit together to compare notes and talk about what the family wishes to highlight as daily routines and which language they prefer to use during each time of the day. The professional(s) can support the family through this process and make recommendations as necessary to ensure that their proposed plan aligns with their language goals for their child. The professional(s) can ask the family if there is an opportunity for the child to be exposed to each language in a variety of settings to ensure language development. While balancing each language in the home is

often an optimal goal, it is not always the appropriate goal for each family. There are many factors to consider in designing a plan that is specific and unique to each individual family, including the language skills of each family member and the resources readily available to that family to support them as they implement their FLP. Also, the professional(s) and families should ensure that the language chosen for an activity or area is practical and natural.

(9) Complete the final family language plan. The professional(s) can identify available resources and provide families with access to additional resources (e.g. sign language classes, sign language tutoring, Deaf mentoring, speech-language pathology services, heritage language classes).

(10) Although the family should be able to ask questions of the professional(s) throughout the process, follow-up should also be undertaken by the professional(s) after a week or so to see how the plan is working and to see if there are any changes that should be made. Follow-up should continue at a frequency that is appropriate for the family and the situation.

Guiding the families through the FLP process requires time and preparation so that families can create plans that will be effective and easy for them to follow. This means ensuring that the families have control of their choices and that the choices are natural and logical for the activity or area of the house. Ultimately, the FLP needs to be aligned with the goals of the family.

Seeking Resources

It is important to provide families with easily accessible resources to aid their success in maintaining their FLP plan. These resources can be from a variety of venues and provide support for the family in various ways. It is important to meet the needs of each individual family, as each has their own strengths and areas where they may wish to grow. Resources to support families may include: programs for learning sign language; associations or organizations for connecting with other families with Deaf and hard-of-hearing children; Deaf mentoring programs; and information about school choices, parental and student rights and negotiating appropriate accommodation for the child in school. Available resources vary by location, so it is important to investigate what is available in the area you serve. Some organizations to investigate that may serve as resources include: the local school for the Deaf or Deaf education unit in a mainstream school; the local chapter of the national Deaf association; local universities; the library; cultural centers to support heritage language development; online groups such as Facebook, Yahoo and Meet-up; online sign language tools or apps for learning sign language; and signing apps for children, including storybook apps with stories read in sign language. Professionals should also continue to support families through regularly scheduled home visits to review what is working and what may need to be adjusted.

In areas where resources are scarce, there are other ways to establish support for families committed to providing plurilingual environments in their homes. Professionals can set up family support groups where families of children of various ages can meet and share successes and struggles, and encourage one another. This could also be a time when the professionals meet with the families as a group to help with connections and sharing information. The local Deaf community can also serve as a resource by providing mentoring and an opportunity to practice learning sign language. Advocacy at the state and local levels is critical in advancing the resources and services available for Deaf and hard-of-hearing children and their families. These support groups and connections to the Deaf community can be places to share and plan for advocacy, such as attending marches, composing letters to local and state officials and petitioning school boards for better services.

Conclusion

As indicated, creating the FLP with families who have Deaf children has benefits and challenges. An FLP can be beneficial for families as it helps to safeguard children's language acquisition and development in one, two or more languages. Families' competence in becoming plurilingual can be increased through explicit language planning. With an FLP, families become more conscious about balancing the input of two or more language with their children throughout the day and locating and utilizing the resources that are available to them. With language planning, families become more committed to putting their goals into action.

An FLP also comes with challenges. As discussed in this chapter, planning for language use with children is not clear cut and depends on a multitude of factors. There is no one-size-fits-all plan. The FLP must be tailored to the unique goals of each family. This includes consideration of their language goals in conjunction with such factors as language skills and available resources. Early intervention specialists are key to getting the family started on a plan that is likely to succeed for that family.

Political and societal pressures based on the biases and assumptions of professionals have proven to be a challenge for many families who navigate the world of plurilingualism. An FLP will be successful if resources are made available to families to successfully practice plurilingualism in their homes. Oftentimes, resources are scarce or non-existent. Families, professionals and community members will need to work together and be creative, and to think outside the box to create resources.

References

Bialystok, E. (2001) *Bilingualism in Development: Language, Literacy, and Cognition.* Cambridge: Cambridge University Press. See https://doi.org/10.1017/CBO9780511605963.

Batamula, C. (2016) Family engagement among immigrant parents with young deaf children. Unpublished doctoral dissertation, George Mason University.

Batamula, C., Keith, C., Kite, B. and Mitchiner, J. (2015) *Family Language Plan.* Washington, DC: Gallaudet University Press.

Bat-Chava, Y. (2000) Diversity of deaf identities. *American Annals of the Deaf* 145 (5), 420–428.

Bauman, H.D. and Murray, J.J. (2014) Deaf gain: An introduction. In H.D. Bauman and J.J. Murray (eds) *Deaf Gain: Raising the Stakes for Human Diversity* (pp. xv–xlii). Minneapolis, MN: University of Minnesota Press.

Chapman, M. and Dammeyer, J. (2017) The significance of deaf identity for psychological well-being. *Journal of Deaf Studies and Deaf Education* 22 (2), 187–194. doi:10.1093/deafed/enw073.

Crowe, K., Fordham, L., Mcleod, S. and Ching, T. (2014) 'Part of our world': Influences on caregiver decisions about communication choices for children with hearing loss. *Deafness & Education International* 16 (2), 61–85. doi:10.1179/1557069X13Y.0000000026.

Curdt-Christiansen, X.L. (2009) Invisible and visible language planning: Ideological factors in the family language policy of Chinese immigrant families in Quebec. *Language Policy* 8 (1), 351–375. doi:10.1007/s10993-009-9146-7.

Davidson, K., Lillo-Martin, D. and Chen Pichler, D. (2013) Spoken English language development in native signing children with cochlear implants. *Journal of Deaf Studies and Deaf Education* 19, 238–250. doi:10.1093/deafed/ent045.

De Houwer, A. (1999) Environmental factors in early bilingual development: The role of parental beliefs and attitudes. In G. Extra and L. Verhoeven (eds) *Bilingualism and Migration* (pp. 75–96). New York: Mouton de Gruyter.

Edwards, V. and Newcombe, L.P. (2005) Language transmission in the family in Wales: An example of innovative language planning. *Language Problems & Language Planning* 29 (2), 135–150.

Eleweke, J. and Rodda, M. (2000) Factors contributing to parents' selection of communication mode to use with their deaf children. *American Annals of the Deaf* 145 (4), 375–383. doi:10.1353/aad.2012.0087.

Fishman, J.A. (1991) *Reversing Language Shift.* Clevedon: Multilingual Matters.

González, N., Moll, L.C. and Amanti, C. (2005) *Funds of Knowledge: Theorizing Practices in Households, Communities, and Classrooms.* Mahwah, NJ: Lawrence Erlbaum.

Hall, M.L., Hall, W.C. and Caselli, N.K. (2019) Deaf children need language, not (just) speech. *First Language* 39 (4), 367–395.

Hall, W.C., Levin, L.L. and Anderson, M.L. (2017) Language deprivation syndrome: A possible neurodevelopmental disorder with sociocultural origins. *Social Psychiatry and Psychiatric Epidemiology* 52, 761–776.

Hassanzadeh, S. (2012) Outcomes of cochlear implantation in deaf children of deaf parents: Comparative study. *Journal of Laryngology & Otology* 126, 989–994. doi:10.1017/S0022215112001909.

Hehir, T. (2002) Eliminating ableism in education. *Harvard Educational Review* 72 (1), 1–32.

Hintermair, M. (2006) Parental resources, parental stress, and socioemotional development of deaf and hard of hearing children. *Journal of Deaf Studies and Deaf Education* 11 (4), 493–513. doi:10.1093/deafed/enl005.

Hintermair, M. (2008) Self-esteem and satisfaction with life of deaf and hard-of-hearing people – a resource-oriented approach to identity work. *Journal of Deaf Studies and Deaf Education* 13, 278–300. doi:10.1093/deafed/enm054.

Hintermair, M. and Albertini, J.A. (2005) Ethics, deafness, and new medical technologies. *Journal of Deaf Studies and Deaf Education* 10 (2), 184–192. doi:10.1093/deafed/eni018.

Humphries, T. (1975) Audism: The making of a word. Unpublished essay.

Humphries, T., Kushalnagar, P., Mathur, G., Napoli, D.J., Padden, C., Rathmann, C. and Smith, S.R. (2012) Language acquisition for deaf children: Reducing the harms of zero tolerance for the use of alternative approaches. *Harm Reduction Journal* 9 (16). doi:10.1186/1477-7517-9-16.

Humphries, T., Kushalnagar, P., Mathur, G., Napoli, D.J., Padde, C. and Rathmann, C. (2014) Ensuring language acquisition for deaf children: What linguists can do. *Language and Public Policy* 90 (2), e31–e52.

Huttunen, K. and Välimaa, T. (2010) Parents' views on changes in their child's communication and linguistic and socioemotional development after cochlear implantation. *Journal of Deaf Studies and Deaf Education* 15 (4), 383–404. doi:10.1093/deafed/enq029.

Hyde, M. and Power, D. (2006) Some ethical dimensions of cochlear implantation for deaf children and their families. *Journal of Deaf Studies and Deaf Education* 11 (1), 102–111. doi:10.1093/deafed/enj009.

Hyde, M., Punch, R. and Komesaroff, L. (2010) Coming to a decision about cochlear implantation: Parents making choices for their deaf children. *Journal of Deaf Studies and Deaf Education* 15 (2), 162–178. doi:10.1093/deafed/enq004.

JCIH (Joint Committee on Infant Hearing) (2007) Year 2007 position statement: Principles and guidelines for early hearing detection and intervention programs. *Pediatrics* 120, 898–921. doi:10.1542/peds.2007-2333.

Kang, H.-S. (2015) Korean families in America: Their family language policies and home-language maintenance. *Bilingual Research Journal* 38 (1), 275–291. doi:10.1080/15235882.2015.1092002.

Kanto, L., Huttunen, K. and Laakso, M.-L. (2013) Relationship between the linguistic environment and early bilingual development of hearing children in Deaf-parented families. *Journal of Deaf Studies and Deaf Education* 18 (2), 242–260. doi:10.1093/deafed/ens071.

Karchmer, M.A. and Mitchell, R.E. (2004) Chasing the mythical ten percent: Parental hearing status of Deaf and hard of hearing in the United States. *Sign Language Studies* 4 (2), 138–163.

King, K. and Fogle, L. (2006) Bilingual parenting as good parenting: Parents' perspectives on family language policy for additive bilingualism. *International Journal of Bilingual Education and Bilingualism* 9 (6), 695–712. doi:10.2167/beb362.0.

King, K. and Fogle, L. (2013) Family language policy and bilingual parenting. *Language Teaching* 46 (2) 172–194. doi:10.1017/S0261444812000493.

King, K., Fogle, L. and Logan-Terry, A. (2008) Family language policy. *Language and Linguistics Compass* 2 (5), 907–922. doi:10.111/j.1749-818X.2008.00076.x.

Kite, B.J. (2020) How the medical professionals impact ASL and English families' language planning policy. *Psychology in the Schools* 57 (3), 402–417. doi:10.1002/pits.22324.

Knoors, H. and Marschark, M. (2012) Language planning for the 21st century: Revisiting bilingual language policy for deaf children. *Journal of Deaf Studies and Deaf Education* 17 (3), 291–305. doi:10.1093/deafed/ens018.

Kopeliovich, S. (2010) Family language policy: A case study of a Russian-Hebrew bilingual family: Toward a theoretical framework. *Diaspora, Indigenous, and Minority Education* 4 (3), 162–178. doi:10.1080/15595692.2010.490731.

Kushalnagar, P., Mathur, G., Moreland, C.J., Napoli, D.J., Osterling, W., Padden, C. and Rathmann, C. (2010) Infants and children with hearing loss need early language access. *Journal of Clinical Ethics* 22 (2), 143–154.

Li, Y., Bain, L. and Steinberg, A. (2003) Parental decision making and the choice of communication modality for the child who is deaf. *Archives of Pediatrics & Adolescent Medicine* 157 (2), 162–168. doi:10.1001/archpedi.157.2.

Liu, L. (2018) 'It's just natural': A critical case of study of family language policy in a 1.5 generation Chinese immigrant family on the west coast of the United States. In M. Siiner, F. Hult and T. Kupisch (eds) *Language Policy and Language Acquisition Planning, Vol. 15*. Cham: Springer.

Mayberry, R.I. (2007) When timing is everything: Age of first-language acquisition effects on second-language learning. *Applied Psycholinguistics* 28 (3), 537–549. doi:10.1017/S0142716407070294.

McKee, R. and Vale, M. (2014) The Vitality of NZSL Project: Parents of Deaf and Hearing Impaired Children: Survey Report. Deaf Studies Research Unit, Victoria University of Wellington. Accessed online at http://www.victoria.ac.nz/lals/centres-and-institutes/ dsru/NZSL-Vitality-Parent-Survey-Report-March-2014.pdf.

McKee, R. and Smiler, K. (2017) Family language policy for deaf children and the vitality of New Zealand Sign Language. In J. Macalister and S.H. Mirvahedi (eds) *Family Language Policies in a Multilingual World: Opportunities, Challenges, and Consequences* (pp. 30–50). New York: Routledge Taylor & Francis Group.

Meadow-Orleans, K.P., Mertens, D. and Sass-Lehrer, M. (2003) *Parents and Their Deaf Children: The Early Years*. Washington, DC: Gallaudet University Press.

Miller, M. (2015) Deafhood: Liberation, healing, and the sign language interpreter. StreetLeverage: Live 2015, Boston, MA. See https://streetleverage.com/live_presentations/deafhood-liberation-healing-sign-language-interpreter/.

Mitchiner, J.C. (2015) Deaf parents of cochlear implanted children: Beliefs on bimodal bilingualism. *Journal of Deaf Studies and Deaf Education* 20 (1), 51–66. doi:10.1093/deafed/enu028.

Moll, L.C., Amanti, C., Neff, D. and Gonzalez, N. (1992) Funds of knowledge for teaching: Using a qualitative approach to connect homes and classrooms. *Theory into Practice* 31 (2), 132–141. doi:10.1080/00405849209543534.

Murray, J.J., Hall, W.C. and Snoddon, K. (2020) The importance of signed languages for deaf children and their families. *The Hearing Journal* 73 (3), 30–32. doi:10.1097/01.HJ.0000657988.24659.f3.

Nicoladis, E. and Genesee, F. (1996) Word awareness in second language learners and bilingual children. *Language Awareness* 5, 80–90. doi:10.1080/09658416.1996.9959894.

Nover, S.M. (1995) Politics & language: American Sign Language and English in deaf education. In C. Lucas (ed.) *Sociolinguistics in Deaf Communities* (pp. 109–163). Washington, DC: Gallaudet University Press.

Piller, I. and Gerber, L. (2018) Family language policy between the bilingual advantage and the monolingual mindset. *International Journal of Bilingual Education and Bilingualism*. doi:10.1080/13670050.2018.1503227.

Pizer, G., Walters, K. and Meier, R.P. (2007) Bringing up baby with baby signs: Language ideologies and socialization in hearing families. *Sign Language Studies* 7 (4), 387–430. doi:10.1353/sls.2007.0026.

Pizer, G., Walters, K. and Meier, R.P. (2013) 'We communicated that way for a reason': Language practices and language ideologies among hearing adults whose parents are deaf. *Journal of Deaf Studies and Deaf Education* 18 (1), 75–92.

Reagan, T. (2011) Ideological barriers to American Sign Language: Unpacking linguistic resistance. *Sign Language Studies* 11 (4), 606–636. doi:10.1353/sls.2011.0006.

Rinaldi, P. and Caselli, M.C. (2014) Language development in a bimodal bilingual child with cochlear implant: A longitudinal study. *Bilingualism: Language and Cognition* 14, 798–809. doi:10.1017/S1366728913000849.

Ruiz, R. (1984) Orientations in language planning. *Journal of the National Association for Bilingual Education* 8 (2), 15–34.

Scarinci, N., Gehrke, M., Ching, T., Marnane, V. and Button, L. (2018) Factors influencing caregiver decision making to change the communication method of their child with hearing loss. *Deafness & Education International* 20 (3–4), 123–153. doi:10.1080/1463154.2018.1511239.

Schwartz, M., Moin, V., Leikin, M. and Breitkopf, A. (2010) Immigrant parents' choices of a bilingual versus monolingual kindergarten for second-generation children: Motives, attitudes, and factors. *International Multilingual Research Journal* 4 (1), 107–124. doi:10.1080/19313152.2010.499038.

Siran, S. and Dettman, S. (2018) Qualitative analysis of caregivers' perspectives regarding using Auslan within a Bilingual-Bicultural (Bi-Bi) approach with their children who use cochlear implants. *Deafness & Education International* 20 (3–4), 205–227. doi:10.1080/14643154.2018.1519965.

Skutnabb-Kangas, T. (2016) Linguistic genocide. In G. Gertz and P. Boudreault (eds) *The Sage Deaf Studies Encyclopedia* (pp. 595–599). SAGE Publications, Inc, https://www.doi.org/10.4135/9781483346489.n191.

Smith-Christmas, C. (2014) Being socialised into language shift: The impact of extended family members on family language policy. *Journal of Multilingual and Multicultural Development* 35 (4), 511–526. doi:10.1080/01434632.2014.882930.

Smith-Christmas, C. (2016) *Family Language Policy: Maintaining an Endangered Language in the Home.* London: Palgrave Macmillan UK.

Snoddon, K. (2008) American Sign Language and early intervention. *The Canadian Modern Language Review/La Revure Canadienne des Langues Vivantes* 64 (4), 581–604.

Spolsky, B. (2012) Family language policy – the critical domain. *Journal of Multilingual & Multicultural Development* 33 (1), 3–11. doi:10.1080/01434632.2011.638072.

Spolsky, B. and Shohamy, E. (1999) *The Languages of Israel: Policy, Ideology and Practice.* Clevedon: Multilingual Matters.

Watson, L.M., Archbold, S.M. and Nikolopoulos, T.P. (2006) Children's communication mode five years after cochlear implantation: Changes over time according to age at implant. *Cochlear Implants International* 7 (2), 77–91. doi:10.1002/cii.301.

Watson, L.M., Hardie, T., Archbold, S.M. and Wheeler, A. (2008) Parents' views on changing communication after cochlear implantation. *Journal of Deaf Studies and Deaf Education* 13 (1), 104–116. doi:10.1093/deafed/enm036.

Wheeler, A., Archbold, S.M., Hardie, T. and Watson, L.M. (2009) Children with cochlear implants: The communication journey. *Cochlear Implants International* 10 (1), 41–62. doi:10.1002/cii.370.

#Why I Sign (2016) #*Why I Sign campaign*, March. See http://www.whyisign.com.

Wong Fillmore, L. (1991) When learning a second language means losing the first. *Early Childhood Research Quarterly* 6 (3), 323–346. doi:10.1016/S0885-2006(05)80059-6.

Young, A. (2010) The impact of early identification of deafness on hearing parents. In M. Marschark and P.E. Spencer (eds) *Oxford Handbook of Deaf Studies, Language, and Education* (2nd edn) (pp. 292–315). New York: Oxford University Press.

Young, A. and Tattersall, H. (2007) Universal newborn hearing screening and early identification of deafness: Parents' responses to knowing early and their expectations of child communication development. *Journal of Deaf Studies and Deaf Education* 12 (2), 209–220. doi:10.1093/deafed/enl033.

Young, A., Carr, G., Hunt, R., McCracken, W., Skipp, A. and Tattersall, H. (2006) Informed choice and deaf children: Underpinning concepts and enduring challenges. *Journal of Deaf Studies and Deaf Education* 11 (3), 322–336. doi:10.1093/deafed/enj041.

10 Critical Perspectives on Education Mediated by Sign Language Interpreters: Inclusion or the Illusion of Inclusion?

Debra Russell

In a climate where inclusive education for deaf learners is the dominant model supported through policies and funding mechanisms, this study invites us to consider the reality of inclusion for deaf learners. This chapter provides an overview of key findings from a multiphase Canadian national research project that examined the ways in which deaf children have access to the classroom content and engagement via a signed language interpreter. Thirty-five interpreters, working in kindergarten to high school settings (five years to 18 years of age), provided video samples of their interpretation. The data were coded using a sociolinguistic model of 'teacher talk' (Cazden, 2001), looking at the techniques of asking metacognitive questions, scaffolding, reconceptualization, sequencing of instructions, peer teaching and the use of feedback, and the ways in which the interpretation managed those elements of classroom discourse. The data provide a challenge to the dominant policy and practice of interpreter-mediated education, in that only six of the 35 interpreters were able to consistently use strategies to convey the discourse elements and to promote engagement in the ways teachers intended. The study also uncovered factors among deaf learners performing well which may serve to guide those making decisions about when a student is ready for an education mediated through an interpreter.

Introduction

At the present time, educational policy and practices in Canada, the United States and other countries outside of North America strongly support an inclusive education model where students who are deaf are to be educated in the local school and supported by educational accommodations. For deaf learners who use a signed language such as American Sign Language (ASL), this can mean that the local school may hire an educational assistant who has some facility with ASL, or that the school is able to secure a qualified, trained signed language interpreter. While there are several bilingual (ASL and English) Canadian schools that specialize in teaching deaf learners, such as the Alberta School for the Deaf and the Ernest C. Drury School for the Deaf, Ontario, most parents outside of the geographic areas of these centers are required to place their child in the local public school. This is because most school districts will not pay for a child to access educational programs outside of their own district. The result is that the children experience learning in a 'mediated education' format (i.e. all the information from teachers and students is mediated through the interpreter). Furthermore, many other children experience no support via interpreters or educational assistants with sign language proficiency. For a more in-depth discussion of learning theory as mediation, see Kozulin *et al.* (2003) and Vygotsky (1978). In this chapter, the phrase 'mediated' is used to describe the mediation process through another human being, the sign language interpreter, while being mediated in an organized learning activity. The phrase is intentionally used instead of 'interpreted education', which has come to reflect the accommodation practice of using a sign language interpreter in an acquisition model of learning that is assumed to provide equal access to the content and language of the classroom.

There are numerous studies suggesting that the vast majority of Deaf students in the United States, Norway and New Zealand do not receive an equitable education when contrasted with their hearing peers, often due to ineffective interpreting services (LaBue, 1998; Locker-McKee & Biederman, 2003; Muruvik Venen, 2009; Ramsey, 1997; Russell, 2008; Schick & Williams, 2004; Schick *et al.*, 1999; Smith, 2013; Winston, 2004). As Russell and Winston (2014: 103) describe, deaf children may *appear* to have access to the language of instruction via sign language interpretation; however, if the linguistic input does not allow for meaningful access to the learning environment, this leads to the *illusion of inclusion*. By this they mean that the child has physical access to the learning environment but not effective linguistic and curricular access. Inclusive education by its very definition means that one is included in all aspects of the educational experience, from the classroom experience of teaching and learning, as well as all other aspects of being a 'learner' during recess and lunch breaks, to having access to after-school clubs and/or sports, to feeling that one has significant relationships with the adults and peers that form the school community. Children in bilingual programs; for example, in French-English programs in Canada, have access to French in every interaction throughout the day, as there is a shared language among the children and adults. For deaf children, it is more likely the case that there are no peers that know ASL, no adults fluent in ASL, and each interaction involving communication is mediated by one adult, the interpreter, who may not be fluent in ASL. By contrast, then, this is not full inclusion.

Further, the social, linguistic and academic development of deaf children has been impeded by myths, assumptions and a general lack of knowledge about the multifaceted, complex nature of learning through an interpreter. The World Federation of the Deaf (WFD) provides support to countries that have signed the United Nations Convention of the Rights of Persons with Disabilities (UNCRPD) by educating governments, Deaf communities and school systems concerning approaches to education through sign language interpreters:

> The WFD is specifically troubled by the current trend in following an operational definition of inclusion for deaf learners as placement in mainstream schools, as these are environments that often do not provide adequate access to and direct instruction in sign language, including instruction from deaf teachers. For many deaf learners, this type of placement does not support inclusion. (WFD, 2018)

This operational definition of inclusion as placement in mainstream schools is contrary to the legislative history of Article 24, where the WFD advocated for a broader definition of inclusion which includes bilingual education for deaf learners as a form of inclusive education. For example, Article 24 of the UNCRPD promotes sign languages in deaf children's education and requires governments to promote education that allows deaf children to thrive and to achieve academically (WFD, 2018). Canada is a signatory to the UNCRPD; however, the level of awareness among most schools about the learning environment required for deaf learners is limited. Most administrators and teachers assume that once they hire a signed language interpreter, a deaf child has a learning experience that is the same as a nondeaf child.

The WFD (2018: 4) Position Paper on Inclusive Education states that in order to achieve inclusive education for deaf learners, it is critical that all deaf children, regardless of where they attend school, are able to do the following:

- access high-quality instruction in a sign language;
- have opportunities to study with other deaf students and with teachers, including deaf teachers, who are themselves fluent in sign language;
- study sign language as a school subject;
- receive instructions from teachers who possess teaching credentials, knowledge of quality bilingual curricula and pedagogy, and awareness of the need for high expectations for deaf learners as bilingual learners;
- experience immersion in school environments that also support parent and deaf community engagement.

While evidence in other countries points to the challenges of educational policy and practices that are not aligned with the WFD position and the UNCRPD tenets (McKee & Biederman, 2003; McKee, 2008; Muruvik Venen, 2009; Ramsey, 1997; Schick & Williams, 2004; Smith, 2013), there has been little research in Canada. As well, rarely does the research include the perspectives of students, parents, teachers, interpreters and administrators. However, these multiple 'voices' of the stakeholders in education are critical to understanding the complexity of mediated education. To date, there has been no empirical evidence from Canada in order to analyze what *actually* happens between interpreters and deaf students, and the nature of the language input that students receive.

Interpreting for Deaf Children: Canadian Evidence

Sociolinguistic research methods have confirmed that interpreters make decisions about how to convey meaningful interpreted utterances, coordinate turn-taking and facilitate interactions (Llewellyn Jones & Lee, 2014; Major & Napier, 2012; Metzger, 1999; Napier, 2007; Roy, 1993; Russell, 2002; Russell & Winston, 2014). Hence, this study drew on sociolinguistic methods in order to examine the ways in which deaf children have access to the classroom content and engagement via a signed language interpreter. The University of Alberta provided ethics approval along with the individual school districts across several Canadian provinces that chose to participate in the study. One of the first phases of the study was to explore the perceptions of deaf students, parents, teachers, interpreters and administrators in order to gain a fuller understanding of the reality of a 'mediated education' (Russell, 2008). This was done through three separate online surveys distributed to interpreters, teachers, administrators and parents (Russell & MacLeod, 2009). In addition to completing the survey, interpreters provided a standard sample of interpretation of classroom discourse for analysis of the effectiveness of the interpreting product to reflect the teacher discourse and interaction patterns in the classroom. Eight other interpreters were observed in classroom settings where the work could not be video-taped for privacy reasons; however, field notes were used by the researcher to capture the findings. The analysis of classroom samples of interpretation and observations of interpreters working in classrooms was then used to identify areas to be explored in semi-structured interviews with interpreters, parents, teachers, administrators and deaf students. Finally, interpreters were selected to participate in a study of their strategies for solving interpretation challenges (Russell & Winston, 2014). We begin by reviewing the online survey data.

Interpreter perceptions on challenges to linguistic access in the classroom

An online survey was distributed to interpreters who were members of the national professional body representing interpreters in Canada, the Association of Visual Language Interpreters of Canada, inviting those who work in kindergarten to high school educational settings to respond. In July 2018, the association changed its name to the Canadian Association of Sign Language Interpreters (CASLI). Seventy-six interpreters responded to the survey. The qualitative data were coded using thematic analysis (Braun & Clarke, 2006; Creswell & Creswell, 2018). Five major themes are described below that are relevant to the ways in which Snoddon and Weber (this volume) describe plurilingualism as embracing partial competences in languages and life experiences that have shaped inadequate language learning environments. The data reveal some of the interpreter experiences that shape inadequate language learning environments. For example, the interpreters describe the challenges of balancing acting as an interpreter while also being expected to be a language and behavior model for the student. The interpreters also identified that the teachers are often very unfamiliar with how to support the language acquisition processes of a deaf learner and have no knowledge of ASL and interpreting processes, both of which affect the language learning environments. As well, there was widespread acknowledgement among the interpreters that they have had no specific training within their interpreting program that would have prepared them to work with children who have incomplete language competences. Additionally, the interpreters recognized that interpreting was insufficient to support language and social development, and that it has an impact on the kinds of relationships that are formed with other students, with teachers, and between the interpreter and the teaching staff. Finally, the theme of no interpretation being available during recess or after-school programs revealed the impact on creating friendships in mediated learning environments. It is against this backdrop that the deaf child is assumed to be developing competency in two languages that are not native to them, such as ASL and English. In contrast, this may not be the case for hearing children that are in a plurilingual learning situation where they could be learning French in an educational setting and using English at home, and switch between languages according to the circumstances.

Based on these themes (see Table 10.1 below), the next aspect of the study involved exploring the actual interpretation provided by the classroom interpreter. We were most interested in the critical outcomes of effective interpretation and the consequences of ineffective interpretation by examining the interpreting performance. We were also interested in the ways in which interpreters approach classroom discourse and learner

Table 10.1 Themes applied to the concept of plurilingualism

Theme	Interpreter comments
Language learning via interpreting	'Some parents I have worked with assume my role is not only to interpret but I am a language model and/or behavior model for their children. Others view us as helpers or as a conduit to impress the language modality of their choice onto their children.'
What is ASL?	'The teachers often view see my work as that of "helping" the deaf student, without any understanding of the nature of ASL and the interpretation process required between English and ASL. They seem to know nothing about language learning for deaf kids.'
Training to work with plurilingual learners	'I have no specific education about educational interpreting – I was trained to work with adults who have full language. It would be useful to have specific PD [professional development] that could help me support the deaf child.'
Interpreting isn't enough	'Other challenges are that the student can become increasingly dependent on the interpreter as the only person who can use their language, or the child's lack of language can lead to failure to understand directions, failure to form peer relations, low self-esteem for student. The fallout of the student not doing well is that leads to poor relationships between interpreters and other staff, and strained relations between staff and student.'
Consequences of lack of language competencies	'The student is not able to use an interpreter often due to a lack of language, so they are inattentive or uncooperative, or are a behavior problem in the class – all that affects social development.'
Consequences of limited interpreting hours	'There is no interpretation during recess or for after-school programs, so the student doesn't have access to peers in the same ways as the hearing kids do...where do they make friends?'

engagement, as described below. The sociolinguistic analysis explored the ways in which interpreters employ strategies to provide appropriate linguistic renditions of teacher discourse for deaf students. The focus was on the interpreters' work from English to ASL when dealing with six common frames that are used by teachers to teach the curriculum and to engage learners academically, socially and intellectually, as identified above.

Interpreting performance: Discourse and engagement

The theoretical framework for this phase of the study was shaped by engagement and learning theory (Willms *et al.*, 2009). Willms *et al.* define student engagement as:

the extent to which students identify with and value school outcomes, have a sense of belonging at school, participate in academic and non-academic activities, strive to meet the formal requirements of schooling, and make a personal investment in learning. (2009: 7)

Three measures of engagement are described:

(1) social (i.e. a sense of belonging and participation in school);
(2) academic (i.e. participation in the formal requirements of schooling); and
(3) intellectual (i.e. the cognitive and emotional investment in learning using higher-ordered thinking skills such as analysis, synthesis, evaluation and problem solving).

These concepts of engagement were chosen as a useful way of understanding the experiences of inclusion for deaf learners, as they serve to move the debate beyond the trend of physical placement as inclusion to considering the linguistic, cognitive and social aspects of inclusion for deaf students. There is widespread agreement that student engagement is key to preparing students for the transition to postsecondary education and the world of work. However, the reality described in Willms *et al.* (2009) is that when students struggle in school or leave school early, they become disadvantaged as they move into adult roles. Further, disengagement is disproportionately experienced by students living in poverty, students with disabilities and students from ethnic minority and Aboriginal communities (Audas & Willms, 2001; Caledon Institute of Social Policy, 2006; Community Health Systems Resource Group, 2005; Richards & Vining, 2004).

Given that engagement in learning is mediated by the language of the classroom, the second layer of analysis came from the application of teachers' use of language in purposeful ways to promote student engagement. Drawing on the work of Cazden (2001), six discourse strategies used by teachers to promote critical thinking and engagement were chosen as the focus of the interpreting skills analysis. These strategies included:

(1) The use of higher-order or *metacognitive questions*;
(2) The application of *scaffolding techniques* to bridge previous learner knowledge with new knowledge;
(3) The *sequencing of instructions*;
(4) *Reconceptualizing strategies* where teachers reframe information in different ways to reach all learners;
(5) *Peer or reciprocal teaching* that occurs through the asking and answering of questions, and small and large group interactions where students share their knowledge with each other; and, lastly,
(6) *Teacher feedback* for learners as individuals and groups, designed to guide learners and keep them engaged in positive ways.

The research questions in this phase of the study were as follows: *What linguistic strategies do interpreters use to represent the teacher's use of language in creating learning environments for deaf learners? What does engagement look like for deaf learners when working with interpreters in mediated learning environments?*

Methodology

A purposive sampling technique (Ritchie *et al.*, 2003) was used to recruit interpreters who regularly work in kindergarten to high school educational settings. Interpreters were recruited via email notices distributed by the national interpreting association, AVLIC, and the interpreters who completed the online survey were also invited to participate in this phase of the study. The data collection included video-recording the participants' interpretation of a 20-minute standard classroom sample that most closely mirrored their regular employment setting: for example, a language arts class from Grade 2, a health class from Grade 6, a science lesson from Grade 8 or a social studies class from Grade 11.

Participants

Thirty-five interpreters participated, including three interpreters working with deaf-blind children who provided sign language input designed for the particular low vision needs of those children. The interpreters were from the Canadian provinces of British Columbia, Alberta, Saskatchewan, Manitoba, Ontario, Nova Scotia, New Brunswick and Newfoundland. The interpreters had a range of experience in interpreting in educational settings, from two years to 35 years. Of the 35 interpreters (three males and 32 females), 29 had formal interpreter training of a minimum of one year of a Deaf Studies program followed by a one-year interpreting program, while the majority had completed one year of Deaf Studies and an interpreter program of two years in length. Six interpreters did not possess formal interpreter training.

Materials and task

The stimuli were professionally produced videotapes of authentic samples of classroom instruction delivered by experienced teachers. The source for the videotapes was the Northwest Connecticut Community-Technical College and a National Interpreter Education Grant (#H160C03000). The classroom samples reflect elementary and junior and senior high school classes. The subject matter included lessons in health, social studies, language arts, spelling and science. The use of professionally produced materials that showed samples of authentic classroom discourse eliminated the problem of securing parental permission to tape in actual classrooms. Four additional interpreters received parental permission to provide samples of actual classroom interpreting which were analyzed in the same manner as the other video samples; however, these data are not reported in this chapter.

A student profile was created for each grade level describing age, family language context, student language preferences, school history, etc. Each interpreter was provided with the profile that matched the classroom stimuli. The description of the deaf student mirrored the type of information that an interpreter would read in a student's Individual Educational Plan (IEP), adding to the ecological validity of this study. The interpreters were instructed to use this description when making decisions about language use and creating the target language interpretation. The interpreters were filmed in a private room, providing 20 minutes of English to ASL interpretation.

Data analysis

The interpretation samples were uploaded into StudioCode (a video annotation software program). Time-coded annotations were added to the footage to explore strategies that represented the six discourse functions chosen for this study. Different tiers were used to identify the discourse functions in the source language of English, and then the strategies used in the target language, ASL.

The researcher and two research assistants analyzed the interpreting samples and reviewed each interpreter sample a minimum of five times. The two research assistants are experienced interpreters, both with 25 years of interpreting experience, and are interpreter educators. Both have Bachelor of Education degrees, and one possesses a Master's degree in education. Both had provided interpretation in educational settings, and one had taught deaf students at the high school level.

The interpreting samples were assessed by using a propositional analysis approach scale for overall effectiveness of the interpretation, ranging from effective, mostly effective, mostly ineffective and ineffective (Dillinger, 1994; Russell, 2002; Russell & Winston, 2014). The stimulus texts were coded for the six discourse features, as mentioned above: (1) higher-order or *metacognitive questions*; (2) the application of *scaffolding techniques* to bridge previous learner knowledge with new knowledge; (3) the *sequencing of instructions*; (4) *reconceptualizing strategies* where teachers reframe information in different ways to reach all learners; (5) *peer or reciprocal teaching* that occurs among learners through the asking and answering of questions and small and large group interactions where students share their knowledge with each other; and (6) *teacher feedback* for learners as individuals and groups, designed to guide learners and keep them engaged in positive ways.

The effective and mostly effective interpreting renditions included being able to manage the teacher discourse function while representing ASL in a manner that was grammatically correct and conventional. Effective and mostly effective work represented the ability to provide the teacher's content as well as the meanings behind the words, which may be explicitly or implicitly coded, to allow for teacher-student engagement and teaching strategies. The ineffective interpreting renditions included the ability to provide lexical representation of the 'teacher's talk' but with frequent grammatical errors in the ASL rendition, content errors and/or significant omissions. These renditions would make it very difficult for deaf students to comprehend the content and participate in the expected student interactions with the teacher in ways that lead to academic, social and intellectual engagement.

Finally, the coding was reviewed by an expert deaf teacher with significant experience teaching deaf learners at the elementary and junior and senior high school levels. This teacher was very familiar with the use of the teacher discourse functions chosen for this study and had a sophisticated understanding of how these strategies could be represented in ASL in order to realize the engagement goals of teachers. This level of expert review was essential in confirming coding and analysis decisions, from the perspective of a first language user of ASL and a highly competent teacher of deaf students.

Results and discussion

The following describes the results and shows the range within interpreting performances. The data reveal that six of the 35 interpreters could use conventional language and interpretation strategies that led to effective interpretation and the potential of realizing engagement in the ways intended by the teacher.

Metacognitive questions

Teachers across the stimulus samples applied Bloom's (1954) Taxonomy and asked a range of questions that reflected lower- to higher-order thinking. Questions at the lowest level ask students to 'remember' in order to recall facts and basic concepts, while the next level of 'understand' asks students to classify, discuss, describe, explain or select. The third level of 'apply' invites students to apply information in new situations, solving, interpreting, demonstrating or implementing solutions. Metacognitive questions at the 'analyze' level ask students to draw connections among ideas, often by comparing, contrasting, questioning, testing, organizing or experimenting. Questions at the 'evaluate' level ask students to justify, support, judge, critique or weigh information. Finally, questions at the highest level ask learners to 'create', which can mean designing, assembling, constructing, authoring or investigating.

Interpreters who were able to demonstrate effective interpreting of the teacher's use of metacognitive questions were able to recognize the type or level of question used by the teacher and find a suitable interpretation. Table 10.2 describes the average percentage of effective and mostly effective work performed by the six interpreters who were consistently able to provide access to the linguistic elements of the classroom in order to promote academic, social and intellectual engagement. The data reveal the six interpreters' use of strategies that could provide a reasonable level of content accuracy to potentially contribute to the engagement of learners.

Table 10.2 Effective and mostly effective interpretation per discourse strategy

Discourse strategy	Average % effective among six interpreters	Range among six interpreters
Metacognitive questions	92%	89–97%
Scaffolding	94%	88–96%
Sequencing	93%	89–94%
Reconceptualize	95%	91–97%
Peer teaching	89%	82–95%
Teacher feedback	90%	85–95%

The successful use of these strategies is contingent upon whether the deaf student possessed the factors necessary for placement in such an environment (as described later in this chapter).

Table 10.3 describes the analysis of the other 29 interpreters who were assessed as providing mostly ineffective or ineffective interpretation across the six discourse strategies. Of the six discourse strategies examined, the interpreters were more successful in recognizing and applying strategies for sequencing and reconceptualizing; however, with rates of effectiveness of 30% and 25%, it means that 70% and 75% of the time the child did not receive an accurate rendition of the 'teacher talk', thus contributing to an impoverished language experience.

The 29 interpreters who were not able to create consistently effective interpretation of a metacognitive question most commonly relied on three strategies, which included substituting a lower-order question (53% of the time), omitting the question (10% of the time), or linking the question and a student response in such a way that there was no time for the deaf child to think and respond as the question had already been answered by another student (37% of the time). Tables 10.4 and 10.5 respectively highlight examples of the reduced cognitive and linguistic renditions offered via interpretation and the frequency of specific strategies that did not represent the teacher's use of questioning.

Table 10.3 Mostly ineffective and ineffective interpretation per discourse strategy

Discourse strategy	Average % effective among 29 interpreters	Range among 29 interpreters
Metacognitive questions	12%	10–16%
Scaffolding	14%	11–15%
Sequencing	30%	28–33%
Reconceptualize	25%	23–29%
Peer teaching	11%	9–14%
Teacher feedback	15%	13–18%

Table 10.4 Reduced cognitive and linguistic renditions

Original teacher utterance	Interpreter rendition
Logically, which answers can you rule out and then explain your thinking ...	*Choose the right answer ...*
I want you to make a prediction based on what we created last week ...	*Remember last week we talked about photosynthesis?*
How can you use this equation? What does the data show? Is that equation the best way to solve this problem?	*What does the data show? Is the equation right or wrong?*
Tell me what you notice about this?	*See? The graph shows the tickets sold in each state.*

Table 10.5 Ineffective interpretation of metacognitive questions

Discourse strategy used	Frequency
Substitute a lower-order question	53%
Omit the question	10%
Link a question and student answer without a pause to allow deaf student to think	37%

The impact of substituting, omitting or linking questions to answers in a manner that tells the student the question has been answered already is to reduce the opportunities for deaf children to learn to think critically and limit opportunities for social, academic and intellectual engagement. The ineffective interpretation was often transcoded ASL signs in English order, with little or none of the natural prosodic elements (Nicodemus, 2009; Winston, 1995) that would contribute to enhanced comprehension for the deaf student. When the interpretation is produced without any of the natural pauses, grammatical structures are lost, and the child will have little access to the content of the message or the interactional patterns within the classroom. Instead of engaging learners, the risk is of distancing the deaf learner from both content and interaction within the classroom and moving him or her to 'bystander status' (Goffman, 1981) instead of being an active participant.

Scaffolding

The second discourse strategy examined scaffolding (Bruner, 1978; Cazden, 2001; Wood *et al.*, 1976). Scaffolding describes strategies based on the teacher modeling or demonstrating the instructional content, then guiding the students through practice activities, eventually releasing more and more responsibility to the student. Scaffolding is often linked with Vygotsky's (1981) construct of 'the zone of proximal development', where the child learns to take over more and more of the responsibility for the task at hand. An example of scaffolding can be seen in the use of questions that help a child create a story, learn to retell the story and then move to independently telling the story. For example, the teacher may ask, *What happened next?*, followed by a *wh*-question that probes for the next piece of information: *What happened when grandpa brought the truck up to the house?*

Teachers may also build in reciprocal teaching within the framework of scaffolded instruction. This often takes the form of dialogue and questions between teacher and students in which participants take turns assuming the role of the teacher (Cazden, 2001). Once again, these strategies make it possible for students to participate in the mature task from the very beginning, moving to independent task completion. In this data set, during the teachers' use of scaffolding strategies, 29 interpreters were effective in representing scaffolding techniques only an average of 14% of the time. The interpreters who were ineffective in representing the scaffolding techniques (see Table 10.6) used two other strategies (i.e. simplified the question to a factual answer or reformulated by including the answer in the context), which changed the complexity and specificity of required answers to the posed question that was originally designed to invite the child to use their thinking in answering the question. Cazden (2001: 109) refers to these as reformulations, which decrease the cognitive tasks faced by the child. The following are examples of reformulations:

Teacher:	What do you think those people are doing?
Reformulation:	What are they planting? (Reformulates with the answer in the question.)
Teacher:	How did they go?
Reformulation with context:	Did they travel by bus, car or airplane?
Teacher:	What kind of a tiger?
Reformulation:	Was he a very SAD tiger? (Reformulation includes a wrong answer, *sad*, but suggests the right semantic set.)

Reciprocal teaching

In terms of peer or reciprocal teaching, the most common approach that the 29 interpreters used in the effective work (11%) was to identify that they needed to pause teachers so only one student was speaking at a time and allow time for the deaf student to see who was speaking, prior

Table 10.6 Ineffective interpretation of scaffolding

Discourse strategy used	Frequency
Reformulation	41%
Use contextualization	33%
Use of wrong answer to suggest right semantic set	26%

to viewing the interpretation of the answer. For the majority of the time, the interpreters did their best to keep up with the teachers and students in the rapid interchange of questions and answers, with a range of processing time between two and four seconds. Such a short processing time means there was no time for the interpreters to use source attribution techniques such as name signs for the nondeaf peers that would give the deaf child a cue to who was speaking, nor was there time for interpreters to manage all of the student comments, especially when there were overlapping utterances among children.

It may be that if the interpreters are dealing with a class that they regularly work in, rather than the stimulus video, they might be comfortable in stopping teachers and reminding them to alter the pacing. However, in the live observations of actual classroom interpretation that occurred in the next phase of the study, the interpreters rarely stopped teachers and nondeaf students. The consequence of this 'rapid-fire' exchange of questions and answers is that the pace of the signing becomes very quick and does not meet the grammatical conventions of a natural use of language. The deaf child is able to view the signing; however, because of the grammatical errors, it can increase the cognitive load for the child attempting to retrieve meaning from it. Once more, this interpreting behavior places the deaf child at risk of becoming a bystander, watching the signs without understanding what they mean and without the opportunity to participate in peer teaching moments.

Sequencing and reconceptualizing

The most effective discourse strategies exhibited by all 29 interpreters providing video samples were sequencing and reconceptualizing. The sequencing of the steps of a science experiment or of solving a math problem were present in the interpretation on average 30% of the time, suggesting that the interpreters were able to recognize sequencing language and represent it visually through ASL indexing or the use of discourse markers that separated the steps. The interpreters who were not able to effectively manage sequencing strategies made frequent errors, such as getting the steps in the wrong order, perhaps due to auditory memory issues or fatigue in managing multiple sequences. For example, one interpreter offered a sequence for a science experiment, getting the first three steps in the correct order, and then transposing Steps 4 and 6.

The analysis of the discourse strategy of reconceptualizing revealed that the ineffective interpreters were able to show this strategy only 25% of the time, allowing the student to see the information in elaborated forms offered by the teacher or restated in different ways. However, when the interpretation was ineffective, the most frequently used approach was to omit the reconceptualization. When interpreters were asked about this strategy in subsequent interviews, many of the interpreters reflected that the repetition used by the teacher was an opportunity for them to 'catch up' with the teacher. Seven interpreters viewed it as unnecessary repetition and made a conscious omission as a strategy for managing their own cognitive fatigue, in ways similar to the interpreters in Napier's (2004) study of strategies used by postsecondary interpreters. However, when viewed from a lens of engagement, the reconceptualization used by teachers would have allowed deaf students greater opportunities to interact with the content and promoted better academic and intellectual engagement.

Teacher feedback

The 'feedback' provided by the teacher to the students revealed that comments, both positive and corrective, were present on average in 15% of the interpreting samples provided by the 29 interpreters. However, teacher feedback is intended for all classroom participants, and positive or corrective feedback offered to one student can have the effect of shaping the future behavior of other students. When teachers praise students for answering, despite the answer being incorrect, it can encourage them to try answering again. When the deaf child misses this information, they are not able to engage in the social and academic expectations for students in the class. An interesting teacher strategy to solicit this level of engagement was demonstrated during subsequent classroom observations. In one classroom, the teacher had a deaf child's name on five of the 'answering sticks' while the nondeaf students had just one stick with their name attached. The teacher then pulled the sticks out to call on students, thus checking in with the deaf learner at least five times during each morning and afternoon. When asked why she did this, the teacher replied:

> It allows me to check comprehension of the deaf student, and to build confidence within the learner as I can call on them when I know they likely have the right answer. And if they don't have the right answer, I can guide them. It works well!

In that classroom context, the interpreter facilitated this strategy through the use of pausing to ensure the deaf child knew that they were being called upon, and then providing the ASL to English spoken interpretation for the teacher and peers. The interpreter did not omit any of the feedback offered to the deaf learner, making linguistic decisions based on teacher discourse and effective interpreting strategies. In that classroom, we see the interpreter and teacher working closely in partnership to ensure that the teacher can accurately assess the deaf student's learning, and peers can also view the student as an equal participant in the class.

Contextual factors among the successful interpreters

Given that only six interpreters were able to consistently provide a level of linguistic access to the content and engagement processes of the classroom, we examined additional contextual factors present in the work of the successful six interpreters (see Table 10.7). All six interpreters had

Table 10.7 Participant variables

Interpreter variables	Effective
Over 8 years of experience	6/35
AVLIC certified	3/35
Provide community interpreting	6/35
Degrees in education	2/35
Foundation of discourse analysis	6/35

over eight years of interpreting experience in the school and in community environments outside of their regular school contracts. In addition, they all shared a background that focused on discourse analysis as part of their early training. Three of the interpreters possessed national certification from AVLIC, and two had degrees in education that would have provided them with additional training about teaching strategies and approaches to education.

Based on the results of the interpreting performances, the next phase included classroom observations of an additional eight interpreters working in elementary schools and junior and senior high schools in Alberta. While permission was not obtained to videotape these classroom sessions, the field notes of observations (Creswell & Creswell, 2018) served as a springboard for targeted semi-structured interviews (Creswell & Creswell, 2018) with interpreters, deaf students, parents, teachers and administrators, in order to learn more about their experiences with interpretation and the engagement of deaf learners in mediated educational settings.

Classroom observations

Eight interpreters (see Table 10.8) agreed to be observed working in language arts, math, science, social studies and physical education classes.

Table 10.8 Classroom observation and interpreter variables

Classes observed	Number of interpreters	Education and experience of interpreter
Grade 3: Language arts and social classes	2 Females	Graduation from Interpreter Education Programs, both had 5 years of experience
Grade 7: Language arts, math and social classes	2 Females	Graduation from Interpreter Education Programs, one interpreter with 5 years of experience, the other with 10 years of experience
Grade 10: Language arts, physical education, science and math	3 Females, 1 Male	Graduation from Interpreter Education Programs, one interpreter with 5 years of experience, the other three with 10 years of experience

The researcher took field notes, observing the teachers using the same discourse strategies as in the stimulus material and the resulting strategies used by the classroom interpreters.

Across all of the classes, the most significant factor that appeared to impact the effectiveness of interpretation was the pace of the teaching. The classrooms were structured for students that can hear, and the teachers appeared to have little knowledge or awareness of the need to accommodate the pacing required for a bilingual and bimodal classroom. While teachers seemed to understand language acquisition in broad terms, they struggled to understand how the deaf child is using a visual-spatial language and how it differs from an auditory language. Hence, teachers did not differentiate instruction in ways that would allow for effective interpretation and engage the deaf students to the same degree as the nondeaf students.

For instance, while three interpreters asked teachers to repeat questions prior to answering them for students, the teachers resumed rapid-fire exchanges which left the interpreters providing summary forms of interpreting in an attempt to catch up. To someone who does not use ASL, it would appear the interpreters were doing a great job. To those who know ASL, it was clear that the interpretation was incomplete, ungrammatical and had no prosodic aspects such as utterance boundaries, affect or topic marking and, in many places, the work simply did not make sense in ASL. Despite the advanced qualifications and experience of the interpreters in this study, the fast-paced sections did not allow for effective interpretation of all discourse features of interest in this study phase. The interpreters that produced effective work had to make conscious omissions of some of the teacher-student exchanges and some of the reconceptualizations used by the teacher. At times, the renditions of teacher discourse were provided in the form of summaries, and at other times there were reformulations that significantly altered the content and teacher intent. Interestingly, the interpreters working in the elementary school classes were consistent in offering the teacher feedback comments to students, even if it meant eliminating other content. Based on the results of the video samples of interpretation and the observations of the 'live' classroom discourse that presented similar patterns, the research moved on to the next phase of conducting interviews with the stakeholders in providing education to deaf children.

Interviews

Semi-structured interviews with interpreters, parents, students, teachers and administrators were conducted to capture multiple perspectives and experiences with inclusive education pertaining to interpreter performance and student engagement (see Table 10.9). The interviews revealed that there were very different perceptions about the ways in which classrooms are inclusive of deaf learners with interpreters (Russell, 2008). In

Table 10.9 Engagement: Perceptions of stakeholders

Engagement type	Students (n = 15)	Parents (n = 10)	Teachers and administrators (n = 56 teachers/ n = 4 administrators)	Interpreters (n = 15)
Social	Lack of participation in school sports or clubs; few friends; limited sense of belonging	My child is not able to participate in school sports or clubs; few friends	Deaf child is fully included; has many friends	Mediated instruction is not a normal social experience for deaf learner
Academic	Yes, if the interpreter is qualified; no, with unqualified interpreter If teacher doesn't control classroom dialogue, no access to group conversations	With qualified interpreter, yes Lack of tutoring and academic supports	With qualified interpreter, yes, equal access Deaf students struggle to meet expectations	Student receives content but seems to struggle with what to do with it; so many school readiness gaps; classes not designed for interpretation
Intellectual	Don't enjoy school Get what I need academically but not socially	How do I keep my child motivated to learn when he/she is struggling?	We provide the tools and up to student to take advantage of them	Students often very disengaged and unmotivated - will they attend postsecondary education?

previous studies, teachers and administrators indicated that they believe that the interpreters do an excellent job, that deaf students are fully included in the life of the school and that the inclusion of deaf learners is working well (Russell, 2008; Russell & MacLeod, 2009). However, in this interview phase, parents painted a different picture, noting that there was no funding for interpreters to ensure that their children could participate in sports and clubs after school, which are key to social engagement. The parents also recognized that schools do not always hire qualified interpreters and there is no one who can assess the interpretation prior to being hired or provide ongoing evaluation and monitoring.

Interpreters commented on the very real challenges of providing interpretation in classrooms with teachers who are unfamiliar with how to teach deaf children and who will not modify classroom activities to allow for successful interpretation. As in the interpreter survey, the interpreters interviewed also commented on the challenges of social engagement, and the realities of deaf children often having no friends or peers with whom to communicate. Some interpreters shared the views of the teachers, adopting the ideology or myth that their interpretations are making the classroom equally accessible. Finally, the views of the deaf students are also illuminating. Students as young as 10 years of age could tell when the interpreting was incomplete and indicated that they felt lost or confused. All of the students believed ineffective interpreters impacted their education in a negative way. In contrast to the teacher and administrator perceptions about deaf students being included and having equal access, students reported being unable to engage in group discussions and debates, and unable to respond to questions. The lack of engagement was partly due to inadequate interpretation and also due to teachers who did not adapt their teaching style and pace to allow for an interpretation to be completed. Equally important is that the students in these interviews revealed that after Grade 3 they did not feel they had friends or meaningful connections with other nondeaf students. While some schools had sign language clubs, the reality for these students was that there were no peers who could use sign language to the degree required for friendship. The most dominant themes that emerged from the stakeholder conversations are summarized in Table 10.9.

However, despite the significant challenges of interpretation, five of the 10 deaf students were doing very well in school. Four common factors emerged across these particular students:

- All had experienced direct education for at least three to five years, meaning they had been in a 'deaf' program where teachers could sign directly.
- All could read and write at or near grade level, which allowed them other ways to access learning when the interpretation was ineffective.
- All had at least one parent who could use sign language and who supported them emotionally.
- And all had deaf friends outside of the school they attended, in order to make up for the lack of social contact with peers in an inclusive setting.

These factors invite much greater attention in the research to help us determine when a child is ready for an 'inclusive' setting. When students have these four factors, they may have resiliency and additional linguistic strategies to bring to inclusive education settings, while understanding that social engagement may have to occur outside of school.

Implications

These data reveal some distinct challenges to the dominant policy and practices of inclusive education. Despite the majority of interpreters possessing formal interpreter education, which is the qualification required by many school districts, only six out of 35 interpreters were able to consistently use strategies that convey teaching discourse elements and promote educational engagement in the manner the teachers intended. The interpreters who recognized teacher discourse and teaching functions through language often made different decisions about the linguistic devices available to them to represent the teacher talk. When one examines the content of Canadian interpreter education programs, there are none that offer additional instruction about teacher discourse and pedagogical principles with kindergarten to high school students. This is a significant gap in the language knowledge needed by interpreters working with teachers, and it affects the quality of linguistic access and level of engagement for deaf learners. If interpreters are taught about direct instruction methods used by teachers who can sign, how teacher discourse affects engagement, and particular discourse strategies used by teachers, will this improve education where everything is mediated through the sign language interpreter?

The study also points to knowledge gaps in the training required of teachers in inclusive settings who are working with deaf students and interpreters. None of the teachers interviewed had any specialized knowledge or in-service training about the nature of plurilingualism or language acquisition in deaf learners, and none of them knew how to work with interpreters in order to ensure their instruction was accessible. There appears to be a widespread myth among educators and policymakers that a deaf child can acquire language by watching an interpreter for the school day; however, language acquisition occurs when children are exposed to adults and other children who share the same language. This is not the context represented in this study, in that the interpreter is the only one in the school who knows ASL; thus, there are reduced natural language learning opportunities. In this study, we can see that the accommodation of interpreters, who are in fact qualified, does not result in full or equal linguistic access to the classroom. While interpreters do their best to keep up, the interpreting performance data show that the work does not realize the teacher discourse and engagement strategies.

Further research needs to explore how we know if a child is ready for the experience of a mediated education and the kinds of environments that need to be constructed to serve that child well. The five children in this study who were succeeding in school had significant experiences that provide critical insight towards reducing the illusion of inclusion, and moving us to a place of determining 'for whom and under what context' inclusion works (MacQuarrie & Parilla, 2009).

Students' experiences provide a starting point for investigating whether classroom practices can be improved to create more effective and engaging learning environments for deaf students. These practices may include the ways in which the curriculum is delivered by the teacher, and other factors such as time, how students are grouped for learning and how the physical environment of classrooms with signed language interpreters can be improved to create more effective and engaging learning environments for deaf students. These Canadian data point to the ways in which inclusive environments are not supporting deaf learners, and this study illustrates some of the reasons why. As Willms *et al.* (2009) stress, when students struggle in school, they are disadvantaged in later life. Based on these findings, in what ways can we re-imagine school environments that support deaf children? Weber (in this volume) describes ways in which she is fostering plurilingualism with deaf learners who have limited linguistic resources available to them. It would seem that many of the students in this study would benefit from the type of direct teaching methods used by a teacher who is fluent in sign language and from the interaction opportunities that are possible within a community of learners that are also developing language competences.

Limitations

This study contributes to our understanding of the actual quality of classroom interpretation provided to represent teacher discourse and to support social, academic and intellectual engagement. A larger study that examines live classroom interpretation versus authentic simulated samples would be a useful addition to our understanding of language learning environments that support or detract from plurilingual development. Based on the results of this multi-phase study, an intervention study is suggested in which interpreters are explicitly taught about the nature of teacher discourse, engagement strategies and pedagogical principles that shape educational processes and the ways in which these can shape interpreting work in the classroom.

Conclusion

Snoddon and Weber (this volume) caution educators to understand the need for teachers who are proficient in a standard sign language variety, in order to support deaf students' access to linguistic complexity. The results presented in this chapter invite us to revisit our assumptions about inclusion and the level of linguistic access and engagement that is realistically possible with classroom interpreters.

These results have implications for interpreters working in educational settings, interpreter educators training interpreters for kindergarten to Grade 12, and teachers who work in inclusive settings with deaf learners. The results will be of interest to administrators and policymakers in examining what inclusion means according to the UNCRPD, and the reality of how current inclusion practices impact deaf children's linguistic and academic experience in Canadian classrooms.

Acknowledgments

Funding for the research project was granted by the Social Sciences and Humanities Research Council of Canada and the Killam Research Fund.

References

Audas, R. and Willms, J.D. (2001) *Engagement and Dropping Out of School: A Life-Course Perspective*. Hull, QC: Human Resources Department Canada Publications Centre.

Bloom, B. (1954) The thought processes of students in discussion. In S.J. French (ed.) *Accent on Teaching: Experiments in General Education* (pp. 23–46). New York: Harperie.

Braun, V. and Clarke, V. (2006) Using thematic analysis in psychology. *Qualitative Research in Psychology* 3, 77–81.

Bruner, J.S. (1978) The role of dialogue in language acquisition. In A. Sinclair, R.J. Jarvella and W.J.M. Levelt (eds) *The Child's Conception of Language*. New York: Springer-Verlag.

Caledon Institute of Social Policy (2006) Improving primary and secondary education on reserves in Canada. *Caledon Commentary*, October. See https://maytree.com/wp-content/uploads/608ENG.pdf.

Cazden, C.B. (2001) *Classroom Discourse: The Language of Teaching and Learning* (2nd edn). Portsmouth, NH: Heinemann.

Community Health Systems Resource Group, The Hospital for Sick Children (2005) *Early School Leavers: Understanding the Lived Reality of Disengagement from Secondary School – Final Report*. Toronto: Ontario Ministry of Education and Training, Special Education Branch. See https://www.tcdsb.org/FORSTAFF/NewTeacherInduction/Documents/schooLeavers.pdf.

Creswell, J.W. and Creswell, J.D. (2018) *Research Design: Qualitative, Quantitative and Mixed Methods and Approaches*. Thousand Oaks, CA: Sage.

Dillinger, M. (1994) Comprehension during interpreting: What do interpreters know that bilinguals don't. In S. Lambert and B. Moser-Mercer (eds) *Bridging the Gap: Empirical Research in Simultaneous Interpreting* (pp. 155–189). Amsterdam: John Benjamins.

Goffman, E. (1981) *Forms of Talk*. Philadelphia, PA: University of Pennsylvania Press.

Kozulin, A., Gindis, B., Ageyev, V. and Miller, S. (2003) *Vygotsky's Educational Theory in Cultural Context*. Cambridge: Cambridge University Press.

LaBue, M.A. (1998) Interpreted education: A study of deaf students' access to the content and form of literacy instruction in a mainstreamed high school English class. Unpublished doctoral dissertation, Harvard Graduate School of Education.

Llewelyn-Jones, P. and Lee, R. (2014) *Re-defining the Role of the Community Interpreter: The Concept of Role-space*. Lincoln: SLI Press.

Major, G. and Napier, J. (2012) Interpreting and knowledge mediation in the healthcare setting: What do we really mean by 'accuracy'? In V. Montalt and M. Shuttleworth (eds) *Linguistica Antverpiensia: Translation & Knowledge Mediation in Medical and Health Settings* (pp. 207–226). Antwerp: Artesius University College.

McKee, R.L. (2008) The construction of deaf children as marginal bilinguals in the mainstream. *International Journal of Bilingual Education and Bilingualism* 11 (5), 519–540. DOI: 10.1080/13670050802149168.

McKee, R.L. and Biederman, Y. (2003) The construction of learning contexts for deaf bilingual learners. In R. Barnard and T. Glynn (eds) *Bilingual Children's Language and Literacy Development: New Zealand Case Studies* (pp. 194–224). Clevedon: Multilingual Matters.

McQuarrie, L. and Parilla, R. (2009) Phonological representations in deaf children: Rethinking the 'functional equivalence' hypothesis. *Journal of Deaf Studies and Deaf Education* 14, 137–154. doi:10.1093/deafed/enn025

Metzger, M. (1999) *Sign Language Interpreting: Deconstructing the Myth of Neutrality*. Washington, DC: Gallaudet University Press.

Muruvik Venen, A. (2009) Ten years of bilingual education in Norway – where are we? In J. Mole (ed.) *International Perspectives on Educational Interpreting* (pp. 164–169). Norbury: Direct Learn.

Napier, J. (2004) Interpreting omissions: A new perspective. *Interpreting* 6 (2), 117–142.

Napier, J. (2007) Cooperation in interpreter-mediated monologic talk. *Discourse and Communication* 1 (4), 407–432.

Nicodemus, B. (2009) *Prosody and Utterance Boundaries in American Sign Language Interpretation.* Washington, DC: Gallaudet University Press.

Ramsey, C. (1997) *Deaf Children in Public Schools: Placement, Context, and Consequences.* Washington, DC: Gallaudet University Press.

Richards, J. and Vining, A. (2004) *Aboriginal Off-Reserve Education: Time for Action.* Commentary No. 198. Toronto: CD Howe Institute.

Ritchie, J., Lewis, J., Elam, G., Tennant, R. and Rahim, N. (2003) Designing and selecting samples. In J. Ritchie and J. Lewis (eds) *Qualitative Research Practice: A Guide for Social Science Students and Researchers* (pp. 77–108). London: Sage.

Roy, C. (1993) A sociolinguistic analysis of the interpreter's role in simultaneous talk in interpreted interaction. *Multilingua* 12 (4), 341–364.

Russell, D. (2002) *Interpreting in Legal Contexts: Consecutive and Simultaneous Interpretation.* Burtonsville, MD: Linstock Press.

Russell, D. (2008) What do others think of our work? Deaf students, teachers, administrators and parents' perspectives on educational interpreting. In C. Roy (ed.) *Diversity and Community in the Worldwide Sign Language Interpreting Profession: Proceedings of the Second World Association of Sign Language Interpreters 2007 Conference* (pp. 34–38). Coleford: Douglas McLean Publishing.

Russell, D. and McLeod, J. (2009) Educational interpreting: Multiple perspectives of our work. In J. Mole (ed.) *International Perspectives on Educational Interpreting* (pp. 128–144). Brassington: Direct Learned Services.

Russell, D. and Winston, E. (2014) Tapping into the interpreting process: Using participant reports to inform the interpreting process in educational settings. *International Journal of Interpreting and Translation Research* 6 (1), 102–127.

Schick, B. and Williams, K. (2004) The educational interpreter performance assessment: Current structure and practices. In E.A. Winston (ed.) *Educational Interpreting: How it Can Succeed* (pp. 186–205). Washington, DC: Gallaudet University Press.

Schick, B., Williams, K. and Bolster, L. (1999) Skill level of educational interpreters working in public schools. *Journal of Deaf Studies and Education* 4 (2), 144–155.

Smith, M. (2013) *More than Meets the Eye: Revealing the Complexities of an Interpreted Education.* Washington, DC: Gallaudet University Press.

Vygotsky, L. (1978) Interaction between learning and development. *Readings on the Development of Children* 23 (3), 34–41.

Vygotsky, L. (1981) The genesis of higher mental functions. In J.V. Wetsch (ed.) *The Concept of Activity in Soviet Psychology.* Armonk, NY: M.E. Sharpe.

Vygotsky, L., Rieber, R.W. and Carton, A.S. (1987) *The Collected Works of L.S. Vygotsky.* New York: Plenum Press.

Willms, J.D., Friesen, S. and Milton, P. (2009) *What Did You Do in School Today? Transforming Classrooms Through Social, Academic, and Intellectual Engagement.* First National Report. Toronto: Canadian Education Association.

Winston, E.A. (1995) Spatial mapping in comparative discourse frames. In K. Emmorey and J. Riley (eds) *Language, Gesture, and Space.* Hillsdale, NJ: Lawrence Erlbaum.

Winston, E.A. (2004) *Educational Interpreting: How it Can Succeed.* Washington, DC: Gallaudet University Press.

Wood, D.J., Bruner, J.S. and Ross, G. (1976) The role of tutoring in problem solving. *Journal of Child Psychiatry and Psychology* 17 (2), 89–10.

WFD (World Federation of the Deaf) (2018) *WFD Position Paper on Inclusive Education.* See https://2tdzpf2t7hxmggqhq3njno1y-wpengine.netdna-ssl.com/wp-content/uploads/2018/06/WFD-Position-Paper-on-Inclusive-Education-5-June-2018-FINAL-without-IS-1.pdf.

Index

Note: References in *italics* are to figures, those in **bold** to tables.

Abbé de l'Épée 83
Abbé Tarra 85
Abbou, Marie-Thérèse 86
Abrams, Stacy 205
action potentials 132
Alexander, R. 134
Allan, J. 38, 39, 40, 52
ALSF (French Sign Language
    Academy) 86
ALTE (Association of Language Testers
    in Europe) 182
American Association of Applied
    Linguistics 1
American Sign Language (ASL) xi, xiv,
    xv, 1, 4, 70, 86
    in Ontario 35, 36–37, 44, 45, 46–47,
    51–52
    in Saskatchewan 103, 109, 115–116
    Signing Naturally 50, 178
    status of 177, 202
    see also bimodal bilingual
    programming
American Society for Deaf Children
    (ASDC) 204–205
Antia, S. 153
assemblages 105–106
Association of Language Testers in
    Europe (ALTE) 182
Association of Visual Language
    Interpreters of Canada
    (CASLI) 221
ATERK NGT 180, 181, 182, 185
'audiophonic' bilingualism 91
August, D. xv
Australia 199, 202

Bagga-Gupta, S. 20, xvI
Batamula, C. 202, 203
Battiste, M. 107, 114
Bell, Alexander Graham 66
bilingual deaf education 1, 2

bilingual parenting 199
bilingualism 3, 7, 61, 198–199
    benefits of 204
    bimodal bilingualism 7
    defined 92, 99, 151
    see also Family Language Policy
    (FLP); plurilingualism
bimodal bilingual education xv, xvii, 30,
    152–154
    see also sign bilingualism in science
    education
bimodal bilingual programming 8–9,
    149–152
    Bimodal Parent Survey 169
    cochlear implants 150, 151
    school background 154–156
    terminology 151
    discussion 165–168
bimodal bilingual programming:
    parent/staff survey outcomes
    162–163, 169
    development of Deaf identity
    163–164
    program benefits 164
    program challenges 164–165
    student academic/language
    progress 163
bimodal bilingual programming:
    student outcomes
    ASL skills 161–162, *162*
    English vocabulary **160**, 160–161
    report cards 161, 162
    speech skills 159–160, **160**
bimodal bilingual programming: study
    overview 156
    classroom context 156–157
    staff/parent survey 159
    student assessment 158–159
    students 156–158
bimodal communication 93, 100–101
bimodal, defined 151

bimodality 92–93
Bloom, B. 226
Bourdieu, Pierre 61, 62–64, 65, 72, 73, 75, 76
  capital 63–64
  doxa 63
  embodied capital 64
  field 63
  habitus 63, 72, 73–74
  institutionalised capital 64
  linguistic capital 64
  linguistic fields 64
  linguistic habitus 64, 65, 66–67, 72
  linguistic marketplaces 63, 64
  objectified capital 64
Bouvet, Danièle 86
Boyd, Marion 46
Branson, J. 42
British Association of Teachers of the Deaf (2017) 67–68
British Deaf and Dumb Association 70
British Sign Language (BSL) 61, 68, 74, 75

Calderon, R. 176
California Association for the Deaf (CAD) 204–205
Canada
  bilingual schools 218–219
  Chinese families in Montreal 198
  cochlear implants xii, 53, 114, 115, 150, 151
  cognitive imperialism 108
  mediated education 218
  racism and ableism 108
  see also bimodal bilingual programming; interpreting for Deaf children; Ontario, Canada; Saskatchewan, Canada
Canadian Association of Educators of the Deaf and Hard of Hearing 38
Canadian Association of Sign Language Interpreters (CASLI) 221
Canadian Charter of Rights and Freedoms 53
Canadian Hearing Society 49
Canagarajah, S. 104, 106
Carbin, C. 40, 41
cartographies 105
Cazden, C.B. 223

CEFR (Common European Framework of Reference for Languages) 1, 3, 173–174, 179–180
  mapping for sign languages 180–182, *181*
CEFR: WeSign4 course–Data and methodology 182–183, *190*
  children and participants 184, **184**
  procedure and materials 183–184
  step 1: teacher assessments 184, 185, **185**
  step 2: self-assessment grid 185, 186
  step 3: evaluation form 186
CEFR: WeSign4 course–Results
  parents' experiences and learning needs 189–190, *190*
  step 1: teacher assessments 186–187, *187*
  step 2: self-assessment grid 187–188, *188*
  step 3: evaluation form results 188–189
CEFR: WeSign4 course–Conclusion 190–191
Cenoz, J. 62
chaining 134
Chavaillaz, J.-F. 83
classroom context 156–157
Clerc, Laurent 83
co-enrollment programs xviii, 151, 152–154
cochlear implants (CI) xvii, 1, 2, 106, 108, 202
  Canada xii, 53, 114, 115, 150, 151
  Netherlands 173
  Sweden 15, 17, 20, 28, 30, 31
  UK 75
cognitive imperialism 107–108, 111, 112, 113, 114, 116
Collier, V.P. 29
colonial languages 72
Common European Framework of Reference for Languages *see* CEFR
communities of practice 130
Compton, S. 39
Conrad, R. 70
Convention on the Rights of Persons with Disabilities (CRPD) 36, 45
  Optional Protocol (2017) 36

Conway, Sean 42, 45, 46
Coste, D. *et al.* 3, 82, 92
Coughlin, Charles 40
Council of Europe xii, 60, 175
    see also CEFR
cued speech 88
Cummins, J. 43, 44, 131
Curdt-Christansen, X.L. 198

Dale, D.M.C. 69
De Houwer, A. 198
Deaf Crows (play; 2016) 104, 105,
    106, 110
    Blossom 120–121
    Jade 117–119
    Oliver 119–120
    Oliver Redux 121–122
    performance space 116–117, *117*
    discussion and conclusion 122–123
deaf, Deaf defined 82
Deaf Education Advisory Forum
    (DEAF) 104, 109, 111–114
Deaf Ontario Now xi, 42, 49
    Ministry review of education
        programs for DHH students
        43–44
    recommendations 35, 36, 44–45
    implementation 46–47
deaf plurilingualism 61–62
Deaf Studies 61
deafness, medical model of 107
Delaporte, Y. 84
Denman, Barry 51
Denmark 2, 177
depicting signs 133
Dettman, S. 202
DHH (deaf and hard-of-hearing)
    students xi–xiii
    bimodal bilingual education xv, xvii,
        30, 152–154
    causes of underachievement xiii–xiv
    early years xiii, xiv
    identification of 195–196
    linguistic interdependence xiii,
        xiv–xvi, 43
    plurilingual instruction xiii, xvi–xvii
    re-imagining school environments
        xvii–xviii
    conclusion xviii–xix
dialogic teaching 134
discrimination xviii–xix, 36

Domfors, L. 20
Dressler, C. xv
Dunant-Sauvin, C. 83
Dutch Foundation for Deaf and Hard-
    of-Hearing Children (NSDSK)
    177–178
    Paedologic Audiologic Institute 177

early years education xiii, xiv, 20–21
Edwards, V. 198
embodied capital 64
Enns, C. *et al.* xi, xvii–xviii
equity of educational opportunities 113
Estève, I. 99
Eurocentrism 107–108
European Centre for Modern
    Languages 180
Ewing, Sir Alexander 70

Fairclough, N. 111, 112, 113
Family Language Policy (FLP) 9,
    195–197
    beliefs, ideologies and attitudes about
        languages 205
    bilingual families using sign language
        201–203
    bilingualism 198–200
    Deaf children's linguistic/listening
        abilities 206
    early identification of children as
        Deaf 195–196
    families' own language experiences/
        identities 205–206
    families with Deaf children 200–201,
        203
    family language plans 206–211, *210*
    framework 197–200, *203*
    macro factors: political and
        sociocultural factors 203–205
    resources 211–212
    sign with hearing babies 204
    conclusion 212
Ferry, Jules 84
fingerspelling 41, 68, 69, 133
Finnish Sign Language 201
FLP *see* Family Language Policy
France 8, 81–82
    2LPE movement 86
    1960s: '*réveil sourd*' and deaf
        community 86–87
    'audiophonic' bilingualism 91

bilingual approach 88
children's bimodal language practices
    100–101
Deaf community 87
deafness and language policy 82–87
Fabius Act (1991) 88–89
first anthropological bilingual model
    83–84
Institution for Young Deaf People 87
International Visual Theatre 86
language(s) and education policies
    87–91
Langue des Signes Française (LSF) 82,
    84, 86, 87, 88–90
Langue des signes québécoise (LSQ)
    xi, 35
legislation 88–89
manual codes 88
medical model of disability 82, 87
Ministry of Education 87–88
Ministry of Health and Social Affairs
    87–88
National Authority for Health (HAS)
    90, 90–91
National Institute for Young Deaf
    People 87
new oralist order: monolingual model
    84–85
oralist approach 88
recommendations to parents 90, 90–91
schooling 87
teaching programme 91
'visuogestural' bilingualism 91
France: exploratory classroom study 92
children's bilingual/bimodal resources
    96, 97–100
individual bilingualism, plurilingualism
    and bimodality 92–93
language profiles 94, 95, **95**, 96
study methodology 93–94, **94**
French Sign Language Academy
    (ALSF) 86

Gallaudet Research Institute 43
Gallaudet University, Washington, DC
    42, 43, 46
García, O. *et al.* 105, 131
Gerber, L. 199
gesture 83, 85, 93, 99, 105
Gibb, Nick 75
Glickman, N.S. 106

Gorter, D. 62
Grenfell, M. 73, 74
Grosjean, F. 92, 176
Gulati, S. 106–107

Hall, M.L. *et al.* 74–75
Hall, W.C. 106
Harris, R. 153
hearing technology 22, 27, 71, 74
Heiling, K. 19
Hendar, O. 19
Hermans, D. *et al.* 153
history of Deaf education xii, 40
Holmström, I. 136
Hornberger, N.H. 45
Houghton, Merv 109
Hult, F. 39, 45
human rights xii, 36, 38, 53, 204
    Saskatchewan 104, 106, 109–110,
        115–116
Hume, C. 74
Humphries, T. *et al.* 174

identification of children as Deaf 195–196
'illusion of inclusion' xii, 218–219
immigrant families 21, 44, 76, 198,
    199–200
inclusive education xvii, 38–39, 218,
    219–220
Indian Sign Language 62, 105
individual self-fulfillment 112–113
International Congress for the
        Improvement of the Conditions
        of Deaf-Mutes, Milan (1880)
        xviii, 40, 66, 72, 85, 107
International Sign 5
interpreter-mediated education 9, 39
interpreting for Deaf children:
        Canadian evidence 217–220
    classroom observations **232**, 232–233
    illusion of inclusion 218
    implications 235–237
    interpreter perceptions on classroom
        challenges 221–222, **222**
    interviews 233–235, **234**
    limitations 237
    conclusion 237
    see also interpreting performance:
        discourse and engagement;
        interpreting performance: results
        and discussion

interpreting performance: discourse and
   engagement 222–223
data analysis 225–226
materials and task 224–225
methodology 224
participants 224
interpreting performance: results and
   discussion 226, **227**, **228**
contextual factors among successful
   interpreters 231–232, **232**
metacognitive questions 226–228,
   227, **228**
reciprocal teaching 229, 230
scaffolding **227**, 228–229, **229**
sequencing and reconceptualizing
   227, 230–231
teacher feedback **227**, 231
Ishaare project 62, 105
Israel: Hebrew-Russian bilinguals
   199–200
Israelite, N. *et al.* 43, 44

Johnson. R. *et al.* 99
Johnson, R.E. *et al.* 43
Johnston, Richard 42, 46

Kamil, M. xv
Kang, H.-S. 199
Kite, B.J. 201–202
Knoors, H. 166, 179
Kopeliovich, S. 199–200
Kozulin, A. *et al.* 218
Kress, G. *et al.* 130
Kusters, A. 105

Lack, A. 68–69
Lamb, T. 73
language 93
language-as-problem 36, 37, 204
language-as-resource 45, 204
language-as-right 45
language deprivation 3, 106–107, 196
language proficiency 131
language repertoire 60
language rights 36, 37, 53
Langue des Signes Française (LSF) 82,
   84, 86, 87, 88–90
Langue des signes québécoise (LSQ)
   xi, 35
Leeson, L. *et al.* 185
legal recognition of sign languages 53

Leigh, I. 167
Lewis, M.M. 69–70
Li Wei 131, 132
Lin, A. 62
Lindahl, C. 30, 130, 133
linguistic deprivation 66
linguistic interdependence xiii,
   xiv–xvi, 43
linguistic standardization 65
Liu, L. 200
Livingston, Robert 109
Lo Bianco, J. 36, 47
Lockert, Bill 109
LSF *see* Langue des Signes Française
LSQ *see* Langue des signes québécoise
Lüdi, G. 92, 99
Lynas, W. *et al.* 69

McKee, R. 204
McLaughlin, M.G. 69
McNeill, D. 93
MacQuarrie, L. 236
Madrid co-enrollment program 153
Mahshie, S.N. 18
Malkowski, Gary 38, 42, 46
manualism 42, 88
mapping for sign languages 180–182
Marschark, M. *et al.* 29, 152, 166
Marshall, S. 5, 6
Martin, M. *et al.* 153
Mason, David 46, 51
Mason, J. 23
Mathison, Robert 40
Matthews, E.S. 107
Mauldin, L. 107
Maxwell-McCaw, D. 167
May, S. 65
Mayer, C. xv
mediated education 218
medical model of deafness 82, 87, 107
Mercer, N. 134–135
Metz, K. 153
Milan Congress (1880) *see* International
   Congress for the Improvement
   of the Conditions of Deaf-
   Mutes, Milan
Miller, D. 42
Miller, M. 195
Millet, A. *et al.* 99
Minority Report 109
Mitchiner, J.C. 150, 202

Moll, L.C. *et al.* 197
monolingualism 65, 112
Moore (2003) 99
Moore, D. 5, 6
multilingualism, defined 61
multimodal social semiotic 131
multimodality 131

Napier, J. 231
nation-states 65
National Academies of Sciences,
    Engineering, and Medicine xiv
Netherlands
    cochlear implants 173
    Kentalis 174, 182
    Kentalis Zoetermeer 175–176
    Koninklijk Effatha Guyot Group
        (KEGG) 178–179
    Twinschool co-enrollment
        program 153
    see also parent sign language teaching
        in the Netherlands; Sign
        Language of the Netherlands;
        Sign Supported Dutch (SSD)
New Zealand 204, 218
Newcombe, L.P. 198
Nilsson, A. 174
nomenclature, diversity of 6–8
Norway 218
NSDSK (Dutch Foundation for Deaf
    and Hard-of-Hearing Children)
    177–178
Nussbaum, D. 152

O'Brien, D. 7
O'Neill, R. 19
Ontario Association of the Deaf (OAD)
    42, 46
    Education Task Force (ETF) 42
Ontario, Canada 8
    ASL/LSQ regulation 35, 36–37, 43,
        44, 45, 46–50, 51–52
    bilingual bicultural education 36–37
    Board of Deaf Education 45
    Centre for Deafness Studies in
        Ontario (CDSO) 45
    Centre Jules-Léger 41, 43
    cochlear implants xii, 53
    Ernest C. Drury School for the Deaf
        36, 41, 46
    French-language instruction 47

heritage language classes 44
International Languages Elementary
    Program 44
IPRC (Identification, Placement, and
    Review Committee) 39–40
Multiculturalism Policy 44
New Democratic Party (NDP) 42
Regional Centres 45
school placement 38–39
schools for the deaf 1
spoken or sign language? xii
see also Deaf Ontario Now
Ontario Education Act 36, 39, 43, 47,
    48, 49
Ontario Institute for Studies in
    Education 43
Ontario Institution for the Education
    and Instruction of the Deaf and
    Dumb 40, 42
Ontario Ministry of Education
    42, 51
Ontario School for the Deaf, Belleville
    37, 40, 41, 42
Ontario School for the Deaf,
    Milton 41
Ontario teacher education 35–37
    ASL/LSQ regulation 43, 44, 45,
        47–50, 51
    background and history 38–42
    Deaf Ontario Now 35, 36, 42–47, 49
    deaf teachers 41
    Letters of Standing 41, 44
    methodology 37–38
    Ontario College of Teachers 37,
        49–50, 51
    Ontario Teaching Certificate 41, 44
    oralism 40
    Professional Training for Teachers of
        the Deaf 40–41
    resistance to sign language rights
        xviii–xix, 35–36, 37, 47–52
    *Review of Ontario Education
        Programs for Deaf and Hard of
        Hearing Students* 36, 43–47, 49
    sign language policy 40, 53
    standard-setting exercise 49–50
    Teacher Education Centre 37, 41
    York University, Toronto 37, 43, 46,
        50–52
    conclusion: looking forward 52–53
oralism 40, 84–85, 88

Paget Gorman signed speech 69
Palmer, Wesley 40
Paludneviciene, R. 153
parent sign language teaching in the
    Netherlands 9, 173–177
  first steps 177–178
  course developments 178–179
  exchange of thoughts with parents
      179–180
  language status 178, 179
  parents' needs 176
  plurilingualism 175
  Policy Nota 178–179
  proficiency level needed 177
  responsibility 176
  Sign Supported Dutch (SSD) 173,
      177, 178, 179
  Total Communication (TC) 177
  see also CEFR
parental choice 112
parenting, bilingual 199
Parilla, R. 236
partiality 7
Pennycook, A. 106
Peterson, David 46
Piller, I. 199
Pizer, G. et al. 201, 204
plurilingual education environments 62
plurilingual instruction xiii, xvi–xvii
plurilingualism xii, xvii, 3–7, 92,
    104–106
  in deaf education 61, 73, 100
  defined 60–62, 92, 104, 131, 175, 181
  in posthumanist onto-epistemology
      105–106
plurilingualism and (in)competence in
    deaf education 1–2
  critical reflections on nomenclature
      6–8
  historical perspective 2–3
  overview of the book 8–9
  theoretical framing 3–6
Poizat, Michel 83
power relations xiii–xiv, xviii
productive signs 133
Py, B. 92, 99

Rae, Bob 46
Report of the Royal Commission on the
    Blind, the Deaf and Dumb etc. of
    the United Kingdom (1889) 66–67

R.J.D. Williams School for the Deaf,
    Saskatchewan 40
Robarts School for the Deaf, London,
    Ontario 41, 46
Rochester Method 41
Ruiz, R. 36, 37, 45, 203
Russell, D. 218, 220

Saskatchewan, Canada 8, 103–104
  American Sign Language (ASL) 103,
      109, 115–116
  challenges to historic reports 115–122
  child development 113
  cochlear implants 114, 115
  cognitive imperialism 107–108, 111,
      112, 113, 114, 116
  Deaf and Hard of Hearing
      Services 116
  Deaf Crows Collective 110
  historic reports 110–114
  language deprivation 106–107
  R.J.D. Williams School for the
      Deaf, 40
  Task Force on Deaf Education
      109–110
  timeline 109–110
  see also Deaf Crows (play; 2016)
Saskatchewan Human Rights
    Commission (SHRC) 104, 106,
    109–110, 115–116
Saskatchewan Pediatric Rehabilitation
    Centre (SPARC) 115–116
Sass-Lehrer, M. 150
Schönström, K. 22, 136, 174
school environments xii, xiii, xvii–xviii,
    76, 114, 219, 237
schools for the deaf xi, 3
Schwartz, M. et al. 199
science education see sign bilingualism
    in science education
Scott, S. 152
Sero-Guillaume, Ph. 84
Shanahan, T. xv
shifting 7
Shores-Hermann, Patty 42
SHRC see Saskatchewan Human Rights
    Commission
sign bilingual science classroom study
    136–143
  dialogue in sign language to
      transcript 136

metalinguistic discussion and the
'right' sign 140–143, *141*, *142*
multimodality and linguistic
repertoire *139*, 139–140, *140*
multimodality and linguistic
resources 137–138, *138*, *139*
translanguaging 136–137
sign bilingualism in science education 8,
129–130
dialogic teaching 145–146
multimodal social semiotics 130–131
multimodality 143–144
science classroom challenges 135
scientific meaning-making through
sign dialogue 134–135
translanguaging 131–133, 144–145
translanguaging as sign bilingual
pedagogical tool 130, 133–134
conclusion 146–147
see also sign bilingual science
classroom study; Sweden
Sign Language of the Netherlands
(SLN) 173–174, 177, 178
see also parent sign language teaching
in the Netherlands
sign languages xi, 3, 53
Sign Supported Dutch (SSD) 173, 177,
178, 179
Sign Supported Speech *see* Total
Communication
Simpson, P. 68
Sir James Whitney School for the Deaf,
Ontario 41, 46
Siran, S. 202
Skutnabb-Kangas, T. 52
Slee, R. 38, 39, 40, 52, 107
SLN *see* Sign Language of the
Netherlands
Smiler, K. 204
Snoddon, K. 1, 3, 6, 177
SPARC (Saskatchewan Pediatric
Rehabilitation Centre) 115–116
speech training 40
SPSM *see* Swedish National Agency for
Education
SSD *see* Sign Supported Dutch
Standard English 65
Stokoe, W. *et al.* 70, 86, 177
STS *see* Swedish Sign Language
Svartholm, K. xvi, 18, 20, 29
Swanwick, R. 30

Sweden xi, xii–xiii, 8, 15–16
bimodal bilingual education 30
cochlear implants 15, 17, 20, 28,
30, 31
deaf schools 17–18, 19–20, 21–22
demographic changes and impact
20–22
early school years 20–21
effectiveness of sign bilingual model
18–20
future of sign bilingualism 27–29
impact of demographic changes
20–22
National Agency for Education 21
plurilingual instruction xvi
qualified teachers 20
refugees and immigrants 21
schools for hard of hearing 22, 28
sign bilingual education 2, 15–18,
29, 130
sign language issues 25–27
sign-supported spoken Swedish 23,
26–27, 30, 132
STS courses 16, 17, 22
students' spoken language skills
18, 27
Swedish literacy 20
teachers' perceptions 22–29, **23**
translanguaging 29–30, 132,
133–134
TUFF courses 16, 20
variability issues 24
discussion 29–30
summary 30–31
see also sign bilingualism in science
education
Swedish National Agency for Education
(SPSM) 19, 20, 25, 130
Swedish Sign Language (STS) xi, xvi,
16, 17, 20–21, 22, 129, 134
symbolic capital 63–64

Task Force on Deaf Education (1989)
104, 109, 111–112
Tervoort, B.T. 177
Thomas, W.P. 29
Thomson, P. 63
timeline 109–110
Tollefson, J.W. 37, 38, 40, 41
Total Communication (TC) 42, 69, 86,
151, 154, 177–178

translanguaging 29–30, 62, 133
  defined xii, 4–5, 131–133, 144–145, 167
  pedagogy xii–xiii, xvii
  as sign bilingual pedagogical tool
      130, 133–134
  status of languages 132
translanguaging space 132
Trofimenkoff, Patti 109

UK deaf education 8, 60–61
  Bourdieu's concepts 62–64, 65
  BSL (British Sign Language) 61, 68,
      74, 75
  cochlear implants 75
  Disability Discrimination Act 67
  family support 74
  fingerspelling 68, 69
  language policy 65–73
  National Association for the Oral
      Instruction of the Deaf 67
  oral education 70
  physical education 69
  plurilingual education environments 62
  plurilingual signed language
      environments 73–75
  plurilingualism defined 60–62
  residential schools 70
  signed languages 61, 66, 68–71
  Teachers of the Deaf (ToD)
      67–68, 70
  Total Communication 69
  Wales 76, 198
  ways forward? 75–76
UN Convention on the Rights of
      Persons with Disabilities
      (UNCRPD) 36, 45, 52, 53, 219
underachievement, causes of xiii–xiv
Underwood, K. 6
United Kingdom 71
  Blind etc. Commission (1889) 66–67
  Board of Education 68
  BSL Act Scotland (2015) 75
  CRIDE (Consortium for Research in
      Deaf Education) 68, 71, 72
  Education Act (1944) 68
  Education Act (1981) 70

Ministry of Education 68
National Curriculum 75
special educational needs (SEN) 71
Special Educational Needs and
      Disability Code of Practice
      (SEND COP) 71
Wales 75–76, 198
Warnock report (1978) 70–71
Welsh Language Act (1993) 75–76
see also UK deaf education
United States
  bilingual families 202
  Centre for ASL and English Bilingual
      Education Research 2
  Chinese families 200
  co-enrollment programs 153
  Council on Education of the Deaf 38
  Deaf students 218
  interpreter-mediated education
      217–218
  Korean-American families 199
  political and sociocultural factors 203
University of Alberta 43, 220
University of Ottawa 41, 43, 51

Van Lier, L. 132
verbal repertoire 93
Virole, B. 85
Visible English 41, 42
VISTA 'Signing Naturally' program
      50, 178
'visuogestural' bilingualism 91
Vygotsky, L. 135, 218, 228

Wacquant, L.J.D. 62, 64, 72
Weber, J. 40
Wells, G. xv
#WhyISign 205
Willms, J.D. et al. 222, 236–237
Winston, E. 218
Woodward, J. 82
World Federation of the Deaf (WFD)
      86, 219
Wynne, Kathleen 48

Young, A.M. 177